Police Officer Exam

The Complete Preparation Guide

3rd Edition

Published in the United States by LearningExpress, LLC, New York.

Library of Congress Cataloging-in-Publication Data:
Police officer exam.—3rd ed.
p. cm.
Includes bibliographical references and index.
ISBN: 978-1-57685-576-8 (alk. paper)
1. Police—United States—Examinations, questions, etc. 2. Police—Vocational guidance—United States. I. LearningExpress (Organization)
HV8143.P635 2007
363.2076—dc22
2006036805

Printed in the United States of America

9 8 7 6 5 4 3

Third Edition

ISBN: 978-1-57685-576-8

Regarding the Information in This Book

We attempt to verify the information presented in our books prior to publication. It is always a good idea, however, to double-check such important information as minimum requirements, application and testing procedures, and deadlines with your local law enforcement agency, as such information can change from time to time.

For more information or to place an order, contact LearningExpress at:
55 Broadway
8th Floor
New York, NY 10006

Or visit us at:
www.learnatest.com

List of Contributors

The following individuals contributed to the content of this book:

Elizabeth Chesla is an adult educator and curriculum developer. She is the author of *TOEFL Exam Success* and coauthor of *ACT Exam Success*, as well as many other writing and reading guides and test-preparation books. She lives in South Orange, New Jersey.

Lieutenant Raymond E. Foster, LAPD (ret.), MPA, is a 24-year veteran of policing. Currently, he is a university lecturer and the author of several books, including *Police Technology*, *Leadership: Texas Hold 'em Style*, and *From LAPD to NYPD: An Introduction to Policing.*

Mary Hesalroad, a police officer for the Austin, Texas, Police Department, has many years of experience as a police recruiter.

Rebecca LaTourneau is a writer and researcher who lives in Forest Lake, Minnesota.

Mary E. Masi is the author and coauthor of several professional books, including *Firefighter Career Starter* and *EMS Essentials Glossary*.

Judith N. Meyers is director of the Two Together Tutorial Program of the Jewish Child Care Association in New York City.

Judith F. Olson is chairperson of the language arts department at Valley High School in West Des Moines, Iowa, where she also conducts test-preparation workshops.

Judith Robinovitz is an independent educational consultant and director of Score at the Top, a comprehensive test preparation program in Vero Beach, Florida.

Judith Schlesinger, PhD, is a writer and psychologist whose background includes years of working with police officers in psychiatric crisis interventions.

Jay Smith is an exercise physiologist and Director of Physical Fitness and Health Maintenance Programs for the Massachusetts Criminal Justice Training Council.

Contents

How to Use This Book

Congratulations on your decision to become a police officer! You will find a career in law enforcement to be both rewarding and financially beneficial. The work is interesting, sometimes exciting, and, of course, extremely important. However, there are some hurdles ahead of you that must be crossed before you can proudly wear a badge. You have to beat out the competition and succeed at each step of an arduous selection process before you can participate in the swearing-in ceremony. The hiring process can take anywhere from a few months to two or even three years or more, so you will want to be sure of your commitment before jumping in.

This book will guide you through each stage of the selection process and will help you strengthen your test-taking skills to improve your chances of success. The following chapters are filled with useful information, advice, and practice exercises that will help you understand both how the hiring process works and how you can best meet the requirements.

► Chapter 1—How Police Officers Are Selected

In this chapter, you will find out how the hiring process works. You will find helpful information about each stage of the process, as well as tips about how to best prepare for each step. You will want to understand this process thoroughly before going any further.

► Chapter 2—The Police Officer Suitability Test

To help you assess your suitability for police work, take the quiz in this chapter. It will help you to evaluate and better understand how your own interests and abilities relate to police work. Be sure to take your time with this test and to reflect upon your answers carefully.

► Chapter 3—The LearningExpress Test Preparation System

Taking a written exam can be very stressful. This chapter will show how to overcome test anxiety and help you to take control of the entire test preparation process. You will discover how to organize your time both before and during the written exam. Take advantage of the study plans offered here so that your written test scores are as high as they can possibly be.

Police departments around the country use different types of exams, so we have included a variety of them in this book—three different types, two of each type. Find out which skills the department you are applying to will be testing (Chapter 3 shows you how to figure this out). Then focus on the practice exams in this book that are similar to the exam you will be taking. The following table is a snapshot of the types of exams included in this book and the relevant chapters to study for each one.

Once you have taken a practice exam and have discovered where any problem areas lie, you can study the relevant subjects in Chapters 7–15. After studying these instructional chapters, take the second practice exam to see if your score improves. You may want to prepare further by getting additional help from a tutor or by studying more on your own.

Chapters 19–21 describe the details of the physical ability test, the personal history statement, and the oral interview. These are important stages in the selection process, so you want to be sure to give them as much attention as you do the written exam. In order to rank high, you want to do well in every step of the selection process.

By reading this book, you will know what police departments across the country are looking for when selecting new recruits. Plus, you will know the best way to approach each step of the selection process. However, even though the basics of the entire process are covered in this book, you will need to get the specific requirements from the municipal office you are applying to. The more effort you put into researching your area of interest, the better your chances of succeeding, so gather as much information as you can. Your success in becoming a police officer depends largely on the amount of work you are willing to do to achieve your goal.

Police Officer Practice Exams	Study Chapters
Exam 1, Chapter 4 Exam 4, Chapter 16 *These exams test your basic reading and writing skills.*	7. Reading Text, Tables, Charts, and Graphs 8. Grammar 9. Vocabulary and Spelling
Exam 2, Chapter 5 Exam 5, Chapter 17 *These exams test job-related skills, such as memory and observation.*	7. Reading Text, Tables, Charts, and Graphs 10. Math 11. Judgment 12. Map Reading 13. Memory and Observation
Exam 3, Chapter 6 Exam 6, Chapter 18 *These exams are similar to the Law Enforcement Candidate Record (LECR) exam.*	9. Vocabulary and Spelling 14. Number and Letter Recall 15. Personal Background

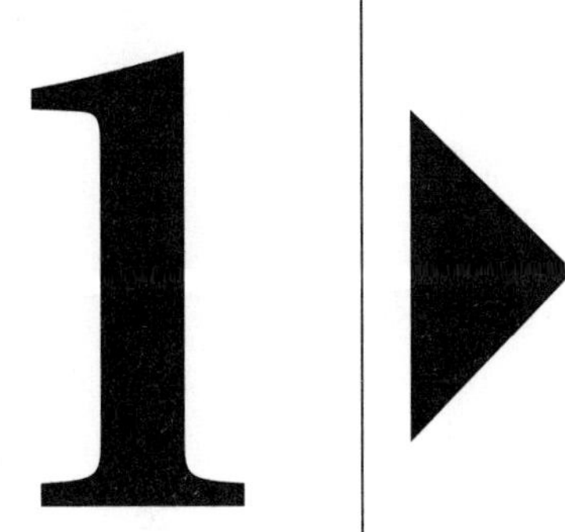

How Police Officers Are Selected

CHAPTER SUMMARY

The hiring process for selecting the best and the brightest police officers varies among police departments. This chapter will give you an overview of the basics common to most municipalities and show you how you can prepare to master each step of the process.

Getting through each phase of the hiring process will require determination and a commitment to your goal of becoming a police officer. The selection process can be challenging, especially for those who don't know what to expect. No doubt, there will be serious competition. But if you use this book and study it thoroughly, you'll get the edge. It will provide you with the vital practice and information you need to succeed.

While there is some variation among cities and towns across the country, most police departments require applicants to successfully complete each of the following steps—although not necessarily in this exact order:

1. Application
2. Written exam
3. Physical ability test
4. Polygraph exam
5. Background investigation
6. Oral board interview

7. Psychological evaluation
8. Medical evaluation

Prepare yourself by taking the practice tests in this book and by reading the chapters that apply to your situation, so you can avoid the pitfalls that prevent many police officer candidates from being hired. In most large cities, many more people apply to be police officers than can ever be accepted. That's one reason you are reading this book—to find out as much as you can about the hiring process and to practice the skills you need to excel at each stage.

This chapter will give you an insider's look at the entire process, so you will be less nervous when facing the tests, interviews, and procedures that can sometimes be intimidating. As you learn what to expect, you are likely to make better choices and get better results than those who are just rushing blindly ahead.

Municipal police departments across the United States use a variety of measures to rank candidates on their eligibility lists. It is from this list that candidates are chosen for hire, so you want to rank as high as possible. The people who plan ahead are the ones who ultimately rise to the top of the eligibility list.

▶ The Eligibility List

Most police departments establish a list of candidates in rank order. How ranks are determined varies from place to place; sometimes the rank is based solely on the written exam score, sometimes on the oral board, and sometimes on a combination of factors. Even if you make it through the entire selection process, the likelihood that you will be hired as a police officer depends on the quality of your performance in one or more parts of the selection process.

Make a commitment now; you need to work hard in advance to do well on the written exam, the physical ability test, and the oral board, so that your name will stand out at the top of your agency's eligibility list.

The first step is to gather as much information as possible. You need to know about the police officer selection process. This chapter outlines the basic process of becoming a police officer. The majority of police departments use most of the steps presented here, though the order may vary, and some departments put more or less emphasis on the various steps.

▶ Basic Qualifications

The basic qualifications you need in order to even think about becoming a police officer vary from city to city, but here are the most common ones:

- A minimum age—sometimes 18, but more often 20 or 21. Maximum ages have been challenged in the courts, with the result that many, if not most, police departments no longer list a maximum age.
- U.S. citizenship or, in a few cities, resident alien status
- A high school diploma or its equivalent and, increasingly, some college credits or even a college degree—sometimes military experience will substitute for college credits
- Excellent physical and mental health, good vision and hearing, and an appropriate weight-to-height ratio
- A valid driver's license and a satisfactory driving record
- No felony convictions

Many jurisdictions, but not all, require that you live in or near the jurisdiction. Most police departments give special consideration to otherwise qualified veterans over civilians. This may take the form of a policy, sometimes called a veteran's preference policy, whereby points are automatically added to the written exam. Is this unfair? No. Military personnel have learned the discipline and many of the skills—such as use of firearms—that are vital to police work. Veterans are simply better qualified than those who haven't served. Also, for older applicants, some departments subtract the number of years served in the military from an applicant's age to satisfy the upper age requirement, if there is one.

Automatic Disqualifiers

There are many things that can disqualify you, the most important being any trouble with the law in the past. Convicted felons are not welcome as police officers in any jurisdiction, no matter how much they might have reformed their lives since their conviction. Misdemeanors and even traffic tickets can disqualify applicants in some cities. People who use illegal drugs or abuse legal ones need not apply. See the section on the personal history statement and background investigation later in this chapter for more information.

Police officers have to be in tip-top physical and emotional shape. Disabilities that would not be a problem in other occupations can become disqualifying conditions for police officers. These disabilities do not have to be obvious or serious ones. For instance, many departments require perfect color vision, so that a simple and common condition like red-green color blindness can disqualify an applicant. Being overweight can also disqualify you. See the section on the medical exam later in this chapter for more information on applicants with disabilities.

Here is a list of other common disqualifiers found in various police departments across the country:

- having a restraining order against you or showing any history of domestic violence
- patterns of drug or alcohol abuse in your history—some cities require absolutely no drug use of any kind within the last one to five years
- selling of marijuana or narcotics in the past
- any felony convictions
- dishonorable discharge from any branch of the U.S. Armed Forces
- being known to habitually associate with criminals
- having a delinquent financial history
- falsifying anything, or giving misleading information during the hiring process

To find out the qualifications necessary to become a police officer in your city of interest, contact the recruiting or personnel office directly; they will send you a list of qualifications as well as the steps you have to go through to apply.

▶ The Exam Announcement

Applying to be a police officer differs from applying for most other jobs. The differences begin with the exam announcement. In most cases, you won't see job openings in the police department advertised in the Help Wanted section of your newspaper. Instead, the city or state starts looking for people who want to be police officers by means of a special announcement. This announcement will outline the basic qualifications necessary to be a police officer as well as the steps you will have to go through in the selection process. It often tells you some of the duties police officers are expected to perform. It may give the date and place of the written exam, which is usually the first step in the selection process.

Get a copy of this announcement. Often, your public library will have a copy. Or you can get one directly from the agency or the city personnel department.

Most jurisdictions now have websites where they post announcements online for job openings, application information, and upcoming tests. If you have access to the Internet, check out the website www.policeone.com/careers. It has direct links to many police department websites around the country where you can obtain helpful employment information, such as

- an exam announcement
- description of duties included in the job
- basic requirements that need to be met at the time of application, such as minimum age, citizenship, high school diploma, or college credits
- brief description of all required tests in the selection process
- benefits of the job
- equal opportunity employment statement
- directions about where to pick up and drop off applications
- veteran's preference statement
- information about who to contact for further details

If the written exams are held irregularly, the police agency or personnel department may maintain a mailing list, so that you can receive an exam announcement the next time an exam is scheduled. If exams are held frequently, you will sometimes be told to simply show up at the exam site on a given day of the week or month. In those cases, you usually get more information about the job and the selection process if you pass the written exam. Study the exam announcement, as well as any other material, such as brochures, that the department sends you. You need to be prepared for the whole selection process in order to be successful.

▶ The Application

Often, the first step in the process of becoming a police officer is filling out an application. These can be obtained from your city's personnel office or from the police recruitment office. Many police departments now offer applications online that you can download, fill out, and send in. If you have access to the Internet, perform a search on any search engine, such as www.yahoo.com, www.google.com, or www.msn.com to find out if the police department you want to apply to has a website and/or an online application process.

Applications vary among municipalities, but usually they request basic information about you that will determine whether or not you may proceed to the next step in the selection process. Questions about your previous education, employment, and military experience are common. In addition, you may find questions that ask about factors that could prove to be disqualifying, such as felony convictions or noncitizen status. In this way, police departments can weed out applicants who are not qualified for police work at the first stage of the hiring process.

Be prepared to have the following information available when filling out an application:

- Social Security number
- birth certificate
- college transcripts or relevant training certificates (if any)

Some police departments require you to attach copies of one or more of these documents to your application when you submit it. A few cities have lengthier applications and will want even more documentation such as a credit report, paycheck stubs, or divorce papers. However, most departments want you to submit an abbreviated application initially, followed by a lengthier, more in-depth personal history statement later on in the process. Either way, be sure you know what information will be required before you go to fill out the application, so you can bring the relevant backup documents with you.

Application Tips

- Neatness and accuracy are critical.
- Make a photocopy of the application.
- Read all directions before you complete the application.
- Use the photocopy to make a practice draft application first. Then, complete the real application in neat block letters, or better yet, type it.
- Keep a photocopy of the application. (Later in the employment screening process, you will complete other forms that will ask for the same information.)
- Do NOT send a resume in place of an application. Civil service rules will most likely require the application form.
- If you mail the application, be sure to include all required supporting documentation and double-check the address.
- If you download the application from the Internet, make sure your printer produces a good, clear copy. Also, if you complete the form online and print a copy, use the spell-check feature and have somebody else proofread it.

Because the initial application is usually for basic information only, don't feel like you have to write your life story for it. There will be plenty of time for more information later, once you pass this first step. Keep your answers brief and to the point. Also, make sure you answer all the questions honestly, as this will become a big issue later during your background check. The importance of honesty and integrity cannot be overestimated when seeking employment in the law enforcement industry.

▶ The Written Exam

In most cities, taking a written exam is the next step in the application process, though in some cases a background interview comes first. (By putting the background interview first, agencies save themselves the expense of testing applicants who don't meet the basic qualifications.)

The written exam is your first opportunity to show that you have what it takes to be a police officer. As such, it's extremely important. People who don't pass the written exam don't go any further in the selection process. Furthermore, the written exam score often figures into applicants' rankings on the eligibility list; in some cases, this score by itself determines your rank, while in others it is combined with other scores, such as physical ability test or oral board scores. In those cities, a person who merely passes the exam with a score of, say, 70, is unlikely to be hired when there are plenty of applicants with scores in the 90s. The exam bulletin usually specifies what the rank will be based on.

An excellent way to boost your score on the exam is to study and complete the practice exams in this book that correspond to the kind of police exam you will be taking.

What the Written Exam Is Like

Most written exams simply test basic skills and aptitudes like how well you understand what you read, your writing ability, your ability to follow directions, your judgment and reasoning skills, and sometimes your memory or your math. In this preliminary written exam, you will not be tested on your knowledge of police policies and procedures, the law, or any other body of knowledge specific to police work. This test is designed only to see if you can read, write, reason, and do basic math.

In a few cities, taking the exam involves studying written materials in advance and then answering questions about them on the exam. Some of these written materials have to do with the law and police procedures—but all you have to do is study the guide you are given. You're still being tested just on your reading skills and memory.

Police officers must be able to read, understand, and act on complex written materials such as laws, policy handbooks, and regulations. They have to write incident reports and other materials that have to be clear and correct enough to stand up in court. They have to be able to think independently, because a patrol officer gets little direct supervision. They have to be able to do enough math to add up the value of stolen material or compute the street price of a drug sold to a dealer for *x* amount per kilo. The basic skills tested on the written exam are the skills police officers use every day.

Most exams are multiple-choice tests of the sort you have often encountered in school. You get an exam book and an answer sheet where you have to fill in circles (bubbles) or squares with a number 2 pencil.

In addition to the multiple-choice test, some cities have applicants write an essay or mock report. You might be asked to write a page or so on a general topic, like something you might write for a school assignment. Or you might be shown a videotape or slides and be told to write about what you saw. In this case, the agency can assess both your writing skills and your short-term memory. By having you actually write something, the agency can assess both your ability to relate facts in a logical order and your skills in grammar, punctuation, spelling, and other important areas.

How to Prepare for the Written Exam

Pay close attention to any material the recruiting unit or city personnel department puts out about the written exam. Many police departments will give you an exam bulletin that describes their written tests in detail. If there's a study guide, study it. Pay close attention to what you are going to be tested on, and then find similar materials to practice with.

For focused, specific preparation that is based on police exams actually given throughout the United States, work through the police officer practice exams, sample exercises, and test instructions in this book. For additional practice, you can take one or more sample exams online. Go to www.learnatest.com to find out more about taking a practice police exam.

Kinds of Questions You Can Expect

Police exams usually cover such subjects as basic reading, writing, English usage, math, memory, attention to detail, and judgment. Sometimes, your ability to read a map or graph is also tested. The exam bulletin or position announcement, available from your recruitment office, should tell you what subjects are on your exam. This information may also be available online at your local police department's website. Some sites even post sample questions to help you practice. For more information on how to find out if your police department has such a website, look in Chapter 22, under the heading "Additional Resources."

Reading Comprehension Questions

Reading comprehension is a part of almost every written police exam. These reading questions are like the ones you have probably encountered in school tests: You are given a paragraph or two to read and then asked questions about it. Questions typically ask you about

- the main idea of the passage as a whole
- specific facts or details contained in the passage
- the meaning of words or phrases as they are used in the passage
- inferences and conclusions you can draw from what is stated in the passage

Writing Questions

For writing questions, you will most likely be asked one or two questions about what you would do in a given situation or what you recall about a particular scenario, perhaps one that you have viewed in a video beforehand. You will be expected to write a few sentences, or, in some cases, a few paragraphs, in order to answer the question. Short essays are more common than they used to be on law enforcement written exams, but multiple-choice tests remain the most popular format.

Grammar Questions

Usually, a grammar question asks you to choose which of four versions of a sentence is most correct. The incorrect choices might contain

- incomplete sentences (fragments)
- two or more sentences put together as if they were one (run-ons)
- verbs that don't agree with their subjects (*he think*) or that use the wrong tense (*yesterday she goes*)
- pronouns that don't match the noun they refer to (*a person . . . they*)
- incorrect modifiers (*good/well, bad/worse/worst*)
- double negatives (*I hadn't never*)

Sometimes, grammar questions also test your punctuation or capitalization skills, usually by giving you a sentence with punctuation marks or capitalized words underlined and asking you to choose which one is wrong.

Spelling Questions

Spelling questions might give you a sentence with a word missing and then ask you which of the choices is the correct spelling of the missing word. Or you might be given several different words and asked which one is spelled wrong.

Vocabulary Questions

Vocabulary questions usually ask you to find a synonym (a word that means the same) or an antonym (a word that means the opposite) of a given word. If you are lucky, that word will come in a sentence that will help you guess its meaning. If you are less lucky, you will just be given the word and have to choose a synonym or antonym without any help from the context.

Another way vocabulary is tested is to give you a sentence with a blank in it and ask you to choose the word that fits best in the sentence.

Other exams include vocabulary questions as a part of the reading comprehension section. One or more of the questions following the reading passage may ask you to choose the correct meaning of a vocabulary word that was used in the passage.

Math Questions

Math is usually a minor part of a police exam, if it's included at all. The questions usually test basic arithmetic: adding, subtracting, multiplying, and dividing whole numbers. Most often, the math questions are word problems that present everyday situations such as the total value of stolen property.

Some tests might ask you to work with fractions, decimals, or percentages, but in real-life situations: how much is left after one person eats half a pizza and another person eats a third; the amount of mileage on a car gauge after a certain number of trips; or how much you have to pay for a shirt at a 15% discount.

Written Exam Tips

- Gather as much information as you can—in advance—about the exam. Some agencies will issue study guides, while others hold study sessions. If your agency has a website, you may find sample test questions online.
- Practice, practice, practice! Review the material in the instructional chapters of this book, which offer tips on how to improve in each skill area on your exam.
- Take all the applicable practice police exams in this book.
- Listen carefully to any and all directions given by the person who administers the test.
- Budget your time during the exam. Don't spend too much time on any one question.
- Read through the entire question before answering it, and make sure you carefully read each answer before choosing the correct one.
- When you read questions, look for words that modify such as *not*, *never*, and *only*.
- Stop to check every now and then to make sure you are filling in the correct bubble or blank for each answer. You don't want to fail the test because of misplaced marks!
- If there is time left after you are finished, go back and double-check your answers.

Memory and Observation Questions

Police officers have to be able to remember details about things they see and things they read, so observation and memory questions are often a part of police exams. You may be given a study booklet in advance of the exam and asked to answer questions about it during the exam without referring to the book. Or you might be given a picture to look at or a passage to read during the exam and then have to answer questions about it, usually without referring to the picture or passage. You may even be shown a videotape and then asked questions about it after you have finished viewing it.

Judgment Questions

Obviously, police officers need to have good judgment, so some exams include multiple-choice questions designed to test your judgment and common sense. You may be given laws or police procedures and asked to apply them to a hypothetical situation, or you may be asked which hypothetical situation is most likely to indicate dangerous or criminal activity. Answering these questions requires both common sense and an ability to read carefully.

Map-Reading Questions

Map-reading questions are usually straightforward: You are given a small city map and told to find the quickest way to get from Point A to Point B without driving the wrong way down a one-way street or through a building. These questions test your ability to orient yourself on a map and read simple symbols such as one-way arrows.

Finding out How You Did

Applicants are generally notified in writing about their performance on the exam. This may take a few weeks, especially if there is a large number of applicants taking tests in your area. The notification may simply say whether or not you passed, but it may tell you what your score was. It may also say when you should show up for the next step in the process, which is often a physical ability test.

Physical Ability Exam Tips

- Begin a rigorous fitness program and stick with it. Work on your upper body strength, reaction time, cardiovascular endurance, and flexibility. Make sure you include daily stretches in your routine.
- Don't forget exercises that strengthen your legs. Strong legs can help you surpass other applicants because most practical physical ability tests (like pulling a dummy, pushing a car, or scaling a wall) involve the use of legs as much as, if not more than, the upper body.
- Maintain a healthy diet; lay off the junk food!
- On the day of your exam, eat lightly and don't overdo the caffeine. You want to be clearheaded and energetic.

▶ The Physical Ability Test

The physical ability test is usually the next step in the process after the written exam. You may have to bring a note from your doctor saying that you are fit enough to undertake this test before you will be allowed to participate. A few agencies give the medical exam before the physical ability test. They all want to make sure that no one has a heart attack in the middle of the test. Expect the test to be tough.

Police work, after all, is physically demanding. The physical ability test isn't even designed to find out whether you are in good enough shape to be a police officer. It assesses only whether you are in good enough shape to do well in the physical training at the police academy. It's the academy that whips recruits into the physical shape necessary to be a police officer.

What the Physical Ability Test Is Like

The exact events that make up the physical ability test vary from city to city, but generally there are three main areas that are tested: cardiovascular fitness, strength, and flexibility. In addition, there may also be a test of hand strength, which helps determine whether you will be able to handle a firearm. Agility, coordination, and reaction time are other factors that may be looked at.

Some common requirements for the physical ability assessment are $\frac{1}{4}$ to $1\frac{1}{2}$ mile timed run, sit-ups, push-ups, sit-and-reach tests (flexibility), bench pressing (upper body strength), and dragging something heavy for a specified distance. Some cities issue very standard physical fitness tests with basic tests, such as the timed run, sit-ups, bench presses, and sit-and-reach exercises, while others conduct tests that are much more varied. In these cases, you may be asked to push a car, drag a dummy body, complete an obstacle course, or vault yourself over a high bar. To find out exactly what the physical ability test is like in your area, contact your hiring agency for a list of specific events. Some agencies post details about the physical ability test on their websites, while others include the information in their published exam announcements.

How to Prepare for the Physical Ability Test

The physical ability test is one area where advance preparation is almost guaranteed to pay off. No matter how good a shape you are in, start an exercise program now. You can design your program around the requirements listed in the exam announcement if you want, but any exercise that will increase your stamina, flexibility, and strength will help.

You should always consult a physician before you begin or increase your exercise regimen. Start gradually, increasing your activity as you go. And remember that you don't have to do all this work alone. Taking an aerobics class or playing football will help increase your stamina, and you can supplement such activities with ones that build your strength.

For more information about the physical ability test, see Chapter 19.

► The Personal History Statement and Background Investigation

Either at the beginning of the whole selection process or after the first couple of cuts are made, the hiring agency will have you fill out a long form about your personal history. You will usually be interviewed about this material by someone from the police or city personnel department. As the department begins to get serious about considering you, it will conduct an investigation into your background, using your personal history statement as a starting point.

This step may be the most important in the whole process, even though the results may not be reflected in your rank on the eligibility list. This is where the police department checks not only your experience and education, but also, and perhaps more importantly, your character. Do you have the integrity, honesty, commitment, personal stamina, and respect for authority and the law that a police officer must have? Police departments go to a lot of trouble and expense to find out.

What the Personal History Statement Is Like

You take part in the background investigation by filling out the personal history form and talking with the interviewer. The form will be long—up to 30 pages—and requires your serious attention and effort. Assume that everything you say will be double-checked by a trained, experienced police investigator. You will be asked where you were born, where you have lived, where you went to school—including elementary school—what you have studied, where you have worked and what you did there, what organizations you have belonged to, and so on. Your whole life will be laid out on paper. You will have to supply names of teachers, employers, neighbors, and relatives, as well as the names of several additional people who can attest to your character and fitness to be a police officer.

How to Fill out the Personal History Statement

Fill out the form completely, looking up dates and places whenever you can rather than relying on your memory. Attach all documents, such as diplomas or transcripts, that are requested. Neatness and accuracy count, but one thing counts even more: honesty.

Be completely honest in everything you write and everything you say to the interviewer. Covering up something in your past, even by just not mentioning it, will in itself be taken as evidence that you don't have the integrity it takes to be a police officer. Yes, past drug use, hospitalizations, scrapes with the law, or family or financial difficulties can hurt your chances, but not as much as omitting them and then having them surface during the investigation. Better to acknowledge, up front, anything that might cause doubt about your fitness to be a police officer, and deal with it. Convince the interviewer that, although you have had difficulties in the past, you have since dealt with them and they will not affect your performance now or in the future. The interviewer may have suggestions about how to resolve past blemishes on your record. For more information, see Chapter 20.

What the Background Investigation Is Like

Starting from your personal history statement, a background investigator from the police department will check you out. The investigator will verify what you have said about yourself: Do you in fact have a high school diploma, an honorable discharge, five years' employment with the same firm?

And then the investigator will start asking the real questions. Your former teachers, landlords, employers, friends, and others will be asked by the investigator how long and how well they knew you and what kind of person they found you to be. Did you meet your obligations? How did you deal with problems? Do they know of anything that might affect your fitness to be a police officer?

The investigator or other personnel will also perform a credit check to see how you have handled your finances and if you have made a habit of paying your bills on time. If you have had financial trouble in the past, it does not mean you will be automatically disqualified, but a long history of problems in this area will raise questions about your ability to conduct your affairs in a responsible manner.

How to Prepare for the Personal History Statement and Background Investigation

As a candidate for the job of police officer, the most important way you can improve your performance on the personal history statement is by improving your personal history. You can't change the past, exactly, but you can use the present to improve your chances in the future. For example, you can take steps to make yourself more attractive to the police department by doing police work as a volunteer, an intern, or a paid cadet.

You can also make sure to pay your bills on time, and clear up any outstanding obligations. Deal with any issues, such as custody cases or legal disputes so that they are resolved in a satisfactory manner. Be sure to give timely notice if leaving a job. In other words, use common sense, meet your obligations, and conduct yourself in a responsible manner.

▶ The Lie Detector Test

Some jurisdictions require a polygraph, or lie detector, test as part of the background investigation process, although the polygraph, if required, is typically one of the last steps you will go through.

There really is no such thing as a lie detector. What the polygraph detects are changes in heart and respiratory rates, blood pressure, and galvanic skin resistance (basically a measure of how much you're perspiring). A cuff like the one your doctor uses to take your blood pressure will be wrapped around your arm. Rubber tubes around your trunk will measure your breathing, and clips on your fingers or palm will measure skin response. The theory is that people who are consciously lying get nervous, and their involuntary bodily responses give them away.

Don't worry about being betrayed by being nervous in the first place. Everyone's a little nervous when confronting a new technology. The polygraph examiner will explain the whole process to you. More importantly, the examiner will ask you a series of questions to establish a baseline both for when you are telling the truth and for when you are not. For instance, the examiner might tell you to answer "No" to every question and then ask you whether your name is George (if it isn't) and whether you drove to the examination today (if you did).

All questions for a polygraph exam have to be in yes-or-no form. You should be told in advance what every question will be. Some questions will be easy ones, like whether you are wearing sneakers. The questions that really count will be ones that will qualify you for a position as a police officer: whether you have committed a crime, whether you have received speeding tickets, or whether you have been arrested. You will probably have been over any problematic areas with the background investigator or other interviewers before, so just tell the truth and try to relax.

▶ The Oral Interview

The selection process in your chosen jurisdiction may include several oral interviews, none of which will be much like other job interviews you have had in the past. There may be an interview connected with your personal history statement, in which the interviewer simply tries to confirm or clarify what you have written. Also, an interview is usually part of the psychological evaluation. In addition, most agencies also conduct an oral interview or board that continues the process of determining whether candidates will make good police officers.

What the Oral Board Is Like

Usually, the interview with the oral board is held at the police department or at city hall. The oral board typically assesses such qualities as interpersonal skills, communication skills, judgment and decision-making abilities, respect for diversity, emotional maturity, problem-solving skills, and adaptability. The board itself may be small, with two or three people, or larger with several people sitting at a long table and facing you. Typically, people on the board are a mixture of police officials, civilians, and other city officials. On some boards, there may be only a couple of police officers and no one else. Other police departments do things more formally and may have city council members sitting on the board, or you may even find yourself face to face with the mayor!

Expect your oral board interview to last for between 20 and 40 minutes. Those who are on the board have already read your application, so they know a bit about you, but seeing you in person will help them complete the picture. Don't underestimate your need to make a good impression. Make sure you are neatly groomed, well dressed, and polite at all times during the interview.

The way the interview is conducted depends on the practices of the individual department. You may be asked a few questions similar to those you would be asked at a normal employment interview: Why do you want to be a police officer? Why in this department? What qualities do you have that would make you a good officer? You may be asked questions about your personal history. Have answers prepared for such questions in case they come.

Instead of or in addition to such questions, you may be presented with hypothetical situations that you will be asked to respond to. A board member may simply tell you what the situation is and ask you what you would do, or one or more board members may role-play the situation, putting you in the place of the officer in charge. You may even see a video that the board members will ask you about after you have seen it.

Often, there is at least one person on the board whose job it is to challenge you a bit. He or she may throw in comments or nonverbal cues meant to throw you off guard or make you second-guess your answers. If you run into this type of situation, don't panic. Just answer as honestly as you can and try to relax. Your best defense is simply being yourself.

This does not mean you shouldn't present your best possible side, however. This is your opportunity to show why you would make a good police officer. Take advantage of questions that leave room for you to mention your positive traits, such as a calm demeanor, a well-developed capacity to settle disputes, and so on. Those on the board have only a few minutes to decide about your personality and character—you want them to see the most positive aspects of these traits.

Increasingly, cities have standardized the oral board questions. The same questions are asked of every candidate, and when the interview is over, the board rates each candidate on a standard scale. This procedure helps the interviewers reach a more objective conclusion about the candidates they have interviewed, and may result in a score that is included in the factors used to generate the eligibility list. Indeed, some departments have decided that the oral board is so important that this score by itself determines candidates' rank on the list.

Here are some of the basic traits most oral boards are looking for in potential police officers:

- honesty, integrity, and a willingness to serve the community
- strong communication skills and an ability to interact with others
- willingness to accept responsibility
- overall reasoning abilities
- emotional maturity
- effective stress management skills
- level of comfort with oneself, including self-confidence level
- problem-solving skills

How to Prepare for the Oral Board

If the police or city personnel department puts out any material about the oral board, study it carefully. It will tell you what the board is looking for. It might even give you some sample questions you can practice with. Chapter 21 in this book can help, too.

Think about your answers to questions you might be asked. You might even try to write your own oral board questions and situations.

Here are a few sample questions to get you started:

- Why do you want to be a police officer?
- What would you do if you saw a driver weaving on the road?
- How well do you know your way around the city?
- Describe a situation in which you encountered someone who was out of control.
- What is your attitude toward those in authority?
- Do you like to take risks?
- Could you shoot someone if you had to?
- What have you done to prepare yourself for this type of work?

Write down your answers if you want. Practice saying them in front of a mirror until you feel comfortable, but don't memorize them. You don't want to sound like you're reciting from a book. Your answers should sound conversational even though you've prepared in advance.

Then enlist friends or family to serve as a mock oral board. If you know a speech teacher, get him or her to help. Give the board your questions, tell them about what you've learned, and then have a practice oral board. Start from the moment you walk into the room. Go through the entire session as if it were the real thing, and then ask your mock board for their feedback on your performance.

It may even help to videotape your mock board session. The camera can reveal things about your body language or habits that you don't even know about.

Here are some common mistakes that you will want to avoid during your oral board:

- *Letting your eyes roam around the room or staring at the floor*. Make sure to look your interviewers directly in the eyes when answering questions.

Oral Board Tips

- Be respectful, courteous, and pleasant throughout the process. Always keep your cool.
- Answer all questions honestly and to the best of your ability. Sincerity counts!
- Listen carefully to the questions. Don't distract yourself by thinking too much about how you might look or what they might be thinking about you. Stay in the moment. If you have to pause and think for a moment before you answer a question, that's okay. It's better than rushing yourself through the process.
- Have a question or two ready for when the board invites you to ask them. This shows your genuine interest in the job.
- Make sure you are on time! Better yet, arrive early.
- Dress conservatively, and go light on jewelry or makeup.
- Don't drink too much caffeine beforehand—you want to be able to relax.

- *Making up something to make yourself sound better.* This is not a good idea, especially because you will most likely be giving yourself away through your body language. Plus, if you are questioned about it further, you may find yourself in serious trouble.
- *Slouching, fidgeting, or sighing a lot.* This is a sure giveaway that you would rather be almost anywhere else than where you are. Sit up straight, pay attention, and stay focused throughout the entire interview. An alert and eager candidate will outshine the jittery, overly anxious one every time.
- *Swaggering, bragging, or acting like a know-it-all.* This is another extreme to avoid. The board members know you are not yet a police officer; they don't expect you to know everything. If you really don't know the answer to a tough question, say so. You might want to add a couple of words about how willing you are to learn, but don't try to bluff your way through a question you cannot answer.

▶ The Psychological Evaluation

Before you get offended at having to go through a battery of psychological tests, consider: Do you want even one emotionally unstable person running around the city maintaining public order and safety with a gun? Neither does the police department.

Of course, you're not unstable, and neither are most of the people applying with you. But remember, police work is one of the most stressful occupations. While no one can guarantee that a given individual will be able to handle the stress, police departments want to weed out as many people with underlying instabilities as they can, in hopes that those remaining will be able to deal with the problems in healthy ways. Sometimes, too, the real purpose of the psychological evaluation is not so much to disclose instabilities as to determine applicants' honesty, habits, and other important characteristics.

What the Written Psychological Evaluation Is Like

More often than not, the psychological evaluation begins with one or more written tests. Typically, these are standard tests licensed from a psychological testing

Psychological Evaluation Tips

- Read over your application and any other written material you have submitted to the department to refresh your memory of events in your past that you described. You may be asked a number of questions about each event, so be prepared ahead of time.
- Be confident when you walk into the room, and greet the psychologist with a firm handshake.
- Focus on answering each question clearly, but try not to draw out your answers into lengthy stories. You want to answer the questions, but not supply unrelated additional information.
- Try not to get defensive if the psychologist seems to be getting too personal. Just be honest and remember that he or she is just doing his or her job.

company; they are often multiple-choice or true-false tests. Both the MMPI (Minnesota Multiphasic Personality Inventory) and the TJTA (Taylor-Johnson Temperament Assessment) tests are commonly used. The tests may take one hour or several; the hiring agency will let you know approximately how much time to allot.

There's only one piece of advice we can offer you for dealing with a written psychological evaluation: Don't try to psych out the test. The people who wrote these tests are experts. They designed the test so that one answer checks against another to find out whether test takers are lying. Just answer honestly, and don't worry too much about how to answer the questions.

What the Oral Psychological Evaluation Is Like

Whether or not there is a written psychological examination, there is usually an oral interview with a psychologist or psychiatrist, who may be either on the city's staff or an independent contractor. The psychologist may ask you questions about your schooling and jobs, your relationships with family and friends, your habits, and your hobbies. Because there is such a broad range of things you could be asked about, there is really no way to prepare. In fact, the psychologist may be more interested in the way you answer—whether you come across as open, forthright, and honest—than in the answers themselves.

Once again, honesty is the best policy; there is no point in playing psychological games with someone who is better trained at it than you are. Try to relax, and answer openly. The psychologist is not trying to trick you.

▶ The Medical Examination

Before passage of the Americans with Disabilities Act (ADA), most police departments conducted a medical examination early in the process, before the physical ability test. Now, the ADA makes it illegal to do any examinations or ask any questions that could reveal an applicant's disability until after a conditional offer of employment has been made. That means that in most cities, you will get such a conditional offer before you are asked to submit to a medical exam. Indeed, you may get such an offer before the polygraph examination, the psychological examination, or, in a few cases, even before the background investigation, precisely because all of these components could reveal a disability.

Drug Testing

However, a test for use of illegal drugs can be administered before a conditional offer of employment is made. If the test comes back positive because of an applicant's use of prescription drugs, the department can ask about and verify that prescription drug use, but cannot use the condition for which the drugs are prescribed to reject an applicant. Being drug-free is a bona fide occupational qualification for a police officer.

Physical Disabilities and the ADA

After the conditional offer of employment, applicants can be rejected for disabilities revealed in the medical or psychological exam, according to the ADA, as long as the disabilities are related to essential job functions, and no reasonable accommodations exist that would make it possible for the applicant to function in the job. For instance, a potential police officer with a heart condition can reasonably be rejected on the basis of that disability. While officers don't spend their lives chasing after suspects on foot, they may have to do so at a moment's notice, and the police department can't accommodate someone who can't safely run several blocks and still get the job done.

Departments have the right, even under the ADA, to reject applicants who have disabilities as minor as color blindness. Being able to provide descriptions of victims, suspects, vehicles, and so on, both for investigative purposes and in court, is an essential function of a police officer, and there is not always someone else available to make the identification.

If you have progressed this far in the selection process, you probably don't have any obvious or seriously disabling conditions. You got through the written exam, physical ability test, psychological evaluation, and oral interview. Any other conditions that you reveal at this point or that come up in the medical exam will probably have to be dealt with on a case-by-case basis. Even conditions such as diabetes or epilepsy need not disqualify you, if your condition is controlled so that you will be able to fulfill the essential functions of a police officer.

What the Medical Exam Is Like

The medical exam itself is nothing to be afraid of. It will be just like any other thorough physical exam. Typical areas of health that are examined in the medical exam include

- range of motion
- reflexes
- spine curvature
- ear, nose, and throat health
- muscle resistance
- vision
- color vision
- hearing
- heart
- lungs
- diabetes

The doctor may be on the staff of the police department or, in smaller departments, someone outside the department with his or her own practice, just like your own doctor. Your blood pressure, temperature, weight, and so on will be measured; your heart and lungs will be listened to; and your limbs will be examined. The doctor will peer into your eyes, ears, nose, and mouth. You will also have to give some blood and some urine for testing. Because of those tests, you won't know the results of the medical exam right away. You will probably be notified in writing in a few weeks, after the test results come in.

▶ Now What?

You have taken all the tests, so what next? Waiting is usually the answer. You have to wait because the results of the tests may take a while. So might the recommendations from the oral board, the psychologist, and the background investigator.

Wait Patiently

You may have several weeks, months, or more to practice patience while waiting to find out how you did on your exams. Even if you are tempted, don't pester the department with phone calls, asking if you made it to the eligibility list or how much longer it will be before you find out your results. For one thing, when you call the department, you will most likely be talking to a receptionist who cannot give you that information anyway. For another, even if you did get through to a higher official, you would be making an impression you don't want to make—that of a pest! They can't indulge the concerns of every new applicant who wants to know how he or she did on a test.

However, you don't have to sit around and do nothing while waiting to find out whether you have been selected. In fact, it will work in your best interest if you actively pursue activities that will help to further your new career. Volunteer somewhere in the community. Work hard at your physical fitness training. Learn more about the law. Even if a problem comes up this time around, you can always try again later or at a different department. Decide now to be successful. Get out there and shine!

▶ If You Get Bad News

The selection process for police officers is a rigorous one. If you fail one or more of the steps, take time for some serious self-evaluation. The good news is that many police officers on the job today failed one or more portions of the test. However, the reason they are on the job is because they, like you, learned from their experience, practiced many of the techniques and tactics in this book, and went on to become police officers.

If you fail the written test, look at the reasons you didn't do well. Was it just that the format was unfamiliar? Well, now you know what to expect.

Do you need to brush up on some of the skills tested? There are lots of books out there to help with reading, writing, and mathematics. Enlist a teacher or a friend to help you, or check out the basic reading and writing courses offered by local high schools and community colleges.

Many cities allow you to retest after a waiting period—a period you can use to improve your skills. If the exam isn't being offered again for years, consider trying another police department.

If you fail the physical ability test, your course of action is clear. Increase your daily physical exercise until you know you can do what is required, and then retest or try another police department.

If you fail the oral board, try to figure out what the problem was. This could be a little trickier to figure out, since you probably won't be told specifics about what exactly the problem was. However, going back over the interview in your mind should provide some clues. How did you feel during the interview? Did you have a hard time expressing yourself? Were you fidgety or inattentive? Were there moments when you lost your temper or found yourself answering questions in a defensive manner?

Practice improving your communication skills. Take a course or read books about effective communication. Talk to other police officers and find out what kinds of answers they gave during their interviews. Go online and visit discussion boards where others are talking about their own oral board interview experiences. Take a look at your opinions and beliefs about the law and the use of force. Are you overly eager to respond aggressively to chaotic situations? Police department officials are looking for candidates with cool heads and sound judgment. They don't want a loose cannon among their new recruits.

If the medical exam eliminates you, you will usually be notified as to what condition caused the problem. Is the condition one that can be corrected? See your doctor for advice. A few minor conditions can eliminate you in one department but be acceptable in another. Contact the recruiting officer at a nearby police department to see if you can apply there.

If you don't make the list and aren't told why, the problem might have been the oral board or, more likely, the psychological evaluation or the background investigation. Did past drug use eliminate you? Different jurisdictions have different criteria when judging the past drug use of an applicant. Some have a zero tolerance policy where they don't allow applicants to have had any previous drug use whatsoever. However, most jurisdictions are more lenient about past drug use and will put a time constraint on their policy, such as no drug use in the past 3–5 years. Other departments have a rule that says you may have used drugs as a juvenile but not as an adult. If past drug use turns out to be a problem for you in the police department you are applying to, it may not be in another jurisdiction. However, if you have had a consistent pattern of drug or alcohol abuse, especially if it is recent, you will most likely have a problem wherever you apply.

If the problem isn't drug use, can you think of anything else in your past that might lead to questions about your fitness to be a police officer? Could any of your personal traits or attitudes raise such questions? Get the opinions of others you know, especially those who are not emotionally connected to you, such as a former teacher or employer. Ask them if there is anything they can think of that might work against you in a psychological evaluation. Encourage them to be honest, and explain why you wish to know.

And then the hard question: Is there anything you can do to change these aspects of your past or your personality? If so, you might have a chance when you reapply or apply to another police department. If not, it may be time to think about another field.

If you feel you were wrongly excluded, most departments have appeals procedures if the rejection was on the basis of a psychological evaluation or background check. However, that word *wrongly* is very important. The psychologist or background investigator almost certainly had to supply a rationale in recommending that the department not hire you. Do you have solid factual evidence that you can use in an administrative hearing to counter such a rationale? If not, you would be wasting your time and money, as well as the police department's, by making an appeal. Move carefully and get legal advice before you take such a step.

▶ Still Waiting?

If you make the eligibility list, go through the waiting game, and still aren't selected, don't despair. Think through all the steps of the selection process, and use them to do a critical self-evaluation.

Maybe your written, physical, and oral board scores were high enough to pass but not high enough to put you near the top of the list. At the next testing, make sure you are better prepared so you can achieve higher scores.

Maybe you had an excellent score that should have put you at the top of the list, and you suspect that you were passed over for someone lower down on the list. That means someone less qualified was selected while you were not, right? Maybe, maybe not.

There were probably a lot of people on the list, and a lot of them may have scored high too. One more point on the written test might have made the difference, or maybe the department had the freedom to pick and choose on the basis of other qualifications. Maybe, in comparison with you, a lot of people on the list had more education or job-related experience. Maybe there was a special need for people with particular skills, like proficiency in Spanish or Cantonese or training in photography. Or maybe the department is focusing on recruiting a specific group or gender to which you don't belong.

What can you do? You may have heard or read about a lot of lawsuits being brought against law enforcement agencies about their selection processes, particularly in large cities. That's a last resort, a step you would take only after getting excellent legal advice and thinking through the costs of time, money, and energy. You would also have to think about whether you would want to occupy a position you got as the result of a lawsuit and whether you would be hurting your chances of being hired somewhere else.

If you are not selected for the exact position you applied for, in the area you wanted to be hired in, this does not mean you should give up altogether. Most people are better off simply trying again. And don't limit your options. There are lots of police departments all over the country, and there are other careers available in law enforcement as well. Do your research. Find out what's available. Find out who's hiring. Consider applying to smaller agencies in small towns or rural agencies, to sheriff's departments, to the state police, or a federal agency. Being turned down by one police department need not be the end of your law enforcement career. See Chapter 22 for information on county, state, and federal job opportunities.

▶ When You Are Selected

Congratulations! The end of the waiting game for you is notification that you have been selected. What happens next, in most cases, is that you'll go to the police academy. Then you are on your way to a career in law enforcement.

In most jurisdictions, you will be hired as a police recruit. You will be paid to go to the academy, usually at a lower rate than you will make when you actually become a member of the force. Academies typically run between 12–30 weeks and include physical and firearms training as well as courses in the laws you will be expected to enforce and in police techniques and procedures. In many jurisdictions, the academy is followed by a period of field training in the jurisdiction that hired you.

After your field training is complete, many states require you to pass a certification exam. This exam is usually based on the same curriculum you studied at the academy, so you should know exactly what to expect. The exam is tough, but the department has already invested a lot of time and money in you and will be sure to prepare you sufficiently beforehand. They want you to succeed!

Once the certification exam is passed, you have passed the finish line. Your hard work and dedication have paid off, and you can stand tall and proud at your swearing-in ceremony, in full dress uniform, as you vow to protect the lives and property of the citizens of your community.

CHAPTER

The Police Officer Suitability Test

CHAPTER SUMMARY

Wanting to be a police officer is one thing; being suited for it is something else. The following quiz can help you decide whether you and this career will make a good match.

There is no one type of person who becomes a police officer. People drawn to law enforcement are as varied as any other group of people in their personalities, experience, and styles. At the same time, there are some attitudes and behaviors that seem to predict success and satisfaction in this profession. These factors have nothing to do with your intelligence and ability—they simply reflect how you interact with other people and how you choose to approach the world. Suitability is therefore key in selecting police officer candidates.

These suitability factors were pulled from research literature and discussions with police psychologists and screeners across the country. They fall into five groups; each group has ten questions in this test.

The LearningExpress Police Officer Suitability Test is not a formal psychological test. For one thing, it is not nearly long enough; the MMPI (Minnesota Multiphasic Personality Inventory) test used in most psychological assessments has 11 times more items than you will find here. For another, it does not focus on your general mental health.

Instead, the test should be viewed as an informal guide—a private tool to help you decide whether being a police officer would suit you, and whether you would enjoy it. It also provides the opportunity for greater self-understanding, which is beneficial no matter what you choose to do for a living.

▶ The Police Officer Suitability Test

Directions

You will need about 20 minutes to answer the following 50 questions. It's a good idea to answer all of the questions in one sitting—scoring and interpretation can be done later. For each question, consider how often the attitude or behavior applies to you. You have a choice between Never, Rarely, Sometimes, Often, and Always; write the number for your answer in the space after each question. To score your answers, see the table below. How the numbers add up will be explained later. If you try to outsmart the test or figure out the "right" answers, you won't get an accurate picture at the end. So just be honest.

Don't read the scoring sections before you answer the questions, or you will defeat the whole purpose of the exercise!

How often do the following statements sound like you? Choose only one answer for each statement.

NEVER	RARELY	SOMETIMES	OFTEN	ALWAYS
0	5	10	20	40

1. I like to know what's expected of me. 10
2. I am willing to admit my mistakes to other people. 10
3. Once I've made a decision, I stop thinking about it. 10
4. I can shrug off my fears about getting physically injured. 20
5. I like to know what to expect. 40
6. It takes a lot to get me really angry. 10
7. My first impressions of people tend to be accurate. 20
8. I am aware of my stress level. 20
9. I like to tell other people what to do. 40
10. I enjoy working with others. 40
11. I trust my instincts. 40
12. I enjoy being teased. 10
13. I will spend as much time as it takes to settle a disagreement. 20
14. I feel comfortable in new social situations. 10
15. When I disagree with a person, I let that person know about it. 40
16. I'm in a good mood. 20
17. I'm comfortable making quick decisions when necessary. 40
18. Rules must be obeyed, even if you don't agree with them. 40
19. I like to say exactly what I mean. 40
20. I enjoy being with people. 20

21. I stay away from doing exciting things that I know are dangerous. ______

22. I don't mind when a supervisor tells me what to do. ______

23. I enjoy solving puzzles. ______

24. The people I know consult me about their problems. ______

25. I am comfortable making my own decisions. ______

26. People know where I stand on things. ______

27. When I get stressed, I know how to make myself relax. ______

28. I have confidence in my own judgment. ______

29. I make my friends laugh. ______

30. When I make a promise, I keep it. ______

31. When I'm in a group, I tend to be the leader. ______

32. I can deal with sudden changes in my routine. ______

33. When I get into a fight, I can stop myself from losing control. ______

34. I am open to new facts that might change my mind. ______

35. I understand why I do the things I do. ______

36. I'm good at calming people down. ______

37. I can tell how a person is feeling even when he or she doesn't say anything. ______

38. I can take criticism without getting upset. ______

39. People follow my advice. ______

40. I pay attention to people's body language. ______

41. It's important for me to make a good impression. ______

42. I remember to show up on time. ______

43. When I meet new people, I try to understand them. ______

44. I avoid doing things on impulse. ______

45. Being respected is important to me. ______

46. People see me as a calm person. ______

47. It's more important for me to do a good job than to get praised for it. ______

48. I make my decisions based on common sense. ______

49. I prefer to keep my feelings to myself when I'm with strangers. ______

50. I take responsibility for my own actions rather than blaming others. ______

▶ Scoring

Attitudes and behaviors can't be measured in units, like distance or weight. Besides, psychological categories tend to overlap. As a result, the numbers and dividing lines between score ranges are approximate, and numbers may vary about 20 points either way. If your score doesn't fall in the optimal range, it doesn't mean a failure—only that an area needs more focus.

It may help to share your test results with some of the people who are close to you. Very often, there are differences between how we see ourselves and how we actually come across to others.

Group 1—Risk Questions

Add up scores for questions 4, 6, 12, 15, 21, 27, 33, 38, 44, and 46.

TOTAL = ______

This group of questions evaluates your tendency to be assertive and take risks. The ideal is in the middle, somewhere between timid and reckless: You should be willing to take risks, but not seek them out just for excitement. Being nervous, impulsive, or afraid of physical injury is an undesirable trait for a police officer. This group also reflects how well you take teasing and criticism, both of which you may encounter every day as a police officer. And as you can imagine, it's also important for someone who carries a gun not to have a short fuse.

- A score between 360 and 400 is rather extreme, suggesting a short temper that could be dangerous in the field.
- If you score between 170 and 360, you are on the right track.
- If you score between 80 and 170, you may want to think about how comfortable you are with the idea of confrontation.
- A score between 0 and 80 indicates that the more dangerous and stressful aspects of the job might be difficult for you.

Group 2—Core Character Traits

Add up scores for questions 2, 8, 16, 19, 26, 30, 35, 42, 47, and 50.

TOTAL = ______

This group reflects such basic traits as stability, reliability, and self-awareness. Can your fellow officers count on you to back them up and do your part? Are you secure enough to do your job without needing praise? In the words of one police psychologist, "If you're hungry for praise, you will starve to death." The public will not always appreciate your efforts, and your supervisors and colleagues may be too busy or preoccupied to pat you on the back.

It is crucial to be able to admit your mistakes and take responsibility for your actions, to be confident without being arrogant or conceited, and to be straightforward and direct in your communication. In a job where lives are at stake, the facts must be clear. Having control of your moods is also very important. While we all have good and bad days, someone who is depressed much of the time is not encouraged to pursue police work; depression affects one's judgment, energy level, and the ability to respond and communicate.

- If you score between 180 and 360, you are in the ballpark. A score of over 360 may indicate that your answers were unrealistic.
- A score of 100–180 indicates that you should look at the questions again and evaluate your style of social interaction.
- Scores between 0 and 100 suggest you may not be ready for this job yet.

Group 3—Judgment Questions

Add up scores for questions 3, 7, 11, 17, 23, 28, 37, 40, 43, and 48.

TOTAL = ______

This group of questions evaluates how you make decisions. Successful police officers are sensitive to unspoken messages, can detect and respond to other people's feelings, and are able to make fair and accurate assessments of a situation, rather than being influenced by their own personal biases and needs. Once the decision to act is made, second-guessing can be dangerous. Police officers must make their best judgments in line with accepted practices, and then act upon these judgments without hesitancy or self-doubt. Finally, it's important to know and accept that you cannot change the world single-handedly. People who seek this career because they want to make a dramatic individual difference in human suffering are likely to be frustrated and disappointed.

- A score over 360 indicates you may be trying too hard.
- If you scored between 170 and 360, your style of making decisions, especially about people, fits with the desired police officer profile.
- Scores between 80 and 170 suggest that you think about how you make judgments and how much confidence you have in them.
- If you scored between 80 and 170, making judgments may be a problem area for you.

Group 4—Authority/Leadership Questions

Add scores for questions 1, 10, 13, 18, 22, 25, 31, 34, 39, and 45.

TOTAL = ______

This group contains the essential attributes of respect for rules and authority—including the personal authority of self-reliance and leadership—and the ability to resolve conflict and work with a team. Once again, a good balance is the key. Police officers must accept and communicate the value of structure and control without being rigid. And even though most decisions are made independently in the field, the authority of the supervisor and the law must be obeyed at all times. Anyone on a personal mission for justice or vengeance will not make a good police officer and is unlikely to make it through the screening process.

- A score between 160 and 360 indicates you have the desired attitude toward authority—both your own and that of your superior officers. Any higher may indicate that you were trying too hard to give the "right" answers.
- If you scored between 100 and 160, you might think about whether a demanding leadership role is something you want every day.
- With scores between 0 and 100, ask yourself whether the required combination of structure and independence would be comfortable for you.

Group 5—Personal Style Attributes

Add up scores for questions 5, 9, 14, 20, 24, 29, 32, 36, 41, and 49.

TOTAL = ______

This is the personal style dimension, which describes how you come across to others. Moderation rules here as well: Police officers should be seen as strong and capable, but not dramatic or heavy-handed; friendly, but not overly concerned with whether they are liked; patient, but not to the point of losing control of a situation. A good sense of humor is essential, not only in the field, but also among one's fellow officers. Flexibility is another valuable trait—especially given all the changes that can happen in one shift—but too much flexibility can be perceived as weakness.

- A score between 160 and 360 is optimal. If you scored over 360, you may be trying too hard.
- Scores between 80 and 160 suggest that you compare your style with the preceding description and consider whether anything needs to be modified.
- If you scored between 0 and 80, you might think about the way you interact with others and whether you would be happy in a job where people are the main focus.

▶ Summary

The Police Officer Suitability Test reflects the fact that being a successful police officer requires moderation rather than extremes. Attitudes that are desirable in reasonable amounts can become a real problem if they are too strong. For example, independence is a necessary trait, but too much of it could result in an officer taking the law into his or her own hands. Going outside accepted police procedure is a bad idea; worse, it can put other people's lives in jeopardy.

As one recruiter said, the ideal police officer is "low key and low maintenance." In fact, there's only one thing you can't have too much of, and that's common sense. With everything else, balance is the key. Keep this in mind as you look at your scores.

CHAPTER

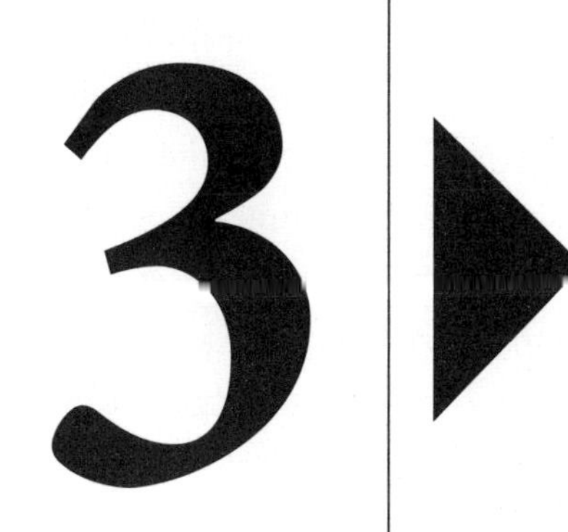

The LearningExpress Test Preparation System

CHAPTER SUMMARY

Taking the police officer written exam can be tough. It demands a lot of preparation if you want to achieve a top score. Your rank on the eligibility list may be determined largely by this score. The LearningExpress Test Preparation System, developed by leading test experts, gives you the discipline and attitude you need to be a winner.

This chapter can help you take control of the entire test preparation process. It clearly explains the steps you need to take to achieve a top score on the written exam. Do not underestimate the importance of doing well on the written exam. Your future career in law enforcement depends on it. This chapter will help you to

- Become familiar with the format of the exam.
- Overcome excessive test anxiety.
- Prepare gradually for the exam instead of cramming.
- Understand and use vital test-taking skills.
- Know how to pace yourself through the exam.
- Learn how to use the process of elimination.
- Know when and how to guess.
- Be in tip-top mental and physical shape on the day of the exam.

Thus, the purpose of this chapter is to ensure that you are in control of the test-prep process. You do not want the exam to control you.

The LearningExpress Test Preparation System puts you in control. In just nine easy-to-follow steps, you will learn everything you need to know to make sure that you are in charge of your preparation and your performance on the exam. Other test takers may let the test get the better of them; other test takers may be unprepared or out of shape, but not you. You will have taken all the steps you need to take to get a high score on the police exam.

Here's how the LearningExpress Test Preparation System works: Nine easy steps lead you through everything you need to know and do to get ready to master your exam. The time next to each of the steps listed below includes both reading about the step and one or more activities. It's important that you do the activities along with the reading, or you won't be getting the full benefit of the system. Each step tells you approximately how much time that step will take you to complete.

We estimate that working through the entire system will take you approximately three hours, though it's perfectly OK if you work faster or slower than the time estimates assume. If you can take a whole afternoon or evening, you can work through the whole LearningExpress Test Preparation System in one sitting. Otherwise, you can break it up, and do just one or two steps a day for the next several days. It's up to you—remember, you are in control.

Nine Steps to Success	**Time**
Step 1. Get Information	30 minutes
Step 2. Conquer Test Anxiety	20 minutes
Step 3. Make a Plan	50 minutes
Step 4. Learn to Manage Your Time	10 minutes
Step 5. Learn to Use the Process of Elimination	20 minutes
Step 6. Know When to Guess	20 minutes
Step 7. Reach Your Peak Performance Zone	10 minutes
Step 8. Get Your Act Together	10 minutes
Step 9. Do It!	10 minutes
Total	**3 hours**

▶ Step 1: Get Information

Time to complete: 30 minutes
Activities: Read Chapter 1, "How Police Officers Are Selected"

Knowledge is power. The first step in the LearningExpress Test Preparation System is finding out everything you can about your police officer written exam. If you have access to the Internet, you can perform a search on any basic search engine to find out if the police department you want to apply to has a website. Or you can check out a site that contains a long list of links to police departments around the country: www.policeone.com/careers. If you find that your targeted police department has a website, review it carefully to see if it contains any information about the written exam. If not, contact the police department you want to apply to and ask for the personnel office. In larger cities, you will be referred to a recruiting unit or to the human resources department. In smaller towns, you may speak to someone right there in the department. Request a position announcement, find out if an exam bulletin is available, and ask when the next written exam is scheduled. If the department issues an exam bulletin, then you'll get a brief outline of what skills will be tested on the written exam.

What You Should Find Out

The more details you can find out about the written exam, either from the bulletin online or from speaking with a recruiter, the more efficiently you'll be able to study. Here's a list of some things you might want to find out about your exam:

- What skills are tested?
- How many sections are on the exam?
- How many questions does each section have?
- Are the questions ordered from easy to hard, or is the sequence random?
- How much time is allotted for each section?
- Are there breaks in between sections?
- What is the passing score and how many questions do you have to answer correctly in order to get that score?
- Does a higher score give you any advantages, like a better rank on the eligibility list?
- How is the test scored: Is there a penalty for incorrect answers?
- Are you permitted to go back to a prior section or move on to the next section if you finish early?
- Can you write in the test booklet or will you be given scratch paper?
- What should you bring with you on exam day?

What's on Most Police Officer Exams

The skills that the police officer written exam tests vary from city to city. That's why it's important to contact the recruiting office of your police department to find out exactly what skills are covered. Below are the most commonly tested subjects:

- Reading Comprehension
- Grammar
- Vocabulary and Spelling
- Math
- Judgment
- Map Reading
- Memory and Observation
- Number and Letter Recall
- Personal Background

If you haven't already done so, stop here and read Chapter 1 of this book, which gives you an overview of the entire police officer selection process. Then move on to the next step to find out how you can get a handle on test anxiety.

▶ Step 2: Conquer Test Anxiety

Time to complete: 20 minutes
Activity: Take the Test Stress Test
Having as much information as possible about the exam is the first step in getting control of the exam. Next, you have to overcome one of the biggest obstacles to test success: test anxiety. Test anxiety cannot only impair your performance on the exam itself, but it can even keep you from preparing! In Step 2, you'll learn stress management techniques that will help you succeed on your exam. Learn these strategies now, and practice them as you work through the exams in this book, so they will be second nature to you by exam day.

Combating Test Anxiety

The first thing you need to know is that a little test anxiety is a good thing. Everyone gets nervous before a big exam—and if that nervousness motivates you to prepare thoroughly, so much the better. It's said that Sir Laurence Olivier, one of the foremost British actors of the twentieth century, was ill before every performance. His stage fright didn't impair his performance; in fact, it probably gave him a little extra edge—just the kind of edge you need to do well, whether on a stage or in an examination room.

Stress Management before the Test

Stress is the difference between your capabilities and the environment. The more prepared you are to handle the examination, the greater your capabilities and the less stress you feel. Preparation for the written exam, oral board, and physical ability test is the only surefire way to increase your score and reduce stress-related anxiety.

If you feel your level of anxiety rising in the weeks before your test, here is what you can do to bring the level down again:

- **Get prepared.** There's nothing like knowing what to expect and being prepared for it to put you in control of test anxiety. That's why you are reading this book. Use it faithfully, and remind yourself that you are better prepared than most of the people who will be taking the test.
- **Practice self-confidence.** A positive attitude is a great way to combat test anxiety. This is no time to be humble or shy. Stand in front of the mirror and say to your reflection, "I'm prepared. I'm full of self-confidence. I'm going to ace this test. I know I can do it." If you hear it often enough, you will believe it.
- **Fight negative messages.** Every time someone starts telling you how hard the exam is or how it's almost impossible to get a high score, fight back by telling them your self-confidence messages above. If the someone with the negative messages is you, telling yourself *you don't do well on exams, you just can't do this,* don't listen. Listen to your self-confidence messages instead.
- **Visualize.** Imagine yourself reporting for duty on your first day of police academy training. Think of yourself wearing your uniform with pride and learning the skills you will use for the rest of your life. Visualizing success can help make it happen—and it reminds you of why you are doing all this work in preparing for the exam.
- **Exercise.** Physical activity helps calm your body down and focus your mind. Being in good physical shape can actually help you do well on the exam, as well as prepare you for the physical ability test. So, go for a run, lift weights, go swimming—and do it regularly.

Stress Management on Test Day

There are several ways you can bring down your level of test anxiety on test day. They will work best if you practice them in the weeks before the test, so you know which ones work best for you.

Test Stress Test

You need to worry about test anxiety only if it is extreme enough to impair your performance. The following questionnaire will provide a diagnosis of your level of test anxiety. In the blank before each statement, write the number that most accurately describes your experience.

0 = Never 1 = Once or twice 2 = Sometimes 3 = Often

___ I have gotten so nervous before an exam that I simply put down the books and didn't study for it.
___ I have experienced disabling physical symptoms such as vomiting and severe headaches because I was nervous about an exam.
___ I have simply not showed up for an exam because I was scared to take it.
___ I have experienced dizziness and disorientation while taking an exam.
___ I have had trouble filling in the little circles because my hands were shaking too hard.
___ I have failed an exam because I was too nervous to complete it.
___ **Total: Add up the numbers in the blanks above.**

Your Test Stress Score

Here are the steps you should take, depending on your score. If you scored

- **Below 3,** your level of test anxiety is nothing to worry about; it is probably just enough to give you that little extra edge.
- **Between 3 and 6,** your test anxiety may be enough to impair your performance, and you should practice the stress management techniques listed in this section to try to bring your test anxiety down to manageable levels.
- **Above 6,** your level of test anxiety is a serious concern. In addition to practicing the stress management techniques listed in this section, you may want to seek additional, personal help. Call your local high school or community college and ask for the academic counselor. Tell the counselor that you have a level of test anxiety that sometimes keeps you from being able to take an exam. The counselor may be willing to help you or may suggest someone else you should talk to.

- **Deep breathing.** Take a deep breath while you count to five. Hold it for a count of one, then let it out on a count of five. Repeat several times.
- **Move your body.** Try rolling your head in a circle. Rotate your shoulders. Shake your hands from the wrist. Many people find these movements very relaxing.
- **Visualize again.** Think of the place where you are most relaxed: lying on the beach in the sun, walking through the park, or wherever is most comforting to you. Now close your eyes and imagine you are actually there. If you practice in advance, you'll find that you need only a few seconds of this exercise to experience a significant increase in your sense of well-being.

When anxiety threatens to overwhelm you right there during the exam, there are still things you can do to manage the stress level:

- **Repeat your self-confidence messages.** You should have them memorized by now. Say them silently to yourself, and believe them!
- **Visualize one more time.** This time, visualize yourself moving smoothly and quickly through the test, answering every question right and finishing just before time is up. Like most visualization techniques, this one works best if you have practiced it ahead of time.
- **Find an easy question.** Skim over the test until you find an easy question, and answer it. Getting even one circle filled in can get you into the test-taking groove.
- **Take a mental break.** Everyone loses concentration once in a while during a long test. It's normal, so you shouldn't worry about it. Instead, accept what has happened. Say to yourself, "Hey, I lost it there for a minute. My brain is taking a break." Put down your pencil, close your eyes, and do some deep breathing for a few seconds. Then you'll be ready to go back to work.

Answer the questions on the Test Stress Test to learn more about your level of test anxiety.

▶ Step 3: Make a Plan

Time to complete: 50 minutes
Activity: Construct a study plan
One of the most important things you can do to get control of yourself and your exam is to make a study plan. Too many people fail to prepare simply because they fail to plan. Spending hours the day before the exam poring over sample test questions not only raises your level of test anxiety, but it also is simply no substitute for careful preparation and practice over time.

Police Officer Exams	Study Chapters
Exam 1, Chapter 4 Exam 4, Chapter 16 *These exams test your basic reading and writing skills.*	7. Reading Text, Tables, Charts, and Graphs 8. Grammar 9. Vocabulary and Spelling
Exam 2, Chapter 5 Exam 5, Chapter 17 *These exams test job-related skills, such as memory and observation.*	7. Reading Text, Tables, Charts, and Graphs 10. Math 11. Judgment 12. Map Reading 13. Memory and Observation
Exam 3, Chapter 6 Exam 6, Chapter 18 *These exams are similar to the Law Enforcement Candidate Record (LECR) exam.*	9. Vocabulary and Spelling 14. Number and Letter Recall 15. Personal Background

Don't fall into the cram trap. Take control of your preparation time by mapping out a study schedule. There are four sample schedules on the following pages, based on the amount of time you have before the exam. If you are the kind of person who needs deadlines and assignments to motivate you for a project, here they are. If you are the kind of person who doesn't like to follow other people's plans, you can use the suggested schedules here to construct your own.

An important aspect of a study plan is flexibility. Your plan should help you, not hinder you, so be prepared to alter your study schedule once you get started, if necessary. You will probably find that one or more steps will take longer to complete than you had anticipated, while others will go more quickly.

In constructing your study plan, you should take into account how much work you need to do. If your score on the first practice test wasn't what you had hoped, consider taking some of the steps from Schedule A and getting them into Schedule D somehow, even if you have only three weeks before the exam.

You can also customize your study plan according to the information you gathered in Step 1. If the exam you have to take doesn't include memory questions, for instance, you can skip Chapter 13 and concentrate instead on some other area that *is* covered. The table on page 32 lists all the chapters you need to study for each exam.

Even more important than making a plan is making a commitment. You can't improve your skills in reading, writing, and judgment overnight. You have to set aside some time every day for study and practice. Try for at least 20 minutes a day. Twenty minutes daily will do you much more good than two hours on Saturday.

If you have months before the exam, you are lucky. Don't put off your study until the week before the exam! Start now. Even ten minutes a day, with half an hour or more on weekends, can make a big difference in your score—and in your chances of making the force!

Schedule A: The Leisure Plan

If no test has been announced yet in your city, you may have a year or more in which to get ready. This schedule gives you six months to sharpen your skills. If an exam is announced in the middle of your preparation, you can use one of the later schedules to help you compress your study program. Study only the chapters that are relevant to the type of exam you will be taking.

Time	Preparation
6 months before the test	Take one of the exams from Chapters 4, 5, or 6. Then study the explanations for the answers until you know you could answer all the questions right. Start going to the library once every two weeks to read books or magazines about law enforcement, or browse through police-related websites.
5 months before the test	Read Chapters 7 and 8 and work through the exercises. Use at least one of the additional resources listed in each chapter. If possible, find other people who are preparing for the test and form a study group.
4 months before the test	Read Chapters 9 and 10 and work through the exercises. Use at least one of the additional resources for each chapter. Start making flash cards of vocabulary and spelling words, and practice your math by making up problems from everyday events.
3 months before the test	Read Chapters 11 and 12 and work through the exercises. Do at least one of the suggested exercises at the end of Chapter 11.
2 months before the test	Read Chapters 13, 14, and 15 and work through the exercises. Exercise your memory by making note of people and places you see each day. Continue to read and work with your flash cards.
1 month before the test	Take one of the sample tests in Chapters 16, 17, or 18. Use your score to help you decide where to concentrate your efforts this month. Go back to the relevant chapters and use the extra resources listed there, or get the help of a friend or teacher.
1 week before the test	Review both of the sample tests you took. See how much you've learned in the past months. Concentrate on what you have done well and resolve not to let any areas where you still feel uncertain bother you.
1 day before the test	Relax. Do something unrelated to police exams. Eat a good meal and go to bed at your usual time.

Schedule B: The Just-Enough-Time Plan

If you have three to six months before your exam, that should be enough time to prepare for the written test, especially if you score above 70% on the first sample test you take. This schedule assumes four months; stretch it out or compress it if you have more or less time, and study only the chapters that are relevant to the type of exam you will be taking.

Time	**Preparation**
4 months before the test	Take one practice exam from Chapters 4, 5, or 6 to determine where you need the most work. Read Chapters 7, 8, and 9 and work through the exercises. Use at least one of the additional resources listed in each chapter. Start going to the library once every two weeks to read books about law enforcement, or visit police-related websites online. Also, make flash cards of vocabulary and spelling words.
3 months before the test	Read Chapters 10 and 11 and work through the exercises. Use at least one of the additional resources for each chapter. Practice your math by making up problems from everyday events. Do at least one of the suggested exercises at the end of Chapter 11.
2 months before the test	Read Chapters 12, 13, and 14 and work through the exercises. Exercise your memory by making note of people and places you see each day. Continue to read and work with your flash cards.
1 month before the test	Take one of the sample tests in Chapters 16, 17, or 18. Use your score to help you decide where to concentrate your efforts this month. Go back to the relevant chapters and use the extra resources listed there, or get the help of a friend or teacher.
1 week before the test	Review both of the sample tests you took. See how much you have learned in the past months. Concentrate on what you have done well, and resolve not to let any areas where you still feel uncertain bother you.
1 day before the test	Relax. Do something unrelated to police exams. Eat a good meal and go to bed at your usual time.

Schedule C: More Study in Less Time

If you have one to three months before the exam, you still have enough time for some concentrated study that will help you improve your score. This schedule is built around a two-month time frame. If you have only one month, spend an extra couple of hours a week to get all these steps in. If you have three months, take some of the steps from Schedule B and fit them in. Study only the chapters that are relevant to the type of exam you will be taking.

Time	Preparation
8 weeks before the test	Take one sample test from Chapters 4, 5, or 6 to find your weakest subjects. Choose the appropriate chapter(s) from among Chapters 7–15 to read in these two weeks. Use some of the additional resources listed there. When you get to those chapters in this plan, review them.
6 weeks before the test	Read Chapters 7–11 and work through the exercises.
4 weeks before the test	Read Chapters 12–15 and work through the exercises.
2 weeks before the test	Take one of the second sample tests in Chapters 16, 17, or 18. Then score it and read the answer explanations until you are sure you understand them. Review the areas where your score is lowest.
1 week before the test	Review Chapters 7–15, concentrating on the areas where a little work can help the most.
1 day before the test	Relax. Do something unrelated to police exams. Eat a good meal and go to bed at your usual time.

Schedule D: The Fast Track

If you have three weeks or less before the exam, you really have your work cut out for you. Carve half an hour out of your day, *every day*, for study. This schedule assumes you have the whole three weeks to prepare in; if you have less time, you'll have to compress the schedule accordingly. Study only the chapters that are relevant to the type of exam you will be taking.

Time	Preparation
3 weeks before the test	Take one practice exam from Chapters 4, 5, or 6. Then read the material in Chapters 7–11 and work through the exercises.
2 weeks before the test	Read the material in Chapters 12–15 and work through the exercises. Take one of the sample tests in Chapter 16, 17, or 18.
1 week before the test	Evaluate your performance on the second sample test. Review the parts of Chapters 7–15 where you had the most trouble. Get a friend or teacher to help you with the section you found to be the most difficult.
2 days before the test	Review both of the sample tests you took. Make sure you understand all of the answer explanations.
1 day before the test	Relax. Do something unrelated to police exams. Eat a good meal and go to bed at your usual time.

▶ Step 4: Learn to Manage Your Time

Time to complete: 10 minutes to read, many hours of practice!
Activities: Practice these strategies as you take the sample tests in this book

Steps 4, 5, and 6 of the LearningExpress Test Preparation System put you in charge of your exam by showing you test-taking strategies that work. Practice these strategies as you take the sample tests in this book, and then you will be ready to use them on test day.

First, you will take control of your time on the exam. The first step in achieving this control is to find out the format of the exam you're going to take. Some police exams have different sections that are each timed separately. If this is true of the exam you'll be taking, you'll want to practice using your time wisely on the practice exams and trying to avoid mistakes while working quickly. Other types of exams don't have separately timed sections. If this is the case, just practice pacing yourself on the practice exams, so you don't spend too much time on difficult questions.

- **Listen carefully to directions.** By the time you get to the exam, you should be familiar with how all the sections work, but listen to the person who is administering the exam just in case something has changed.
- **Pace yourself.** Glance at your watch every few minutes, and compare the time to how far you've gotten in the sections. When one-quarter of the time has elapsed, you should be a quarter of the way through the sections and so on. If you're falling behind, pick up the pace a bit.
- **Keep moving.** Don't spend too much time on any one question. If you don't know the answer, skip the question and move on. Circle the number of the question in your test booklet in case you have time to come back to it later.
- **Keep track of your place on the answer sheet.** If you skip a question, make sure you skip that space on the answer sheet too. Check yourself every 5–10 questions to make sure the question number and the answer sheet number are still the same.
- **Don't rush.** Though you should keep moving steadily through the test, rushing won't help. Try to keep calm and work methodically and quickly.

▶ Step 5: Learn to Use the Process of Elimination

Time to complete: 20 minutes
Activity: Complete worksheet on Using the Process of Elimination

After time management, your next most important tool for taking control of your exam is using the process of elimination wisely. It's standard test-taking wisdom that you should always read all the answer choices before choosing your answer. This practice helps you find the right answer by eliminating wrong answer choices. And, sure enough, that standard wisdom applies to your exam, too.

Let's say you're facing a vocabulary question that goes like this:

13. "Biology uses a binomial system of classification." In this sentence, the word *binomial* most nearly means
a. understanding the law.
b. having two names.
c. scientifically sound.
d. having a double meaning.

If you happen to know what *binomial* means, of course, you don't need to use the process of elimination, but let's assume that, like many people, you don't. So you look at the answer choices. "Understanding the law" sure doesn't sound very likely for something having to do with biology. So you eliminate choice **a**—and now you have only three answer choices to deal with. Mark an **X** next to choice **a** so you never have to read it again.

On to the other answer choices. If you know that the prefix *bi*- means *two*, as in *bicycle*, flag answer **b** as a possible answer. Mark a check mark beside it, meaning "good answer, I might use this one."

Choice **c**, "scientifically sound," is a possibility. At least it's about science, not law. It could work here, though, when you think about it, having a "scientifically sound" classification system in a scientific field is kind of redundant. You remember the *bi* thing in *binomial*, and probably continue to like answer **b** better. But you are not sure, so you put a question mark next to **c**, meaning "well, maybe."

Now, choice **d**, "having a double meaning." You are still keeping in mind that *bi*- means *two*, so this one looks possible at first. But then you look again at the sentence the word belongs in, and you think, "Why would biology want a system of classification that has two meanings? That wouldn't work very well!" If you are really taken with the idea that *bi* means *two*, you might put a question mark here. But if you are feeling a little more confident, you'll put an **X**. You have already got a better answer picked out.

Now your question looks like this:

13. "Biology uses a binomial system of classification." In this sentence, the word *binomial* most nearly means

X **a.** understanding the law.
✔ **b.** having two names.
? **c.** scientifically sound.
? **d.** having a double meaning.

You have just one check mark, for a good answer. If you are pressed for time, you should simply mark choice **b** on your answer sheet. If you have got the time to be extra careful, you could compare your check-mark answer to your question-mark answers to make sure that it's better. (It is: The *binomial* system in biology is the one that gives a two-part genus and species name like *homo sapiens*.)

It's good to have a system for marking good, bad, and maybe answers. We're recommending this one:

X = bad
✔ = good
? = maybe

If you don't like these marks, devise your own system. Just make sure you do it long before test day—while you are working through the practice exams in this book—so you won't have to worry about it during the test.

Even when you think you're absolutely clueless about a question, you can often use the process of elimination to get rid of at least one answer choice. If so, you're better prepared to make an educated guess, as you will see in Step 6. More often, the process of elimination allows you to get down to only two possibly right answers. Then you're in a strong position to guess. And sometimes, even though you don't know the right answer, you can find it simply by getting rid of the wrong ones, as you did in the last example.

Try using your powers of elimination on the questions in the worksheet entitled Using the Process of Elimination that begins page 40. The answer explanations there show one possible way you might use the process to arrive at the right answer.

The process of elimination is your tool for the next step, which is knowing when to guess.

Using the Process of Elimination

Use the process of elimination to answer the following questions.

1. Ilsa is as old as Meghan will be in five years. The difference between Ed's age and Meghan's age is twice the difference between Ilsa's age and Meghan's age. Ed is 29. How old is Ilsa?

- **a.** 4
- **b.** 10
- **c.** 19
- **d.** 24

2. "All drivers of commercial vehicles must carry a valid commercial driver's license whenever operating a commercial vehicle." According to this sentence, which of the following people need NOT carry a commercial driver's license?

- **a.** a truck driver idling his engine while waiting to be directed to a loading dock
- **b.** a bus operator backing her bus out of the way of another bus in the bus lot
- **c.** a taxi driver driving his personal car to the grocery store
- **d.** a limousine driver taking the limousine to her home after dropping off her last passenger of the evening

3. Smoking tobacco has been linked to

- **a.** increased risk of stroke and heart attack.
- **b.** all forms of respiratory disease.
- **c.** increasing mortality rates over the past ten years.
- **d.** juvenile delinquency.

4. Which of the following words is spelled correctly?

- **a.** incorrigible
- **b.** outragous
- **c.** domestickated
- **d.** understandible

Answers

Here are the answers, as well as some suggestions as to how you might have used the process of elimination to find them.

1. d. You should have eliminated choice **a** off the bat. Ilsa can't be four years old if Meghan is going to be Ilsa's age in five years. The best way to eliminate the other answer choices is to try plugging them into the information given in the problem. For instance, for choice **b**, if Ilsa is 10, then Meghan must be 5. The difference in their ages is 5. The difference between Ed's age, 29, and Meghan's age, 5, is 24. Is 24 two times 5? No. Then choice **b** is wrong. You could eliminate choice **c** in the same way and be left with choice **d**.

2. c. Note the word *not* in the question, and go through the answers one by one. Is the truck driver in choice **a** "operating a commercial vehicle"? Yes, idling counts as "operating," so he needs to have a commercial driver's license. Likewise, the bus operator in choice **b** is operating a commercial vehicle; the question doesn't say the operator has to be on the street. The limo driver in **d** is operating a commercial vehicle, even if it doesn't have passenger in it. However, the cabbie in choice **c** is not operating a commercial vehicle, but his own private car.

Using the Process of Elimination (continued)

3. a. You could eliminate choice **b** simply because of the presence of the word *all*. Such absolutes hardly ever appear in correct answer choices. Choice **c** looks attractive until you think a little about what you know—aren't *fewer* people smoking these days, rather than more? So how could smoking be responsible for a higher mortality rate? (If you didn't know that *mortality rate* means the rate at which people die, you might keep this choice as a possibility, but you'd still be able to eliminate two answers and have only two to choose from.) And choice **d** seems seems unlikely, so you could eliminate that one, too. And you're left with the correct choice, **a**.

4. a. How you used the process of elimination here depends on which words you recognized as being spelled incorrectly. If you knew that the correct spellings were *outrageous*, *domesticated*, and *understandable*, then you were home free.

▶ Step 6: Know When to Guess

Time to complete: 20 minutes
Activity: Complete worksheet on Your Guessing Ability

Armed with the process of elimination, you're ready to take control of one of the big questions in test taking: Should I guess? Unless the exam has a guessing penalty, you have nothing to lose and everything to gain from guessing. The more complicated answer depends both on the exam and on you—your personality and your guessing intuition.

Most police officer written exams don't use a guessing penalty. The number of questions you answer correctly yields your score, and there's no penalty for wrong answers. So most of the time, you don't have to worry—simply go ahead and guess. But if you find that your exam does have a guessing penalty, you should read the section below to find out what that means to you.

How the Guessing Penalty Works

A guessing penalty really works only against *random* guessing—filling in the little circles to make a nice pattern on your answer sheet. If you can eliminate one or more answer choices, as outlined previously, you're better off taking a guess than leaving the answer blank, even on the sections that have a penalty.

Here's how a guessing penalty works: Depending on the number of answer choices in a given exam, some proportion of the number of questions you get incorrect is subtracted from the total number of questions you got correct. For instance, if there are four answer choices, typically the guessing penalty is one-third of your wrong answers. Suppose you took a test of 100 questions. You answered 88 of them correctly and 12 incorrectly.

If there's no guessing penalty, your score is simply 88. But if there's a one-third point guessing penalty, the scorers take your 12 incorrect answers and divide by 3 to come up with 4. Then they subtract that 4 from your correct-answer score of 88 to leave you with a score of 84. Thus, you would have been better off if you had simply not answered those 12 questions that you weren't sure of. Then your total score would still be 88, because there wouldn't be anything to subtract.

What You Should Do about the Guessing Penalty

That's how a guessing penalty works. The first thing this means for you is that marking your answer sheet at random doesn't pay. If you're running out of time on

Your Guessing Ability

The following are ten really hard questions. You're not supposed to know the answers. Rather, this is an assessment of your ability to guess when you don't have a clue. Read each question carefully, just as if you did expect to answer it. If you have any knowledge at all of the subject of the question, use that knowledge to help you eliminate wrong answer choices. Use this answer grid to fill in your answers to the questions.

1.	ⓐ	ⓑ	ⓒ	ⓓ	**5.**	ⓐ	ⓑ	ⓒ	ⓓ	**9.**	ⓐ	ⓑ	ⓒ	ⓓ
2.	ⓐ	ⓑ	ⓒ	ⓓ	**6.**	ⓐ	ⓑ	ⓒ	ⓓ	**10.**	ⓐ	ⓑ	ⓒ	ⓓ
3.	ⓐ	ⓑ	ⓒ	ⓓ	**7.**	ⓐ	ⓑ	ⓒ	ⓓ					
4.	ⓐ	ⓑ	ⓒ	ⓓ	**8.**	ⓐ	ⓑ	ⓒ	ⓓ					

1. September 7 is Independence Day in
- **a.** India.
- **b.** Costa Rica.
- **c.** Brazil.
- **d.** Australia.

2. Which of the following is the formula for determining the momentum of an object?
- **a.** $p = mv$
- **b.** $F = ma$
- **c.** $P = IV$
- **d.** $E = mc^2$

3. Because of the expansion of the universe, the stars and other celestial bodies are all moving away from each other. This phenomenon is known as
- **a.** Newton's first law.
- **b.** the big bang.
- **c.** gravitational collapse.
- **d.** Hubble flow.

4. American author Gertrude Stein was born in
- **a.** 1713.
- **b.** 1830.
- **c.** 1874.
- **d.** 1901.

5. Which of the following is NOT one of the Five Classics attributed to Confucius?
- **a.** *I Ching*
- **b.** *Book of Holiness*
- **c.** *Spring and Autumn Annals*
- **d.** *Book of History*

6. The religious and philosophical doctrine that holds that the universe is constantly in a struggle between good and evil is known as
- **a.** Pelagianism.
- **b.** Manichaeanism.
- **c.** neo-Hegelianism.
- **d.** Epicureanism.

7. The third chief justice of the Supreme Court was
- **a.** John Blair.
- **b.** William Cushing.
- **c.** James Wilson.
- **d.** John Jay.

8. Which of the following is the poisonous portion of a daffodil?
- **a.** the bulb
- **b.** the leaves
- **c.** the stem
- **d.** the flowers

Your Guessing Ability (continued)

9. The winner of the Masters golf tournament in 1953 was

a. Sam Snead.
b. Cary Middlecoff.
c. Arnold Palmer.
d. Ben Hogan.

10. The state with the highest per capita personal income in 1980 was

a. Alaska.
b. Connecticut.
c. New York.
d. Texas.

Answers

Check your answers against the correct answers below.

1. c.
2. a.
3. d.
4. c.
5. b.
6. b.
7. b.
8. a.
9. d.
10. a.

How Did You Do?

You may have simply gotten lucky and actually known the answers to one or two questions. In addition, your guessing was more successful if you were able to use the process of elimination on any of the questions. Maybe you didn't know who the third Chief Justice was (question 7), but you knew that John Jay was the first. In that case, you would have eliminated choice **d** and, therefore, improved your odds of guessing correctly from one in four to one in three.

According to probability, you should get $2\frac{1}{2}$ answers correct by guessing, so getting either two or three correct would be average. If you got four or more correct, you may be a really terrific guesser. If you got one or none correct, you may not be a very strong guesser.

Keep in mind, though, that this is only a small sample. You should continue to keep track of your guessing ability as you work through the practice questions in this book. Circle the numbers of questions you guess on as you make your guess, or, if you don't have time while you take the practice exams, go back afterward and try to remember which questions you guessed at. Remember, on a test with four answer choices for each question, your chances of getting a right answer is one in four. So keep a separate "guessing" score for each exam. How many questions did you guess on? How many did you get correct? If the number you got correct is at least one-fourth of the number of questions you guessed on, you are at least an average guesser, maybe better—and you should go ahead and guess on the real exam. If the number you got correct is significantly lower than one-fourth of the number you guessed on, you should not guess on exams where there is a guessing penalty unless you can eliminate a wrong answer. If there's no guessing penalty, however, you would be safe in guessing anyway.

an exam that has a guessing penalty, you should not use your remaining seconds to mark a pretty pattern on your answer sheet. Take those few seconds to try to answer one more question right.

But as soon as you get out of the realm of random guessing, the guessing penalty no longer works against you. If you can use the process of elimination to get rid of even one incorrect answer choice, the odds stop being against you and start working in your favor.

Sticking with our example of an exam that has four answer choices, eliminating just one incorrect answer makes your odds of choosing the correct answer one in three. That's the same as the one-out-of-three guessing penalty—even odds. If you eliminate two answer choices, your odds are one in two—better than the guessing penalty. In either case, you should go ahead and choose one of the remaining answer choices.

But what if you're not much of a risk-taker, *and* you think of yourself as the world's worst guesser? Complete the Your Guessing Ability worksheet to get an idea of how good your intuition is.

▶ Step 7: Reach Your Peak Performance Zone

Time to complete: 10 minutes to read; weeks to complete!
Activity: Complete the Physical Preparation Checklist

To get ready for a challenge like a big exam, you have to take control of your physical, as well as your mental, state. Exercise, proper diet, and rest will ensure that your body works with, rather than against, your mind on test day, as well as during your preparation.

Exercise

If you don't already have a regular exercise program, the time during which you're preparing for your written exam is an excellent time to start one. You'll have to be in shape to pass the physical ability test and to make it through the first weeks of basic training anyway. And if you're already keeping fit—or trying to get that way—don't let the pressure of preparing for the written exam be an excuse for quitting now. Exercise helps reduce stress by pumping wonderful good-feeling hormones called endorphins into your system. It also increases the oxygen supply throughout your body, including your brain, so you'll be at peak performance on test day.

A half hour of vigorous activity—enough to raise a sweat—every day should be your aim. If you're really pressed for time, every other day is OK. Choose an activity you like and get out there and do it. Jogging with a friend always makes the time go faster, or take a radio.

But don't overdo it. You don't want to exhaust yourself so much that you can't study. Moderation is the key.

Diet

First of all, cut out the junk food. Go easy on caffeine, and try to eliminate alcohol and nicotine from your system at least two weeks before the exam. Promise yourself a celebration the night after the exam, if need be.

What your body needs for peak performance is simply a balanced diet. Eat plenty of fruits and vegetables, along with protein and complex carbohydrates. Foods that are high in lecithin (an amino acid), such as fish and beans, are especially good brain foods.

Rest

You probably know how much sleep you need every night to be at your best, even if you don't always get it. Make sure you do get that much sleep, though, for at least a week before the exam. Moderation is important here, as well. Too much extra sleep could just make you groggy.

If you're not a morning person and your exam will be given in the morning, you should reset your internal clock so that your body doesn't think you're taking an exam at 3 A.M. You have to start this process well before the exam. The way it works is to get up half an hour earlier each morning, and then go to bed half an hour earlier that night. Don't try it the other way around; you'll just toss and turn if you go to bed early without having gotten up early. The next morning, get up another half an hour earlier, and so on. How long you will have to do this depends on how late you're used to getting up.

▶ Step 8: Get Your Act Together

Time to complete: 10 minutes to read; time to complete will vary
Activity: Complete Final Preparations worksheet

You're in control of your mind and body; you're in charge of test anxiety, your preparation, and your test-taking strategies. Now it's time to take charge of external factors, like the testing site and the materials you need to take the exam.

Find out Where the Test Is and Make a Trial Run

The exam bulletin or notice the recruiting office sent you will tell you when and where your exam is being held. Do you know how to get to the testing site? Do you know how long it will take you to get there? If not, make a trial run, preferably on the same day of the week at the same time of day. Make note, on the Final Preparations worksheet, of the amount of time it will take you to get to the exam site. Plan on arriving 10–15 minutes early so you can get the lay of the land, use the bathroom, and calm down. Then figure out how early you will have to get up that morning, and make sure you get up that early every day for a week before the exam.

Gather Your Materials

The night before the exam, lay out the clothes you will wear and the materials you have to bring with you to the exam. Plan on dressing in layers; you won't have any control over the temperature of the examination room. Have a sweater or jacket you can take off if it's warm or put on if the air conditioning is on full blast. Use the checklist on the Final Preparations worksheet on page 48 to help you pull together what you will need.

Don't Skip Breakfast

Even if you don't usually eat breakfast, do so on exam morning. A cup of coffee doesn't count. Don't eat doughnuts or other sweet foods, either. A sugar high will leave you with a sugar low in the middle of the exam. A mix of protein and carbohydrates is best: Cereal with milk or eggs with toast will do your body a world of good.

Physical Preparation Checklist

During the week before the test, write down (1) what physical exercise you engaged in and for how long and (2) what you ate for each meal. Remember, you're trying for at least a half an hour of exercise every other day (preferably every day) and a balanced diet that's light on junk food.

7 Days before the Exam

Exercise: _______ for _______ minutes

Breakfast: ________________________________

Lunch: ________________________________

Dinner: ________________________________

Snacks: ________________________________

6 Days before the Exam

Exercise: _______ for _______ minutes

Breakfast: ________________________________

Lunch: ________________________________

Dinner: ________________________________

Snacks: ________________________________

5 Days before the Exam

Exercise: _______ for _______ minutes

Breakfast: ________________________________

Lunch: ________________________________

Dinner: ________________________________

Snacks: ________________________________

4 Days before the Exam

Exercise: _______ for _______ minutes

Breakfast: ________________________________

Lunch: ________________________________

Dinner: ________________________________

Snacks: ________________________________

3 Days before the Exam

Exercise: _______ for _______ minutes

Breakfast: ________________________________

Lunch: ________________________________

Dinner: ________________________________

Snacks: ________________________________

2 Days before the Exam

Exercise: _______ for _______ minutes

Breakfast: ________________________________

Lunch: ________________________________

Dinner: ________________________________

Snacks: ________________________________

1 Day before the Exam

Exercise: _______ for _______ minutes

Breakfast: ________________________________

Lunch: ________________________________

Dinner: ________________________________

Snacks: ________________________________

▶ Step 9: Do It!

Time to complete: 10 minutes, plus test-taking time
Activity: Ace the Police Officer Written Exam!

Fast forward to exam day. You're ready. You made a study plan and followed through. You practiced your test-taking strategies while working through this book. You're in control of your physical, mental, and emotional state. You know when and where to show up and what to bring with you. In other words, you're better prepared than most of the other people taking the exam with you.

Just one more thing. When you're done with the police officer written exam, you will have earned a reward. Plan a celebration. Call up your friends and plan a party, or have a nice dinner for two—whatever your heart desires. Give yourself something to look forward to.

And then do it. Go into the exam, full of confidence, armed with the test-taking strategies you've practiced till they're second nature. You're in control of yourself, your environment, and your performance on the exam. You're ready to succeed. So do it. Go in there and ace the exam. And look forward to your future career in law enforcement!

Final Preparations

Getting to the Exam Site

Location of exam: ______________________________

Date of exam: ______________________________

Time of exam: ______________________________

Do I know how to get to the exam site? Yes ___ No ___ (If no, make a trial run.)

Time it will take to get to exam site: ________________

Things to Lay out the Night Before

Clothes I will wear ___

Sweater/jacket ___

Watch ___

Photo ID ___

Admission card ___

4 No. 2 pencils ___

____________ ______________________

____________ ______________________

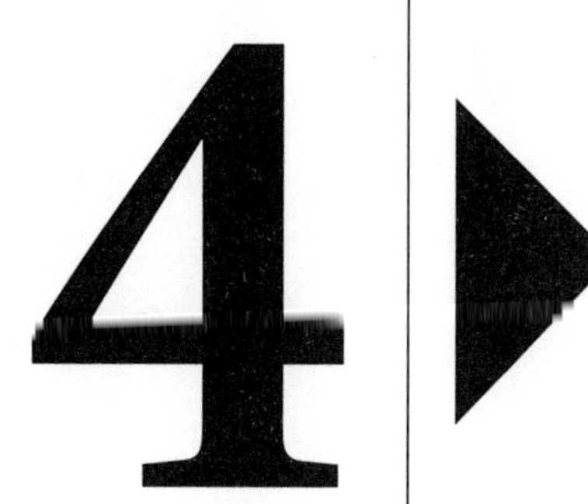

Police Officer Practice Exam 1

CHAPTER SUMMARY

This first practice exam gives you an example of one type of police officer exam often used by police departments around the country. It tests your basic reading and writing skills.

Some cities and towns use exams similar to the following one to test potential police recruits. This kind of exam simply tests your reading and writing skills. The police department wants to know whether you have the basic skills that will enable you to succeed in your academy and on-the-job training.

The following multiple-choice exam is divided into four parts:

- Part One: 30 reading comprehension questions
- Part Two: 25 questions on the grammatical skills needed for clear writing
- Part Three: 25 vocabulary questions
- Part Four: 20 spelling questions

For the best results, treat this exam like the real thing. Get out your number 2 pencils, and give yourself two hours to take the exam. The answer sheet is on the following page. Then comes the exam itself, and after that is the answer key, with each correct answer explained. The answer key is followed by a section on how to score your exam.

Police Officer Practice Exam 1

1.	ⓐ	ⓑ	ⓒ	ⓓ	**36.**	ⓐ	ⓑ	ⓒ	ⓓ	**71.**	ⓐ	ⓑ	ⓒ	ⓓ
2.	ⓐ	ⓑ	ⓒ	ⓓ	**37.**	ⓐ	ⓑ	ⓒ	ⓓ	**72.**	ⓐ	ⓑ	ⓒ	ⓓ
3.	ⓐ	ⓑ	ⓒ	ⓓ	**38.**	ⓐ	ⓑ	ⓒ	ⓓ	**73.**	ⓐ	ⓑ	ⓒ	ⓓ
4.	ⓐ	ⓑ	ⓒ	ⓓ	**39.**	ⓐ	ⓑ	ⓒ	ⓓ	**74.**	ⓐ	ⓑ	ⓒ	ⓓ
5.	ⓐ	ⓑ	ⓒ	ⓓ	**40.**	ⓐ	ⓑ	ⓒ	ⓓ	**75.**	ⓐ	ⓑ	ⓒ	ⓓ
6.	ⓐ	ⓑ	ⓒ	ⓓ	**41.**	ⓐ	ⓑ	ⓒ	ⓓ	**76.**	ⓐ	ⓑ	ⓒ	ⓓ
7.	ⓐ	ⓑ	ⓒ	ⓓ	**42.**	ⓐ	ⓑ	ⓒ	ⓓ	**77.**	ⓐ	ⓑ	ⓒ	ⓓ
8.	ⓐ	ⓑ	ⓒ	ⓓ	**43.**	ⓐ	ⓑ	ⓒ	ⓓ	**78.**	ⓐ	ⓑ	ⓒ	ⓓ
9.	ⓐ	ⓑ	ⓒ	ⓓ	**44.**	ⓐ	ⓑ	ⓒ	ⓓ	**79.**	ⓐ	ⓑ	ⓒ	ⓓ
10.	ⓐ	ⓑ	ⓒ	ⓓ	**45.**	ⓐ	ⓑ	ⓒ	ⓓ	**80.**	ⓐ	ⓑ	ⓒ	ⓓ
11.	ⓐ	ⓑ	ⓒ	ⓓ	**46.**	ⓐ	ⓑ	ⓒ	ⓓ	**81.**	ⓐ	ⓑ	ⓒ	ⓓ
12.	ⓐ	ⓑ	ⓒ	ⓓ	**47.**	ⓐ	ⓑ	ⓒ	ⓓ	**82.**	ⓐ	ⓑ	ⓒ	ⓓ
13.	ⓐ	ⓑ	ⓒ	ⓓ	**48.**	ⓐ	ⓑ	ⓒ	ⓓ	**83.**	ⓐ	ⓑ	ⓒ	ⓓ
14.	ⓐ	ⓑ	ⓒ	ⓓ	**49.**	ⓐ	ⓑ	ⓒ	ⓓ	**84.**	ⓐ	ⓑ	ⓒ	ⓓ
15.	ⓐ	ⓑ	ⓒ	ⓓ	**50.**	ⓐ	ⓑ	ⓒ	ⓓ	**85.**	ⓐ	ⓑ	ⓒ	ⓓ
16.	ⓐ	ⓑ	ⓒ	ⓓ	**51.**	ⓐ	ⓑ	ⓒ	ⓓ	**86.**	ⓐ	ⓑ	ⓒ	ⓓ
17.	ⓐ	ⓑ	ⓒ	ⓓ	**52.**	ⓐ	ⓑ	ⓒ	ⓓ	**87.**	ⓐ	ⓑ	ⓒ	ⓓ
18.	ⓐ	ⓑ	ⓒ	ⓓ	**53.**	ⓐ	ⓑ	ⓒ	ⓓ	**88.**	ⓐ	ⓑ	ⓒ	ⓓ
19.	ⓐ	ⓑ	ⓒ	ⓓ	**54.**	ⓐ	ⓑ	ⓒ	ⓓ	**89.**	ⓐ	ⓑ	ⓒ	ⓓ
20.	ⓐ	ⓑ	ⓒ	ⓓ	**55.**	ⓐ	ⓑ	ⓒ	ⓓ	**90.**	ⓐ	ⓑ	ⓒ	ⓓ
21.	ⓐ	ⓑ	ⓒ	ⓓ	**56.**	ⓐ	ⓑ	ⓒ	ⓓ	**91.**	ⓐ	ⓑ	ⓒ	ⓓ
22.	ⓐ	ⓑ	ⓒ	ⓓ	**57.**	ⓐ	ⓑ	ⓒ	ⓓ	**92.**	ⓐ	ⓑ	ⓒ	ⓓ
23.	ⓐ	ⓑ	ⓒ	ⓓ	**58.**	ⓐ	ⓑ	ⓒ	ⓓ	**93.**	ⓐ	ⓑ	ⓒ	ⓓ
24.	ⓐ	ⓑ	ⓒ	ⓓ	**59.**	ⓐ	ⓑ	ⓒ	ⓓ	**94.**	ⓐ	ⓑ	ⓒ	ⓓ
25.	ⓐ	ⓑ	ⓒ	ⓓ	**60.**	ⓐ	ⓑ	ⓒ	ⓓ	**95.**	ⓐ	ⓑ	ⓒ	ⓓ
26.	ⓐ	ⓑ	ⓒ	ⓓ	**61.**	ⓐ	ⓑ	ⓒ	ⓓ	**96.**	ⓐ	ⓑ	ⓒ	ⓓ
27.	ⓐ	ⓑ	ⓒ	ⓓ	**62.**	ⓐ	ⓑ	ⓒ	ⓓ	**97.**	ⓐ	ⓑ	ⓒ	ⓓ
28.	ⓐ	ⓑ	ⓒ	ⓓ	**63.**	ⓐ	ⓑ	ⓒ	ⓓ	**98.**	ⓐ	ⓑ	ⓒ	ⓓ
29.	ⓐ	ⓑ	ⓒ	ⓓ	**64.**	ⓐ	ⓑ	ⓒ	ⓓ	**99.**	ⓐ	ⓑ	ⓒ	ⓓ
30.	ⓐ	ⓑ	ⓒ	ⓓ	**65.**	ⓐ	ⓑ	ⓒ	ⓓ	**100.**	ⓐ	ⓑ	ⓒ	ⓓ
31.	ⓐ	ⓑ	ⓒ	ⓓ	**66.**	ⓐ	ⓑ	ⓒ	ⓓ					
32.	ⓐ	ⓑ	ⓒ	ⓓ	**67.**	ⓐ	ⓑ	ⓒ	ⓓ					
33.	ⓐ	ⓑ	ⓒ	ⓓ	**68.**	ⓐ	ⓑ	ⓒ	ⓓ					
34.	ⓐ	ⓑ	ⓒ	ⓓ	**69.**	ⓐ	ⓑ	ⓒ	ⓓ					
35.	ⓐ	ⓑ	ⓒ	ⓓ	**70.**	ⓐ	ⓑ	ⓒ	ⓓ					

▶ Police Officer Practice Exam 1

Part One: Reading Comprehension

Answer questions 1–30 on the basis of the reading passages that precede them.

In order for our society to make decisions about the kinds of punishments we will impose on convicted criminals, we must understand why we punish criminals. Some people argue that retribution is the purpose of punishment and that, therefore, the punishment must in some direct way fit the crime. This view is based on the belief that a person who commits a crime deserves to be punished. Because the punishment must fit the specific crime, the theory of retribution allows a sentencing judge to consider the circumstances of each crime, criminal, and victim in imposing a sentence.

Another view, the deterrence theory, promotes punishment in order to discourage commission of future crimes. In this view, punishment need not relate directly to the crime committed, because the point is to deter both a specific criminal and the general public from committing crimes in the future. However, punishment must necessarily be uniform and consistently applied, in order for the members of the public to understand how they would be punished if they committed a crime. Laws setting sentencing guidelines are based on the deterrence theory and do not allow a judge to consider the specifics of a particular crime in sentencing a convicted criminal.

1. According to the passage, punishment
- **a.** is rarely an effective deterrent to future crimes.
- **b.** must fit the crime in question.
- **c.** is imposed solely at the discretion of a judge.
- **d.** may be imposed for differing reasons.

2. The retribution theory of punishment
- **a.** is no longer considered valid.
- **b.** holds that the punishment must fit the crime committed.
- **c.** applies only to violent crimes.
- **d.** allows a jury to recommend the sentence that should be imposed.

3. The passage suggests that a person who believes that the death penalty results in fewer murders most likely also believes in
- **a.** the deterrence theory.
- **b.** the retribution theory.
- **c.** giving judges considerable discretion in imposing sentences.
- **d.** the integrity of the criminal justice system.

4. A good title for this passage would be
- **a.** Sentencing Reform: A Modest Proposal.
- **b.** More Criminals Are Doing Time.
- **c.** Punishment: Deterrent or Retribution?
- **d.** Why I Favor Uniform Sentencing Guidelines.

5. A person who believes in the deterrence theory would probably also support
- **a.** nonunanimous jury verdicts.
- **b.** early release of prisoners because of prison overcrowding.
- **c.** a broad definition of the insanity defense.
- **d.** allowing television broadcasts of court proceedings.

6. The theories described in the passage differ in
- **a.** the amount of leeway they would allow judges in determining sentences.
- **b.** the number of law enforcement professionals who espouse them.
- **c.** their concern for the rights of the accused.
- **d.** their concern for protecting society from crime.

DNA is a powerful investigative tool because, with the exception of identical twins, no two people have the same DNA. In other words, the sequence, or order of the DNA building blocks, is different in particular regions of the cell, making each person's DNA unique. Therefore, DNA evidence collected from a crime scene can link a suspect to a crime or eliminate one from suspicion in the same way that fingerprints are used. DNA can also link evidence to a victim through the DNA of relatives if the victim's body cannot be found. For example, if technicians have a biological sample from the victim, such as a bloodstain left at a crime scene, the DNA taken from that evidence can be compared with DNA from the victim's biological relatives to determine whether the bloodstain belongs to the victim. When a DNA profile developed from evidence at one crime scene is compared with a DNA profile developed from evidence found at another crime scene, they can be linked to each other or to the same perpetrator, whether the crime was committed locally or in another state.

7. What is the primary purpose of this paragraph?
- **a.** to show that DNA is a powerful investigative tool
- **b.** to illustrate how the unique characteristics of DNA make different types of comparisons and eliminations possible
- **c.** to teach the reader that identical twins have the same DNA
- **d.** to show how laboratory technicians develop DNA profiles

8. All of the following are true EXCEPT
- **a.** everyone, except for identical twins, has different DNA.
- **b.** the sequence of DNA building blocks is the same in particular regions of the cell, making comparisons possible.
- **c.** DNA can be used for comparisons or eliminations of offenders from different states.
- **d.** DNA from relatives can be used to identify victims.

9. According to the passage, DNA should be collected from a crime scene because
- **a.** it is better than fingerprints.
- **b.** there is DNA left at every crime scene.
- **c.** it can be used to eliminate potential suspects.
- **d.** DNA is a new investigative tool.

10. Which of the following conclusions can be drawn from the paragraph?
- **a.** DNA can be collected from sources other than blood.
- **b.** DNA can be collected only from bloodstains.
- **c.** DNA cannot be collected from bloodstains.
- **d.** DNA can connect crime scenes only if it is taken from bloodstains.

Adolescents are at high risk for violent crime. Although they make up only 14% of the population age 12 and over, 30% of all violent crimes—1.9 million—are committed against them. Because crimes against adolescents are likely to be committed by offenders of the same age (as well as the same sex and race), preventing violence among and against adolescents is a twofold challenge. Adolescents are at risk of being both victims and perpetrators of violence. New violence-prevention programs in urban middle schools help reduce the crime rate by teaching both victims and perpetrators the skills of conflict resolution and how to apply reason to disputes, as well as by changing attitudes toward achieving respect through violence and toward the need to retaliate. These programs provide a safe place for students to discuss their conflicts and therefore prove appealing to students at risk.

11. What is the main idea of the passage?
- **a.** Adolescents are more likely to commit crimes than older people and must therefore be taught nonviolence in order to protect society.
- **b.** Middle school students appreciate the conflict resolution skills they acquire in violence-prevention programs.
- **c.** Middle school violence-prevention programs are designed to help to lower the rate of crimes against adolescents.
- **d.** Violence against adolescents is increasing.

12. Which of the following is NOT mentioned in the passage as a skill taught by middle school violence-prevention programs?
- **a.** keeping one's temper
- **b.** settling disputes without violence
- **c.** avoiding the need for vengeance
- **d.** being reasonable in emotional situations

13. According to the passage, which of the following statements about adolescents is true?
- **a.** Adolescents are disproportionately likely to be victims of violent crime.
- **b.** Adolescents are more likely to commit violent crimes than other segments of the population.
- **c.** Adolescents are the victims of 14% of the nation's violent crimes.
- **d.** Adolescents are reluctant to attend violence-prevention programs.

14. According to the passage, why is preventing violence against adolescents a "twofold challenge"?
- **a.** because adolescents are twice as likely to be victims of violent crime as members of other age groups
- **b.** because adolescents must be prevented from both perpetrating and being victimized by violent crime
- **c.** because adolescents must change both their violent behavior and their attitudes towards violence
- **d.** because adolescents are vulnerable yet reluctant to listen to adult advice

In the 1966 Supreme Court case *Miranda v. Arizona*, the Court concluded that police officers must advise a suspect of his or her Fifth Amendment right against self-incrimination, commonly known as the Miranda Admonition. The Supreme Court further outlined two general principles to guide police officer behavior. Essentially, the court stated that if a suspect was in custody, and the police were going to ask accusatory questions, the suspect must be advised of Miranda. Subsequent court decisions have further detailed police custody to include in-field detention, transportation, arrest, and booking. Moreover, police officers can ask non-accusatory questions, such as a suspect's name, without making the Miranda advisement. As time has passed, courts have repeatedly interpreted police actions against Miranda and have set many more restrictions on how, when, and where questioning can be conducted.

15. What would be the best title for this passage?
- **a.** How to Interrogate Suspects
- **b.** Supreme Court Decisions of the 1960s
- **c.** In-Custody Interviews
- **d.** Court Decisions on Police Interrogations

16. Based on information from the passage, which statement is correct?
 a. Police officers must always read a suspect the Miranda Admonition.
 b. Police officers cannot ask accusatory questions.
 c. Miranda regulates police behavior.
 d. Police custody does not include detention.

17. From the passage, it can be inferred that which of the following is NOT an example of a non-accusatory question?
 a. the suspect's name
 b. the suspect's date of birth
 c. the suspect's alibi
 d. the suspect's telephone number

18. Based on the passage, which of the following is a true statement?
 a. The Miranda decision applies only in Arizona.
 b. Miranda involves a two-part test of police behavior.
 c. Miranda involves only in-field detentions.
 d. A suspect must invoke his or her Miranda rights.

Police officers, researchers, and other criminal justice practitioners have been struggling to find a uniform definition for the term *gang*. It may be that the different forms and structures of street gangs complicate the difficulty in finding one all-purpose definition. For example, some researchers have drawn a distinction between street gangs and drug gangs. Drug gangs are seen as much more organized than street gangs, and are generally smaller, more cohesive, and hierarchical. They are organized for the sole purpose of selling drugs and protecting their individual members from discovery.

On the other hand, street gangs can be characterized as having organized themselves for the protection of their perceived territory and of the gang membership itself. Because a street gang's mission is to protect its territory, a street gang by nature is more visible than a drug gang, since it must mark the boundaries of that territory. To further complicate this issue, other types of gangs, like motorcycle gangs and prison gangs, share some characteristics with both street gangs and drug gangs, as well characteristics unique to themselves.

19. What would be the best title for this passage?
 a. Drug Gangs and Street Gangs
 b. Defining Street Gangs
 c. Defining Gangs
 d. Problems for Gang Researchers

20. Based on the passage, which of the following sentences is true?
 a. Gangs are completely disorganized groups of criminals.
 b. Gangs are always highly organized.
 c. Motorcycle gangs are more organized than prison gangs.
 d. Street gangs are less organized than drug gangs.

21. Based on the passage, which of the following is NOT true?
 a. Street gangs are organized to protect the identities of individual members.
 b. A street gang's mission is to protect its territory.
 c. Prison gangs share some characteristics with street gangs.
 d. Drug gangs tend to be smaller.

Detectives who routinely investigate violent crimes can't help but become somewhat jaded. Paradoxically, the victims and witnesses with whom they work closely are often in a highly vulnerable and emotional state. The emotional fallout from a sexual assault, for example, can be complex and long lasting. Detectives must be trained to handle people in emotional distress and must be sensitive to the fact that for the victim, the crime is not routine. At the same time, detectives must recognize the limits of their role and resist the temptation to act as therapists or social workers, instead referring victims to the proper agencies.

22. What is the main idea of the passage?
- **a.** Detectives who investigate violent crimes must not become emotionally hardened by the experience.
- **b.** Victims of violent crime should be referred to therapists and social workers.
- **c.** Detectives should be sensitive to the emotional state of victims of violent crimes.
- **d.** Detectives should be particularly careful in dealing with victims of sexual assault.

23. According to the passage, what is "paradoxical" about the detective's relationship to the victim?
- **a.** Detectives know less about the experience of violent crime than do victims.
- **b.** What for the detective is routine is a unique and profound experience for the victim.
- **c.** Detectives must be sensitive to victims' needs but can't be social workers or psychologists.
- **d.** Not only must detectives solve crimes, but they must also handle the victims with care.

24. Which of the following is NOT advocated by the passage for detectives who investigate violent crimes?
- **a.** They should refer victims to appropriate support services.
- **b.** They should be aware of the psychological consequences of being victimized.
- **c.** They should not become jaded.
- **d.** They should not become too personally involved with victims' problems.

In many police departments, detectives who want to be promoted further must first spend an extended period of time working in the internal affairs division. Not only do these officers become thoroughly versed in detecting police misconduct, they also become familiar with the circumstances and attitudes out of which such conduct might arise. Placement in internal affairs reduces the possibility that a commanding officer might be too lenient in investigating or disciplining a colleague. The transfer to internal affairs also separates a detective from his or her precinct, reducing the prospect of cronyism, and it familiarizes the detective with serving in a supervisory capacity.

25. According to the passage, detectives are transferred to internal affairs in order to
- **a.** enable them to identify situations that might lead to police misconduct.
- **b.** familiarize them with the laws regarding police misconduct.
- **c.** ensure that they are closely supervised.
- **d.** increase the staff of the internal affairs division.

26. Who, according to the passage, must spend an extended period working for the internal affairs department?

a. detectives interested in police misconduct
b. all detectives
c. detectives interested in advancement
d. officers who want to become detectives

27. The internal affairs requirement is apparently intended to

a. teach detectives how to conduct their own police work properly.
b. demonstrate to the community that the police department takes internal affairs seriously.
c. strengthen the internal affairs division.
d. make supervisors more effective in preventing police misconduct.

Police officers need to be informed about different cultural practices so that they can make decisions about whether or not a crime has actually occurred. For example, a medicinal technique known as *coining*, commonly practiced in some Southeast Asian cultures, often produces red marks across a patient's back, neck, and shoulders. These marks often appear to be very similar to those a police officer would see on a child who has been beaten with a strap, and this has led to instances in the United States in which a police officer has arrested a parent for abuse when no abuse occurred. Often, this misunderstanding of the culture is compounded by the parent's and/or child's inability to speak fluent English.

A police officer who understands that coining is a non-painful, alternative technique used as a medicinal treatment will make different decisions than a police officer who is totally unfamiliar with the culture. Examples like this illustrate why communities are better served by officers who have an understanding of their makeup, culture, and values.

28. What is the main idea of this passage?

a. Coining can cause red marks.
b. Cultural understanding can influence decision making.
c. Different cultures use different medical techniques.
d. Coining is an accepted medical treatment.

29. According to the passage, which of the following is true?

a. Coining is painful.
b. People who use coining do not speak English.
c. Coining can leave red marks.
d. People who use coining are always arrested.

30. The passage suggests that in police work, awareness of other cultural practices

a. is completely unnecessary and a waste of valuable time.
b. is ultimately a benefit to both the officer and the community.
c. should be every police officer's first priority.
d. often leads to mistrust of the police department.

Part Two: Writing

Answer questions 31–55 by choosing the sentence that is correct in both grammar and punctuation.

31. **a.** The search took place without incident. Except for a brief argument between two residents.
b. The search took place. Without incident except for a brief argument between two residents.
c. The search, took place without incident except, for a brief argument between two residents.
d. The search took place without incident, except for a brief argument between two residents.

32. a. They finished their search, left the building, and return to police headquarters.
b. They finished their search, left the building, and returns to police headquarters.
c. They finished their search, left the building, and returned to police headquarters.
d. They finished their search, left the building, and returning to police headquarters.

33. a. Searching for evidence, police officers, must be mindful of the Fourth Amendment.
b. Searching for evidence. Police officers must be mindful of the Fourth Amendment.
c. When searching for evidence. Police officers, must be mindful of the Fourth Amendment.
d. When searching for evidence, police officers must be mindful of the Fourth Amendment.

34. a. The evidence had been improperly gathered, the case was dismissed.
b. Because the evidence had been improperly gathered, the case was dismissed.
c. Because the evidence had been improperly gathered. The case was dismissed.
d. The evidence had been improperly gathered the case was dismissed.

35. a. Officer Alvarez was able to search the suspect's car, where she found $200,000 worth of cocaine. Because she had a warrant.
b. $200,000 worth of cocaine was found. The result of a search by Officer Alvarez of the suspect's car, because she had a warrant.
c. Because of a warrant and a search of the suspect's car. $200,000 worth of cocaine was found by Officer Alvarez.
d. Because Officer Alvarez had a warrant, she was able to search the suspect's car, where she found $200,000 worth of cocaine.

36. a. The guard, like the prisoners, were sick of the food in the prison mess hall, and yesterday he went to the warden and complained.
b. The guard, like the prisoners, was sick of the food in the prison mess hall, and yesterday he goes to the warden and complains.
c. The guard, like the prisoners, was sick of the food in the prison mess hall, and yesterday he went to the warden and complained.
d. The guard, like the prisoners, were sick of the food in the prison mess hall, and yesterday he goes to the warden and complained.

37. a. Mr. Lowell felt it was time to move away from the crime-ridden neighborhood, but he could not afford to do so.
b. Mr. Lowell felt it was time to move away from the crime-ridden neighborhood, he could not afford to do so.
c. Mr. Lowell felt it was time to move away from the crime ridden neighborhood he could not afford to do so.
d. Mr. Lowell felt it was time to move away. From the crime-ridden neighborhood, but he could not afford to do so.

38. a. Lieutenant Wells did not think the prisoner could be capable to escape.
b. Lieutenant Wells did not think that the prisoner capable of escaping.
c. Lieutenant Wells did not think the prisoner capable of escape.
d. Lieutenant Wells did not think that the prisoner capable to escape.

39. a. The masked gunman ordered the bank customers to remove their jewelry and lie down on the floor, with a growl.
b. The masked gunman ordered the bank customers to remove their jewelry, with a growl, and lie down on the floor.
c. The masked gunman ordered the bank customers with a growl. To remove their jewelry and lie down on the floor.
d. With a growl, the masked gunman ordered the bank customers to remove their jewelry and lie down on the floor.

40. a. Of all the dogs in the K-9 Corps, Zelda is the most bravest.
b. Of all the dogs in the K-9 Corps, Zelda is the bravest.
c. Of all the dogs in the K-9 Corps, Zelda is the braver.
d. Of all the dogs in the K-9 Corps, Zelda is the more brave.

41. a. When her workday is over, Officer Hernandez likes to watch TV, preferring sitcoms to police dramas.
b. When her workday is over. Officer Hernandez likes to watch TV, preferring sitcoms to police dramas.
c. When her workday is over, Officer Hernandez likes to watch TV. Preferring sitcoms to police dramas.
d. When her workday is over, Officer Hernandez likes to watch TV, preferring sitcoms. To police dramas.

42. a. All day the exhausted volunteers had struggled through snake-ridden underbrush. In search of the missing teenagers, who still had not been found.
b. All day the exhausted volunteers had struggled through snake-ridden underbrush in search of the missing teenagers, who still had not been found.
c. All day the exhausted volunteers had struggled through snake-ridden underbrush in search of the missing teenagers. Who still had not been found.
d. All day the exhausted volunteers had struggled through snake-ridden underbrush. In search of the missing teenagers. Who still had not been found.

43. a. My partner Rosie and I, we did not like each other at first, but now we get along fine.
b. My partner Rosie and I did not like each other at first, but now her and I get along fine.
c. My partner Rosie and me did not like each other at first, but now she and I get along fine.
d. My partner Rosie and I did not like each other at first, but now we get along fine.

44. a. A sharpshooter for many years, Miles Johnson could shoot a pea off a person's shoulder from 70 yards away.
b. Miles Johnson could shoot a pea off a person's shoulder from 70 yards away, a sharpshooter for many years.
c. A sharpshooter for many years, a pea could be shot off a person's shoulder by Miles Johnson from 70 yards away.
d. From 70 yards away, a sharpshooter for many years, Miles Johnson could shoot a pea off a person's shoulder.

45. **a.** Sergeant Cooper was the most toughest commander we had ever had, yet she was also the fairest.
b. Sergeant Cooper was the toughest commander we had ever had, yet she was also the most fair.
c. Sergeant Cooper was the toughest commander we had ever had, yet she was also the most fairly.
d. Sergeant Cooper was the tough commander we had ever had, yet she was also the most fair.

46. **a.** Officer Chen thought they should call for backup; moreover, Officer Jovanovich disagreed.
b. Officer Chen thought they should call for backup; meanwhile, Officer Jovanovich disagreed.
c. Officer Chen thought they should call for backup; however, Officer Jovanovich disagreed.
d. Officer Chen thought they should call for backup; furthermore, Officer Jovanovich disagreed.

47. **a.** The TV show *Colombo* is said to have been inspired in part of the classic Russian novel *Crime and Punishment.*
b. The TV show *Colombo* is said to have been inspired in part by the classic Russian novel *Crime and Punishment.*
c. The TV show *Colombo* is said to have been inspired in part off of the classic Russian novel *Crime and Punishment.*
d. The TV show *Colombo* is said to have been inspired in part from the classic Russian novel *Crime and Punishment.*

48. **a.** Corky and Moe, respected members of the K-9 Corps, has sniffed out every pound of marijuana in the warehouse.
b. Corky and Moe, respected members of the K-9 Corps, sniffs out every pound of marijuana in the warehouse.
c. Corky and Moe, respected members of the K-9 Corps, sniffing out every pound of marijuana in the warehouse.
d. Corky and Moe, respected members of the K-9 Corps, sniffed out every pound of marijuana in the warehouse.

49. **a.** When ordered to be removing their jewelry and lying down on the floor, not a single bank customer resisted.
b. When ordered to have removed their jewelry and to have lain down on the floor, not a single bank customer resisted.
c. When ordered to remove their jewelry and lie down on the floor, not a single bank customer resisted.
d. When ordered to remove their jewelry and be lying down on the floor, not a single bank customer resisted.

50. **a.** Recession, like budget cuts, is hard on the beat cop.
b. Recession and budget cuts is hard on the beat cop.
c. Recession, like budget cuts, are hard on the beat cop.
d. Budget cuts, like the recession, is hard on the beat cop.

51. **a.** Jury members become impatient with both prosecution and defense when they were sequestered for months.
b. When jury members are sequestered for months, they are becoming impatient with both prosecution and defense.
c. Jury members became impatient with both prosecution and defense when they are sequestered for months.
d. When jury members are sequestered for months, they become impatient with both prosecution and defense.

52. **a.** Sergeant Falk believes that neither suspect Hamm nor suspect Kozorez is responsible for the theft.
b. Sergeant Falk believes that neither suspect Hamm nor suspect Kozorez are responsible for the theft.
c. Sergeant Falk believes that suspect Hamm and suspect Kozorez is not responsible for the theft.
d. Sergeant Falk believes that both suspect Hamm and suspect Kozorez is not responsible for the theft.

53. **a.** A police officer can expect danger when you respond to a domestic dispute.
b. A police officer can expect danger when one responds to a domestic dispute.
c. A police officer can expect danger when responding to a domestic dispute.
d. A police officer can expect danger when we respond to a domestic dispute.

54. **a.** Officer DeAngelo phoned his partner every day when he was in the hospital.
b. When his partner was in the hospital, Officer DeAngelo phoned him every day.
c. When in the hospital, a phone call was made every day by Officer DeAngelo to his partner.
d. His partner received a phone call from Officer DeAngelo every day while he was in the hospital.

55. **a.** Some of the case transcripts I have to type are very long, but that doesn't bother one if the cases are interesting.
b. Some of the case transcripts I have to type are very long, but that doesn't bother you if the cases are interesting.
c. Some of the case transcripts I have to type are very long, but it doesn't bother a person if the cases are interesting.
d. Some of the case transcripts I have to type are very long, but that doesn't bother me if the cases are interesting.

Part Three: Vocabulary

Answer questions 56–80 by choosing the correct definition of the underlined word.

56. Special equipment is required to find <u>latent</u> fingerprints.
a. obvious
b. hidden
c. human
d. mammal

57. As soon as the Department of Corrections' recommendations for prison reform were released, the department was inundated with calls from people who said they approved.
- **a.** provided
- **b.** bothered
- **c.** rewarded
- **d.** flooded

58. Research indicates that facing rearward in a car seat protects an infant's fragile head and neck during a collision.
- **a.** small
- **b.** extended
- **c.** extemporaneous
- **d.** delicate

59. The Marion Police Department's policy of aggressively recruiting women officers is unique.
- **a.** rigorous
- **b.** admirable
- **c.** unparalleled
- **d.** remarkable

60. These unfortunate changes would result in the elimination of five positions in the department.
- **a.** addition
- **b.** reversal
- **c.** removal
- **d.** recall

61. The warning stated that a terrorist attack was imminent, and we should immediately take precautions.
- **a.** soon
- **b.** powerful
- **c.** unlikely
- **d.** distant

62. The police department recruited Officer Long because she was proficient in the use of computers.
- **a.** helpful
- **b.** unequaled
- **c.** efficient
- **d.** skilled

63. Most people thought the police officers' new hats were ostentatious because of all the gold braid around the brim.
- **a.** hilarious
- **b.** outrageous
- **c.** pretentious
- **d.** obnoxious

64. The report was entirely fact based—it did not include the intangible benefits of the new policies.
- **a.** real
- **b.** concrete
- **c.** insurmountable
- **d.** indefinable

65. The Adamsville Police Department's computer system was outmoded.
- **a.** worthless
- **b.** unusable
- **c.** obsolete
- **d.** unnecessary

66. The integrity of the entire department was jeopardized by one officer's ill-advised actions.
- **a.** data
- **b.** honesty
- **c.** information
- **d.** facts

67. The profiler concentrated on the abnormal psychology of criminal behavior.
- **a.** educational
- **b.** standard
- **c.** unusual
- **d.** youth

68. The police officer testified that the suspect's actions were totally overt, and there was no question he was the guilty party.
- **a.** open
- **b.** closed
- **c.** hidden
- **d.** unknown

69. Mayor Owly regarded budget cuts as a panacea for all the problems faced by the police department.
- **a.** cure
- **b.** result
- **c.** cause
- **d.** necessity

70. The attorney's glib remarks irritated the judge.
- **a.** angry
- **b.** superficial
- **c.** insulting
- **d.** dishonest

71. The jury was surprised that the suspect, who was accused of several high-profile murders, appeared nondescript.
- **a.** lethargic
- **b.** undistinguished
- **c.** respectable
- **d.** impeccable

72. Joe's spiteful remarks about other officers he had worked with made the whole precinct careful about what they said in front of him.
- **a.** malicious
- **b.** changeable
- **c.** approving
- **d.** dangerous

73. There was no precedent for the city council's shocking actions.
- **a.** vote
- **b.** tax
- **c.** support
- **d.** example

74. The terrorist group's ideologies seemed to be downright evil and contradicted all decency and common sense.
- **a.** technologies
- **b.** beliefs
- **c.** members
- **d.** inadequacies

75. One of the duties of a captain is to delegate responsibility.
- **a.** analyze
- **b.** respect
- **c.** criticize
- **d.** assign

76. Warrantless searches are allowed under some exigent circumstances.
- **a.** serious
- **b.** written
- **c.** verbal
- **d.** ordinary

77. Officer Albaghadi was called upon to articulate the philosophy of her entire department.
- **a.** trust
- **b.** refine
- **c.** verify
- **d.** express

78. After the party in his honor, he was in an expansive mood.
- **a.** outgoing
- **b.** relaxed
- **c.** humorous
- **d.** grateful

79. The ruling proved to be detrimental to the investigation.
- **a.** decisive
- **b.** harmful
- **c.** worthless
- **d.** advantageous

80. According to the code of conduct, "Every officer will be accountable for his or her decisions."
- **a.** applauded
- **b.** compensated
- **c.** responsible
- **d.** approached

Part Four: Spelling

Answer questions 81–100 by choosing the correct spelling of the word that belongs in the blank.

81. In many states, road tests require ____________ parking.
- **a.** paralel
- **b.** paralell
- **c.** parallal
- **d.** parallel

82. The paramedics attempted to ____________ the victim.
- **a.** stablize
- **b.** stableize
- **c.** stableise
- **d.** stabilize

83. Prosecutors argued that testimony concerning the past behavior of the accused was ____________.
- **a.** irelevent
- **b.** irelevant
- **c.** irrelevant
- **d.** irrelevent

84. The mayor pointed to the ____________ drop in crime rate statistics.
- **a.** encouredging
- **b.** encouraging
- **c.** incurraging
- **d.** incouraging

85. The mentally ill suspect will have a ____________ hearing on Friday.
- **a.** commitment
- **b.** committment
- **c.** comittment
- **d.** comitment

86. The prisoner's alibi seemed ____________ from the outset.
- **a.** rediculous
- **b.** rediculus
- **c.** ridiculous
- **d.** ridiculus

87. It was a ___________ day for the department's annual picnic.
a. superb
b. supperb
c. supurb
d. sepurb

88. The first time Officer Lin drove the squad car into town, all his old friends were ___________.
a. jellous
b. jealous
c. jealuse
d. jeolous

89. When we were halfway up the hill, we heard a ___________ explosion.
a. teriffic
b. terriffic
c. terific
d. terrific

90. If elected, Deputy Gana will make a fine ___________.
a. sherrif
b. sherriff
c. sherif
d. sheriff

91. Catching the persons responsible for the fire has become an ___________ for Officer Beatty.
a. obssession
b. obsessian
c. obsession
d. obsessiun

92. Officer Alvarez would have fired her weapon, but she did not want to place the hostage in ___________.
a. jeoperdy
b. jepardy
c. jeapardy
d. jeopardy

93. Because of the danger they were in, the soldiers were unable to enjoy the ___________ scenery.
a. magniffisent
b. magnifisent
c. magnificent
d. magnifficent

94. From inside the box came a strange ___________ whirring sound.
a. mechinical
b. mechanical
c. mechenical
d. machanical

95. The community was shocked when Cindy Pierce, the president of the senior class, was arrested for selling ___________ drugs.
a. elicitt
b. ellicit
c. illicit
d. illicet

96. There will be an immediate ___________ into the mayor's death.
a. inquiry
b. inquirry
c. enquirry
d. enquery

97. Dimitry Mansky was subject to a lawsuit after he attempted to ____________ his contract.

a. termenate
b. terrminate
c. termanate
d. terminate

98. Ben Alshieka feels that he is being ____________ for his religious beliefs.

a. persecuted
b. pursecuted
c. presecuted
d. perrsecuted

99. The warehouse exuded a ____________ odor.

a. peculior
b. peculiar
c. peculliar
d. puculior

100. Understanding a criminal's ____________ can help decrease certain crimes.

a. psycology
b. pyschology
c. psychology
d. psychollogy

► Answers

Part One: Reading Comprehension

1. **d.** The passage presents two reasons for punishment. The second sentence notes a view that "some people" hold. The first line of the second paragraph indicates "another view."
2. **b.** This is the main idea of the first paragraph.
3. **a.** This is an application of the main idea of the second paragraph to a specific crime.
4. **c.** The first sentence indicates that the passage is about punishment. The first paragraph is about retribution; the second is about deterrence.
5. **d.** The second paragraph notes that one reason behind the deterrence theory is the effect of deterring not only criminals but also the public.
6. **a.** The last sentence of each paragraph specifies the effect of the theory discussed on the amount of discretion allowed to judges in sentencing.
7. **b.** This choice most completely summarizes the primary purpose of the paragraph. The other choices are all supporting details in the passage.
8. **b.** See the second sentence of the passage: "The sequence or order of the DNA building blocks is *different* in particular regions of the cell. . . "
9. **c.** The passage states that DNA collected from crime scenes can either link or eliminate a suspect.
10. **a.** The passage states that DNA testing may be performed "if technicians have a biological sample from the victim, such as a bloodstain." From this statement, you can infer that DNA is collected from biological samples, of which bloodstains are one example.
11. **c.** The other choices, though mentioned in the passage, are not the main idea.
12. **a.** While keeping one's temper is probably an aspect of the program, it is not explicitly mentioned in the passage.
13. **a.** See the second sentence of the passage.
14. **b.** This idea is explicitly stated in the fourth sentence.
15. **d.** The passage begins with an explicit reference to the Supreme Court and then proceeds to outline how Supreme Court decisions and other court decisions have impacted police interviewing and interrogation techniques.
16. **c.** See the third sentence of the passage: "The Supreme Court further outlined two general principles to guide police officer behavior."
17. **c.** Asking a suspect's name is specifically given in the fifth sentence as an example of a non-accusatory question, so you can infer that similar informational questions, such as asking for a suspect's birth date and telephone number, are also reasonably non-accusatory. Asking for a suspect's alibi (where he or she was when the crime occurred) is accusatory.
18. **b.** The passage states that the Supreme Court provides two guidelines and then gives examples of those guidelines. Moreover, all the other statements can be disproved by facts from the passage.
19. **c.** The primary purpose of the passage is to discuss the struggle "to find a uniform definition for the term *gang*."
20. **d.** The fourth sentence of the passage states that "drug gangs are seen as much more organized than street gangs."
21. **a.** The passage states that drug gangs are organized to protect their members' identities,

whereas street gangs are organized to protect territory. This statement directly contradicts choice **a**, which makes that choice the correct answer.

22. c. Choice **a** is incorrect because the first sentence suggests that becoming jaded is unavoidable. Choices **b** and **d** are mentioned in the passage but do not reflect the main idea.

23. b. See the first two sentences of the passage.

24. c. The passage claims that becoming jaded is inevitable.

25. a. See the second sentence of the passage.

26. c. See the first sentence.

27. d. This reason is implied throughout the passage.

28. b. The main idea of the passage is that having an understanding of different cultures can influence decision making. The passage uses the example of coining to support and illustrate this main idea; coining itself is not what the passage is about.

29. c. The second sentence of the passage states that coining "often produces red marks." Don't be fooled by choice **a**—though coining may seem painful, the passage never states this, and in fact, it is not.

30. b. As illustrated by the coining example, an officer who is aware of other cultural practices is a benefit to the community because the community is better served, and a knowledgeable officer can more effectively perform his or her duty.

Part Two: Writing

31. d. Choices **a** and **b** contain sentence fragments. Choice **c** uses commas incorrectly.

32. c. The word *returned* is in the past tense, as are *finished* and *left* in the first part of the sentence, so this sentence is the only one that uses proper parallel structure.

33. d. Choices **b** and **c** contain sentence fragments. The first part of choice **a** is a dangling modifier; in addition, no comma should separate *police officers* from *must*.

34. b. Choices **a** and **d** are run-on sentences; choice **c** contains a sentence fragment.

35. d. Each of the other choices includes a sentence fragment.

36. c. The verb should be *was*, not *were*, to agree with *the guard*. The verbs in the second half of the sentence should be in the past tense to match the first half of the sentence.

37. a. This is a complete sentence. Choice **b** is a comma splice; choice **c** is a run-on sentence; choice **d** contains a sentence fragment.

38. c. The correct preposition is *of. Think that* in choices **b** and **d** would require a complete clause with a verb, rather than the phrase that actually completes the sentence.

39. d. The modifier *with a growl* should be placed next to *the masked gunman*.

40. b. *Bravest* is the correct form of the adjective.

41. a. The other choices contain sentence fragments.

42. b. The other choices contain sentence fragments.

43. d. The correct pronoun case forms are used; choice **a** contains a redundant subject (*My partner Rosie and I, we . . .*); choices **b** and **c** contain incorrect pronoun case forms.

44. a. The modifier a *sharpshooter for many years* is clearly and correctly placed only in this choice.

45. b. This choice is the only one that contains the correct forms of the adjectives *tough* and *fair*.

46. c. *However* is the clearest and most logical transitional word.

47. b. The correct preposition is *by*; choices **a**, **c**, and **d** contain incorrect prepositions: *of*, *off*, and *from*.

48. d. The correct form of the verb is *sniffed*.

49. c. *To remove* and *lie* are the logical forms of these verbs.

50. a. The subject *recession* agrees in number with its verb is; in choices **b**, **c**, and **d** the subjects and verbs do not agree.

51. d. The verbs *are sequestered* and *become* are consistently in the present tense; in choices **a**, **b**, and **c** there are unnecessary shifts in tense.

52. a. The *neither . . . nor* construction always takes a singular verb, while the *both . . . and* construction always takes a plural verb.

53. c. There is no unnecessary shift in person; the other answers contain unnecessary shifts in person from *police officer* to *you*, *one*, and *we*.

54. b. In the other choices, the pronoun reference is ambiguous—who's in the hospital? Choice **c** also contains a misplaced modifier, *When in the hospital*, which seems to refer to *a phone call*.

55. d. The other answers contain unnecessary shifts in person from *I* to *one*, *you*, and *a person*.

Part Three: Vocabulary

56. b. Something *latent* is something that is hidden or unseen, but is capable of being exposed or revealed.

57. d. To be *inundated* is to be flooded.

58. d. Something *fragile* is delicate and must be handled with care.

59. c. *Unique* means one of a kind.

60. c. To *eliminate* something is to remove or eradicate it.

61. a. Something that is *imminent* is ready to take place, or going to happen soon.

62. d. To be *proficient* at something is to be skilled at it.

63. c. Something that is *ostentatious* is pretentious or showy.

64. d. Something *intangible* is something that is apparent, but not easily definable.

65. c. When something is *outmoded*, it is out of date or obsolete.

66. b. *Integrity* is a strong adherence to a set of values, it is a synonym of honesty.

67. c. Something characterized as *abnormal* is not normal; it is unusual.

68. a. An action that is *overt* is one that is highly visible, completely open to view.

69. a. A *panacea* is a remedy or cure-all.

70. b. A *glib* remark is one that is quick or fluent but seems insincere.

71. b. Someone who is *nondescript* appears ordinary or lacking in distinction.

72. a. A person who is *spiteful* is malicious and intends harm.

73. a. A *precedent* is a prior example that often serves to authorize subsequent actions.

74. b. *Ideologies* are a set of rigid beliefs held by specific groups.

75. d. To *delegate* something is to assign it to someone else.

76. a. Something that is *exigent* requires immediate attention or action because of its serious nature.

77. d. To *articulate* an idea is to express it clearly.

78. a. An *expansive* mood is one that is open and outgoing.

79. b. Something that is *detrimental* is damaging.

80. c. To be held *accountable* is to be held responsible or answerable.

Part Four: Spelling

Consult a dictionary if you are not sure why the answers in Part Four are correct.

81. d.
82. d.
83. c.
84. b.
85. a.
86. c.
87. a.
88. b.
89. d.
90. d.
91. c.
92. d.
93. c.
94. b.
95. c.
96. a.
97. d.
98. a.
99. b.
100. c.

▶ Scoring

Most U.S. cities require a score of at least 70% to pass a police officer exam. Because this exam has 100 questions, the number you answered correctly is your percentage: If you got 70 questions correct, your score is 70%.

What you should do next depends not only on how you score, but also on whether the city you're applying to uses your written score to help determine your rank on the eligibility list. Some cities use other factors, such as your performance in an oral board or interview, to decide whether or not to hire you. In that case, all you need to do is to pass the written exam in order to make it to the next step in the process, and a score of at least 70% is good enough. In other cities, however, your written score, either by itself or in combination with other factors, is used to place you on the eligibility list. The higher your score, the more likely you are to be hired.

Use this practice exam as a way to analyze your performance. Pay attention to the areas in which you miss the most questions. If most of your mistakes are in the reading comprehension questions, then you know you need to practice your reading skills. Or perhaps you had difficulty with the spelling section. Once you see where you need help, then your mission will be to study the chapters in this book on the relevant skills to develop your test-taking strategies.

To help you see where your trouble spots are, break down your scores according to the four sections below:

Part One: ______ questions correct
Part Two: ______ questions correct
Part Three: ______ questions correct
Part Four: ______ questions correct

Write down the number of correct answers for each section, and then add up all three numbers for your overall score. Each question is worth one point and the total you arrive at after adding all the numbers is also the percentage of questions that you answered correctly on the test.

And now forget about your total score; what's more important right now is your score on the individual sections of the exam.

Below is a table that shows you which of the instructional chapters correspond to the three parts of the exam. Your best bet is to review all of the chapters carefully, but you'll want to spend the most time on the chapters that correspond to the kind of question that gave you the most trouble.

EXAM PART	CHAPTER
One	7
Two	8
Three	9
Four	9

Remember, reading and writing skills are important not only for the exam, but also for your job as a police officer. So the time you spend improving those skills will pay off—not only in higher exam scores, but also in career success.

After you've read the relevant chapters, take the second exam of this type, in Chapter 16, to see how much you've improved.

CHAPTER

5 Police Officer Practice Exam 2

CHAPTER SUMMARY

The practice exam in this chapter is an example of the kind of job-related exam used by many police departments around the country. It tests skills police officers actually use on the job—not only basic skills like math and reading, but also map reading, memory, and good judgment and common sense.

The first practice exam in this book showed you an example of a police exam that simply tests your reading and writing skills. This second practice exam shows you a somewhat different kind of test. It still includes reading comprehension—most police exams do, because reading is such a vital job-related skill—but it also tests your ability to memorize pictures and written material, your map-reading skills, and your ability to use judgment to solve the kinds of problems police officers typically encounter, including simple math problems. There are 100 questions on this test, broken down into three sections:

- Part One: Memorization and Visualization consists of a set of pictures and text that you have to study and then a set of questions that you must answer based on the visuals and the text. You will not be allowed to look back at the material as you respond to these questions.
- Part Two: Reading covers map reading and reading comprehension.
- Part Three: Judgment and Problem Solving gives you questions that test deductive and inductive reasoning, your ability to apply good judgment and common sense in specific situations, and your ability to solve problems involving numbers (math word problems).

For best results, approach this exam as if it were the real thing. Find a quiet place where you can take the exam, and arm yourself with a few sharp number 2 pencils. Give yourself 15 minutes to study the memory material at the beginning of the exam. Then start the practice test, which begins with questions about what you memorized. Give yourself two and a half hours to complete the test, in addition to the 15 minutes you spent memorizing.

After the exam is an answer key complete with explanations of why the correct answer is the best choice. An explanation of how to interpret your test score follows the answer key.

Police Officer Practice Exam 2

1.	ⓐ	ⓑ	ⓒ	ⓓ
2.	ⓐ	ⓑ	ⓒ	ⓓ
3.	ⓐ	ⓑ	ⓒ	ⓓ
4.	ⓐ	ⓑ	ⓒ	ⓓ
5.	ⓐ	ⓑ	ⓒ	ⓓ
6.	ⓐ	ⓑ	ⓒ	ⓓ
7.	ⓐ	ⓑ	ⓒ	ⓓ
8.	ⓐ	ⓑ	ⓒ	ⓓ
9.	ⓐ	ⓑ	ⓒ	ⓓ
10.	ⓐ	ⓑ	ⓒ	ⓓ
11.	ⓐ	ⓑ	ⓒ	ⓓ
12.	ⓐ	ⓑ	ⓒ	ⓓ
13.	ⓐ	ⓑ	ⓒ	ⓓ
14.	ⓐ	ⓑ	ⓒ	ⓓ
15.	ⓐ	ⓑ	ⓒ	ⓓ
16.	ⓐ	ⓑ	ⓒ	ⓓ
17.	ⓐ	ⓑ	ⓒ	ⓓ
18.	ⓐ	ⓑ	ⓒ	ⓓ
19.	ⓐ	ⓑ	ⓒ	ⓓ
20.	ⓐ	ⓑ	ⓒ	ⓓ
21.	ⓐ	ⓑ	ⓒ	ⓓ
22.	ⓐ	ⓑ	ⓒ	ⓓ
23.	ⓐ	ⓑ	ⓒ	ⓓ
24.	ⓐ	ⓑ	ⓒ	ⓓ
25.	ⓐ	ⓑ	ⓒ	ⓓ
26.	ⓐ	ⓑ	ⓒ	ⓓ
27.	ⓐ	ⓑ	ⓒ	ⓓ
28.	ⓐ	ⓑ	ⓒ	ⓓ
29.	ⓐ	ⓑ	ⓒ	ⓓ
30.	ⓐ	ⓑ	ⓒ	ⓓ
31.	ⓐ	ⓑ	ⓒ	ⓓ
32.	ⓐ	ⓑ	ⓒ	ⓓ
33.	ⓐ	ⓑ	ⓒ	ⓓ
34.	ⓐ	ⓑ	ⓒ	ⓓ
35.	ⓐ	ⓑ	ⓒ	ⓓ
36.	ⓐ	ⓑ	ⓒ	ⓓ
37.	ⓐ	ⓑ	ⓒ	ⓓ
38.	ⓐ	ⓑ	ⓒ	ⓓ
39.	ⓐ	ⓑ	ⓒ	ⓓ
40.	ⓐ	ⓑ	ⓒ	ⓓ
41.	ⓐ	ⓑ	ⓒ	ⓓ
42.	ⓐ	ⓑ	ⓒ	ⓓ
43.	ⓐ	ⓑ	ⓒ	ⓓ
44.	ⓐ	ⓑ	ⓒ	ⓓ
45.	ⓐ	ⓑ	ⓒ	ⓓ
46.	ⓐ	ⓑ	ⓒ	ⓓ
47.	ⓐ	ⓑ	ⓒ	ⓓ
48.	ⓐ	ⓑ	ⓒ	ⓓ
49.	ⓐ	ⓑ	ⓒ	ⓓ
50.	ⓐ	ⓑ	ⓒ	ⓓ
51.	ⓐ	ⓑ	ⓒ	ⓓ
52.	ⓐ	ⓑ	ⓒ	ⓓ
53.	ⓐ	ⓑ	ⓒ	ⓓ
54.	ⓐ	ⓑ	ⓒ	ⓓ
55.	ⓐ	ⓑ	ⓒ	ⓓ
56.	ⓐ	ⓑ	ⓒ	ⓓ
57.	ⓐ	ⓑ	ⓒ	ⓓ
58.	ⓐ	ⓑ	ⓒ	ⓓ
59.	ⓐ	ⓑ	ⓒ	ⓓ
60.	ⓐ	ⓑ	ⓒ	ⓓ
61.	ⓐ	ⓑ	ⓒ	ⓓ
62.	ⓐ	ⓑ	ⓒ	ⓓ
63.	ⓐ	ⓑ	ⓒ	ⓓ
64.	ⓐ	ⓑ	ⓒ	ⓓ
65.	ⓐ	ⓑ	ⓒ	ⓓ
66.	ⓐ	ⓑ	ⓒ	ⓓ
67.	ⓐ	ⓑ	ⓒ	ⓓ
68.	ⓐ	ⓑ	ⓒ	ⓓ
69.	ⓐ	ⓑ	ⓒ	ⓓ
70.	ⓐ	ⓑ	ⓒ	ⓓ
71.	ⓐ	ⓑ	ⓒ	ⓓ
72.	ⓐ	ⓑ	ⓒ	ⓓ
73.	ⓐ	ⓑ	ⓒ	ⓓ
74.	ⓐ	ⓑ	ⓒ	ⓓ
75.	ⓐ	ⓑ	ⓒ	ⓓ
76.	ⓐ	ⓑ	ⓒ	ⓓ
77.	ⓐ	ⓑ	ⓒ	ⓓ
78.	ⓐ	ⓑ	ⓒ	ⓓ
79.	ⓐ	ⓑ	ⓒ	ⓓ
80.	ⓐ	ⓑ	ⓒ	ⓓ
81.	ⓐ	ⓑ	ⓒ	ⓓ
82.	ⓐ	ⓑ	ⓒ	ⓓ
83.	ⓐ	ⓑ	ⓒ	ⓓ
84.	ⓐ	ⓑ	ⓒ	ⓓ
85.	ⓐ	ⓑ	ⓒ	ⓓ
86.	ⓐ	ⓑ	ⓒ	ⓓ
87.	ⓐ	ⓑ	ⓒ	ⓓ
88.	ⓐ	ⓑ	ⓒ	ⓓ
89.	ⓐ	ⓑ	ⓒ	ⓓ
90.	ⓐ	ⓑ	ⓒ	ⓓ
91.	ⓐ	ⓑ	ⓒ	ⓓ
92.	ⓐ	ⓑ	ⓒ	ⓓ
93.	ⓐ	ⓑ	ⓒ	ⓓ
94.	ⓐ	ⓑ	ⓒ	ⓓ
95.	ⓐ	ⓑ	ⓒ	ⓓ
96.	ⓐ	ⓑ	ⓒ	ⓓ
97.	ⓐ	ⓑ	ⓒ	ⓓ
98.	ⓐ	ⓑ	ⓒ	ⓓ
99.	ⓐ	ⓑ	ⓒ	ⓓ
100.	ⓐ	ⓑ	ⓒ	ⓓ

▶ Police Officer Practice Exam 2

Study Booklet

You have 15 minutes to study the following Wanted posters and to read the article on police procedure. After 15 minutes are up, turn the page and go on to answer the test questions, beginning with questions about the study material. **Do not refer back to this study booklet to answer the questions.** When you have finished with Part One: Memorization and Visualization, you may continue with the rest of the exam.

MISSING
Valeria Guerra

DESCRIPTION:

Age: 11
Race: Hispanic
Height: 5′1″
Weight: 90 lbs.
Hair: Black, straight, shoulder-length
Eyes: Brown
Skin: Dark brown

REMARKS: Last seen alone at Beachfront Candy Shop in Ridgepoint Mall in Clarktown at noon on Saturday, April 1. Wearing red shorts, white T-shirt, with her hair in a ponytail. Front right tooth missing.
IF LOCATED: Call Clarktown Sheriff's Department, Juvenile Unit, at 344-555-1220.

WANTED
Michael Hagan Finan

ALIASES: Robbie Hagan
WANTED BY: New York City Police Department
CHARGES: Drug Possession
DESCRIPTION:

Age: 24
Race: White
Height: 6′3″
Weight: 195 lbs.
Hair: Blond
Eyes: Green

IDENTIFYING SCARS OR MARKS: Tattoo on inner right bicep of black peace symbol.
REMARKS: Rides a black Suzuki RM250 with cracked headlight. Last seen in Brooklyn and believed to be headed for Camden, New Jersey.

WANTED
Lin Yang

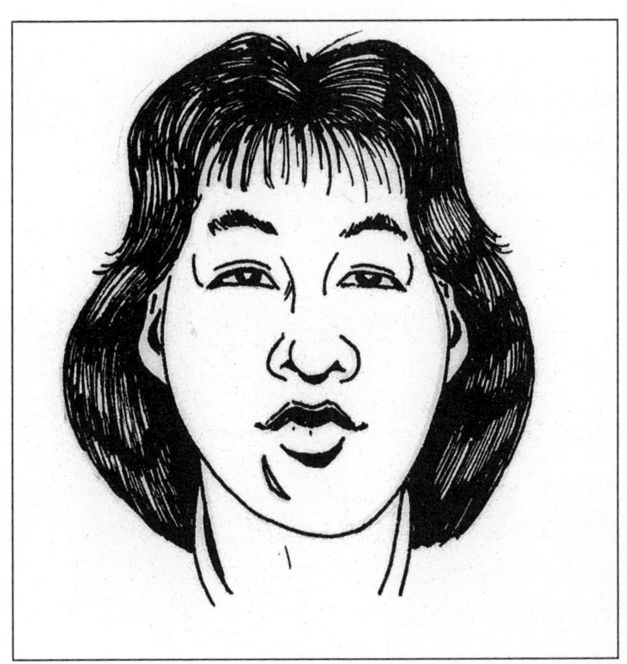

ALIASES: Lisa Yang
WANTED BY: North Dakota State Police
CHARGES: Burglary
DESCRIPTION:

Age: 36
Race: Asian
Height: 5′2″
Weight: 110 lbs.
Hair: Black
Eyes: Brown

IDENTIFYING SCARS OR MARKS: Scar on chin.
REMARKS: Last seen at 3 Elks Casino in Grand Forks, North Dakota. Yang may be headed for Fresno, California, driving a white Firebird.

WANTED
Louis Robert Hart

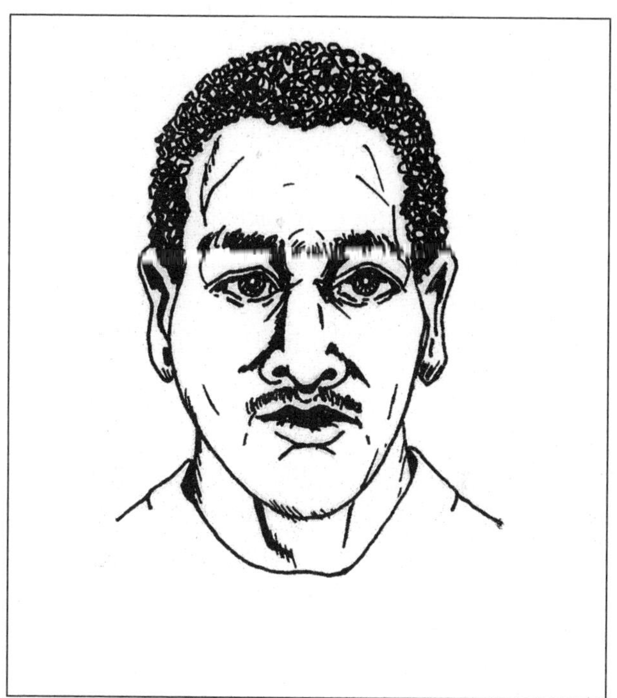

ALIASES: Hart-Break; Robert Louis
WANTED BY: FBI
CHARGES: Conspiracy
DESCRIPTION:

Age: 45
Race: Black
Height: 6′3″
Weight: 255 lbs.
Hair: Black
Eyes: Brown

REMARKS: Hart is addicted to gambling and frequents the Blue Streak Greyhound Raceway in Jacksonville, Mississippi. Is thought to still be in the area.
CAUTION: Hart is known to carry a diving knife strapped to his right leg.

WANTED
Barry Edward Brand

ALIASES: Eddie One-Eye, Bold Larry
WANTED BY: Florida State Police
CHARGES: Auto Theft
DESCRIPTION:

Age: 55
Race: White
Height: $5'8\frac{1}{2}''$
Weight: 165 lbs.
Hair: None
Eyes: Blue

IDENTIFYING SCARS OR MARKS: Wears black patch over missing right eye, shaves head.
REMARKS: Last seen in Pensacola. Is known to frequent the Dew Drop Inn downtown and drives a stolen sky blue Cadillac Coupe Deville. Sources say he is moving to Peoria, Illinois.

Terry Stops

Often in the course of routine patrol, a police officer needs to briefly detain a person for questioning without an arrest warrant or even probable cause. The officer may also feel that it is necessary to frisk this person for weapons. This type of detention is known as a Terry Stop, after the U.S. Supreme Court case *Terry vs. State of Ohio*. In that case, the Court determined that a Terry Stop does not violate a citizen's right to be free from unreasonable search and seizure, as long as certain procedures are followed. First, the person must be behaving in some manner that arouses the police officer's suspicion. Second, the officer must believe that swift action is necessary to prevent a crime from being committed or a suspect from escaping. Finally, in order to frisk the individual, the officer must reasonably believe that the person is armed and dangerous.

In determining whether an individual is acting in a suspicious manner, a police officer must rely on his or her training and experience. Circumstances in each case will be different, but an officer must be able to articulate what it was about a person's behavior that aroused suspicion, whether it was one particular action or a series of actions taken together. For example, it may not be unusual for shoppers in a store to wander up and down the aisles looking at merchandise. However, it may be suspicious if a person does this for an inordinate period of time, seems to be checking the locations of surveillance equipment, and is wearing loose clothing that would facilitate shoplifting. Similarly, it is not unusual for a person wearing gym shorts and a T-shirt to be running through a residential neighborhood; however, a person dressed in regular clothes might legitimately be suspect. It is important to note that a person who simply appears out of place based on the manner in which he or she is dressed is not sufficient cause for suspicion on the part of a police officer.

In addition to the behavior that arouses an officer's attention, the officer must believe that immediate action must be taken to prevent the commission of a crime or a suspect from escaping. In some situations, it may be better to wait to develop probable cause and arrest the person. One important element of this decision is the safety of any other people in the area. In addition, a police officer may determine that his or her immediate action is necessary to avert the commission of a crime, even if no people are in danger. If the suspect appears, for example, to be checking out parked cars for the possibility of stealing one, an officer may well be able to wait until the crime is in progress (thereby having probable cause for an arrest) or even until the crime is actually committed, when patrol cars can be dispatched to arrest the individual. On the other hand, a person who appears to be planning a carjacking should be stopped before the occupants of a car can be hurt. Again, an officer must make a quick decision based on all the circumstances.

Once an officer has detained a suspicious person, the officer must determine if he or she feels it is necessary to frisk the individual for weapons. Again, an officer should rely on her or his training and experience. If the officer feels that the detainee poses a threat to the officer's safety, the suspect should be frisked. For example, although there may certainly be exceptions, a person suspected of shoplifting is not likely to be armed. On the other hand, a person suspected of breaking and entering may very well be carrying a weapon. In addition, the officer should be aware of the behavior of the person once the stop is made. Certain behavior indicates the person is waiting for an opportunity to produce a weapon and threaten the officer's safety. The safety of the officer and any civilians in the area is the most important consideration.

Part One: Memorization and Visualization

Answer the following 30 questions based on the wanted posters and police procedure article you have just studied. **Do not refer back to the study material to answer these questions.**

1. Michael Hagan Finan is wanted for
- **a.** theft
- **b.** fraud.
- **c.** conspiracy.
- **d.** drug possession.

2. Michael Hagan Finan wears a tattoo on his right arm depicting a
- **a.** peace symbol.
- **b.** motorcycle.
- **c.** ring.
- **d.** greyhound.

3. How old is Valeria Guerra?
- **a.** 18
- **b.** 11
- **c.** 30
- **d.** 17

4. Barry Edward Brand also goes by which of the following names?
- **a.** Eddie One-Eye
- **b.** Robert Louis
- **c.** Edward Cloud
- **d.** Willie James

5. When last seen, Valeria Guerra wore her hair in
- **a.** tight curls.
- **b.** braids.
- **c.** a ponytail.
- **d.** a spike cut.

6. Identifying scars or marks on Barry Edward Brand include which of the following?
- **a.** missing right eye
- **b.** tattoo of a swastika
- **c.** a scar above the right eye
- **d.** tattoo of an eye on the inner right forearm

7. Lin Yang weighs approximately
- **a.** 180 lbs
- **b.** 110 lbs.
- **c.** 120 lbs.
- **d.** 80 lbs.

8. Lin Yang was last seen driving a
- **a.** Cadillac Coupe Deville.
- **b.** Ford F-150.
- **c.** Firebird.
- **d.** Suzuki RM250.

9. Louis Robert Hart is wanted by the
- **a.** FBI.
- **b.** Jacksonville Police.
- **c.** North Dakota State Police.
- **d.** Florida State Police.

10. Lin Yang is wanted for
- **a.** carrying a concealed weapon.
- **b.** conspiracy.
- **c.** reckless driving.
- **d.** burglary.

11. Louis Robert Hart is believed to be in which state?
- **a.** New Mexico
- **b.** Mississippi
- **c.** Illinois
- **d.** Florida

12. Which of the following best describes Louis Robert Hart's facial hair?
a. He is clean-shaven.
b. He wears a full beard and mustache.
c. He wears a goatee.
d. He wears a thin mustache.

13. Which of these females is listed as missing?
a. Guerra
b. Yang
c. Cho
d. both Yang and Guerra

14. Which of the suspects is wanted for conspiracy?
a. Hart
b. Yang
c. Brand
d. Finan

15. Which suspect frequents the Dew Drop Inn in Pensacola?
a. Hart
b. Guerra
c. Finan
d. Brand

16. Which suspect may be moving to Peoria, Illinois?
a. Brand
b. Finan
c. Yang
d. Hart

17. Which suspect is known to strap a diving knife to his or her leg?
a. Yang
b. Hart
c. Brand
d. both Yang and Brand

18. Which suspect is bald?
a. Hart
b. Yang
c. Finan
d. Brand

19. Based on the wanted posters, which of the following statements is true?
a. Both Hart and Brand have tattoos.
b. Both Hart and Brand are under 40.
c. Hart is younger than Brand.
d. Brand is taller than Hart.

20. Based on the wanted posters, which of the following statements is false?
a. Finan has red hair.
b. Hart has a goatee.
c. Finan and Hart are both under 50.
d. Finan and Hart are not close in age.

21. According to the reading passage, a Terry Stop is
a. an arrest for shoplifting.
b. the brief detention and questioning of a suspicious person.
c. an officer's frisking a suspect for weapons.
d. the development of a case that results in an arrest warrant.

22. According to the passage, a Terry Stop includes frisking a suspect if
a. the officer sees evidence of a weapon.
b. the person is suspected of breaking and entering.
c. there are civilians in the area.
d. the officer or others are in danger.

23. An officer on foot patrol notices two people standing on a street corner. The officer observes the two and, after a moment, one of the people walks slowly down the street, looks in the window of a store called McFadden's, walks forward a few feet, and then turns around and returns to the other person. They speak briefly, and then the other person walks down the street, performing the same series of motions. They repeat this ritual five or six times each. The officer would be justified in performing a Terry Stop, based on her suspicion that the people

a. appeared to be carrying weapons.
b. looked out of place.
c. might be planning to rob McFadden's.
d. were obstructing the sidewalk.

24. According to the passage, an officer may choose to conduct a Terry Stop to

a. discourage loitering.
b. prevent a crime from being committed or a suspect from escaping.
c. find out if a person is carrying a concealed weapon.
d. rule out suspects after a crime has been committed.

25. According to the passage, the determination that a person is suspicious

a. depends on the circumstances of each situation.
b. means someone looks out of place.
c. usually means someone is guilty of planning a crime.
d. usually indicates a person is carrying a concealed weapon.

26. An officer has stopped a suspicious individual. The suspect seems to be trying to reach for something under her coat. The officer should

a. call for backup.
b. arrest the suspect.
c. frisk the suspect.
d. handcuff the suspect.

27. An officer observes a person sitting on a bench outside a bank at 4:30 P.M. The officer knows the bank closes at 5:00. The person checks his watch several times and watches customers come and go through the door of the bank. He also makes eye contact with a person driving a blue sedan that appears to be circling the block. Finally, a parking space in front of the bank becomes vacant, and the sedan pulls in. The driver and the man on the bench nod to each other. The officer believes the two are planning to rob the bank just before it closes. The officer should

a. immediately begin questioning the man on the bench, because it appears he's going to rob the bank.
b. immediately begin questioning the driver of the sedan, because it appears she's driving the get away car.
c. go into the bank, warn the employees, and ask all the customers to leave for their own safety.
d. call for backup, because it appears the potential robbers are waiting for the bank to close.

28. According to the U.S. Supreme Court, a Terry Stop

a. is permissible search and seizure.
b. often occurs in the course of police work.
c. should be undertaken only when two officers are present.
d. requires probable cause.

29. According to the passage, persons suspected of shoplifting

a. should never be frisked, as shoplifters rarely carry weapons.

b. may legitimately be the subjects of a Terry Stop.

c. always wear loose clothing and wander in the store a long time.

d. may be handcuffed immediately for the safety of the civilians in the area.

30. An officer in a squad car is patrolling a wealthy residential neighborhood. She notices one house in which a light will come on in one part of the house for a few minutes, then go off. A moment later, a light will come on in another part of the house, then go off. This happens several times in different parts of the house. The officer also notes that the garage door is standing open and that there are no cars parked there or in the driveway. The officer believes there may be a burglary in progress, and pulls over to observe the house. While she is watching the house, a man wearing torn jeans and a dirty T-shirt walks by the house. According to the passage, the officer should NOT

a. allow the man to see her, as he may be dangerous.

b. involve the neighbors by asking them if they have information.

c. stop the man, as there is no indication he is involved in criminal activity.

d. radio headquarters until she is absolutely sure a crime is being committed.

Part Two: Reading

Answer questions 31–34 solely on the basis of the following passage.

On May 19, 2006, at 5:20 A.M., Officers Garcia and Norwood were on patrol in a marked black and white police vehicle. The officers received a radio call to respond to a reported burglary at 945 Allen Street. The officers drove to the location, a retail electronics store, arriving ten minutes after receiving the call. The officers noted that the store's front window was smashed out. The officers deployed on the location by having Garcia watch the front and Norwood walk down a small alley and watch the back.

While waiting for other officers to assist them in searching the location, one of the officers was approached by Tom Sharp, who stated he lived in the upstairs apartment directly across the street, and that he had heard the window breaking and called the police. Five minutes after Garcia and Norwood called for backup, Officers Roberts and Short arrived. Short walked down the alley to assist Norwood while Roberts stayed with Garcia. Roberts and Garcia entered the store through the smashed out large display window and searched for the suspects. During a search of the interior, Roberts and Garcia discovered a stairway leading to a storage attic. The officers thoroughly searched the location and determined that the suspects were gone.

31. Based on the passage, which officer most likely first spoke with Tom Sharp?

a. Norwood

b. Garcia

c. Roberts

d. Short

32. Approximately what time did Roberts and Short arrive?
- **a.** 5:15 A.M.
- **b.** 5:20 A.M.
- **c.** 5:30 A.M.
- **d.** 5:35 A.M.

33. Where did the burglary occur?
- **a.** an apartment building
- **b.** a retail electronics shop
- **c.** an electronics repair shop
- **d.** an alleyway

34. How did the suspect(s) most likely enter the location?
- **a.** through a broken rear door, off the side alley
- **b.** through a roof access in the attic
- **c.** through the smashed front window
- **d.** through the smashed rear window

Answer questions 35–37 solely on the basis of the map on the next page. The arrows indicate traffic flow; one arrow indicates a one-way street going in the direction of the arrow; two arrows represent a two-way street. You are not allowed to go the wrong way on a one-way street.

35. Officers Kamena and Bean are completing a call in the Raymond Avenue Mall at the southeast corner of the building. Dispatch notifies them of a silent alarm going off in a residence located at the northwest corner of Arroyo Drive and Linda Lane. What is the quickest route for Officers Kamena and Bean to take to the residence?
- **a.** Turn north on Spivey Road, then east on Linda Lane, and then north on Arroyo Drive.
- **b.** Turn east on John Street, then north on Vincente, then west on Linda Lane, then north on Malinda Road, and then east on Brigham Boulevard to Arroyo Drive.
- **c.** Turn north on Spivey Road, then east on Brigham Boulevard, and then south on Arroyo Drive.
- **d.** Turn north on Spivey Road, then east on Battery Road, then north on Malinda Road, and then east on Brigham Boulevard.

36. Officers Montinari and Schmidt are southbound on Arroyo Drive and have just crossed Needle Street. They receive a call of an altercation between a bus driver and a passenger, with the bus parked at a bus stop located at Raymond Avenue and Battery Road. What is the quickest route for Officers Montinari and Schmidt to take to the bus stop?
- **a.** Continue south on Arroyo Drive, then west on John Street, then north on Malinda Road, then west on Needle Street, then north on Spivey Road, and then west on Battery Road to Raymond Avenue.
- **b.** Continue south on Arroyo Drive, then west on Shore Drive, and then north on Raymond Avenue to Battery Road.
- **c.** Make a U-turn on Arroyo Drive and then go west on Battery Road to Raymond Avenue.
- **d.** Continue south on Arroyo Drive, then east on Shore Drive, then north on Vincente, and then west on Battery Road to Raymond Avenue.

37. Officer Ricardo is driving west on Battery Road. She makes a right onto James Avenue, then a left onto Linda Lane, then a right onto Raymond, and then a right onto Brigham Road. What direction is she facing?
- **a.** east
- **b.** south
- **c.** west
- **d.** north

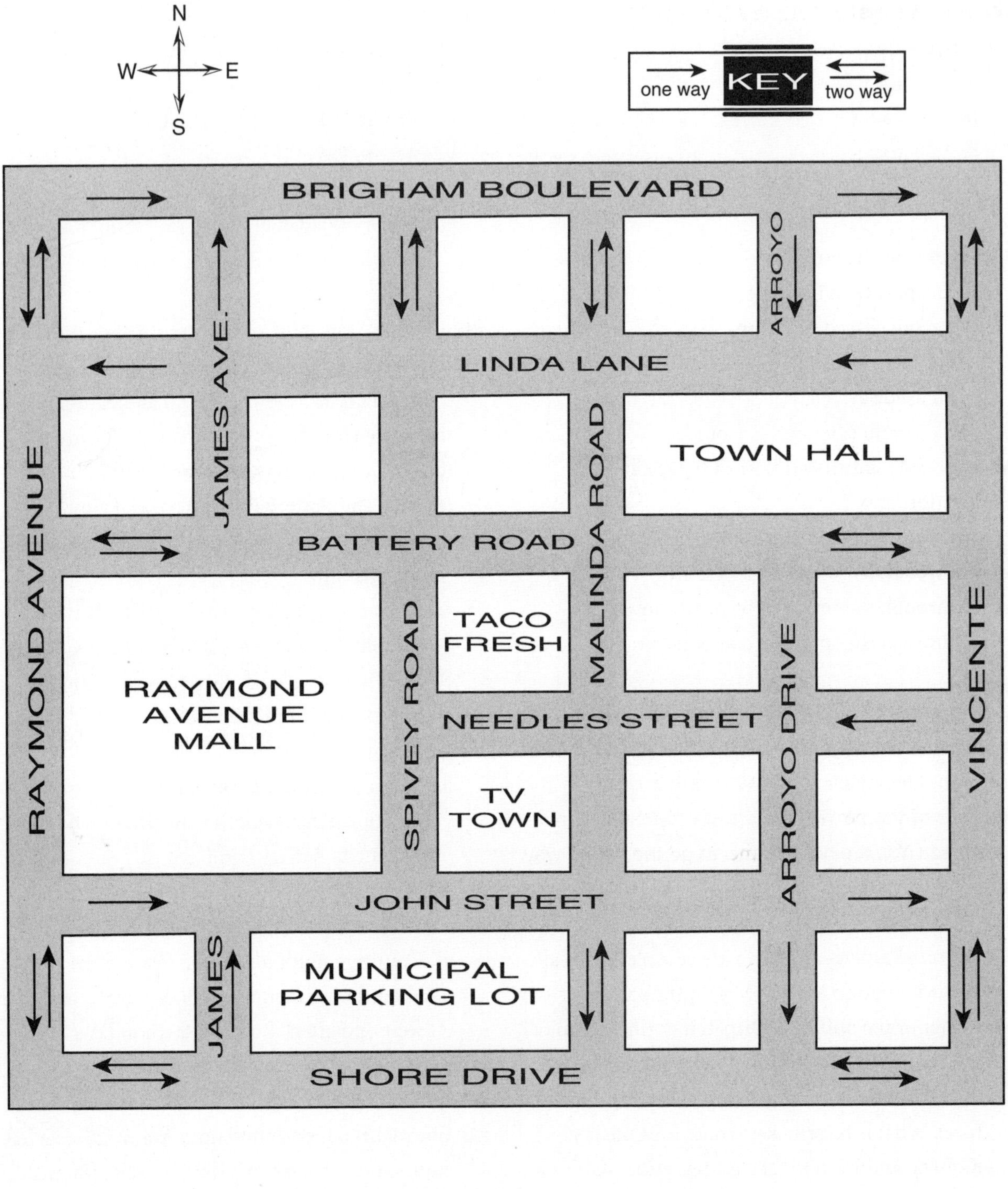

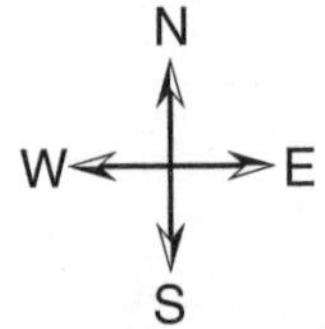

BRIGHAM BOULEVARD
ARROYO
LINDA LANE
JAMES AVE.
MALINDA ROAD
TOWN HALL
RAYMOND AVENUE
BATTERY ROAD
TACO FRESH
SPIVEY ROAD
VINCENTE
RAYMOND AVENUE MALL
NEEDLES STREET
ARROYO DRIVE
TV TOWN
JOHN STREET
JAMES
MUNICIPAL PARKING LOT
SHORE DRIVE

Answer questions 38–43 solely on the basis of the following passage.

Many public safety officials, especially police officers, have certain restrictions on the protections provided by the Bill of Rights. While most Americans can express themselves freely thanks to the First Amendment, police officers, due to the nature of their employment, cannot. Police officers who are on duty, and especially those in uniform, are generally restricted from making political speeches and from endorsing political candidates. A police officer's diminished First Amendment right extends to his or her off-duty hours; if the officer's conduct would tend to reflect negatively on his or her department or the profession, his or her freedom of speech is limited.

If a police officer questions a suspect about an incident, the Fifth Amendment—sometimes referred to the right to avoid self-incrimination—allows the suspect the right to not answer those questions. On the other hand, a police officer under suspicion of wrongdoing does not have the right to refuse to answer questions. An excessive force complaint against a police officer could result in any number of criminal filings. While an officer's statements made in conjunction with the incident cannot generally be used against him or her in court, officers still cannot refuse to answer questions.

According to the Fourth Amendment, the government cannot search or seize property except with probable cause. Police officers daily use areas and containers that are not protected in the same manner as the general public. A police officer's supervisor can, within certain limits, search a police officer's locker, police vehicle, and perhaps an equipment bag without the probable cause necessary to search similar areas belonging to the public.

38. Which constitutional amendment generally covers issues surrounding freedom of speech?
- **a.** First
- **b.** Second
- **c.** Fourth
- **d.** Fifth

39. According to the passage, which of the following is true?
- **a.** The Constitution provides that police officers can carry firearms.
- **b.** An excessive force complaint violates the Fifth Amendment.
- **c.** A police officer's freedom of speech can be limited during his or her off-duty hours.
- **d.** A police officer can always refuse to answer questions.

40. Which of the following is the best title for the passage?
- **a.** An Overview of the Constitution
- **b.** Drug Use and the Police Department
- **c.** The Powers of the Police
- **d.** The Bill of Rights and Public Safety Officials

41. According to the passage, the Fifth Amendment generally covers which of the following?
- **a.** self-incrimination
- **b.** search and seizure
- **c.** free association
- **d.** freedom of speech

42. According to the passage, all of the following are areas wherein police officers might have diminished Fourth Amendment rights EXCEPT
- **a.** their homes.
- **b.** their lockers.
- **c.** their squad cars.
- **d.** their equipment bags.

43. Based on the information in the passage, you can assume that a police officer should refrain from the use of racial slurs because

a. he or she can be arrested.
b. it reflects poorly on the officer and the department.
c. he or she is completely unprotected by the First Amendment.
d. it might lead to a search and seizure of the officer's personal belongings.

Answer questions 44–48 based on the map on the following page, and the information below.

A police officer is often required to assist civilians who seek travel directions or referral to city agencies and facilities.

This map is a section of the city where some public buildings are located. Each of the squares represents one city block. Street names are as shown. If there is an arrow next to the street name, it means the street is one way only in the direction of the arrow. If there is no arrow next to the street name, two-way traffic is allowed.

44. While you are on foot patrol, an elderly man stops you in front of the firehouse and asks you to help him find the Senior Citizens' Center. You should tell him to

a. walk across the street to the Senior Citizens' Center.
b. walk south to Avenue C, make a right and walk west on Avenue C, make a right on Grand Street, and walk up to the Senior Citizens' Center.
c. walk north to Avenue B and then west on Avenue B to the end of the park, make a right, and go one block.
d. walk north to Avenue B and then west on Avenue B to Lafayette Street, make a right, and go one block.

45. The head librarian needs gasoline for his automobile. He is leaving the Avenue D garage exit from the library. His quickest legal route is to go

a. north on Central Street to Avenue C and west on Avenue C to the gas station.
b. west on Brooklyn Street to Avenue B and north on Avenue B to the gas station.
c. west on Avenue D to Grand Street and north on Grand Street to the gas station.
d. west on Avenue D to Lafayette Street and north on Lafayette Street to the gas station.

46. You are dispatched from the police station to an altercation taking place at the northwest corner of the public park. Which is the most direct legal way to drive there?

a. east to Central Street, north on Central Street to Avenue B, and west on Avenue B to Grand Street
b. west to Grand Street and north on Grand Street to Avenue B
c. east to Brooklyn Street, north on Brooklyn Street to Avenue B, and west on Avenue B to Grand Street
d. west to Greene Street, north on Greene Street to Avenue C, and east on Avenue C to Brooklyn Street

47. A nurse at the city hospital goes to the public library every Monday as a volunteer. What would be her shortest legal route from the hospital to the library?

a. west on Avenue A, south on Lafayette Street, east on Avenue C, and south on Central Street to the library entrance
b. east on Avenue B and south on Central Street to the library entrance
c. west on Avenue A, south on Lafayette Street, and east on Avenue D to the library entrance
d. east on Avenue A and south on Central Street to the library entrance

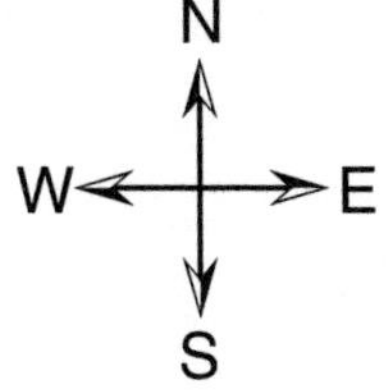

AVENUE A

SENIOR CITIZENS' CENTER

STREET

CITY HOSPITAL

CLINIC

AVENUE B

STREET

GAS STATION

STREET

PUBLIC PARK

STREET

FIRE-HOUSE

STREET

AVENUE C

LAFAYETTE

GRAND

HIGH SCHOOL

GREENE

BROOKLYN

PUBLIC LIBRARY

CENTRAL

PARKING GARAGE

AVENUE D

HEALTH CENTER

POLICE STATION

1st AVENUE

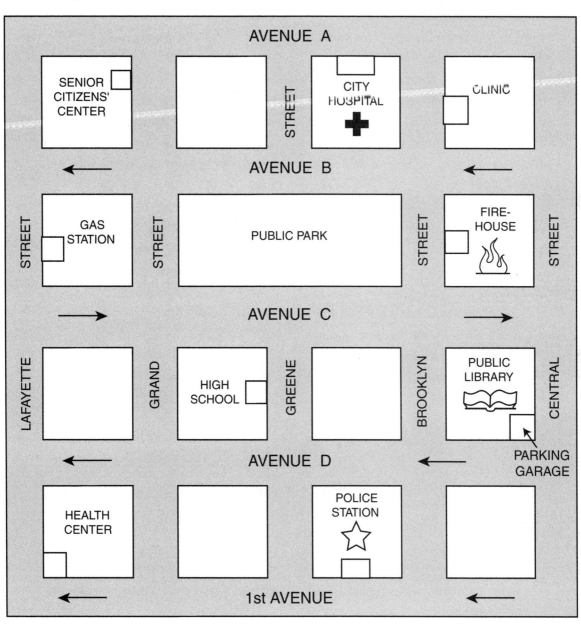

48. After responding to a call at the firehouse, you are ready to drive back to the police station for the end of your shift. What is the quickest legal route?
  a. south on Brooklyn Street and west on 1st Avenue to the police station
  b. north on Brooklyn Street, west on Avenue A, south on Lafayette Street, and east on 1st Avenue to the police station
  c. north on Brooklyn Street and east on 1st Avenue to the police station
  d. south on Brooklyn Street, west on Avenue C, south on Grand Street, and east on 1st Avenue to the police station

Answer questions 49–53 solely on the basis of the following passage.

On April 20, 2006, at 2:00 P.M., Officers Watts and Johnson were on patrol in a marked black and white police vehicle. Watts was driving the police vehicle westbound on First Street approaching Broadway when the officers observed Daniel Bardus driving a green Chevrolet northbound on Broadway. Both police officers noted that Bardus continued northbound through the intersection, failing to come to a complete stop for the posted stop sign.

Watts negotiated a right turn and began to follow Bardus. Watts activated the vehicle's emergency lights while Johnson radioed in Bardus's license number. Instead of stopping, Bardus accelerated to 60 mph. Johnson radioed the dispatch center, stating that the officers were in pursuit of Bardus. The dispatch center acknowledged the pursuit and informed Watts and Johnson that the car being driven by Bardus was stolen.

A few minutes into the pursuit, Watts and Johnson were joined by a second police vehicle driven by Sergeant Ducis. Shortly after Ducis joined the pursuit, Bardus attempted a left turn off of Broadway onto Platea Street, but Bardus was traveling too fast and his vehicle's tires lost traction, sending him into a violent spinout. Bardus's vehicle spun out of control and struck a light post approximately 150 feet west of Broadway. Bardus exited his vehicle and ran northbound between the houses.

The passenger officer in the police car was the first to begin chasing Bardus on foot between the houses and tackled him with the partner officer. The sergeant followed seconds behind. Officer Watts handcuffed Bardus and helped him to his feet. The last officer on the scene searched Bardus and found a small handgun in Bardus's left front pocket.

49. Why did the officers initially try to stop Bardus?
  a. He was driving a stolen car.
  b. He failed to stop for the officers.
  c. He violated a stop sign.
  d. He was carrying a gun.

50. What is the most likely address of Bardus's capture?
  a. 250 Platea Street
  b. 250 Broadway
  c. 100 Broadway
  d. 250 First Street

51. Which officer tackled Bardus?
  a. Watts
  b. Johnson
  c. Ducis
  d. unknown

52. Who found the handgun?
  a. Watts
  b. Johnson
  c. Ducis
  d. unknown

53. According to the passage, how many total vehicles were involved in the pursuit?
  a. one
  b. two
  c. three
  d. four

Answer questions 54–56 solely on the basis of the map on the next page. The arrows indicate traffic flow: One arrow indicates a one-way street going in the direction of the arrow; two arrows represent a two-way street. You are not allowed to go the wrong way on a one-way street.

54. Officer Tenney is eastbound on Kent Avenue at Lee Lane. He receives a call about a vicious dog at a residence located at the northeast corner of Lynch Road and Mill Road. What is the quickest route for Officer Tenney to take?
  a. Continue east on Kent Avenue, then north on Main Street to Mill Road, and then west on Mill Road to the northeast corner of Lynch Road and Mill Road.
  b. Continue east on Kent Avenue, then north on Main Street, then west on Pomeroy Boulevard, and then south on Lynch Road.
  c. Continue east on Kent Avenue, then south on Main Street, then west on Pine Avenue, then north on Grove Street, and then east on Mill Road to Lynch Road.
  d. Continue east on Kent Avenue, then north on Main Street, then west on Palmer Avenue, and then north on Lynch Road to Mill Road.

55. Officers McElhaney and Calhoun are driving by the courthouse, northbound on Upton Street. They receive a call about a fight among four juveniles at Ross Park on the Grove Street side of the park. What is the most direct route for Officers McElhaney and Calhoun?
  a. Continue north on Upton Street, west on Pomeroy Boulevard, then south on Main Street, and then west on Kent Avenue to Grove Street.
  b. Continue north on Upton Street, then west on Pomeroy Boulevard, and then south on Grove Street to Ross Park.
  c. Continue north on Upton Street, then west on Pomeroy Boulevard, then south on Main Street, then west on Palmer Avenue, and then south on Grove Street to Ross Park.
  d. Make a U-turn on Upton Street and then go west on Palmer Avenue and then south on Grove Street to Ross Park.

56. Officer Kearney is leaving Jim's Deli, heading west on Pine Avenue. She turns left on Lee Lane, then left again onto Pecan Avenue. She turns left on Main Street and finally turns right on Palmer Avenue. What direction is she facing?
  a. west
  b. south
  c. north
  d. east

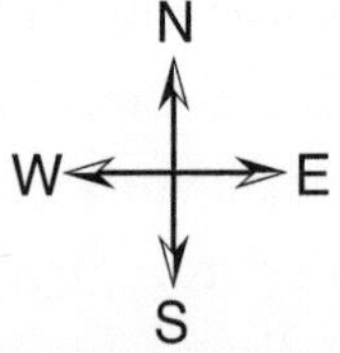

POMEROY BOULEVARD
MILL ROAD
COURT-
HOUSE
LYNCH ROAD
LEE LANE
BOND ROAD
PALMER AVENUE
GROVE STREET
COMMUNITY CENTER
MAIN STREET
KENT AVENUE
ROSS PARK
LEE LANE
BOND ROAD
JIM'S
DELI
UPTON STREET
PINE AVENUE
PECAN AVENUE

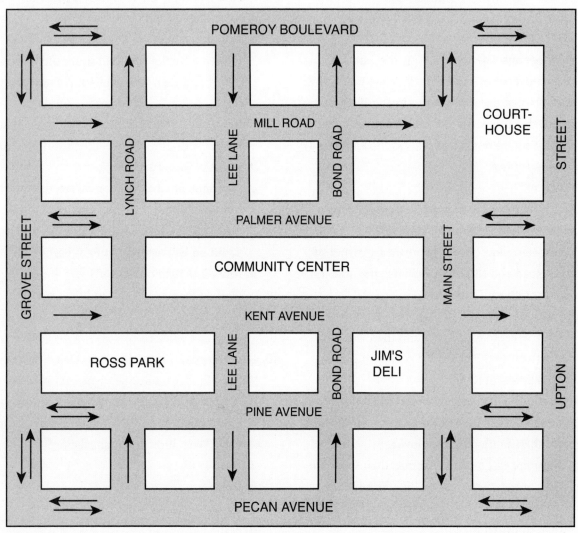

Answer questions 57–60 solely on the basis of the following passage.

Most criminals do not suffer from antisocial personality disorder; however, nearly all persons with this disorder have been in trouble with the law. Sometimes labeled sociopaths, they are a grim problem for society. Their crimes range from con games to murder, and they are set apart by what appears to be a complete lack of conscience. Often attractive and charming, and always inordinately self-confident, they nevertheless demonstrate a disturbing emotional shallowness, as if they had been born without a faculty as vital as sight or hearing. These individuals are not legally insane, nor do they suffer from the distortions of thought associated with mental illness; however, some experts believe they are mentally ill. If so, it is an illness that is exceptionally resistant to treatment, particularly since these individuals have a marked inability to learn from the past. It is this latter trait that makes them a special problem for law enforcement officials. Their ability to mimic true emotion enables them to convince prison officials, judges, and psychiatrists that they feel remorse. When released from incarceration, however, they go back to their old tricks, their con games, their impulsive destructiveness, and their sometimes lethal deceptions.

57. Based on the passage, which of the following is NOT likely to be a characteristic of the person with antisocial personality disorder?
a. delusions of persecution
b. feelings of superiority
c. inability to suffer deeply
d. inability to feel joy

58. Which of the following careers would probably best suit the person with antisocial personality?
a. soldier with ambition to make officer
b. warden of a large penitentiary
c. loan officer in a bank
d. salesperson dealing in nonexistent real estate

59. Based on the passage, which of the following words best sums up the inner emotional life of the person with antisocial personality?
a. angry
b. anxious
c. repressed
d. empty

60. According to the passage, which of the following characteristics is most helpful to the person with antisocial personality in getting out of trouble with the law?
a. inability to learn from the past
b. ability to mimic the emotions of others
c. attractiveness and charm
d. indifference to the suffering of others

Part Three: Judgment and Problem Solving

Use good judgment and common sense, as well as the information provided in the question, to answer the following questions.

61. While on foot patrol downtown, Officer Gutierrez is approached by Ms. Louise Herald, who says that a man snatched a shopping bag full of gifts from her arm and ran away. Ms. Herald remembers the contents of the shopping bag as follows:

- 1 cashmere sweater valued at $260
- 3 diamond bracelets, each valued at $365
- 1 computer game valued at $78
- 1 cameo brooch valued at $130

Later, Officer Gutierrez receives a call from Ms. Herald, who says she has found the receipts for the stolen merchandise. She says that what she told the officer was correct except that there were only two diamond bracelets, not three, and that the value of the cashmere sweater was $245. What should Officer Gutierrez write as the total value of the stolen property?

a. $833
b. $1,183
c. $1,198
d. $1,563

62. Lieutenant Magnus is attempting to determine which motorcycle officer to commend for issuing the most citations during the month. She knows that Officer Slack issued more citations than Officer Diamond, who issued 270. Officer Diamond issued 30 more than Officer Sharp, but ten fewer than officer than Officer Elia. How many citations did Officer Elia issue?

a. 270
b. 240
c. 280
d. 220

63. Officer DeMarco is on routine patrol at about 3 A.M. on a Sunday morning. He drives his police vehicle to the rear alley of a shopping center and discovers a man lying face down on the ground. Officer DeMarco approaches the man and finds that he is breathing. Officer DeMarco also sees drug paraphernalia, including a hypodermic syringe, on the ground next to the man. Officer DeMarco tries to wake the man, but is unable. What is Officer DeMarco's best course of action?

a. Presume the man is sleeping, move him out of the way of the alley traffic, and continue routine patrol.
b. Arrest the man for possession of the drug paraphernalia.
c. Call for an ambulance and have the man transported to a medical facility.
d. Call for a supervisor.

64. Police officers do not always issue citations if there has been a clear violation of the traffic law. In which of the following situations would it be most appropriate for an officer NOT to issue a citation?

a. At a four-way stop sign, you see a woman in a van slowly roll through the stop sign without coming to a complete stop. The woman looks in your direction, waves, and silently mouths the word *sorry*.

b. You are transporting a prisoner from the scene of the arrest to the station. You observe an elderly man make a U-turn from a left-turn lane that is clearly posted "No Left Turn."

c. You see a city councilperson driving on the wrong side of the road.

d. You see a delivery van double parked, causing a traffic jam.

65. Four eyewitnesses saw a vehicle being stolen and noted the license plate number. Each wrote down a different number listed below. Which one is probably right?

a. KLV 017

b. XIW 007

c. XIW 017

d. XIV 017

66. Randy Wade comes home and surprises a burglar in his house. The burglar runs past Randy out the door. Which one of the following parts of Randy's description of the burglar will be most helpful to police in identifying him?

a. He walked with a limp.

b. He carried a VCR.

c. He wore a ski mask.

d. He smelled like fish.

67. Officer Madeira has noticed that daytime residential burglaries in her district have increased during the past two months. Which of the following situations, occurring around 1:00 P.M., should Officer Madeira investigate?

a. a teenaged boy dancing down the sidewalk, holding a large radio to his ear and singing

b. a woman walking door to door carrying a small suitcase

c. a man parked in the shade eating a sandwich and watching some children play

d. a man walking down the street carrying a medium-sized television set

Use the following information to answer questions 68–70.

Officers responding alone to the scene of a burglar alarm should do the following in the order given:

1. Turn off siren and emergency lights as soon as possible to keep from alerting suspects.
2. Park the patrol car away from the building.
3. Notify the dispatcher of their arrival and location.
4. Begin checking the outside of the building for signs of entry.
5. Notify the dispatcher if signs of entry are discovered.
6. Wait for backup if it is available before going inside a building where entry has been made.
7. Tell backup officers where to position themselves as they arrive.

68. Officer Celer is on patrol by herself at about 4 A.M. She is driving down a residential street when she sees dark smoke coming out of a house. As she pulls to the curb, she observes a man carrying a gas can exit the house and run down the street. What is her best course of action?

a. Call for backup before pursuing the man with a gas can.
b. Notify dispatch of the fire, request backup, and pursue the man with the gas can.
c. Notify dispatch of the fire and the man running from the scene, then use the garden hose at the front of the house to fight the fire.
d. Notify dispatch about both the fire and the man running from the scene, then attempt to wake anyone in the house and render aid if it is safe to do so.

69. On a Sunday afternoon at about 2 P.M., Officer Dodrill is on routine patrol when he receives a radio call to respond to a silent burglary alarm in a commercial district. Dodrill knows that most of the businesses in that area are manufacturing firms that are generally closed on Sunday. Dodrill also knows that most silent burglary alarms are false activations. Which of the following is his best course of action?

a. Because most of the calls are false, he should ignore it and request a dinner break from dispatch.
b. Although most of the calls are false, the area is filled with closed manufacturing businesses, so he should activate his emergency lights and siren and proceed rapidly to the location.
c. Although most of the calls are false, he should proceed directly to the location.
d. Because most of the calls are false, he should continue to patrol his assigned area until he is nearer the location.

70. Officer Carmine was requested to transport two prisoners from the department holding facility to the county regional jail. After completing the transport, she checks the back seat of the police vehicle and notices two ten-dollar bills. What is her best course of action?

a. Give the money to the regional jail personnel and tell them to give each prisoner ten dollars.
b. Complete the appropriate department form explaining the circumstances and deposit the money with the department property or evidence officer.
c. Take the money and send it to a local charity.
d. Interview the prisoners and give the money to the one most likely to have misplaced it.

71. On Monday morning, Officers Rosen and McNalty respond to a call of a burglary that apparently took place over the weekend at Datamation Computer Consultants. The owner of the business says that the following equipment is missing:

- 3 telephone sets, each valued at $125
- 2 computers, each valued at $1,300
- 2 computer monitors, each valued at $950
- 1 printer valued at $600
- 1 fax machine valued at $50

Officer McNalty is preparing a complaint report on the burglary. What should he write as the total value of the missing property?

a. $3,025
b. $5,400
c. $5,525
d. $6,525

72. The police are staking out a suspected crack house. Officer Michaels is in front of the house. Officer Roth is in the alley behind the house. Officer Jensen is covering the windows on the north side, Officer Sheen those on the south. If Officer Michaels switches places with Officer Jensen, and Jensen then switches places with Officer Sheen, where is Officer Sheen?

a. in the alley behind the house
b. on the north side of the house
c. in front of the house
d. on the south side of the house

73. Downtown merchants have complained to Sergeant Ramos about a recent rash of auto thefts. Mr. Smith says that six of his best customers have had their cars stolen in the past two weeks while parked in the downtown area. Sergeant Ramos alerts Officer Hammond to patrol the area closely. Which following situation should Officer Hammond investigate?

a. a transient approaching people as they get out of their cars to ask them for a cigarette
b. two young men sitting on the hood of a car parked in front of Mr. Smith's store
c. a tow truck operator attempting to open the door of a vehicle for a man who is standing nearby
d. a man walking from parked car to parked car pulling on the door handles

74. Officer Gomez is off-duty and driving in his personal vehicle. Gomez is on his way to work, so he has his badge, gun, and cell phone. He sees a traffic accident occur two blocks ahead of him at an intersection. As Gomez gets closer, he sees one of the drivers involved in the accident quickly exit his car and run away from the scene of the accident. What is Gomez's best course of action?

a. Use his cell phone to report the accident, then stop and render aid.
b. Use his cell phone to report the accident, then continue on to work.
c. Report both the accident and the man running away, then use his personal vehicle to follow the man.
d. Presume someone else will report the accident, and use his personal vehicle to pursue the man running from the accident.

75. Sergeant Janikowski is responsible for determining the vacation schedule for the coming year. According to the department vacation policy, choice of vacation is ranked according to seniority. Janikowski knows that Ducale is the least senior, James is more senior than Smyth, and Barton has less seniority than Smyth. Which officer should have first choice for his or her vacation?

a. Ducale
b. Smyth
c. James
d. Barton

76. Police officers may find themselves in situations where using a normal, conversational tone of voice is not enough to get an individual to do what the officer requires. Which situation below calls for an officer to shout using a firm, authoritative tone of voice?

- **a.** asking to see a driver's proof of automobile insurance after an accident
- **b.** advising a new partner of a recently implemented departmental policy
- **c.** chasing a burglar out of a house
- **d.** asking a boy why he is not in school on a Monday morning

77. The police department needs to appoint a new captain, which will be based on seniority. Sergeant West has less seniority than Sergeant Temple, but more than Sergeant Brody. Sergeant Rhodes has more seniority than Sergeant West, but less than Sergeant Temple. Sergeant Temple doesn't want the job. Who will be the new captain?

- **a.** Rhodes
- **b.** Temple
- **c.** West
- **d.** Brody

Use the following information to answer questions 78–81.

Officers frequently handle domestic disturbance calls. Since these calls are dangerous for both the families involved and the officers, officers called to the scene of a domestic disturbance should carry out the following steps in the order listed:

1. Inform the dispatcher when they arrive.
2. Park the patrol car away from the residence.
3. Before knocking, listen carefully at the door to get an idea of what is happening inside.
4. Stand on either side of the door while knocking, in order to be less vulnerable to gunshots or immediate attack.
5. Knock and identify themselves as police officers.
6. Once inside, restore order as calmly as possible by separating those who are arguing.
7. Administer first aid if immediately necessary.
8. Talk to the participants separately and find out what happened.
9. Let the dispatcher know if the situation is under control or if assistance is needed.

78. Officers Charles and Washington have been dispatched to 2104 Maple Avenue. Neighbors called 911 and said that they could hear Jeff threatening his wife Sara and that they were afraid he was about to beat her. Officer Charles notifies the dispatcher that they have arrived. He parks the car in front of 2102 Maple, and he and Officer Washington begin walking up the sidewalk to 2104 Maple Ave. What should the two officers do next?

- **a.** Knock on the front door and request entry.
- **b.** Listen at the door to see if they can tell what is going on inside.
- **c.** Talk to the neighbors who called before taking any action.
- **d.** Administer first aid to those who are injured.

79. Officer Wallace arrives at the scene of a domestic disturbance. After notifying the dispatcher of her arrival and parking her car a few houses away, Officer Wallace is at the house's front door. She listens for a few minutes and hears a woman sobbing. The house is dark and quiet except for the sounds of the woman crying. The next step Officer Wallace should take is to
a. walk around to the rear of the house and listen at the back door.
b. knock on the door and identify herself.
c. call to the woman through the door to ask if she is injured.
d. step to one side of the door before knocking.

80. Officers Stanley and DiMartino have just pulled up to the curb near 9000 Block Parkway on a domestic disturbance call. Neighbors are reporting sounds of breaking glass, yelling, and gunshots. What is the first thing the officers should do?
a. Listen at the door to see if they can tell what is happening.
b. Get the dispatcher to have a neighbor meet them outside to tell them what they heard.
c. Radio in to the dispatcher when they arrive at the scene.
d. Immediately run into the residence.

81. Officer Roberts is dispatched to a domestic disturbance at 3412 Runnymeade. When he arrives, he radios in to the dispatcher and parks at 3410 Runnymeade. As he approaches the house, the door flies open and a woman runs out. She is bleeding heavily from a cut on her arm and collapses at his feet, crying, "Help me, officer!" The next thing Officer Roberts should do is to
a. apply first aid to the woman's wound.
b. search the house for the suspect.
c. separate the victim and the suspect.
d. identify himself to the victim.

82. Four people witnessed a mugging. Each gave a different description of the mugger. Which description is probably right?
a. He was average height, thin, and middle-aged.
b. He was tall, thin, and middle-aged.
c. He was tall, thin, and young.
d. He was tall, of average weight, and middle-aged.

83. Officer Kim reports to the scene of a burglary at 125 Eastside Avenue, apartment 3D. The resident, Anthony Blake, who is a musician, says that he returned from his girlfriend's house this morning to find his lock picked and his instruments missing:

- 1 violin valued at $3,500
- 2 violin bows, each valued at $850
- 2 music stands, each valued at $85
- 1 cello valued at $2,300

In addition, Mr. Blake says that his watch, valued at $250, and $85 in cash are missing. When Officer Kim writes her report on the burglary, what should she write as the total value of the stolen property and cash?
a. $6,735
b. $7,070
c. $7,670
d. $8,005

84. Police officers must sometimes exceed posted speed limits in order to enforce the law. In which situation below would it be most appropriate for an officer to go faster than the speed limit?

a. on the way to a call of a burglary that took place the day before
b. while chasing a suspected bank robber who is speeding down the highway
c. on the way to the local hospital, transporting a prisoner who has had recurrent headaches
d. while late for an appointment to testify in a case of breaking and entering

85. Officer Hesalroad has responded to the scene of a robbery. On the officer's arrival, the victim, Ms. Margaret Olsen, tells the officer that the following items were taken from her by a man who threatened her with a knife:

■ 1 gold watch, valued at	$240
■ 2 rings, each valued at	$150
■ 1 ring, valued at	$70
■ Cash	$95

Officer Hesalroad is preparing her report on the robbery. Which one of the following is the total value of the cash and property Ms. Olsen reported stolen?

a. $545
b. $555
c. $705
d. $785

86. Officers are required to immediately report to their supervisor any damage to a patrol car. In which situation below should an officer call the supervisor to report a damaged patrol car?

a. A disgruntled citizen kicks a tire on the patrol car as she walks past it.
b. The driver's door is dented in by an irate man under arrest for public intoxication.
c. The officer bumps a pole while backing out of an alley but finds no dents or scratches on the vehicle.
d. The officer finds a dozen eggs smashed on the windshield.

Use the following information to answer question 87.

When a police officer makes an arrest for the crime of driving under the influence, the officer should:

1. Have the driver get out of the vehicle.
2. Request that the driver perform field sobriety tests.
3. Demonstrate each sobriety test before allowing the driver to attempt the tests.
4. If the driver fails the sobriety tests, arrest the driver and explain why.
5. Have the driver's vehicle towed to a holding facility by the department's designated towing company.

87. Officer Marcos is on patrol when he sees a white Ford Thunderbird run a red light at the intersection of Maple and Walnut. The vehicle is weaving back and forth over the double yellow line in the center of the roadway. The driver pulls over to the side of the road for Officer Marcos five blocks later and gets out of his car. When Officer Marcos smells a strong odor of alcohol on the man's breath, he asks the driver to perform several sobriety tests. The driver says, "Okay," and immediately tries to stand on one leg, but cannot do so. Officer Marcos tells the driver he is under arrest for driving under the influence, and places him in the patrol car. He then calls for a tow truck to impound the Thunderbird. Under these circumstances, the actions taken by Officer Marcos were

a. improper, because he failed to demonstrate the sobriety tests for the driver.
b. proper, because it was obvious by the driver's actions that he would not pass a field sobriety test.
c. improper, because he did not tell the driver to get out of his car.
d. proper, because the driver could not stand on one leg.

Use the following information to answer questions 88–91.

All police officers are expected to know how to properly package evidence after the decision has been made to collect it. The following steps should be carried out in the order listed:

1. Place each item in a separate container.
2. Seal each container in such a way that it cannot be opened without breaking the seal.
3. The officer collecting the evidence should write his or her name or employee number on the seal.
4. Place a tag on the container that identifies the case number, the date and time collected, where the item was found, what the item is, who collected it, and what condition the item is in.
5. Turn the evidence in personally to the Property Room without breaking the chain of custody by allowing someone else to do it.

88. Officer Schwartz is the first officer to arrive at the scene of a burglary at Wiggin's Liquor Store. After making sure the scene is secure, she begins to collect evidence. The first item she finds is a screwdriver lying on the sidewalk in front of the glass doors leading into the store. The second item she sees is a small flashlight on the floor inside the building. Officer Schwartz places the screwdriver in a small plastic bag. What is the next thing she should do?

a. Lock the screwdriver in the trunk of her car.
b. Seal the bag with evidence tape so that the bag cannot be opened.
c. Write the case number and other information about the evidence on the outside of the bag.
d. Put the flashlight in the bag with the screwdriver.

89. Officer Jackson is dispatched to a fatality collision scene involving a person suspected of driving while intoxicated. The suspect is under arrest, and Officer Jackson is searching his vehicle for evidence. He finds an empty glass beer bottle in the front seat, along with a receipt from Evy's Liquor Emporium for a 12-pack of beer. The first thing Officer Jackson should do with this evidence is to

a. put the bottle and the receipt in a bag, and seal it.
b. attach a tag to the neck of the bottle and write the case number on the tag.
c. place the bottle and the receipt in different bags.
d. turn the bottle and the receipt in to the Property Room.

90. Two officers are dispatched to the scene of a robbery. Officer McGregor is assigned to collect all of the physical evidence. Officer Sterne is in charge of the scene and is responsible for interviewing the victim and the witnesses and for keeping the crime scene from being contaminated by onlookers. As Officer McGregor is labeling the bag in which she has placed a knife dropped by the suspect, a witness points out a button on the sidewalk, which she says may have come from the suspect's jacket. What should Officer McGregor do next?

a. Seal the button in a container by itself, write her name on the seal, label the container, and give it to Officer Sterne.
b. Let Officer Sterne collect and package the button and label its container, and then receive the container from Officer Sterne to deliver it to the Property Room.
c. Place the button in a container, seal the container, write her name and information about the button on the label, and then turn in the container to the Property Room.
d. Leave the button on the sidewalk, because the witness is not certain it came from the suspect's jacket.

91. Officer Patel has collected evidence at a crime scene and placed it in a container. The first thing Officer Patel should write on the evidence tag is

a. his employee number.
b. the case number.
c. the date.
d. the time he arrived at the crime scene.

92. Four police officers are chasing a suspect on foot. Officer Calvin is directly behind the suspect. Partners Jenkins and Burton are side by side behind Calvin. Officer Zeller is behind Jenkins and Burton. Burton trips and falls, and Calvin turns back to help him. An officer tackles the suspect. Which officer caught the suspect?

a. Burton
b. Zeller
c. Jenkins
d. Calvin

Use the following information to answer questions 93–94.

Police officers follow certain procedures when placing a person under arrest and transporting that person in a patrol car. Officers are expected to:

1. Handcuff the prisoner securely.
2. Search the prisoner carefully for possible weapons and contraband.
3. Check the area where the prisoner will be seated in the patrol car for possible weapons and contraband from a previous arrest.
4. Place the prisoner in the patrol car and place a seat belt around the individual.
5. Transport the prisoner directly to jail.
6. Check the seat and floorboard area where the prisoner was seated after arrival at the jail for possible contraband or weapons from the prisoner.

93. Officer Ling responded to a backup request by Officer Seamus. When Ling arrived at the scene, Officer Seamus had Michelle Bradley in custody for assault. Ling knew that Seamus is a 15-year veteran of the police department and very well respected by his peers, supervisors, and managers. Seamus asked Ling to transport Bradley to the station. Ling walked Bradley to his police car and began to search her. Seamus said to Ling, "I have already searched her." What is Ling's best course of action?

a. Discontinue searching Bradley and transport her to the station.
b. Discontinue searching Bradley, transport her out of Seamus's sight and re-search Bradley.
c. Call a supervisor to the scene to make a decision about re-searching Bradley.
d. Conduct a search of Bradley and tell Seamus that she would be more comfortable double-checking.

94. Officer Vitry is called to the scene of a traffic accident by Sergeant Medford. One of the drivers involved in the accident is an 82-year-old woman whose license expired three days ago. Medford tells Vitry to transport the woman to the station and stay with her until her son picks her up. Which of the following is Vitry's best course of action?

a. Transport the woman after searching, handcuffing, and securing her seat belt.
b. Search, seat belt, and transport the woman.
c. Transport the woman.
d. Transport the woman after securing her seat belt.

95. Officers Roberts and Reed are on bicycle patrol in the downtown area. Sergeant McElvey tells them that a white male has been committing robberies along the nearby bike path by stepping out of the bushes and threatening bicyclists with an iron pipe until they give him their bicycles. There have been three separate incidents, and the suspect descriptions are from three different victims.

Robbery #1: Suspect is a white male, 20–25 years old, 5′9″, 145 pounds, with a shaved head, wearing a skull earring in the left ear, floppy white T-shirt, worn light blue jeans, and black combat boots.

Robbery #2: Suspect is a white male, 25–30 years old, dark brown hair in a military-style crew cut, 6′2″, 200 pounds, wearing a white T-shirt with the words "Just Do It" on the back, blue surgical scrub pants, and black combat boots.

Robbery #3: Suspect is a white male, 23 years old, 5′10″, skinny build, no hair, wearing a tie-dyed T-shirt, blue baggy pants, dark shoes, and one earring.

Three days after Sergeant McElvey told the officers about the robberies, Officer Reed arrested a suspect for attempting to take a woman's mountain bike from her on the bicycle path.

The description of the suspect is as follows:
Robbery #4: Suspect is a white male, 22 years old, 140 pounds, 5′10″, with a shaved head and one pierced ear, wearing a plain white T-shirt two sizes too large for him, faded baggy blue jeans, and scuffed black combat boots.

After comparing the suspect description with those in the first three robberies, Officer Reed should consider the arrested man as a suspect in which of the other robberies?

a. Robbery #1, Robbery #2, and Robbery #3
b. Robbery #1, but not Robbery #2 or Robbery #3
c. Robbery #1 and Robbery #3, but not Robbery #2
d. Robbery #1 and Robbery #2, but not Robbery #3

96. Officer Troy arrives at the scene of a hit-and-run traffic accident. Ms. Chen tells him she was waiting for the light to change when a car struck her from behind. The driver backed up and left the scene. She saw his license plate as he left, as did three teenaged witnesses waiting for the school bus. The choices below list what each one reported. Which license plate number below is most likely the license plate of the hit-and-run vehicle?

a. JXK 12L
b. JYK 12L
c. JXK 12I
d. JXX I2L

97. Captain Forest likes to let her officers choose who their partners will be; however, no pair of officers may patrol together more than seven shifts in a row. Officers Adams and Baxter patrolled together seven shifts in a row. Officers Carver and Dennis have patrolled together three shifts in a row. Officer Carver does not want to work with Officer Adams. Who should Officer Baxter be assigned with?

a. Carver
b. Adams
c. Dennis
d. Forest

98. Four eyewitnesses give descriptions of the getaway car used in a bank robbery. Which description is probably right?

a. dark blue with a white roof
b. dark green with a gray roof
c. black with a gray roof
d. dark green with a tan roof

Use the following information to answer questions 99–100.

The first officer to respond to the scene of a sexual assault has many responsibilities. The officer should take the following steps in the order listed:

1. Aid the victim if necessary by calling for an ambulance or administering first aid.
2. Try to calm and comfort the victim as much as possible.
3. If the attack is recent, get a suspect description from the victim and radio the dispatcher to put out a be-on-the-lookout broadcast.
4. Find out from the victim where the crime occurred.

5. Determine if there is any physical evidence on the victim that may need to be preserved, such as pieces of the suspect's skin or blood under the victim's fingernails.
6. If possible, have the victim change clothing, and then take the clothing he or she was wearing as evidence.
7. Convince the victim that he or she should undergo a medical exam for health and safety purposes, and so that evidence may be gathered.

99. At 2 A.M., Officer Maxwell is sent to the scene of a sexual assault at 1201 Roxy St. He arrives and finds the victim, Susan Jackson, sitting on the front porch crying. She tells him that a man crawled through her window and raped her. When the rapist ran out the front door, she called the police immediately. The next step Officer Maxwell should take is to

a. take a look around the house to make sure the suspect is really gone.
b. ask Jackson if she is injured and in need of medical attention.
c. talk Jackson into going to the hospital for a medical exam.
d. ask Jackson to describe her attacker.

100. Officer Augustine is at 2101 Reynolds Street talking to Betty Smith, the victim of a sexual assault. She is uninjured and is very calm. She gives Officer Augustine a detailed description of her attacker and says she thinks he may be headed for a nearby tavern. At this point, Officer Augustine should

a. get into her patrol car and drive to the tavern.
b. give the dispatcher the description of the suspect.
c. take the victim straight to the hospital for a medical exam.
d. have the victim change clothing.

► Answers

Part One: Memorization and Visualization

1. **d.** Refer to the Charges section on Finan.
2. **a.** Refer to the Identifying Scars or Marks section on Finan.
3. **b.** Refer to the Description section where Guerras's age is listed.
4. **a.** Refer to the Aliases section on Brand.
5. **c.** Refer to the drawing of Guerra and to the Remarks section.
6. **a.** Refer to the Identifying Scars or Marks section on Brand. Remembering the alias *Eddie One-Eye* would also give you the answer to this question.
7. **b.** Refer to the Description section on Yang.
8. **c.** Refer to the Remarks section on Yang.
9. **a.** Refer to the Wanted By section on Hart.
10. **d.** Refer to the Charges section on Yang.
11. **b.** Refer to the Remarks section on Hart.
12. **d.** Refer to the drawing of Hart.
13. **a.** Guerra is listed as "missing," while Yang is listed as "wanted."
14. **a.** Refer to the Charges section on Hart.
15. **d.** Refer to the Remarks section on Brand.
16. **a.** Refer to the Remarks section on Brand.
17. **b.** Refer to the Caution section on Hart.
18. **d.** Refer to the Description section on Brand.
19. **c.** Refer to the Description sections of both Hart and Brand. None of the other options is true.
20. **b.** Hart has only a moustache, not a full goatee.
21. **b.** See the first three sentences of the first paragraph of the passage.
22. **d.** See the fourth paragraph.
23. **c.** Based on the actions described, an officer's training and experience would indicate that the people were planning a robbery.
24. **b.** See the sixth sentence of the first paragraph.
25. **a.** See the second sentence of the second paragraph.
26. **c.** See the fourth paragraph.
27. **d.** See the third paragraph.
28. **a.** See sentences three and four of the first paragraph.
29. **b.** Refer to the second paragraph, the fourth sentence.
30. **c.** See the sixth sentence of the second paragraph.

Part Two: Reading

31. **b.** Garcia was guarding the front of the location, so he was the one most likely to have spoken to Sharp, who lived across the street.
32. **d.** According to the passage, the call was received at 5:20, the first officers arrived at 5:30, and backup officers (Roberts and Short) arrived five minutes later, at 5:35.
33. **b.** The passage identifies the location as a retail electronics shop.
34. **c.** All of the information tends to support the suspect's entering through the smashed front window. Nothing else was presented to indicate another point of entry.
35. **c.** This is the simplest way around the one-way streets and Town Hall. Because Linda Lane is one-way the wrong way, some backtracking is inevitable. However, the residence is only one block off of Brigham Boulevard, and so turning eastbound on Brigham requires the least amount of backtracking. Choice **a** directs the officers to turn the wrong way down a one-way street. Choice **b** requires too much backtracking. Choice **d** leaves the officers on Brigham Boulevard, not Linda Lane.

36. b. This route is most direct because it requires the fewest turns. Choice **a** requires the officers to go the wrong way on John Street. Choice **c** is not correct because Arroyo Drive is a one-way street south. Choice **d** takes the officers too far east.

37. a. If Officer Ricardo turns right onto James Avenue, she will be facing north. A left turn onto Linda Lane turns her west again, and a right turn onto Raymond Avenue turns her north. The final right turn onto Brigham Boulevard turns her east.

38. a. The first paragraph outlines the connection between the First Amendment and freedom of speech.

39. c. According to the passage, a police officer's off-duty speech can be limited if it reflects negatively on his or her department or profession. No information regarding choice **a** is provided. The third paragraph uses an excessive force complaint as an example of how the Fifth Amendment is diminished, and choice **d** states the opposite of information provided in the passage.

40. d. The passage is about how some amendments found in the Bill of Rights do not necessarily apply to public safety officials, of which (as stated in the first sentence) police officers are a subset.

41. a. The third paragraph relates self-incrimination with the Fifth Amendment.

42. a. The passage never states that an officer's Fourth Amendment rights may be diminished in his or her home.

43. b. The passage states that an officer's First Amendment rights may be diminished, not eradicated, so choices **a** and **c** are incorrect. Choice **d** relates to the Fourth Amendment and is irrelevant.

44. c. Choice **a** takes the man to the park, not to the Senior Citizens' Center. Choice **b** takes the man too far south. Choice **d** takes him to Lafayette Street, while the entrance to the Senior Citizens' Center is on Grand Street.

45. d. Choice **a** takes the librarian the wrong way on Avenue C. Choice **b** shows the wrong directions for the streets—Brooklyn Street runs north-south, and Avenue D runs east-west. Choice **c** leaves the librarian one block east of the gas station.

46. b. Choices **a** and **c** take you the wrong way on 1st Avenue. Choice **d** will get you to the southeast, not the northwest, corner of the park.

47. d. Choice **a** is less direct. Choice **b** does not start from the hospital, and involves going the wrong way on Avenue B. Choice **c** is indirect and involves going the wrong way on Avenue D.

48. a. Choice **b** is less direct and involves going the wrong way on 1st Avenue. Choice **c** will lead away from 1st Avenue, not toward it. Choice **d** takes you the wrong way on Avenue C and 1st Avenue.

49. c. The last sentence of the first paragraph states that the initial violation was failing to stop for a stop sign.

50. a. Bardus exited his vehicle on Platea, 150 feet west of Broadway, and ran between the buildings. The only possible address is on Platea Street.

51. b. Because Jones was driving the police car, Johnson must have been the passenger who gave chase.

52. a. Sergeant Ducis was the last police officer on the scene, and he performed the search that yielded the gun.

53. c. Watts's and Johnson's, Bardus's, and Ducis's vehicles were all involved in the pursuit.

54. **d.** This is the most direct route because it does not require any backtracking. Choice **a** is not correct because it would require the officer to go the wrong way on Mill Road. Choice **b** requires some backtracking and takes the officer the wrong way on Lynch Road. Choice **c** is not as direct because it requires the officer to move in the opposite direction from the call.

55. **b.** This is the fastest route, requiring the fewest turns. Choice **a** is not correct because Kent is a one-way street going east. Choice **c** requires too many turns and is not the most direct route. Choice **d** is not correct because Upton Street is one-way going north.

56. **d.** A left turn onto Lee Lane turns Officer Kearney south. Another left turn onto Pecan Avenue turns her east. Left onto Main Street turns her north and the final right turn onto Palmer turns her back east.

57. **a.** The discussion of the traits of a person with antisocial personality disorder in the middle of the passage specifies that such a person does not have distortions of thought. The passage speaks of the antisocial person as being *inordinately self-confident* (choice **b**), and of the person's *emotional shallowness* (choices **c** and **d**).

58. **d.** The third sentence of the passage speaks of *con games*. None of the other professions would suit an impulsive, shallow person who has been in trouble with the law.

59. **d.** The passage mentions *emotional shallowness*. The other choices hint at the capability to feel meaningful emotion.

60. **b.** The passage says that a person with antisocial personality disorder can mimic real emotion, thereby conning prison officials, judges, and psychiatrists. The other choices are mentioned in the passage, but not in connection with getting out of trouble with the law.

Part Three: Judgment and Problem Solving

61. **b.** Add the corrected value of the sweater ($245) to the value of the two, not three, bracelets ($730), plus the other two items ($78 and $130).

62. **c.** The text states that Officer Diamond issued 270 summonses, which was ten fewer than Officer Elia. Therefore, Officer Elia issued 280 summonses.

63. **c.** There is something seriously wrong with a person who can sleep through a police officer trying to wake him or her up. Although the man is likely a drug user, human life always takes precedent over an arrest. After the man receives medical treatment, he may still be arrested. Calling a supervisor (choice **d**) to the scene of any call where an officer should be able to make the decision is not the best option.

64. **b.** The least appropriate time to issue a citation for a minor traffic violation is when you are transporting a prisoner, especially from the scene of the arrest to the station. If you make the traffic stop, you are opening yourself up to a number of problems, such as the prisoner trying to escape by taking advantage of your being distracted.

65. **c.** The elements of the license plate number that most often repeat in the eyewitnesses descriptions are XIW and 017. Therefore, the correct license number is most likely XIW 017.

66. **a.** The fact that the burglar walked with a limp is the only element of the description likely to remain constant over time and will therefore be most helpful to the police.

67. d. A man walking down the street in the afternoon carrying a television set is the most likely of all the choices to be the daytime burglar, since people do not regularly carry appliances on the street. The teenaged boy is drawing attention to himself and so is unlikely to have stolen the radio. There is also less reason to suspect the woman, who is probably a door-to-door salesperson. It is likely that the man in the car is having a late lunch.

68. d. In all situational questions, human life takes precedent over property. Additionally, any time a police officer pursues a suspect, the officer should be weighing the risks associated with capturing the suspect against the risk to human life, particularly the lives of innocent people. In this instance, the officer's best course of action is to notify dispatch of the fire and the description of the man, and then to attempt to wake anyone in the house. If the officer pursues the probable suspect, she puts people who might be asleep in the house at greater risk. Because the officer is a not a trained firefighter and the garden hose is not a viable firefighting option, her best course is to attempt to wake the residents, render aid, and then assist in the pursuit of the suspect after the arrival of the fire department.

69. c. Although most silent alarm calls are false, the fact that this one is occurring in an area of predominately closed manufacturing businesses slightly increases the chances that the alarm is reporting an actual break-in. Therefore, Dodrill should not ignore the call. Because there is nothing in the scenario to indicate that human life is at risk, the use of the emergency lights and siren is inappropriate. Any time an officer uses that equipment, there is an increased risk of causing or becoming involved in a traffic accident.

70. b. Neither choice **a** nor choice **d** is likely to return the money to the rightful owner. More importantly, the money may not have been misplaced; it may have been dropped by one of the prisoners because it is somehow connected to a crime. The best course of action is to complete a report and deposit the money with the department.

71. c. The total value of all three telephone sets at $125 each is $375. The total value of both computers at $1,300 each is $2,600. The two computer monitors, each valued at $950, have a total value of $1,900. Add those three totals to the printer at $600 and the fax machine at $50 for a grand total of $5,525 for all the stolen property.

72. c. After all the switches were made, Officer Sheen is in front of the house. Officer Roth is in the alley behind the house; Officer Michaels is on the north side; and Officer Jensen is on the south.

73. d. An officer who is looking for auto thieves should pay attention to a man who is trying to open car doors. The transient in choice **a** may be panhandling, but there is no reason to suspect car theft. People often sit on car hoods, as in choice **b**. The man in choice **c** probably owns the vehicle he's standing near.

74. a. Gomez's best course of action is to report the accident, stop, and render aid. When a police officer is off duty, he or she does not have many of the advantages of an on-duty officer. While Gomez has his gun and badge, he does not have any other police equipment like his body armor, police radio, or partner officer. Generally, off-duty police officers are better off being good witnesses and rendering aid. In this scenario, Gomez lacks sufficient information as to the action of the man who is running away. The man could be fleeing the scene or running toward a telephone for help.

75. c. The order of seniority would be James, Smyth, Barton, and then Ducale.

76. c. It would not be appropriate to shout in the situations described in choices **a**, **b**, or **d**. An officer would shout at a burglar because the situation calls for identifying himself or herself as a police officer. A loud, authoritative shout in this situation is part of the voice control officers should exercise as the first step in the use of force.

77. a. Sergeant Temple has the most seniority, but does not want the job. Next in line is Sergeant Rhodes, who has more seniority than West or Brody.

78. b. The officers have accomplished steps 1 and 2. Step 3 is to listen at the door.

79. d. Standing to one side of the door before knocking is the next step in the procedure after listening at the door.

80. c. The first step is for the officers to tell the dispatcher they have arrived at the scene.

81. a. The woman is bleeding and needs first aid. Choice **b** is not an option in the list of procedures. There aren't two people to separate as suggested in choice **c**. The woman knows he is a police officer, so there is no need to identify himself as suggested in choice **d**.

82. b. Tall, thin, and middle-aged are the elements of the description repeated most often and are therefore the most likely to be accurate.

83. d. The two violin bows, each worth $850, have a total value of $1,700. The two music stands, each worth $85, have a total value of $170. Add those totals to $3,500 for the violin and $2,300 for the cello to get $7,670. Finally, don't forget to add the $250 watch and $85 in cash, for a grand total of $8,005.

84. b. No emergency situation exists in choices **a**, **c**, or **d**. (Choice **c** might seem reasonable at first, but the headaches are described as *recurrent*, not sudden in onset.)

85. c. The two rings, each valued at $150, have a total value of $300, but then it's important to note that there's another ring, worth $70. Add $370 for the three rings to $240 for the gold watch and $95 in cash for a total of $705 in stolen property and cash.

86. b. No damage has been done to the patrol car in choice **a**, **c**, or **d**.

87. a. Step 3 in the procedures instructs the officer to demonstrate each sobriety test, which Officer Marcos did not do.

88. b. Sealing the bag is step 2 on the list of procedures.

89. c. Putting each item of evidence in a separate container is step 1 on the list of procedures.

90. c. This choice includes all of the procedures listed from step 1 to step 5. Choices **a** and **b** are incorrect because the procedures insist that the same officer who collects and labels the evidence should turn it in. In choice **d**, whether the witness is certain or not has no bearing on whether the officer should collect what might be important evidence.

91. b. Step 4 says that the first thing to be written on the evidence tag is the case number. The officer's employee number (choice **a**) goes on the seal, not on the evidence tag.

92. c. After all the switching was done, Officer Jenkins was directly behind the suspect. Officer Burton had fallen and Officer Calvin turned back to help him. Officer Zeller remained in the rear.

93. **d.** Police officers should always follow safety-related procedures. In this instance, the instructions imply that a police officer transporting a suspect is required to search that person. Although Seamus is a well-respected, experienced officer, Ling will be responsible for Bradley's safe transportation to the scene. If Seamus missed a weapon during the search, Ling will ultimately be responsible for the outcome. Police officers must be able to do the right thing even when their peers have offered advice contrary to policy and are watching.

94. **d.** Although the woman is driving on an expired license, it is clear from Sergeant Medford's instructions that he intends for the woman to be released to her son and that she is not under arrest. The woman's age and the other circumstances indicate that she is not subject to the policy. However, the use of seat belts is a good practice and is required by most state laws.

95. **c.** The suspect described in Robbery #2 has a crew-cut hair style, is at least five inches taller than the other suspects, and is about 60 pounds heavier. The other three descriptions are much more likely to be of the same man because they all describe a similar build and mention one earring or a pierced ear.

96. **a.** The witnesses seem to agree that the plate starts out with the letter J. Three witnesses agree that the plate ends with 12L. Three witnesses think that the second letter is X, and a different three think that the third letter is K. The plate description that has all of these common elements is choice **a**.

97. **a.** Baxter should be assigned to patrol with Carver. Baxter cannot be assigned with Adams, because they have already been together for seven shifts. If Baxter is assigned to Dennis, that would leave Carver with Adams. Adams does not want to work with Carver.

98. **b.** *Dark green and gray roof* are the elements repeated most often by the eyewitnesses and are therefore most likely correct.

99. **b.** Getting medical attention for the victim is the first step on the list of procedures. Choice **a** is not on the list of procedures, choice **c** is the last step on the list, and choice **d**, while important, is less urgent than determining whether Jackson is injured.

100. **b.** The officer has already taken care of steps 1 and 2: The victim doesn't need immediate medical help, and she is calm. Step 3 tells the officer to radio the suspect description to the dispatcher so a be-on-the-lookout bulletin can be issued.

▶ Scoring

A passing score for police exams in most cities is 70%. If the real exam consists of 100 questions, like the test you just took, each question would be worth one point. Thus, your score on this exam is the same as your percentage.

While a total score of at least 70 usually lands you on the eligibility list, in many cities, you need to do much better than just pass the exam to have a chance at a job. Many cities rank applicants according to their test scores, so that the higher you score on the exam, the better your chance of being called to go through the next steps in the selection process. In addition, veterans and/or residents of the city may have points added to their test scores, so that the best possible score is actually more than 100. If your city conducts this kind of ranking, your goal isn't just to score 70 and pass—you need the highest score you can possibly reach.

Use this practice exam as a way to analyze your performance. Pay attention to the areas where you miss the most questions. If most of your mistakes are in the reading comprehension questions, then you know you need to practice your reading skills. Or perhaps you had difficulty memorizing the wanted posters. Once you see where you need help, then you should study the chapters in this book on the relevant skills to develop your test-taking strategies.

To help you see where you should concentrate, break down your scores according to the three sections below:

Part One: _____ questions correct
Part Two: _____ questions correct
Part Three: _____ questions correct

Write down the number of correct answers for each section and then add up all three numbers for your overall score. Each question is worth one point, and the total you arrive at after adding all the numbers is also the percentage of questions that you answered correctly on the test.

For now, forget about your total score; what's more important right now is your scores on the individual sections of the exam.

Below is a table that will show you which of the instructional chapters correspond to the three parts of the exam. Your best bet is to review all of the chapters carefully, but you will want to spend the most time on the chapters that correspond to the kind of question that you found most difficult.

EXAM PART	CHAPTER
One	7 and 13
Two	7 and 12
Three	10 and 11

Depending on your score on the exam you just took, you might breeze through these instructional chapters, or really buckle down and study hard. Either way, the chapters give you what you need to score your best.

After you've read the relevant chapters, take the second exam of this type, in Chapter 17, to see how much you've improved.

CHAPTER

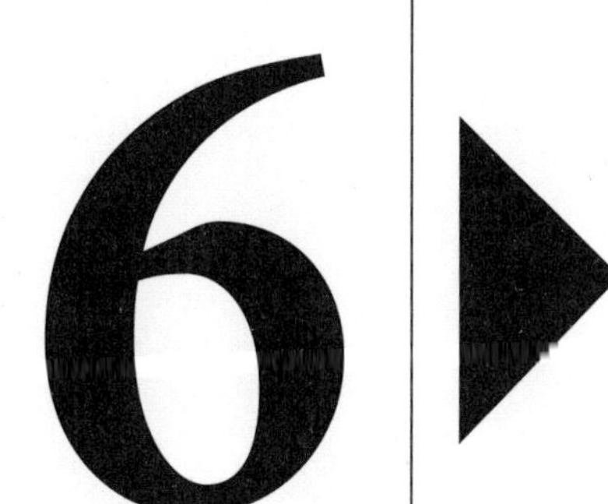

Police Officer Practice Exam 3

CHAPTER SUMMARY

This is the third practice exam in this book based on the entry-level civil service exam that police departments around the country administer to prospective police officers. If the police department you're applying to uses an exam called the LECR (Law Enforcement Candidate Record), this is the exam for you.

This practice police exam has two parts. The first part has two sections: verbal comprehension and number and letter recall. In the verbal section, you are given ten minutes to answer questions on synonyms and antonyms. The number and letter recall section lasts only nine minutes and consists of 100 questions. You are asked to remember certain number-letter combinations from a given table. You will have the table in front of you as you complete these questions.

The second part of the exam consists of 185 questions about your personal background. This exam includes 20 sample personal background questions to help familiarize you with the format.

Incorrect answers count against you in the first part of the exam. It's better to leave questions blank than to close your eyes and point at an answer. A good rule of thumb is to guess only if you can definitely eliminate at least two of the four given answers.

When you finish the exam, check the answer key at the end of the test, and see how well you scored. Because there are no correct or incorrect answers on the personal background questions, no answer key is included for this section.

Police Officer Practice Exam 3

Verbal Section

1.	a	b	c	d
2.	a	b	c	d
3.	a	b	c	d
4.	a	b	c	d
5.	a	b	c	d
6.	a	b	c	d
7.	a	b	c	d
8.	a	b	c	d
9.	a	b	c	d
10.	a	b	c	d
11.	a	b	c	d
12.	a	b	c	d
13.	a	b	c	d
14.	a	b	c	d
15.	a	b	c	d
16.	a	b	c	d
17.	a	b	c	d
18.	a	b	c	d
19.	a	b	c	d
20.	a	b	c	d
21.	a	b	c	d
22.	a	b	c	d
23.	a	b	c	d
24.	a	b	c	d
25.	a	b	c	d
26.	a	b	c	d
27.	a	b	c	d
28.	a	b	c	d
29.	a	b	c	d
30.	a	b	c	d
31.	a	b	c	d
32.	a	b	c	d
33.	a	b	c	d
34.	a	b	c	d
35.	a	b	c	d
36.	a	b	c	d
37.	a	b	c	d
38.	a	b	c	d
39.	a	b	c	d
40.	a	b	c	d
41.	a	b	c	d
42.	a	b	c	d
43.	a	b	c	d
44.	a	b	c	d
45.	a	b	c	d
46.	a	b	c	d
47.	a	b	c	d
48.	a	b	c	d
49.	a	b	c	d
50.	a	b	c	d

Number and Letter Recall Section

1.	a	b	c	d	e
2.	a	b	c	d	e
3.	a	b	c	d	e
4.	a	b	c	d	e
5.	a	b	c	d	e
6.	a	b	c	d	e
7.	a	b	c	d	e
8.	a	b	c	d	e
9.	a	b	c	d	e
10.	a	b	c	d	e
11.	a	b	c	d	e
12.	a	b	c	d	e
13.	a	b	c	d	e
14.	a	b	c	d	e
15.	a	b	c	d	e
16.	a	b	c	d	e
17.	a	b	c	d	e
18.	a	b	c	d	e
19.	a	b	c	d	e
20.	a	b	c	d	e
21.	a	b	c	d	e
22.	a	b	c	d	e
23.	a	b	c	d	e
24.	a	b	c	d	e
25.	a	b	c	d	e
26.	a	b	c	d	e
27.	a	b	c	d	e
28.	a	b	c	d	e
29.	a	b	c	d	e
30.	a	b	c	d	e
31.	a	b	c	d	e
32.	a	b	c	d	e
33.	a	b	c	d	e
34.	a	b	c	d	e
35.	a	b	c	d	e
36.	a	b	c	d	e
37.	a	b	c	d	e
38.	a	b	c	d	e
39.	a	b	c	d	e
40.	a	b	c	d	e
41.	a	b	c	d	e
42.	a	b	c	d	e
43.	a	b	c	d	e
44.	a	b	c	d	e
45.	a	b	c	d	e
46.	a	b	c	d	e
47.	a	b	c	d	e
48.	a	b	c	d	e
49.	a	b	c	d	e
50.	a	b	c	d	e
51.	a	b	c	d	e
52.	a	b	c	d	e
53.	a	b	c	d	e
54.	a	b	c	d	e
55.	a	b	c	d	e
56.	a	b	c	d	e
57.	a	b	c	d	e
58.	a	b	c	d	e
59.	a	b	c	d	e
60.	a	b	c	d	e
61.	a	b	c	d	e
62.	a	b	c	d	e
63.	a	b	c	d	e
64.	a	b	c	d	e
65.	a	b	c	d	e
66.	a	b	c	d	e
67.	a	b	c	d	e
68.	a	b	c	d	e
69.	a	b	c	d	e
70.	a	b	c	d	e
71.	a	b	c	d	e
72.	a	b	c	d	e
73.	a	b	c	d	e
74.	a	b	c	d	e
75.	a	b	c	d	e

Number and Letter Recall Section (continued)

76. ⓐ ⓑ ⓒ ⓓ ⓔ
77. ⓐ ⓑ ⓒ ⓓ ⓔ
78. ⓐ ⓑ ⓒ ⓓ ⓔ
79. ⓐ ⓑ ⓒ ⓓ ⓔ
80. ⓐ ⓑ ⓒ ⓓ ⓔ
81. ⓐ ⓑ ⓒ ⓓ ⓔ
82. ⓐ ⓑ ⓒ ⓓ ⓔ
83. ⓐ ⓑ ⓒ ⓓ ⓔ
84. ⓐ ⓑ ⓒ ⓓ ⓔ
85. ⓐ ⓑ ⓒ ⓓ ⓔ
86. ⓐ ⓑ ⓒ ⓓ ⓔ
87. ⓐ ⓑ ⓒ ⓓ ⓔ
88. ⓐ ⓑ ⓒ ⓓ ⓔ
89. ⓐ ⓑ ⓒ ⓓ ⓔ
90. ⓐ ⓑ ⓒ ⓓ ⓔ
91. ⓐ ⓑ ⓒ ⓓ ⓔ
92. ⓐ ⓑ ⓒ ⓓ ⓔ
93. ⓐ ⓑ ⓒ ⓓ ⓔ
94. ⓐ ⓑ ⓒ ⓓ ⓔ
95. ⓐ ⓑ ⓒ ⓓ ⓔ
96. ⓐ ⓑ ⓒ ⓓ ⓔ
97. ⓐ ⓑ ⓒ ⓓ ⓔ
98. ⓐ ⓑ ⓒ ⓓ ⓔ
99. ⓐ ⓑ ⓒ ⓓ ⓔ
100. ⓐ ⓑ ⓒ ⓓ ⓔ

Personal Background Section

1. ⓐ ⓑ ⓒ ⓓ
2. ⓐ ⓑ ⓒ ⓓ ⓔ ⓕ
3. ⓐ ⓑ ⓒ ⓓ ⓔ ⓕ
4. ⓐ ⓑ ⓒ ⓓ
5. ⓐ ⓑ ⓒ ⓓ ⓔ ⓕ ⓖ ⓗ
6. ⓐ ⓑ ⓒ ⓓ ⓔ ⓕ
7. ⓐ ⓑ ⓒ ⓓ
8. ⓐ ⓑ ⓒ ⓓ ⓔ
9. ⓐ ⓑ ⓒ ⓓ ⓔ
10. ⓐ ⓑ ⓒ ⓓ
11. ⓐ ⓑ ⓒ ⓓ
12. ⓐ ⓑ ⓒ ⓓ ⓔ
13. ⓐ ⓑ ⓒ ⓓ ⓔ
14. ⓐ ⓑ ⓒ ⓓ ⓔ ⓕ
15. ⓐ ⓑ ⓒ ⓓ ⓔ
16. ⓐ ⓑ ⓒ ⓓ
17. ⓐ ⓑ ⓒ ⓓ
18. ⓐ ⓑ ⓒ ⓓ ⓔ ⓕ
19. ⓐ ⓑ ⓒ ⓓ
20. ⓐ ⓑ ⓒ ⓓ ⓔ ⓕ

▶ Police Officer Practice Exam 3

Part One: Verbal Section

You have ten minutes for this section. Choose the correct answer for each question.

1. Which word means the *same* as COERCE?
a. compel
b. permit
c. waste
d. deny

2. Which word means the *same* as COLLABORATE?
a. cooperate
b. coordinate
c. entice
d. elaborate

3. Which word means the *opposite* of ABSTRACT?
a. concentrated
b. simple
c. concrete
d. understandable

4. Which word means the *opposite* of DESPONDENT?
a. pessimistic
b. dejected
c. exultant
d. miserable

5. Which word means the *same* as HEFTY?
a. robust
b. slight
c. trivial
d. unimportant

6. Which word means the *same* as NOCTURNAL?
a. dawn
b. night
c. morning
d. afternoon

7. Which word means the *opposite* of IMPARTIAL?
a. complete
b. prejudiced
c. unbiased
d. erudite

8. Which word means the *same* as IMPERATIVE?
a. immaterial
b. important
c. insignificant
d. irrelevant

9. Which word means the *opposite* of JUDICIOUS?
a. partial
b. litigious
c. imprudent
d. unrestrained

10. Which word means the *opposite* of TREPIDATION?
a. apprehension
b. anxiety
c. concern
d. confidence

11. Which word means the *same* as EGRESS?
a. opening
b. access
c. exit
d. entrance

12. Which word means the *same* as GARBLED?
a. lucid
b. unintelligible
c. devoured
d. outrageous

13. Which word means the *same* as COMPLIANCE?
a. defiance
b. destitute
c. conformity
d. combination

14. Which word means the *opposite* of PRESUMPTION?
a. guess
b. guidance
c. certainty
d. comportment

15. Which word means the *opposite* of AMBIGUOUS?
a. apathetic
b. certain
c. equivocal
d. indefinite

16. Which word means the *same* as EXPOSE?
a. relate
b. develop
c. reveal
d. pretend

17. Which word means the *opposite* of CHRONIC?
a. fatal
b. quick
c. bucolic
d. infrequent

18. Which word means the *same* as BOUNDARY?
a. limit
b. external
c. internal
d. litigation

19. Which word means the *opposite* of DETAIN?
a. promote
b. increase
c. incur
d. release

20. Which word means the *opposite* of AUDIBLE?
a. mandatory
b. planned
c. optical
d. silent

21. Which word means the *opposite* of REVERENCE?
a. disrespect
b. loyalty
c. frustration
d. prosperity

22. Which word means the *same* as ECSTATIC?
a. inconsistent
b. positive
c. wild
d. exhilarated

23. Which word means the *same* as APATHY?
a. hostility
b. depression
c. indifference
d. concern

24. Which word means the *opposite* of NEUTRAL?
a. partisan
b. adamant
c. fertile
d. aggravated

25. Which word means the *same* as COMPLY?
a. subdue
b. entertain
c. flatter
d. obey

26. Which word means the *same* as COURTESY?
a. civility
b. congruity
c. conviviality
d. rudeness

27. Which word means the *opposite* of CRITICAL?
a. inimical
b. judgmental
c. trivial
d. massive

28. Which word means the *opposite* of CREDIBILITY?
a. harmony
b. disharmony
c. honesty
d. dishonesty

29. Which word means the *opposite* of DETERRENT?
a. encouragement
b. obstacle
c. proponent
d. advantage

30. Which word means the *same* as DESPAIR?
a. mourning
b. disregard
c. despondency
d. pessimism

31. Which word means the *opposite* of HIERARCHICAL?
a. monarchical
b. egalitarian
c. placid
d. oligarchical

32. Which word means the *same* as CONTINUOUS?
a. intermittent
b. adjacent
c. incessant
d. contiguous

33. Which word means the *same* as EVOKE?
a. summon
b. satisfy
c. emancipate
d. eradicate

34. Which word means the *opposite* of EXPLICIT?
a. modest
b. innocent
c. suggested
d. embodied

35. Which word means the *opposite* of LABORIOUS?
a. arduous
b. easy
c. complex
d. specific

36. Which word means the *opposite* of FORTUNATE?
a. excluded
b. hapless
c. hardworking
d. lucky

37. Which word means the *same* as ANTERIOR?
a. outside
b. inside
c. back
d. front

38. Which word means the *same* as DISPARITY?
a. imbalance
b. insensitive
c. incognito
d. interpret

39. Which word means the *opposite* of INCOHERENT?
a. comprehensible
b. tentative
c. disciplined
d. muddled

40. Which word means the *same* as INTIMIDATE?
a. condescend
b. convince
c. coerce
d. cooperate

41. Which word means the *same* as RECOGNIZE?
a. indemnity
b. identify
c. petition
d. pardon

42. Which word means the *opposite* of INTENTIONAL?
a. accidental
b. calculated
c. willful
d. amicable

43. Which word means the *opposite* of ATTAIN?
a. achieve
b. answer
c. futile
d. fail

44. Which word means the *same* as INACCESSIBLE?
a. reality
b. rendezvous
c. remote
d. random

45. Which word means the *opposite* of IRRATIONAL?
a. logical
b. incorrect
c. disregard
d. damaged

46. Which word means the *opposite* of DECENCY?
a. civility
b. vulgarity
c. wastefulness
d. jagged

47. Which word means the *same* as ADJOINING?
a. distance
b. secluded
c. rancorous
d. adjacent

48. Which word means the *same* as CURSORY?
- **a.** careful
- **b.** hasty
- **c.** coordinated
- **d.** dissimilar

49. Which word means the *opposite* of MISCONSTRUE?
- **a.** understand
- **b.** injure
- **c.** massive
- **d.** minor

50. Which word means the *same* as REVISION?
- **a.** blond
- **b.** modification
- **c.** moderate
- **d.** repulse

Recall Section

In this section, each set of 25 questions is preceded by a key that consists of letter sets and numbers. Each question consists of one of the letter sets followed by numbers. Use the key to pick the number that goes with each letter set, and then fill in the appropriate circle on the answer sheet. You have nine minutes for this section.

KEY 1

NUB	FED	SRT	AXZ	JIK	DGB	IFA	CSB	LEW
12	92	44	24	16	55	36	99	26
LGF	VGB	QOP	WQA	BCV	PLG	YTR	RCJ	MAZ
32	88	31	17	78	27	61	23	45
GYH	KLV	PON	FAS	QLG	XEG	RIF	NDF	HUN
25	68	74	21	91	56	11	89	33

		a	b	c	d	e
1.	LEW	26	78	99	43	33
2.	KLV	18	44	68	89	25
3.	WQA	27	17	55	32	71
4.	PON	63	22	74	81	59
5.	QLG	19	34	25	72	91
6.	RIF	21	11	53	39	70
7.	MAZ	15	73	93	45	31
8.	QOP	73	44	14	31	59
9.	NUB	12	21	88	53	36
10.	BCV	56	78	32	94	11
11.	LGF	57	19	55	32	78
12.	VGB	23	21	59	49	88
13.	XEG	63	41	56	39	92

		a	b	c	d	e
14.	HUN	75	33	39	54	38
15.	SRT	19	44	91	13	31
16.	DGB	55	24	64	18	39
17.	YTR	11	87	35	52	61
18.	RCJ	65	23	47	23	31
19.	NDF	63	41	81	78	89
20.	FAS	96	18	32	21	11
21.	FED	71	36	41	92	38
22.	GYH	25	90	32	28	19
23.	AXZ	78	24	74	91	26
24.	JIK	16	27	39	42	63
25.	PLG	43	27	54	41	59

KEY 2

OGF	EGO	JOK	DJA	OXE	KOG	OGI	IXJ	NAA
23	88	24	45	68	35	14	32	41
NFO	**FED**	**HIG**	**AXA**	**JIV**	**DGO**	**IFA**	**XHO**	**OED**
43	93	47	36	75	11	25	73	55
GOH	**KOE**	**KON**	**FAH**	**JOG**	**XEG**	**IIF**	**NAF**	**HFN**
31	58	54	34	94	15	44	83	22

		a	b	c	d	e
26.	OED	35	45	11	23	55
27.	KOE	68	47	54	83	58
28.	DJA	35	58	33	45	92
29.	KON	34	54	12	23	50
30.	JOG	15	58	23	34	94
31.	IIF	44	64	88	12	25
32.	NAA	47	52	32	41	24
33.	JOK	62	33	54	24	13
34.	NFO	52	43	47	64	63
35.	OXE	43	24	68	53	34
36.	OGF	11	36	54	48	23
37.	EGO	32	88	13	43	86
38.	XEG	52	46	15	23	33
39.	HFN	61	22	23	14	28
40.	HIG	51	32	45	47	24
41.	DGO	15	43	11	23	58
42.	OGI	24	85	21	14	54
43.	IXJ	32	47	34	62	24
44.	NAF	52	94	84	47	83
45.	FAH	35	48	23	34	41
46.	FED	93	35	23	43	52
47.	GOH	54	25	90	31	28
48.	AXA	42	36	14	42	13
49.	JIV	31	60	23	38	75
50.	KOG	98	35	54	64	37

KEY 3

NAM	KAE	YAD	FBM	JAN	XEN	IYD	DBF	MFD
51	58	54	94	74	15	44	85	22
ANF	**ENA**	**LAK**	**DJB**	**AXY**	**KAN**	**ANI**	**IXJ**	**DBB**
27	88	24	95	18	59	14	52	41
DFA	**FEQ**	**MIN**	**BXY**	**XIV**	**DNA**	**IFB**	**XMA**	**AED**
45	75	43	56	35	11	25	35	55

		a	b	c	d	e
51.	AED	55	45	11	25	99
52.	KAE	68	43	54	85	58
53.	DJB	55	58	19	95	72
54.	KAN	58	74	12	25	59
55.	JAN	15	58	25	51	74
56.	IYD	44	64	88	12	25
57.	DBF	43	85	52	41	24
58.	LAK	62	17	54	24	15
59.	DFA	52	45	43	69	65
60.	AXY	45	24	18	59	54
61.	ANF	11	96	94	48	27
62.	ENA	52	88	15	42	86
63.	XEN	52	46	15	25	99

		a	b	c	d	e
64.	MFD	61	82	22	14	28
65.	MIN	51	12	43	48	24
66.	DNA	15	11	85	25	58
67.	ANF	27	85	21	14	54
68.	IXJ	52	43	54	62	24
69.	DBF	92	74	84	43	85
70.	FBM	15	48	25	94	41
71.	FEQ	75	65	25	45	52
72.	NAM	54	25	70	51	28
73.	BXY	42	56	14	59	15
74.	XIV	51	60	25	58	35
75.	KAN	78	45	59	64	56

KEY 4

LFA	FRQ	MAT	BLY	LAV	DTA	AFB	LMA	ARD
45	75	43	56	35	11	25	35	55
TAK	CAR	YAR	KMB	JAT	LRT	AKD	RBF	MRD
51	58	54	94	74	15	44	85	22
ATF	RTA	LAC	DJB	ALY	CAK	ATB	ALJ	DBK
27	88	24	95	18	59	14	52	41

		a	b	c	d	e
76.	ARD	43	85	55	41	24
77.	CAR	58	45	43	69	65
78.	DJB	45	24	18	59	95
79.	CAK	58	74	12	25	59
80.	JAT	68	43	74	85	58
81.	AKD	62	17	54	44	15
82.	DBK	41	64	88	12	25
83.	LAC	55	45	11	24	99
84.	DTA	11	96	94	48	27
85.	ALJ	55	52	19	95	72
86.	ATF	15	11	85	27	58
87.	RTA	52	86	15	42	88
88.	LRT	52	46	15	25	99

		a	b	c	d	e
89.	MRD	61	82	22	14	28
90.	MAT	51	12	43	48	24
91.	LFA	78	45	59	64	56
92.	ATF	52	43	54	62	27
93.	ALJ	27	85	21	14	52
94.	RBF	92	74	85	43	84
95.	YAR	15	54	25	94	41
96.	FRQ	54	75	70	51	28
97.	TAK	51	60	25	58	35
98.	BLY	42	56	14	42	15
99.	LAC	75	65	25	24	52
100.	CAK	15	59	25	51	74

Part Two: Personal Background Section

Answer each question honestly. Mark only one answer unless the question directs you otherwise. There is no time limit for this section.

1. If I were to witness a coworker involved in employee theft, my initial reaction would be to
a. report the person to my superiors.
b. reprimand the person myself.
c. ignore the person's actions.
d. document the person's actions.

2. As a job applicant, my most important goal in an employment interview is to
a. impress the interviewer.
b. learn about the position.
c. learn about salary and benefits.
d. demonstrate my positive characteristics.
e. demonstrate my commitment and professionalism.
f. demonstrate my sense of humor.

3. My favorite type of movie is
a. action/adventure.
b. suspense.
c. romance.
d. comedy.
e. drama.
f. other.

4. I feel the primary role of a parent is to
a. educate.
b. discipline.
c. protect.
d. provide.

5. On a typical weekend afternoon, I am likely to (Mark all that apply)
a. catch up on work.
b. go to a movie.
c. go to a cultural event.
d. go to a sporting event.
e. spend quiet time alone.
f. spend time with family or friends.
g. engage in physical activity.
h. do chores around the house.

6. If a close family member were in a local nursing home, I would prefer to visit
a. several times a week.
b. once a week.
c. once or twice a month.
d. irregularly.
e. on holidays and special occasions.
f. not at all.

7. If I come across a difficult word while reading or working, I am most likely to
a. try to determine its meaning based on context.
b. look it up in the dictionary.
c. jot it down and ask someone about its meaning.
d. skip over it on the assumption that I can understand what I am reading without knowing the word.

8. I believe my most productive work period is during
a. the morning.
b. the afternoon.
c. the evening.
d. the late night.
e. any time period.

9. The word that best describes my driving style is
a. patient.
b. impatient.
c. observant.
d. aggressive.
e. cautious.

10. If I observe a vehicle broken down along a busy highway, I am most likely to
a. stop and offer assistance.
b. call the police to report what I saw.
c. continue driving, assuming someone else will help out.
d. respond if I am not in a hurry.

11. In school, I generally completed assignments
a. ahead of time.
b. just in time.
c. on time sometimes and late sometimes.
d. most often late.

12. Other than gaining an education, my main priority in school was
a. making friends.
b. participating in sports.
c. determining a career path.
d. participating in extracurricular activities.
e. having a good time.

13. If I disagreed with the methods of a teacher, I would
a. approach him or her directly.
b. write him or her a note.
c. approach his or her supervisor.
d. not do anything about it.
e. drop the class.

14. In school, I demonstrated the most enthusiasm for
a. math classes.
b. science classes.
c. social science/social studies classes.
d. liberal arts classes.
e. physical education classes.
f. industrial arts classes.

15. When I complete a major project at work, I am most likely to
a. begin focusing immediately on another project.
b. expect immediate feedback from colleagues.
c. expect feedback from supervisors.
d. appreciate the sense of accomplishment.
e. desire some time off.

16. I feel that becoming romantically involved with a coworker is
a. wrong.
b. sometimes unwise but unavoidable.
c. acceptable under most circumstances.
d. acceptable if kept discreet.

17. When I am given a rush assignment at work, I am most likely to feel
a. challenged.
b. that I am being treated unfairly.
c. flustered or overwhelmed.
d. energized.

18. If a coworker asks for a loan, I will
- **a.** provide it without hesitation.
- **b.** say yes if it is a small amount.
- **c.** say no.
- **d.** provide it, but set up a specific repayment date.
- **e.** base my decision on my evaluation of the particular coworker's trustworthiness.
- **f.** base my decision on the closeness of my relationship with this coworker.

19. In a small-class setting at school, I would
- **a.** speak up often.
- **b.** prefer that the teacher did not call on me.
- **c.** respond only if asked to.
- **d.** feel self-conscious about expressing myself.

20. If someone I know tells me he or she is considering dropping out of high school, my first reaction would be to
- **a.** express my disappointment.
- **b.** describe how the person's life might be with and without an education.
- **c.** try hard to convince him or her to remain in school.
- **d.** list his or her options and let the person decide for himself or herself.
- **e.** refer him or her to someone else.
- **f.** tell him or her dropping out is not an option.

▶ Answers

Verbal

1. a.
2. a.
3. c.
4. c.
5. a.
6. b.
7. b.
8. b.
9. c.
10. d.
11. c.
12. b.
13. c.
14. c.
15. b.
16. c.
17. d.
18. a.
19. d.
20. d.
21. a.
22. d.
23. d.
24. a.
25. d.
26. a.
27. c.
28. d.
29. a.
30. c.
31. b.
32. c.
33. a.
34. c.
35. b.
36. b.
37. d.
38. a.
39. a.
40. c.
41. b.
42. a.
43. d.
44. c.
45. a.
46. b.
47. d.
48. b.
49. a.
50. b.

Recall

1. a.
2. c.
3. b.
4. c.
5. e.
6. b.
7. d.
8. d.
9. a.
10. b.
11. d.
12. e.
13. c.
14. b.
15. b.
16. a.
17. e.
18. b.
19. e.
20. d.
21. d.
22. a.
23. b.
24. a.
25. b.
26. e.
27. e.
28. d.
29. b.
30. e.
31. a.
32. d.
33. d.
34. b.
35. c.
36. e.
37. b.
38. c.
39. b.
40. d.
41. c.
42. d.
43. a.
44. e.
45. d.
46. a.
47. d.
48. b.
49. e.
50. b.
51. a.
52. e.
53. d.
54. e.
55. e.
56. a.
57. b.
58. d.
59. b.
60. c.
61. e.
62. b.
63. c.
64. c.
65. c.
66. b.
67. a.
68. a.
69. e.
70. d.
71. a.
72. d.
73. b.
74. e.
75. c.
76. c.
77. a.
78. e.
79. e.
80. c.
81. d.
82. a.
83. d.
84. a.
85. b.
86. d.
87. e.
88. c.
89. c.
90. c.
91. b.
92. e.
93. e.
94. c.
95. b.
96. b.
97. a.
98. b.
99. d.
100. b.

▶ Scoring

The passing score for the exam is computed using formulas that subtract for incorrect answers and take into consideration the personal background section. Scoring on the personal background section varies, so focus on the first section in determining your score.

Verbal Score

First, count the questions you answered correctly. Then, count the number of questions you answered incorrectly and divide by four. Subtract the results of the division from the number you got correct for your raw score. Questions you didn't answer don't count either way.

1. Number of correct questions: ______
2. Number of incorrect questions: ______
3. Divide number **2** by 4: ______
4. Subtract number **3** from number 1: ______

The result of number **4** above is your raw score on the verbal section.

Recall Score

Count the recall questions you answered correctly. Then, count the number of questions you answered incorrectly and divide by five. Subtract the results of the division from the number you got correct, and that's your score. Questions you didn't answer don't count.

1. Number of correct questions: ______
2. Number of incorrect questions: ______
3. Divide number **2** by 5: ______
4. Subtract number **3** from number 1: ______

The result of number **4** above is your raw score on the recall section.

What the Scores Mean

Generally, if you scored at least 70% on each section—that's 35 on verbal and 70 on recall—you can figure that you would probably pass the first part of the test if you took it today. But then, your goal isn't just to pass. Because your rank on the eligibility list may be based on your written exam score among other factors, you want to score as high as you can. Unless you scored nearly 100%, you will want to spend some time in study and practice.

Your score isn't the main point of taking this practice exam. Analyzing your performance is much more important. Use this analysis to focus your study and practice between now and exam day.

- **Did you find that you didn't know many of the words in the verbal section?** Then you should plan to spend a lot of time on the vocabulary section of Chapter 9.
- **Did you have trouble with the recall section?** Then you need to study and practice the material in Chapter 14, Number and Letter Recall.
- **Did you feel that you would have been able to get the correct answers if only you'd had enough time?** Chapters 9 and 14 have numerous tips on time management for an exam. You might also review Chapter 3, The LearningExpress Test Preparation System.
- **Did you do pretty well overall but feel you could use an extra edge?** That's the point of this whole book. Stick with it, and you will do well on exam day.

Whether you feel you performed well or poorly on this practice exam, your next step is to work with Chapters 9, 14, and 15, which cover the three kinds of questions on the exam. You can decide whether to spend a lot of time or just a little on the individual chapters based on how you did on the practice exam.

After you've read the relevant chapters, take the second exam of this type, in Chapter 18, to see how much you've improved.

CHAPTER

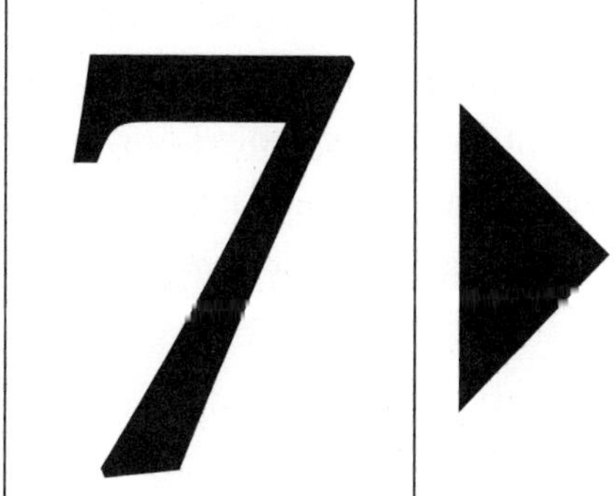

Reading Text, Tables, Charts, and Graphs

CHAPTER SUMMARY

Police officers need to have the ability to read—pure and simple. They also need to be able to understand what they are reading. Reports, procedure explanations, forms, suspect descriptions, and many other documents are regularly referred to in the law enforcement profession. This chapter provides tips and exercises that will help you improve your reading comprehension and improve your test score in this area.

The reading comprehension portion of the written test is designed to measure how well applicants understand what they read. The tests are usually multiple choice and will likely have questions based on brief passages, much like the standardized tests offered in schools. This chapter focuses on the specifics you will need to know to ace the reading comprehension questions on your exam. Once you are armed with the strategies that are explained in this chapter, you will be better able to understand what you read. Be sure to spend plenty of time with this chapter so that you can accurately assess your reading comprehension ability and increase your level of skill in this area. There are also additional resources available at the end of this chapter to help you build on what you learn. Reading is a skill that can always be improved, no matter what your current level of reading comprehension. And it is a skill that you will use for the rest of your life, not just on the police officer written exam.

▶ Types of Reading Comprehension Questions

You have probably encountered reading comprehension questions before, where you are given a passage to read and then have to answer multiple-choice questions about it. This kind of question has two advantages for you as a test taker:

1. Any information you need to know is right in front of you.
2. You're being tested only on the information provided in the passage.

The disadvantage, however, is that you have to know where and how to find that information quickly in an unfamiliar text. This makes it easy to fall for one of the incorrect answer choices, especially since they're designed to mislead you.

The best way to excel on this passage/question format is to be very familiar with the kinds of questions that are typically asked on the test. Questions most frequently fall into one of the following four categories:

1. fact or detail
2. main idea or title
3. inference or interpretation
4. vocabulary definition

In order to succeed on a reading comprehension test, you need to thoroughly understand each of these four types of questions.

Fact or Detail

Facts and details are the specific pieces of information that support the passage's main idea. Generally speaking, facts and details are indisputable—things that don't need to be proven, like statistics (18 million people) or descriptions (a green overcoat). While you may need to decipher paraphrases of facts or details, you should be able to find the answer to a fact or detail question directly in the passage. This is usually the simplest kind of question; however, you must be able to separate important information from less important information. The main challenge in answering this type of question is that the answer choices can be confusing because they are often very similar to each other. You should read each answer choice carefully before selecting one.

Main Idea or Title

The main idea of a passage is the thought, opinion, or attitude that governs the whole passage. It may be clearly stated, or only implied. Think of the main idea as an umbrella that is general enough to cover all of the specific ideas and details in the passage. Sometimes, the questions found after a passage will ask you about the main idea, while others use the term *title*. Don't be misled; main idea and title questions are the same. They both require you to know what the passage is mostly about. Often, the incorrect answers to a main idea or title question are too detailed to be correct. Remember that the main idea of a passage or the best title for a passage is general, not specific.

If you are lucky, the main idea will be clearly stated in the first or last sentence of the passage. At other times, the main idea is not stated in a topic sentence but is implied in the overall passage, and you will need to determine the main idea by inference. Because there may be a lot of information in the passage, the trick is to understand what all that information adds up to—what it is that the author wants you to know. Often, some of the wrong answers to main idea questions are specific facts or details from the passage. A good way to test yourself is to ask, "Can this answer serve as a net to hold the whole passage together?" If not, chances are you have chosen a fact or detail, not a main idea.

Inference or Interpretation

Inference or interpretation questions ask you what the passage means, implies, or suggests, not just what it says. They are often the most difficult type of reading comprehension question.

Inference questions can be the most difficult to answer because they require you to draw meaning from the text when that meaning is implied rather than directly stated. Inferences are conclusions that we draw based on the clues the writer has given us. When you draw inferences, you have to be something of a detective, looking for clues such as word choice, tone, and specific details that suggest a certain conclusion, attitude, or point of view. You have to read between the lines in order to make a judgment about what an author was implying in the passage.

A good way to test whether you've drawn an acceptable inference is to ask, "What evidence do I have for this inference?" If you can't find any, you probably have the wrong answer. You need to be sure that your inference is logical and that it is based on something that is suggested or implied in the passage itself—not by what you or others might think. Like a good detective, you need to base your conclusions on evidence—facts, details, and other information—not on random hunches or guesses.

Vocabulary Definitions

Questions designed to test vocabulary are really trying to measure how well you can figure out the meaning of an unfamiliar word from its context. *Context* refers to the words and ideas surrounding a vocabulary word. If the context is clear enough, you should be able to substitute a nonsense word for the one being sought, and you would still make the correct choice because you could determine meaning strictly from the sense of the sentence. For example, you should be able to determine the meaning of the following italicized nonsense word based on its context:

> The speaker noted that it gave him great *terivinix* to announce the winner of the Outstanding Leadership Award.

In this sentence, *terivinix* most likely means

- **a.** pain.
- **b.** sympathy.
- **c.** pleasure.
- **d.** anxiety.

Clearly, the context of an award makes choice **c**, *pleasure*, the best choice. Awards don't usually bring pain, sympathy, or anxiety.

When confronted with an unfamiliar word, try substituting a nonsense word and see if the context gives you the clue. If you're familiar with prefixes, suffixes, and word roots, you can also use this knowledge to help you determine the meaning of an unfamiliar word.

You should be careful not to guess at the answer to vocabulary questions based on how you may have seen the word used before or what you think it means. Many words have more than one possible meaning, depending on the context in which they're used, and a word you've seen used one way may mean something else in a test passage. Also, if you don't look at the context carefully, you may make the mistake of confusing the vocabulary word with a similar word. For example, the vocabulary word may be *taut* (meaning *tight*), but if you read too quickly or don't check the context, you might think the word is *taunt* (meaning *tease*). Always make sure you read carefully and that what you think the word means fits into the context of the passage you're being tested on.

Now it is time to practice answering the four types of reading comprehension questions.

Tips for Improving Your Reading Comprehension Score

Before the test:

- Practice, practice, practice!
- Working with a friend or family member, select paragraphs from an article in the newspaper and have your partner create questions to ask you about it.
- Read short passages from articles or books and make up questions for yourself.
- Take advantage of online resources (information is available at the end of this chapter).

During the test:

- Read the questions first, before you read the passage, so you will know what words and ideas to look out for.
- Focus your attention; don't let your mind wander during the reading of the test passages.
- If one part of a passage confuses you, just read on until you are finished. Then go back and look at the confusing part again.
- Look at each one of the multiple-choice answers, then compare each with the paragraph to see which ones can be eliminated.
- Focus on the main idea of the text. What is the passage mostly about?
- Don't skip any sentences when reading the passage.
- Don't let your own knowledge of the subject matter interfere with your answer selection. Stick with the information that is given in the passage.
- Read the passage actively, asking yourself questions about the main idea and jotting down notes in the margin.

Practice Passage 1

The following is a sample test passage, followed by four questions. Read the passage carefully, and then answer the questions, based on your reading of the text, by circling your choice. Note under your answer which type of question has been asked. Correct answers appear immediately after the questions.

In the last decade, community policing has been frequently touted as the best way to reform urban law enforcement. The idea of putting more officers on foot patrol in high crime areas, where relations with police have frequently been strained, was initiated in Houston in 1983 under the leadership of then-Commissioner Lee Brown. He believed that officers should be accessible to the community at the street level. If officers were assigned to the same area over a period of time, those officers would eventually build a network of trust with neighborhood residents. That trust would mean that merchants and residents in the community would let officers know about criminal activities in the area and would support police intervention. Since then, many large cities have experimented with Community-Oriented Policing (COP) with mixed results. Some have found that police and citizens are grateful for the opportunity to work together. Others have found that unrealistic expectations by citizens and resistance from officers have combined to hinder the effectiveness of COP. It seems possible, therefore, that a good idea may need improvement before it can truly be considered a reform.

1. Community policing has been used in law enforcement since
 a. the late 1970s.
 b. the early 1980s.
 c. the Carter administration.
 d. Lee Brown was New York City police commissioner.

 Question type: ______________________

2. The phrase *a network of trust* in this passage suggests that
 a. police officers can rely only on each other for support.
 b. community members rely on the police to protect them.
 c. police and community members rely on each other.
 d. community members trust only each other.

 Question type: ______________________

3. The best title for this passage would be
 a. Community Policing: The Solution to the Drug Problem.
 b. Houston Sets the Pace in Community Policing.
 c. Communities and Cops: Partners for Peace.
 d. Community Policing: An Uncertain Future?

 Question type: ______________________

4. The word *touted* in the first sentence of the passage most nearly means
 a. praised.
 b. denied.
 c. exposed.
 d. criticized.

 Question type: ______________________

Answers

Don't just look at the correct answers and move on. The explanations are the most important part, so read them carefully. Use these explanations to help you understand how to tackle each kind of question the next time you come across it.

1. b. Question type: 1, fact or detail. The passage says, "The idea of putting more officers on foot patrol in high crime areas, where relations with police have frequently been strained, was initiated in Houston in 1983 under the leadership of then-Commissioner Lee Brown." Do not be confused by the opening phrase, *In the last decade* because the passage does not include the current date, so you have no way of knowing which decade the passage is referring to. This information doesn't help you even if you know that a decade is a period of ten years. Don't be misled by trying to figure out when Carter was president. Also, if you happen to know that Lee Brown was New York City's police commissioner at one time, don't let that information lead you away from the information contained in the passage alone. Brown was commissioner in Houston when he initiated community policing.

2. c. Question type: 3, inference. The *network of trust* referred to in this passage is between the community and the police, as you can see from the sentence where the phrase appears. The key phrase in the question is in this passage. You may think that police can rely only on each other, or one of the other answer choices may appear equally plausible to you. But your choice of answers must be limited to the one suggested in this passage. Another tip for questions like this: Beware of absolutes! Be suspicious of any answer containing words like *only*, *always*, or *never*.

3. d. Question type: 2, main idea. A good title usually expresses the main idea. In this passage, the main idea comes at the end. The sum of all the details in the passage suggests that community policing is not without its critics and that therefore its future is uncertain. Another key phrase is *mixed results*, which means that some communities haven't had full success with community policing.

4. a. Question type: 4, vocabulary. The word *touted* is linked in this passage with the phrase *the best way to reform*. Most people would think that a good way to reform something is praiseworthy. In addition, the next few sentences in the passage describe the benefits of community policing. Criticism or a negative response to the subject doesn't come until later in the passage.

Practice Passage 2

Answer the questions that follow this passage. Circle the answers to the questions, and note under your answer which type of question has been asked. Then check your answers against the key that appears immediately after the questions.

> There is some evidence that crime rates are linked to social trends such as demographic and socioeconomic changes. Crime statistics showed a decline in the post-World War II era of the 1940s and '50s. Following the Vietnam War in the 1970s, however, reported crimes were on the rise again, only to be followed by lower numbers of such reports in the 1980s. One of the reasons for these fluctuations appears to be age. When the population is younger, as in the 1960s when the baby boomers came of age, there is a greater incidence of crime nationwide. A second cause for the rise and fall of crime rates appears to be economic. Rising crime rates appear to follow falling economies. A third cause cited for the cyclical nature of crime statistics appears to be the ebb and flow of public policy decisions, which sometimes protect personal freedoms at the expense of government control. A youthful, economically disadvantaged population that is not secured by social controls of family and community or by government authority is likely to see an upswing in reported crimes.

1. Crime statistics seem to rise when populations are

a. younger.
b. older.
c. veterans
d. richer.

Question type: ____________

2. The main idea of the passage is that

a. times of prosperity show lower crime statistics.
b. when the economy slows, crime statistics rise.
c. incidence of reported crime is related to several social and economic variables.
d. secure families are less likely to be involved in crime.

Question type: ____________

3. The best title for this passage would be

a. Wars and Crime Statistics.
b. Why Crime Statistics Rise and Fall.
c. Youth and Crime Statistics.
d. Poverty and Crime Statistics.

Question type: ____________

4. Crime statistics show that crime is
   a. random.
   b. cyclical.
   c. demographic.
   d. social.

   Question type: Fact

Answers

1. a. Question type: 1, detail. This is a fairly clear example of how you can look quickly through a passage and locate a clearly stated detail. The word *young* appears in relation to the baby boomers; the idea is also suggested in the last sentence by the word *youthful.*

2. c. Question type: 2, main idea. The other answer choices are details—they're all in the passage, but they're not what the passage is *mostly* about. Choice **c** is the only one that combines several details into a statement that reflects the first sentence, which is also the topic sentence, of the paragraph.

3. b. Question type: 2, main idea. Each of the other choices expresses a detail, one of the reasons listed in the passage for fluctuation in crime rates. Choice **b** is the only one that expresses the sum of those details.

4. b. Question type: 1, detail. The passage mentions *the cyclical nature of crime statistics.* Other phrases that suggest this answer include *fluctuations, rise and fall, and ebb and flow.*

Practice Passage 3

Answer the questions that follow this passage. Circle the answers to the questions, and note under your answer which type of question has been asked. Then check your answers against the key that appears immediately after the questions.

In recent years, issues of public and personal safety have become a major concern to many Americans. Violent incidents in fast-food restaurants, libraries, hospitals, schools, and offices have led many to seek greater security inside and outside of their homes. Sales of burglar alarms and high-tech security devices such as motion detectors and video monitors have skyrocketed in the last decade. Convenience stores and post offices have joined banks and jewelry stores in barricading staff behind iron bars and safety glass enclosures. Communities employ private security forces and encourage homeowners to keep trained attack dogs on their premises. While some people have sympathy for the impetus behind these efforts, there is also some concern that these measures will create a siege mentality leading to general distrust among people that could foster a dangerous isolationism within neighborhoods and among neighbors.

1. The passage suggests which of the following about community security?
   a. Communities are more dangerous today than they were ten years ago.
   b. Too much concern for security can destroy trust among neighbors.
   c. Poor security has led to an increase in public violence.
   d. Isolated neighborhoods are safe neighborhoods.

   Question type: interpret

2. The word *foster* in the last sentence of the passage most nearly means

a. adopt.
b. encourage.
c. prevent.
d. secure.

Question type: ____________________

3. The author believes that

a. more security is needed to make neighborhoods safer.
b. people should spend more on home security.
c. people should not ignore the problems created by excessive safety concerns.
d. attack dogs and high-tech devices are the best protection against violent crime.

Question type: ____________________

4. In the last sentence, the phrase *siege mentality* means

a. hostility.
b. defensiveness.
c. fear.
d. corruption.

Question type: ____________________

Answers

1. b. Question type: 4, inference. The key word here is *distrust*, which implies that neighbors become suspicious of each other if they are worried about safety.

2. b. Question type: 3, vocabulary. The first answer choice is meant to confuse you if you associate the word *foster* with foster care and, by extension, with adoption. *Foster* means *nurture* or *help to grow*. Look again at the sentence. What could *a general distrust* (the thing that fosters) do to *a dangerous isolationism* (the thing being fostered)? A general distrust could *encourage* a dangerous isolationism.

3. c. Question type: 4, inference. By using phrases like *dangerous isolationism*, the author suggests that he or she doesn't approve of the move toward more use of security devices. The other answer choices all indicate the author's approval of the trend being discussed.

4. b. Question type: 3, vocabulary. The key word here is *siege*. People who perceive themselves to be under attack tend to stick together in the face of a common enemy. They become quick to defend themselves against that enemy.

▶ Create Your Own Questions

A good way to solidify what you've learned about reading comprehension questions is for you to write the questions. Here's a passage, followed by space for you to create your own questions. Write one question of each of the four types: fact or detail, main idea or title, inference or interpretation, and vocabulary definition.

As you create your own questions and answers, you will have the chance to understand how multiple-choice questions work. Typically, incorrect answers are incorrect because the reader has misunderstood, has a predisposition, uses unsound reasoning, or is only casually reading the passage. Knowing how multiple-choice questions work gives you a definite advantage when taking your written exam.

In recent years, law enforcement officers have welcomed the advent of a number of new technologies that have aided them greatly in their work. These include long-range eavesdropping devices and computer scanners that allow police to identify possible suspects by merely typing a license number into a computer in the patrol car. The scanner allows instant access to motor vehicle and criminal records and gives officers the opportunity to snare wrongdoers, even when they are not involved in criminal activity at the time. Police departments have praised the use of the computers, which they say help them get criminals off the streets and out of the way of honest citizens. Not all of those citizens agree with this attitude, however; some believe that arrests made solely on the basis of scanner identification constitute an invasion of privacy. They regard the accessing of records as illegal search and seizure. In New Jersey, Florida, and Arizona, lawsuits have been filed by citizens who believe that their constitutional rights have been violated. They believe that much computer-generated information is inaccurate and vulnerable to hackers who invade computer databases. Some believe that such information from scanners could be used to charge innocent citizens with crimes, or to target particular neighborhoods for harassment.

1. Detail question: ______________________

____

a.
b.
c.
d.

2. Main idea question: ______________________

____

a.
b.
c.
d.

3. Inference question: ______________________

____

a.
b.
c.
d.

4. Vocabulary question: ______________________

____

a.
b.
c.
d.

Possible Questions

Following is one question of each type, based on the passage. Your questions may be very different, but these will give you an idea of the kinds of questions that could be asked.

1. *Main idea question:* Which of the following best expresses the main idea of the passage?
a. New technologies are available to police officers.
b. Police are skeptical of new policing technologies.
c. New technologies raise questions of privacy.
d. New technologies may be discriminatory.

2. *Detail question:* Computer scanners allow police to
a. identify suspects.
b. access computer databases.
c. locate wrongdoers.
d. all of the above

3. *Vocabulary question:* In this passage, the word *snare* means
a. question.
b. interrupt.
c. capture.
d. free.

If English Isn't Your First Language

When nonnative speakers of English have trouble with reading comprehension tests, it's often because they lack the cultural, linguistic, and historical frame of reference that native speakers enjoy. People who have not lived in or been educated in the United States often don't have the background information that comes from reading American newspapers, magazines, and textbooks.

A second problem for nonnative English speakers is the difficulty in recognizing vocabulary and idioms (expressions like *chewing the fat*) that assist comprehension. In order to read with good understanding, it's important to have an immediate grasp of as many words as possible in the text. Test takers need to be able to recognize vocabulary and idioms immediately so that the ideas those words express are clear.

The Long View

Read newspapers, magazines, and other periodicals that deal with current events and matters of local, state, and national importance. Pay special attention to articles that are related to law enforcement.

Be alert to new or unfamiliar vocabulary or terms that occur frequently in the popular press. Use a highlighter pen to mark new or unfamiliar words as you read. Keep a list of those words and their definitions. Review them for 15 minutes each day. Though at first you may find yourself looking up a lot of words, don't be frustrated—you will look up fewer and fewer words as your vocabulary expands.

During the Test

When you are taking your written exam, make a picture in your mind of the situation being described in the passage. Ask yourself, "What did the writer mostly want me to think about this subject?"

Locate and underline the topic sentence that carries the main idea of the passage. Remember that the topic sentence—if there is one—may not always be the first sentence. If there doesn't seem to be one, try to determine what idea summarizes the whole passage.

4. *Inference question:* The writer implies, but does not directly state, that

- **a.** computer technologies must be used with care.
- **b.** high-tech policing is the wave of the future.
- **c.** most citizens believe that high-tech policing is beneficial.
- **d.** most police officers prefer using the new technologies.

Answers

1. c.
2. d.
3. c.
4. d.

▶ Reading Tables, Graphs, and Charts

Police officer exams may also include a section testing your ability to read tables, charts, and graphs. These sections are really quite similar to regular reading comprehension sections, but instead of pulling information from a passage of text, you will need to answer questions about a graphic representation of data. The types of questions asked about tables, charts, and graphs are actually quite similar to those about reading passages, though there usually aren't any questions on vocabulary. The main difference in reading tables, charts, or graphs is that you're reading or interpreting data represented in tabular (table) or graphic (picture) form rather than textual (sentence and paragraph) form.

Tables

Tables present data in rows and columns. The following is a very simple table that shows the number of accidents reported in one county over a 24-hour period. Use it to answer question 1.

TIME OF DAY	NUMBER OF ACCIDENTS
6:00 A.M.–9:00 A.M.	11
9:00 A.M.–12:00 P.M.	3
12:00 P.M.–3:00 P.M.	5
3:00 P.M.–6:00 P.M.	7
6:00 P.M.–9:00 P.M.	9
9:00 P.M.–12:00 A.M.	6
12:00 A.M.–3:00 A.M.	5
3:00 A.M.–6:00 A.M.	3

1. Based on the information provided in this table, at what time of day do the most accidents occur?

a. noon
b. morning rush hour
c. evening rush hour
d. midnight

The correct answer is **b**, morning rush hour. You can clearly see that the highest number of accidents (11) occurred between 6:00 A.M. and 9:00 A.M.

Graphs

Now, here's the same information presented as a graph. A graph uses two axes rather than columns and rows to create a visual picture of the data.

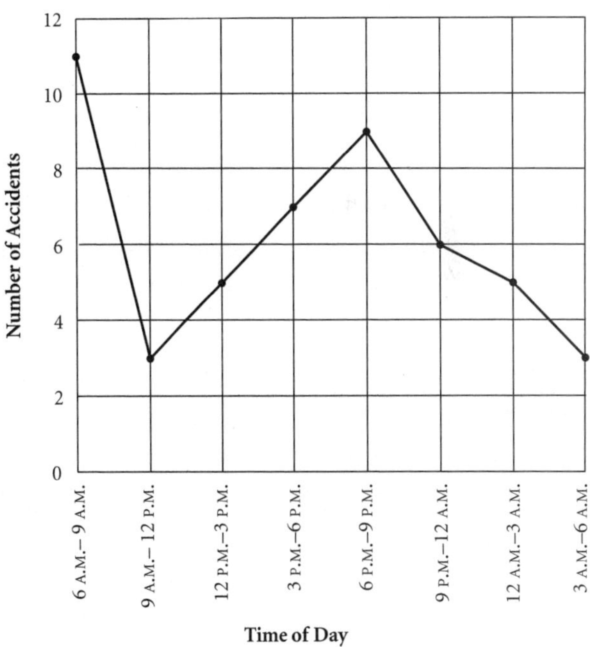

Here you can actually see the time of the greatest number of accidents represented by a line that corresponds to the time of day and number. These numbers can also be represented by a box in a bar graph, as follows.

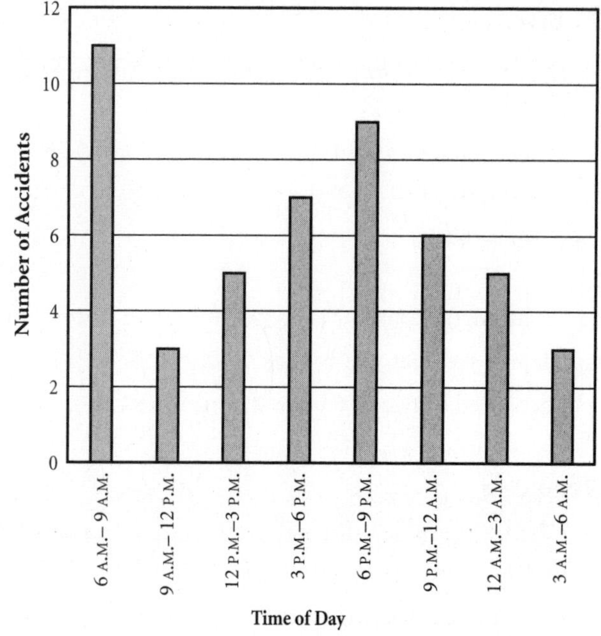

When reading graphs, the key is to be sure that you know exactly what the numbers on each axis represent. Otherwise, you're likely to misinterpret the information. On the bar graph, you see that the horizontal axis represents the time of day, and the vertical axis represents the number of accidents that occurred. Thus, the tallest box shows the time of day with the most accidents.

Practice

Like regular reading comprehension questions, questions on tables, charts, and graphs may also ask you to make inferences and maybe even do basic math using the information and numbers presented on the table, chart, or graph. For example, you may be asked questions like the following on the information presented in the preceding table, line graph, and bar graph. The answers follow immediately after the questions.

2. What is the probable cause for the high accident rate between 6:00 A.M. and 9:00 A.M.?

a. People haven't had their coffee yet.
b. A lot of drivers are rushing to work.
c. There is a glare from the morning sun.
d. Highway construction is heaviest during those hours.

3. What is the total number of accidents?

a. 48
b. 51
c. 49
d. 53

Answers

2. b. A question like this tests your common sense as well as your ability to read the graph. Though there may indeed be sun glare and many drivers may have not yet had their coffee, these items are too variable to account for the high number of accidents. In addition, choice **d** is not logical because construction generally slows traffic down. Choice **b** is the best answer, because from 6:00 to 9:00 A.M. there is consistently a lot of rush-hour traffic. In addition, many people do rush, and this increases the likelihood of accidents.

3. c. This question, of course, tests your basic ability to add. To answer this question correctly, you need to determine the value of each bar and then add those numbers together if you are given the bar graph. If you are given the table, you merely add up the column of numbers to find the total.

Charts

Finally, you may be presented information in the form of a chart like the pie chart below. Here, the accident figures have been converted to percentages. In this figure, you don't see the exact number of accidents, but you see how accidents for each time period compare to the others.

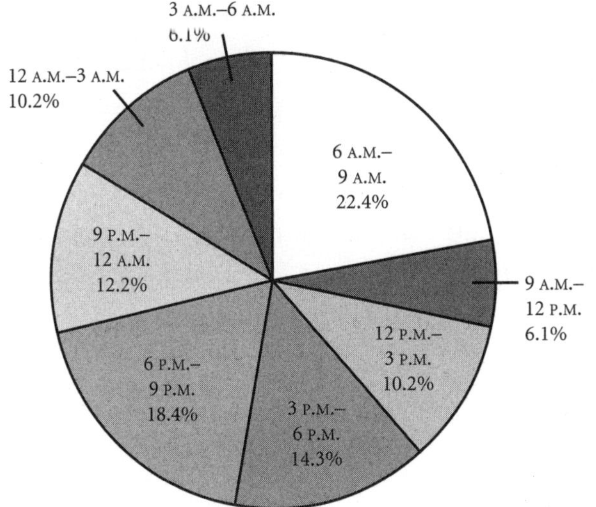

Practice

Try the following questions to hone your skill at reading tables, graphs, and charts.

Answer questions 1 and 2 on the basis of the pie chart shown below.

Causes of household fires

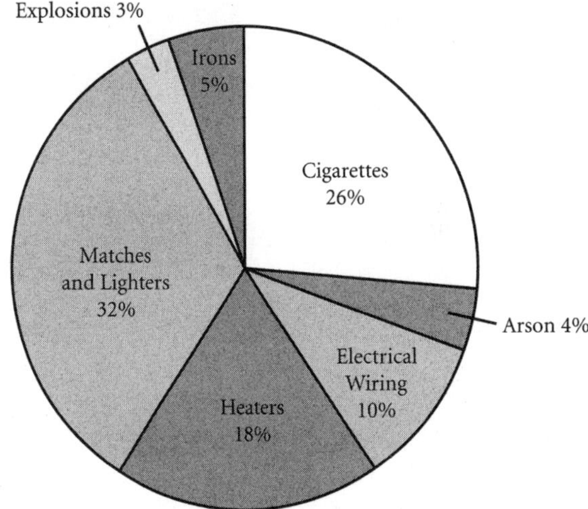

1. What is the percentage of smoking-related fires?
  a. 26%
  b. 32%
  c. 58%
  d. 26–58%

2. Based on the information provided in the chart, which of the following reasons applies to the majority of these fires?
  a. malicious intent to harm
  b. violation of fire safety codes
  c. carelessness
  d. faulty products

Answer questions 3 and 4 on the basis of the following graph.

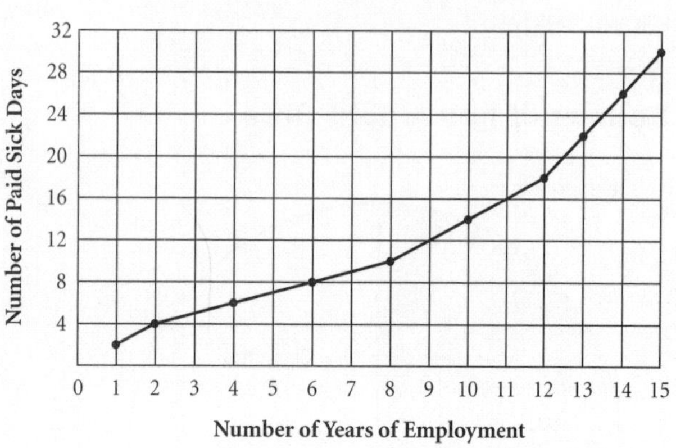

3. At what point does the rate of increase of sick days change?

a. one year of employment
b. four years of employment
c. three years of employment
d. nine years of employment

4. During what years of employment is the number of sick days equal to double the number of years of employment?

a. 1, 4, and 12
b. 13, 14, and 15
c. 1, 2, and 15
d. 2, 4, and 10

Answers

1. d. Of the causes presented in the chart, both cigarettes (26%) and matches and lighters (32%) are related to smoking. But not all match fires are necessarily smoking related. Thus, the best answer allows for a range between 26% and 58%.

2. c. Fires from cigarettes, heaters, irons, and matches and lighters—81% in total—are generally the result of carelessness. Only 4% of fires are arsons, so choice **a** cannot be correct. Electrical, heater, and explosion fires may be the result of fire safety code violations, but even so, they total only 31%. Finally, there's no indication in this chart that there were faulty products involved.

3. c. In the first two years of employment, employees gain an additional two sick days. In the third year, employees gain only one additional day, that is, from four to five days.

4. c. In the first year, the number of sick days is two; in the second, four; and not until the fifteenth year does the number of sick days (30) again double the number of years of employment.

▶ Additional Resources

Here are some other ways you can build the vocabulary and knowledge that will help you do well on reading comprehension questions.

- Practice asking the four sample question types about passages you read for information or pleasure.
- If you have access to the Internet, visit several websites that are related to law enforcement. For example, www.policeone.com and www.criminaljustice-online.com. Many other sites are available—just perform a basic search on any search engine to find more. Exchanging views with others on the Internet will help expand your knowledge of job-related material that may appear in a passage on the test.

- Use your library. Many public libraries have sections, sometimes called Lifelong Learning Centers, that contain materials for adult learners, such as books with exercises in reading and study skills. It's also a good idea to enlarge your base of information by reading books and articles related to law enforcement. Many libraries have computer systems that allow you to access information quickly and easily. Library personnel can show you how to use the computers and access the Internet.
- Begin now to build a broad knowledge of your potential profession. Get in the habit of reading articles in newspapers and magazines on job-related issues. Keep a clipping file of those articles. This will help keep you informed of trends in the profession and familiarize you with pertinent vocabulary.
- Consider reading or subscribing to professional journals. The journals listed below are written for a general readership among law enforcement personnel and are available for a reasonable annual fee. They may also be available in your public library.

American Police Beat
1 Brattle Square 4th Floor
Cambridge, MA 02138
800-234-0056
www.apbweb.com/subscribe.htm

FBI Law Enforcement Bulletin
Government Printing Office
Superintendent of Documents
P.O. Box 371954
Pittsburgh, PA 15250-7954
202-512-1800
www.fbi.gov/publications/leb/leb.htm

Law Officer Magazine
52 B Street
Suite 1900
San Diego, CA 92101-4495
www.lawofficermagazine.com

Police Chief
International Association of Chiefs of Police, Inc.
515 North Washington Street
Alexandria, VA 22314
703-836-6767 or 800-THE IACP
www.theiacp.org/pubinfo/pc

POLICE Magazine
3520 Challenger Street
Torrance, CA 90503
310-533-2400
www.policemag.com

If you need more help building your reading skills and taking reading comprehension tests, consider *501 Reading Comprehension Questions, 3rd Edition*, and *Reading Comprehension Success in 20 Minutes a Day, 3rd Edition*, both published by LearningExpress.

Additionally, you may want to check out the following websites that can help build your reading skills:

Helpful Websites

- Reading Strategies
  www.utexas.edu/student/utlc/lrnres/handouts.html
- Reading Comprehension Resources
  www.resourceroom.net
- Reading Better and Faster
  http://english.glendale.cc.ca.us/speed1.html

CHAPTER

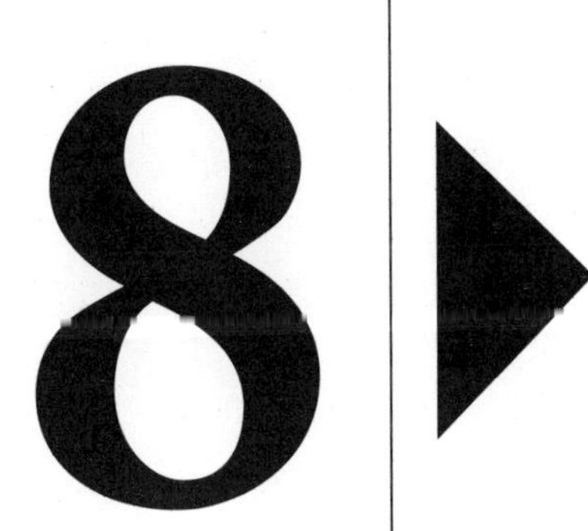

Grammar

CHAPTER SUMMARY

Besides being able to read well, police officers must be able to write correctly and have a good grasp of the English language. This chapter reviews the sentence-level writing skills often tested on multiple-choice exams, including complete sentences, capitalization, punctuation, subject-verb agreement, verb tenses, pronouns, and confusing word pairs.

There is plenty of writing involved in police work; just ask any law enforcement official you see. The grammar section of the written exam helps the department determine whether or not applicants are capable of this aspect of the job. The tips and exercises in this chapter will help you improve your skills in this area and assess how much practice you need before taking the actual test.

▶ Complete Sentences

Sentences are the basic unit of written language. Most writing is done using complete sentences, so it's important to distinguish sentences from fragments. A sentence expresses a complete thought, while a fragment requires something more to express a complete thought.

Fragments

Look at the following pairs of word groups. The first in each pair is a sentence fragment; the second is a complete sentence.

FRAGMENT	COMPLETE SENTENCE
The officer on foot patrol.	The officer was on foot patrol.
Exploding from the barrel of the gun.	The bullet exploded from the barrel of the gun.

These examples show that a sentence must have a subject and a verb to complete its meaning. The first fragment has a subject, but it needs a helping verb. Adding *was* before *on* completes the sentence. The second fragment has neither a subject nor a verb. Only when a subject and verb are added is the sentence complete.

Now look at the next set of word groups. Mark those that are complete sentences.

1. **a.** We saw the squad car approaching.
   b. When we saw the squad car approaching.

2. **a.** Before the prison was built in 1972.
   b. The prison was built in 1972.

3. **a.** Because we are on duty in the morning.
   b. We are on duty in the morning.

If you chose 1. a., 2. b., and 3. b., you were correct. You may have noticed that the groups of words are the same, but the fragments have an extra word at the beginning. These words are called *subordinating conjunctions.* If a group of words that would normally be a complete sentence is preceded by a subordinating conjunction, something more is needed to complete the thought.

In the following three sentences, the thoughts have been completed.

- When we saw the squad car approaching, we flagged it down.
- Before the prison was built in 1972, the old jailhouse was demolished.
- Because we were on duty in the morning, we went to bed early.

Here is a list of words that can be used as subordinating conjunctions.

after	that
although	though
as	unless
because	until
before	when
if	whenever
once	where
since	wherever
than	while

Run-On Sentences

If you can tell when a group of words isn't a sentence, then you can tell when one or more sentences have been run together, sometimes with a comma in between. Some tests will ask you to find run-on sentences. Each of the sentences below is a run-on sentence. Can you find where to put a period and begin a new sentence?

1. We went to the academy we had a good time.
2. Without exception, the prisoners conformed to the new ruling they kept their cells clean.
3. The defense needed time to examine the new evidence, the lawyer asked for an extension.

If you noticed that a new sentence begins after *academy* in the first sentence, after *ruling* in the second, and after *evidence* in the third, you were right. Generally, you can tell whether you're looking at a run-on by covering the second half of the sentence and asking yourself whether the first half by itself is a sentence. Then cover the first half. Is the second half a sentence by itself? If your answer to one or both questions is *no*, then the sentence is fine. If you answered both questions with *yes*—both halves of the sentence could be sentences by themselves—then you've got a run-on, unless there happens to be a semicolon (;) between the two halves.

Practice

Some of the questions on a police officer exam may test your ability to distinguish a sentence from a fragment or a run-on. Check for a subject and a verb, as well as for subordinating conjunctions. Practice answering the following sample questions.

1. Which of the following groups of words is a complete sentence?
- **a.** The contraband buried beneath the floorboards beside the furnace.
- **b.** After we spent considerable time examining all of the possibilities before making a decision.
- **c.** In addition to the methods the detective used to solve the crime.
- **d.** The historical account of the incident bore the most resemblance to fact.

2. Which of the following groups of words is a complete sentence?
- **a.** This was fun to do.
- **b.** We looking.
- **c.** Before the door opened.
- **d.** If we ever see you again.

3. Which of the following groups of words is a run-on?
- **a.** Whenever I put on my uniform, I am filled with a sense of pride.
- **b.** The special services unit completed its work and made its report to the chief.
- **c.** Unless we hear from the directors of the board before the next meeting, we will not act on the new proposal.
- **d.** We slept soundly, we never heard the alarm.

Answers

1. d.
2. a.
3. d.

▶ Capitalization

You may encounter questions that test your ability to capitalize correctly. Here is a quick review of the most common capitalization rules.

- Capitalize the first word of a sentence. If the first word is a number, write it as a word.
- Capitalize the pronoun *I*.
- Capitalize the first word of a quotation: I said, "What's the name of your dog?" Do not capitalize the first word of a partial quotation: He called me "the most diligent officer" he had ever seen.
- Capitalize proper nouns and proper adjectives. See the table on the next page for more about proper nouns and adjectives.

The following passage contains no capitalized words. Circle those letters that should be capitalized.

when I first saw the black hills on january 2, 2005, i was shocked by their beauty. we had just spent new

CAPITALIZATION	
CATEGORY	**EXAMPLE (PROPER NOUNS)**
days of the week, months of the year	Friday, Saturday; January, February
holidays, special events	Christmas, Halloween; Two Rivers Festival, Dilly Days
names of individuals	John Jay, Rudy Giuliani, George Billeck
names of structures, buildings	Lincoln Memorial, Principal Building
names of trains, ships, aircraft	Queen Elizabeth, Chicago El
product names	Corn King hams, Ford Mustang
cities and states	Des Moines, Iowa; Juneau, Alaska
streets, highways, roads	Grand Avenue, Interstate 29, Deadwood Road
landmarks, public areas	Continental Divide, Grand Canyon, Glacier National Park
bodies of water	Atlantic Ocean, Mississippi River
ethnic groups, languages, nationalities	Asian-American, English, Arab
official titles	Mayor Daley, President Johnson
institutions, organizations, businesses	Dartmouth College, Lions Club, General Motors Corporation
proper adjectives	English muffin, Polish sausage

year's day in sioux falls, south dakota and had headed west toward our home in denver, colorado. as we traveled along interstate 90, i could see the black hills rising slightly in the distance. president calvin coolidge had called them "a wondrous sight to behold." i understood why. after driving through the badlands and stopping at wall drug in wall, south dakota, we liked the way the evergreen-covered hills broke the barren monotony of the landscape. my oldest daughter said, "dad, look! there's something that's not all white." we could see why the lakota regarded the hills as a native american holy ground. we saw mount rushmore and custer state park, the home of the largest herd of buffalo in north america. we also drove the treacherous spearfish canyon road. fortunately, our jeep cherokee had no trouble with the ice and snow on the winding road.

Check your circled version against the corrected version of the passage that follows.

When I first saw the Black Hills on January 2, 2005, I was shocked by their beauty. We had just spent New Year's Day in Sioux Falls, South Dakota and had headed west toward our home in Denver, Colorado. As we traveled along Interstate 90, I could see the Black Hills rising slightly in the distance. President Calvin Coolidge had called them "a wondrous sight to behold." I understood why. After driving through the Badlands and stopping at Wall Drug in Wall, South Dakota, we liked the way the evergreen-covered hills broke the barren monotony of the landscape. My oldest daughter said, "Dad, look! There's something that's not all white." We could see why the Lakota regarded the hills as a Native American holy ground. We saw Mount Rushmore and Custer State Park, the home of the largest herd of buffalo in North America. We also drove the treacherous Spearfish Canyon Road. Fortunately, our Jeep Cherokee had no trouble with the ice and snow on the winding road.

Practice

Now try these sample questions. Choose the option that is capitalized correctly.

4. **a.** This year we will celebrate christmas on Tuesday, December 25 in Manchester, Ohio.
   b. This year we will celebrate Christmas on Tuesday, December 25 in manchester, Ohio.
   c. This year we will celebrate Christmas on Tuesday, December 25 in Manchester, Ohio.
   d. This year we will celebrate christmas on Tuesday, December 25 in manchester, Ohio.

5. **a.** Abraham Adams made an appointment with Mayor Burns to discuss the building plans.
   b. Abraham Adams made an appointment with Mayor Burns to discuss the Building Plans.
   c. Abraham Adams made an appointment with mayor Burns to discuss the building plans.
   d. Abraham Adams made an appointment with mayor Burns to discuss the Building Plans.

6. **a.** Abigail Dornburg, MD, was named head of the review board for Physicians Mutual.
   b. Abigail Dornburg, MD, was named Head of the Review Board for Physicians Mutual.
   c. Abigail Dornburg, MD Was named head of the review board for Physicians mutual.
   d. Abigail dornburg, MD, was named head of the review board for Physicians Mutual.

Answers

4. c.
5. a.
6. a.

▶ Punctuation

A section on the written exam may test your punctuation skills. Make sure you know how to use periods, commas, and apostrophes correctly.

Periods

Here is a quick review of the rules regarding the use of a period.

- Use a period at the end of a sentence that is not a question or an exclamation.
- Use a period after an initial in a name: Millard K. Furham.
- Use a period after an abbreviation, unless the abbreviation is an acronym.
  Abbreviations: Mr., Ms., Dr., A.M., General Motors Corp., Allied Inc.
  Acronyms: NASA, AIDS, MTV
- If a sentence ends with an abbreviation, use only one period. (We brought food, tents, sleeping bags, etc.)

Commas

Using commas correctly can make the difference between presenting information clearly and distorting the facts. The following chart demonstrates the necessity of commas in written language. How many people are listed in the sentence?

COMMAS AND MEANING	
Number undetermined	My sister Diane John Carey Melissa and I went to the fair.
Four people	My sister Diane, John Carey, Melissa, and I went to the fair.
Five people	My sister, Diane, John Carey, Melissa, and I went to the fair.
Six people	My sister, Diane, John, Carey, Melissa, and I went to the fair.

Here is a quick review of the most basic rules regarding the use of commas.

- Use a comma before *and, but, so, or, for, nor,* and *yet* when they separate two groups of words that could be complete sentences.
  Example: The S.W.A.T. leader laid out the attack plan, and the team executed it to perfection.
- Use a comma to separate items in a series.
  Example: The student driver stopped, looked, and listened when she got to the railroad tracks.
- Use a comma to separate two or more adjectives modifying the same noun.
  Example: The hot, black, rich coffee tasted great after an hour in below-zero weather. (Notice that there is no comma between *rich* [an adjective] and *coffee* [the noun *rich* describes]).
- Use a comma after introductory words, phrases, or clauses in a sentence.
  Examples: *Usually,* the class begins with a short writing assignment. [introductory word]
  Racing down the street, the yellow car ran a stoplight. [introductory phrase]
  After we responded to the call, we returned to our normal patrol. [introductory clause]
- Use a comma after a name followed by Jr., Sr., or some other abbreviation.
  Example: The class was inspired by the speeches of Martin Luther King, Jr.
- Use a comma to separate items in an address.
  Example: The car stopped at 1433 West G Avenue, Orlando, Florida, 36890.
- Use a comma to separate a day and a year, as well as after the year.
  Example: I was born on July 21, 1954, during a thunderstorm.
- Use a comma after the greeting of a friendly letter and after the closing of any letter.
  Example: Dear Uncle Jon,
  Sincerely yours,
- Use a comma to separate contrasting elements in a sentence.
  Example: Your essay needs strong arguments, not strong opinions, to convince me.
- Use commas to set off appositives (words or phrases that explain or identify a noun).
  Example: My partner, a rookie, is named Ron.

The following passage contains no commas or periods. Add commas and periods as needed.

Dr Newton Brown Jr a renowned chemist has held research positions for OPEC Phillips Petroleum Inc Edward L Smith Chemical Designs and R J Reynolds Co His thorough exhaustive research is recognized in academic circles as well as in the business community as the most well-designed reliable data available Unfortunately on July 6 1988 he retired after a brief but serious illness He lives in a secluded retirement community at 2401 Beach Sarasota Springs Florida

Check your version against the following corrected version.

Dr. Newton Brown, Jr., a renowned chemist, has held research positions for OPEC, Phillips Petroleum Inc., Edward L. Smith Chemical Designs, and R.J.Reynolds Co. His thorough, exhaustive research is recognized in academic circles, as well as in the business community, as the most well-designed, reliable data available. Unfortunately, on July 6, 1988, he retired after a brief but serious illness. He lives in a secluded retirement community at 2401 Beach, Sarasota Springs, Florida.

Apostrophes

Apostrophes communicate important information in written language. Here is a quick review of the two most important rules regarding the use of apostrophes.

- Use an apostrophe to show that letters have been omitted from a word to form a contraction.
  Examples: do not = don't; national = nat'l;
  I will = I'll; it is = it's
- Use an apostrophe to show possession. See the table below for more examples.
  Examples: Juan's dog; Nikia's house

Practice

Practice with these sample test questions. For each question, choose which of the four options is punctuated correctly.

7. a. Although it may seem strange, my partners purpose in interviewing Dr. E.S. Sanders Jr. was to eliminate him as a suspect in the crime.
b. Although it may seem strange my partner's purpose in interviewing Dr. E.S. Sanders, Jr. was to eliminate him, as a suspect in the crime.
c. Although it may seem strange, my partner's purpose in interviewing Dr. E.S. Sanders, Jr., was to eliminate him as a suspect in the crime.
d. Although it may seem strange, my partner's purpose in interviewing Dr. E.S. Sanders, Jr. was to eliminate him, as a suspect in the crime.

8. a. After colliding with a vehicle at the intersection of Grand, and Forest Ms. Anderson saw a dark hooded figure crawl through the window, reach back and grab a small parcel, and run north on Forest.
b. After colliding with a vehicle at the intersection of Grand, and Forest, Ms. Anderson saw a dark hooded figure crawl through the window, reach back and grab a small parcel, and run north on Forest.
c. After colliding with a vehicle at the intersection of Grand and Forest Ms. Anderson saw a dark, hooded figure crawl through the window, reach back and grab a small parcel, and run north on Forest.
d. After colliding with a vehicle at the intersection of Grand and Forest, Ms. Anderson saw a dark, hooded figure crawl through the window, reach back and grab a small parcel, and run north on Forest.

APOSTROPHES TO SHOW POSSESSION		
SINGULAR NOUNS (ADD 'S)	**PLURAL NOUNS ENDING IN S (ADD ')**	**PLURAL NOUNS NOT ENDING IN S**
boy's	boys'	men's
child's	kids'	children's
lady's	ladies'	women's

9. a. When we interviewed each of the boys and their fathers, we determined that the men's stories did not match the boy's versions.
b. When we interviewed each of the boys and their fathers, we determined that the men's stories did not match the boys' versions.
c. When we interviewed each of the boys and their fathers, we determined that the mens' stories did not match the boys' versions.
d. When we interviewed each of the boys' and their fathers', we determined that the men's stories did not match the boys' versions.

Answers

7. c.
8. d.
9. b.

▶ Verbs

Subject-Verb Agreement

In written language, a subject must agree with its verb in number. In other words, if a subject is singular, the verb must be singular. If the subject is plural, the verb must be plural. If you are unsure whether a verb is singular or plural, apply this simple test. Fill in the blanks in the two sentences below with the matching form of the verb. The verb form that best completes the first sentence is singular. The verb form that best completes the second sentence is plural.

One person _____. [Singular]
Two people _____. [Plural]

Look at these examples using the verbs *speak* and *do.* Try it yourself with any verb that confuses you.

One person *speaks.*	One person *does.*
Two people *speak.*	Two people *do.*

Pronoun Subjects

Few people have trouble matching noun subjects and verbs, but pronouns are sometimes difficult for even the most sophisticated writers. Some pronouns are always singular, others are always plural, and still others can be either singular or plural, depending on the usage.

These pronouns are always singular:

each	everyone
either	no one
neither	nobody
anybody	one
anyone	somebody
everybody	someone

The indefinite pronouns *each, either*, and *neither* are most often misused. You can avoid a mismatch by mentally adding the word *one* after the pronoun and removing the other words between the pronoun and the verb. Look at the following examples.

Each **of the officers** wants his own squad car.
Each **one** wants his own squad car.

Either **of the suspects** knows where the stolen merchandise is located.
Either **one** knows where the stolen merchandise is located.

These sentences may sound awkward because many speakers misuse these pronouns, and you are probably used to hearing them used incorrectly. Despite that, the substitution trick (inserting *one* for the words following the pronoun) will help you avoid this mistake.

Some pronouns are always plural and require a plural verb:

both	many
few	several

Other pronouns can be either singular or plural:

all	none
any	some
most	

The words or prepositional phrases following these pronouns determine whether they are singular or plural. If what follows the pronoun is plural, the verb must be plural. If what follows is singular, the verb must be singular.

All of the **work is** finished.
All of the **jobs are** finished.
Is any of the **pizza** left?
Are any of the **pieces** of pizza left?

None of the **time was** wasted.
None of the **minutes were** wasted.

Subjects Joined by *and*

If two nouns or pronouns are joined by *and*, they require a plural verb.

He **and** she want to buy a new house.
Jack **and** Jill want to buy a new house.

Subjects Joined by *or* or *nor*

If two nouns or pronouns are joined by *or* or *nor,* they require a singular verb. Think of them as two separate sentences and you'll never make a mistake in agreement.

He **or** she wants to buy a new house.
He wants to buy a new house.
She wants to buy a new house.

Neither Jack **nor** Jill is good at basketball.
Jack is not good at basketball.
Jill is not good at basketball.

Practice

Circle the correct verb in each of the following sentences.

10. Every other day either Bert or Ed (takes, take) out the trash.
11. The woman in question (works, work) at the Civic Center box office.
12. A good knowledge of the rules (helps, help) you understand the game.
13. Each of these factors (causes, cause) the crime rate to increase.
14. (Have, Has) either of them ever arrived on time?

Answers

10. takes
11. works
12. helps
13. causes
14. Has

Verb Tense

The tense of a verb tells a reader when the action occurs. Present tense verbs tell the reader to imagine the action happening as it is being read, while past tense verbs tell the reader that the action has already happened. Read the following two paragraphs. The first one is written in the present tense, the second in the past tense. Notice the difference in the verbs. They are highlighted to make them easier to locate.

As Officer Horace **opens** the door, he **glances** around cautiously. He **sees** signs of danger everywhere. The centerpiece and placemats from the dining room table **are scattered** on the floor next to the table. An end table in the living room **is lying** on its side. He **sees** the curtains flapping and **notices** glass on the carpet in front of the window.

As Officer Horace **opened** the door, he **glanced** around cautiously. He **saw** signs of danger everywhere. The centerpiece and placemats from the dining room table **were scattered** on the floor next to the table. An end table in the living room **was lying** on its side. He **saw** the curtains flapping and **noticed** glass on the carpet in front of the window.

You can distinguish present tense from past tense by simply fitting the verb into a sentence.

VERB TENSE	
PRESENT TENSE (TODAY, I ___ . . .)	**PAST TENSE (YESTERDAY, I ___ . . .)**
drive	drove
think	thought
rise	rose
catch	caught

The important thing to remember about verb tense is to keep it consistent. If a passage begins in the present tense, keep it in the present tense unless there is a specific reason to change—to indicate that some action occurred in the past, for instance. If a passage begins in the past tense, it should remain in the past tense. Verb tense should never be mixed as it is in the following sentence.

Wrong: Officer Terry **opens** the door and **saw** the unruly crowd.

Correct: Officer Terry **opens** the door and **sees** the unruly crowd.

Officer Terry **opened** the door and **saw** the unruly crowd.

However, sometimes it is necessary to use a different verb tense in order to clarify when an action occurred. Read the following sentences and the explanations following them.

The sergeant **sees** the criminal that you **caught**. [The verb *sees* is in the present tense, indicating that the action is occurring in the present. However, the verb *caught* is in the past tense, indicating that the criminal was caught at some earlier time.]

The prison that **was built** over a century ago **sits** on top of the hill. [The verb phrase *was built* is in the past tense, indicating that the prison was built in the past. However, the verb *sits* is in the present tense, indicating that the action is still occurring.]

Practice

Check yourself with these sample questions. Choose the option that uses verb tense correctly. Answers are at the end of the chapter.

15. **a.** When I work hard, I always get what I want.
b. When I work hard, I always got what I want.
c. When I worked hard, I always got what I want.
d. When I worked hard, I always get what I wanted.

16. **a.** It all started after I came home and am in my room studying for a big test.
b. It all started after I came home and was in my room studying for a big test.
c. It all starts after I come home and was in my room studying for a big test.
d. It all starts after I came home and am in my room studying for a big test.

17. **a.** The suspect became nervous and dashes into the house and slams the door.
b. The suspect becomes nervous and dashed into the house and slammed the door.
c. The suspect becomes nervous and dashes into the house and slammed the door.
d. The suspect became nervous and dashed into the house and slammed the door.

Answers

15. a.
16. b.
17. d.

▶ Pronouns

Pronoun Case

Most of the time, a single pronoun in a sentence is easy to use correctly. In fact, most English speakers would readily identify the mistakes in the following sentences.

Me went to the prison with **he**.
My partner gave **she** a ride to work.

Most people know that *Me* in the first sentence should be *I* and that *he* should be *him*. They would also know that *she* in the second sentence should be *her*. Such errors are easy to spot when the pronouns are used alone in a sentence. The problem occurs when a pronoun is used with a noun or another pronoun. See if you can spot the errors in the following sentences.

The rookie rode with Jerry and **I**.
Belle and **him** are going to the courthouse.

The errors in these sentences are not as easy to spot as those in the sentences with a single pronoun. The easiest way to attack this problem is to turn the sentence with two pronouns into two separate sentences. Then the error once again becomes very obvious.

The rookie rode with Jerry.
The rookie rode with **me** (not I).

Belle **is** going to the courthouse. [Notice the singular verb *is* in place of *are*.]
He (not *him*) is going to the ice courthouse.

Pronoun Agreement

Another common error in using pronouns involves singular and plural pronouns. Like subjects and verbs, pronouns must match the number of the nouns they represent. If the noun a pronoun represents is singular, the pronoun must be singular. On the other hand, if the noun a pronoun represents is plural, the pronoun must be plural. Sometimes a pronoun represents another pronoun. If so, either both pronouns must be singular or both pronouns must be plural. Consult the list of singular and plural pronouns you saw earlier in this chapter.

The **officer** must take a break when **she** (or **he**) is tired. [singular]
Officers must take breaks when **they** are tired. [plural]

One of the rookies misplaced **her** file. [singular]
All of the rookies misplaced **their** files. [Plural]

If two or more singular nouns or pronouns are joined by *and*, use a plural pronoun to represent them.

Buddha and Muhammad built religions around **their** philosophies.
If **he and the sergeant** want to know where I was, **they** should ask me.

If two or more singular nouns or pronouns are joined by *or*, use a singular pronoun. If a singular and a plural noun or pronoun are joined by *or*, the pronoun should agree with the closest noun or pronoun it represents.

Matthew or Jacob will loan you **his** extra radio.
The elephant or the moose will furiously protect **its** young.

Neither **the officers** nor **the sergeant** was sure of **his** location.
Neither **the sergeant** nor **the officers** was sure of **their** location.

Practice

Circle the correct pronoun in the following sentences.

18. Andy or Arvin will bring (his, their) camera so (he, they) can take pictures of the party.

19. One of the file folders isn't in (its, their) drawer.

20. The uniform store sent Bob and Ray the shirts (he, they) had ordered.

21. Benny and (he, him) went to the courthouse with Bonnie and (I, me).

22. Neither my cousins nor my uncle knows what (he, they) will do tomorrow.

Answers

18. his, he
19. its
20. they
21. he, me
22. he

► Easily Confused Word Pairs

The following word pairs are often misused in written language. By reading the following explanations and looking at the examples, you can learn to use these words correctly every time.

Its/It's

Its is a possessive pronoun that means "belonging to it." *It's* is a contraction for *it is* or *it has.* The only time you will ever use *it's* is when you can also substitute the words *it is* or *it has.*

Who/That

Who refers to people. *That* refers to things.

There is the officer **who** helped me recover my car.
The woman **who** invented the copper-bottomed kettle died in 1995.
This is the house **that** was burglarized.
The bullets **that** I needed were no longer in stock.

There/Their/They're

Their is a possessive pronoun that shows ownership. *There* is an adverb that tells where an action or item is located. *They're* is a contraction for the words *they are.* Here is an easy way to remember these words.

- *Their* means belonging to them. Of the three words, *their* can be most easily transformed into the word *them.* Extend the *r* on the right side and connect the *i* and the *r* to turn *their* into *them.* This clue will help you remember that *their* means "belonging to them."
- If you examine the word *there,* you can see that it contains the word *here.* Whenever you use *there,* you should be able to substitute *here.* The sentence should still make sense.
- Imagine that the apostrophe in *they're* is actually a very small letter *a.* Use *they're* in a sentence only when you can substitute *they are.*

Your/You're

Your is a possessive pronoun that means "belonging to you." *You're* is a contraction for the words *you are.* The

Answering Multiple-Choice Questions about Grammar

As you take the portion of the test that assesses your writing skills, apply what you know about the rules of grammar:

- Look for complete sentences.
- Check for periods, commas, and apostrophes.
- Look for subject-verb agreement and consistency in verb tense.
- Check the pronouns to make sure the correct form is used and that the number (singular or plural) is correct.
- Check those easily confused pairs of words.
- When determining which answer is correct to any one question, don't go back and review answer choices that you have already eliminated as being wrong.
- Always read all of the answer choices before selecting one. You may find an even better answer if you keep looking.

only time you should use *you're* is when you can substitute the words *you are.*

To/Too/Two

To is a preposition or an infinitive.

- As a preposition: *to* the jail, *to* the bottom, *to* my church, *to* our garage, *to* his school, *to* his hideout, *to* our disadvantage, *to* an open room, *to* a ballad, *to* the precinct
- As an infinitive (*to* followed by a verb, sometimes separated by adverbs): *to* walk, *to* leap, *to* see badly, *to* find, *to* advance, *to* read, *to* build, *to* sorely want, *to* badly misinterpret, *to* carefully peruse

Too means also. Whenever you use the word *too*, substitute the word *also*. The sentence should still make sense.

Two is a number, as in *one, two*. If you memorize this, you will never misuse this form.

Practice

The key is to think consciously about these words when you see them in written language. Circle the correct form of these easily confused words in the following sentences.

23. (Its, It's) (to, too, two) late (to, too, two) remedy the problem now.

24. This is the officer (who, that) gave me the directions I needed.

25. (There, Their, They're) going (to, too, two) begin construction as soon as the plans are finished.

26. We left (there, their, they're) house after the storm subsided.

27. I think (your, you're) going (to, too, two) get at least (to, too, two) extra shifts.

28. The crime syndicate moved (its, it's) home base of operations.

Answers

23. It's, too, to
24. who
25. They're, to
26. their
27. you're, to, two
28. its

▶ Additional Resources

This chapter was a very basic review of only a few aspects of written English. For more help with these aspects and more, consult the following books.

For Nonnative Speakers of English

- *Errors in English and Ways to Correct Them* by Harry Shaw (HarperCollins)
- *Living in English* by Betsy J. Blosser (Passport Books)

For Everyone

- *Grammar Essentials,* 3rd Edition (Learning-Express)
- *Writing Skills Success in 20 Minutes a Day, 3rd Edition* (LearningExpress)
- *501 Grammar and Writing Questions, 3rd Edition* (LearningExpress)
- *Grammar Smart: A Guide To Perfect Usage*, The Princeton Review Series *(Princeton Review)*
- *English Grammar for Dummies* by Geraldine Woods (John Wiley & Sons)

Grammar-Related Websites

- English Grammar Help
  http://owl.english.purdue.edu/handouts/general/index.html
- Ask Miss Grammar
  www.protrainco.com/info/grammar.htm
- Grammar Rules and Practice Exercises
  www.chompchomp.com/menu.htm
- Grammar & Style (a complete online grammar guide)
  http://andromeda.rutgers.edu/~jlynch/Writing
- Grammar Slammer
  http://englishplus.com/grammar
- Common Errors In English
  www.wsu.edu/~brians/errors

CHAPTER 9 Vocabulary and Spelling

CHAPTER SUMMARY

Your grasp of the English language will be measured on the written exam in the areas of vocabulary and spelling. This chapter covers both areas, providing useful tips and exercises that can increase your chances of success.

Police officers need the ability to communicate effectively with others. Using good vocabulary and correct spelling is important when writing or speaking. Law enforcement officials need to be able to speak, understand, read, and write the English language efficiently. Use this chapter to improve your vocabulary and spelling skills.

▶ Vocabulary

If your written exam has a section that tests your vocabulary, the questions will most likely deal with synonyms, antonyms, word parts, context, and/or homophones.

- **Synonyms** are words that share the same meaning or nearly the same meaning as other words.
- **Antonyms** are words that are the opposite or nearly the opposite of other words.
- **Word parts** are made up of prefixes, roots, and suffixes.

- **Context** refers to the text surrounding a word.
- **Homophones** are words that sound the same but have different meanings, such as *heard* and *herd.*

Synonym and Antonym Questions

A word is a *synonym* of another word if it has the same or nearly the same meaning as the other word. *Antonyms* are words with opposite meanings. Test questions often ask you to find the synonym or antonym of a word. If you're lucky, the word will be surrounded by a sentence that helps you guess what the word means. If you're less lucky, you will get just the word, and then you have to figure out what the word means without any help.

Questions that ask for synonyms and antonyms can be tricky because they require you to recognize the meanings of several words that may be unfamiliar—not only the words in the questions but also the answer choices. Usually, the best strategy is to look at the structure of the word and to listen for its sound. See if a part of a word—the root—looks familiar. The meaning of a word is located within its root. For instance, the root of *credible* is *cred,* which means to trust or believe. Knowing what common root parts mean can help you understand the meaning of words you don't know. Other words with the root *cred* are *incredible, sacred,* and *credit.* Looking for related words that have the same root as the word in question can help you to choose the right answer, even if it is only by process of elimination.

Synonym Practice

Try your hand at identifying the root and other word parts and the related words in these sample synonym questions. Circle the word that means the same or about the same as the underlined word. Answers and explanations appear right after the questions.

1. a set of <u>partial</u> prints
  a. identifiable
  b. incomplete
  c. visible
  d. enhanced

2. <u>substantial</u> evidence
  a. inconclusive
  b. weighty
  c. proven
  d. alleged

3. <u>corroborated</u> the statement
  a. confirmed
  b. negated
  c. denied
  d. challenged

4. <u>ambiguous</u> questions
  a. meaningless
  b. difficult
  c. simple
  d. vague

Answers

The explanations are just as important as the answers, because they show you how to go about choosing a synonym if you don't know the word.

1. **b.** *Partial* means *incomplete.* The root of the word here is *part.* A partial print is only part of the whole.
2. **b.** *Substantial* evidence is *weighty.* The key part of the word here is *substance.* Substance has weight.
3. **a.** *Corroboration* is *confirmation.* Notice the prefix *co-*, which means *with* or *together*. Some related words are *cooperate, coworker,* and *collide.* Corroboration means that one statement fits with another.

4. d. *Ambiguous* questions are *vague* or uncertain. The key part of this word is *ambi-*, which means *two* or *both*. An ambiguous question can be taken two ways.

Antonym Practice

The main danger in answering questions with antonyms is forgetting that you are looking for opposites rather than synonyms. Most antonym questions will include one or more synonyms as answer choices. The trick is to keep your mind on the fact that you are looking for the opposite of the word. If you're allowed to mark in the books or on the test papers, circle the word *antonym* or *opposite* in the directions to help you remember.

Otherwise, the same tactics that work for synonym questions work for antonyms as well: Try to determine the meaning of part of the word or to remember a context where you've seen the word before.

Circle the word that means the *opposite* of the underlined word in the sentences below. Answers are immediately after the questions.

5. zealous pursuit
- **a.** envious
- **b.** eager
- **c.** idle
- **d.** comical

6. inadvertently left
- **a.** mistakenly
- **b.** purposely
- **c.** cautiously
- **d.** carefully

7. exorbitant prices
- **a.** expensive
- **b.** unexpected
- **c.** reasonable
- **d.** outrageous

8. compatible partners
- **a.** comfortable
- **b.** competitive
- **c.** harmonious
- **d.** experienced

9. belligerent attitude
- **a.** hostile
- **b.** reasonable
- **c.** instinctive
- **d.** ungracious

Answers

Be sure to read the explanations as well as the right answers.

5. c. *Zealous* means *eager*, so *idle* is most nearly opposite. Maybe you've heard the word *zeal* before. One trick in this question is not to be misled by the similar sounds of *zealous* and *jealous*. The other trick is not to choose the synonym, *eager*.

6. b. *Inadvertently* means *by mistake*, so *purposely* is the antonym. The key element in this word is the prefix *in-*, which usually means *not* or *the opposite of*. Consider related words like *involuntary*, *inappropriate*, and *ineligible*. As usual, one of the answer choices (**a**) is a synonym.

7. c. The key element here is *ex-*, which means *out of* or *away from*. *Exorbitant* literally means *out of orbit*. The opposite of an *exorbitant* or *outrageous* price would be a *reasonable* one.

8. b. The opposite of *compatible* is *competitive*. Here you have to distinguish among three words that contain the same prefix, *com-*, and to let the process of elimination work for you. The other choices are too much like synonyms.

9. b. The key element in this word is the root *belli-*, which means *warlike*. The synonym choices, then, are *hostile* and *ungracious*; the antonym is *reasonable*.

Context Questions

Context is the surrounding text in which a word is used. Most people use context to help them determine the meaning of an unknown word. A vocabulary question that gives you a sentence around the vocabulary word is usually easier to answer than one with little or no context. The surrounding text can help you as you look for synonyms for the specified words in the sentences.

The best way to take meaning from context is to look for key words in sentences or paragraphs that convey the meaning of the text. If nothing else, the context will give you a means to eliminate wrong answer choices that clearly don't fit. The process of elimination will often leave you with the correct answer.

Context Practice

Try these sample questions. Circle the word that best describes the meaning of the underlined word in the sentence.

10. The members of the jury were appalled by the wild and uncontrolled behavior of the witness in the case.
- **a.** horrified
- **b.** amused
- **c.** surprised
- **d.** dismayed

11. Despite the fact that he appeared to have financial resources, the defendant claimed to be destitute.
- **a.** wealthy
- **b.** ambitious
- **c.** solvent
- **d.** impoverished

12. Though she was distraught over the disappearance of her child, the woman was calm enough to give the officer her daughter's description.
- **a.** punished
- **b.** distracted
- **c.** composed
- **d.** anguished

13. The unrepentant criminal expressed no remorse for his actions.
- **a.** sympathy
- **b.** regret
- **c.** reward
- **d.** complacency

Some tests may ask you to fill in the blank by choosing a word that fits the context. In the following questions, circle the word that best completes the sentence.

14. Professor Washington was a very ____________ woman known for her reputation as a scholar.
- **a.** stubborn
- **b.** erudite
- **c.** illiterate
- **d.** disciplined

15. His ______________________ was demonstrated by his willingness to donate large amounts of money to worthy causes.
- **a.** honesty
- **b.** loyalty
- **c.** selfishness
- **d.** altruism

Answers

Check to see whether you were able to pick out the key words that help you define the target word, as well as whether you got the right answer.

10. **a.** The key words *wild* and *uncontrolled* signify *horror* rather than the milder emotions described by the other choices.

11. **d.** The key words here are *financial resources,* but this is a clue by contrast. The introductory *Despite the fact* signals that you should look for the opposite of the idea of having financial resources.

12. **d.** The key words here are *though* and *disappearance of her child*, signalling that you are looking for an opposite of *calm* in describing how the mother spoke to the officer. The only word strong enough to match the situation is *anguished.*

13. **b.** *Remorse* means *regret for one's actions.* The part of the word here to beware of is the prefix *re-*. It doesn't signify anything in this word, though it often means *again* or *back.* Don't be confused by the two choices that also contain the prefix *re-*. The strategy here is to see which word sounds better in the sentence. The key words are *unrepentant* and *no,* indicating that you're looking for something that shows no repentance.

14. **b.** The key words here are *professor* and *scholarly*. Even if you don't know the word *erudite,* the other choices don't fit the description of the professor.

15. **d.** The key phrase here is *large amounts of money to worthy causes.* They give you a definition of the word you're looking for. Again, even if you don't know the word *altruism*, the other choices seem inappropriate to describe someone so generous.

For Nonnative Speakers of English

Be very careful not to be confused by the sound of words that may mislead you. Be sure you look at the word carefully, and pay attention to the structure and appearance of the word as well as its sound. You may be used to hearing English words spoken with an accent. The sounds of those words may be misleading in choosing a correct answer.

Questions about Word Parts

Some tests may ask you to find the meaning of a part of a word: roots, which are the main part of the word; prefixes, which go before the root word; or suffixes, which go after. Any of these elements can carry meaning or change the use of a word in a sentence. For instance, the suffix *-s* or *-es* can change the meaning of a noun from singular to plural: *boy, boys.* The prefix *un-* can change the meaning of a root word to its opposite: *necessary, unnecessary.*

To identify most parts of words, the best strategy is to think of words you already know that carry the same root, suffix, or prefix. Let what you know about those words help you to see the meaning of words that are less familiar.

On the following two pages are some of the word parts that appear most often on vocabulary tests. If you read the following lists of word parts and their meanings for five to ten minutes every day, you will soon have the level of recognition you need to score high on this portion of the exam. You may also wish to create flash cards to carry around with you—write the word part on one side of the card and its meaning and some examples of it on the other.

Word Part Practice

Circle the word or phrase below that best describes the meaning of the underlined portion of the word. Answers appear after the questions.

16. <u>pro</u>active
- **a.** after
- **b.** forward
- **c.** toward
- **d.** behind

17. <u>re</u>cession
- **a.** against
- **b.** see
- **c.** under
- **d.** back

18. <u>con</u>temporary
- **a.** with
- **b.** over
- **c.** apart
- **d.** time

19. etymo<u>logy</u>
- **a.** state of
- **b.** prior to
- **c.** study of
- **d.** quality of

20. vandal<u>ize</u>
- **a.** to make happen
- **b.** to stop
- **c.** to fill
- **d.** to continue

Common Prefixes and Their Meanings

a (not, without) *ex*: amoral, apolitical	**ab** (away from, off) *ex*: abnormal, abhor	**bi** (two) *ex*: bifocals, bicentennial
contra (against, opposite) *ex*: contradict, contraceptive	**de** (take away from, down, do the opposite of) *ex*: deflate, derail	**dis** (not, opposite of, exclude) *ex*: disown, disarm
im, in, il (not, negative) *ex*: impossible, inappropriate, illegal	**inter** (between, among) *ex*: interstate, intervene	**mis** (wrong) *ex*: misspell, misplace
non (not, no) *ex*: nonsense, nonconformity	**ob, op** (toward, against, in the way of) *ex*: objection, oppose	**per** (through, very) *ex*: persecute, persuade
pre (before) *ex*: precede, predict	**pro** (forward, for) *ex*: protect, propel, provide	**port** (carry) *ex*: portable, portfolio
re (back, again) *ex*: remember, reply	**term** (end, boundary, limit) *ex*: terminology, termination	**trans** (across, beyond, change) *ex*: transformation, transfer
un (not, against, opposite) *ex*: unstoppable, untrustworthy, unhappy	**voc** (to call) *ex*: vocation, vocal	

Common Root Words and Their Meanings

anim (mind, life, spirit, anger) *ex*: animal, animated, animosity	**cede, ceed, cess** (go, yield) *ex*: concede, success, exceed	**cred** (trust, believe) *ex*: credible, sacred, incredible
dic, dict (say, speak) *ex*: indication, dictionary, edict	**fid** (belief, faith) *ex*: confide, affidavit, fidelity	**flu, flux** (to flow, flowing) *ex*: fluid, fluctuate
form (shape) *ex*: conform, format, formality	**ject** (throw) *ex*: interject, object, intersect	**man** (by hand, make, do) *ex*: manage, craftsmanship, command
oper (work) *ex*: operation, cooperate	**path** (feel) *ex*: homeopathic, sympathy, psychopath	**pict** (paint, show, draw) *ex*: depiction, picture
pel/pulse (push) *ex*: impulse, compel	**rog** (ask) *ex*: interrogate	**rupt** (break) *ex*: interrupt, corrupt
sent, sens (feel, think) *ex*: resentment, sensitive	**sist** (to withstand, make up) *ex*: insist, resist, persist	**spir** (breath, soul) *ex*: inspire, perspire

Common Suffixes and Their Meanings

ance, ence (quality or process) *ex*: dominance, dependence	**ant, ent** (something or someone that performs an action) *ex*: client, applicant	**ate** (office or function) *ex*: dedicate, candidate
dom (state of being) *ex*: boredom, wisdom	**er, or** (person or thing that does something) *ex*: officer, director	**ful** (amount or quality that fills) *ex*: handful, cheerful
ian, an (related to, one that is) *ex*: custodian, human	**ia** (names, diseases) *ex*: malaria, anorexia	**ile** (capability, aptitude) *ex*: fragile, docile
ing (action, result of action) *ex*: singing, jumping, clinging	**ion** (condition or action) *ex*: abduction, selection, deduction	**ive** (condition) *ex*: motive, directive
ity (expressing state or condition) *ex*: sincerity, brevity	**ment** (action, product, result) *ex*: fragment, ornament, judgment	**ness** (state, condition, quality) *ex*: happiness, goodness, nervousness
or (property, condition) *ex*: candor, squalor, splendor	**otic** (relationship to action, process, or condition) *ex*: patriotic, psychotic, hypnotic	**ship** (status, condition) *ex*: partnership, friendship, courtship
ty (quality or state) *ex*: unity, civility, anonymity	**ure** (act, condition, process or function) *ex*: exposure, composure, assure	**y** (inclination, result of an activity) *ex*: dreamy, pesky, whiny

Answers

Even if the word in the question was unfamiliar, you might have been able to guess the meaning of the prefix or suffix by thinking of some other word that has the same prefix or suffix.

16. **b.** Think of a *propeller*. A propeller sends an airplane *forward*.

17. **d.** Think of *recall*: Manufacturers *recall* or *bring back* cars that are defective; people *recall* or *bring back* past events in memory.

18. **a.** Think of *congregation*: a group of people gather *with* each other in a house of worship.

19. **c.** Think of *biology*, the *study of* life.

20. **a.** Think of *scandalize*: to *make* something shocking *happen*.

How to Answer Vocabulary Questions

- Look for word parts that you know, such as the root, prefix, or suffix, and think of similar words that may give clues to the meaning of the word in question.
- Pay close attention to the directions. Make sure you know when to look for the opposite meaning rather than a similar one.
- Think of how the word makes sense in a sentence.
- Sound out the word inside your head to make sure you aren't reading it wrong.
- Don't be fooled by words that sound the same but have different spellings and meanings.
- Check back over your work if you have time remaining to make sure you haven't made any careless mistakes.

Homophone Questions

Don't be fooled by words that sound alike but have entirely different meanings. The best way to identify these easily confused words is by studying them and quizzing yourself until you have the meanings and spellings memorized. On the next page is a list of homophones that are often found on written exams. Review the list carefully and consult your dictionary to determine the meanings of any words that you are unsure of.

Homophone Practice

Each sentence below contains two words in parentheses that are homophones. Circle the word that makes sense in the sentence. Answers and explanations follow the questions.

21. He slammed on his (break, brake) just before the stop sign.

22. The mayor decided to (higher, hire) a few more police officers.

23. His family advised him to seek (council, counsel) before going any further.

24. She told him to get his (facts, fax) straight before speaking to her again.

25. No one (new, knew) exactly what had happened.

26. They wondered if someone would try to (steel, steal) the jewelry.

Answers

Check to see if you selected the correct word in each sentence.

21. **brake**—a stopping device, such as the brake in a truck or car. (*Break* means to damage something.)

22. **hire**—to pay for the services of someone. (*Higher* means something or someone is more high than someone or something else.)

23. **counsel**—advice. (*Council* means a group of people who meet for a purpose.)

24. **facts**—something that is really true. (*Fax*—short for facsimile—means a document sent or received from a fax machine.)

25. **knew**—having known something. (*New* is the opposite of old.)

26. **steal**—taking something that belongs to someone else. (*Steel* is a metal.)

Homophones

ad, add
affect, effect
allowed, aloud
bare, bear
bored, board
boulder, bolder
brake, break
bred, bread
build, billed
cent, scent
cereal, serial
cite, sight, site
counsel, council
course, coarse
days, daze
died, dyed
due, do, dew
facts, fax
fair, fare
feat, feet
find, fined
flour, flower
for, fore, four
great, grate
groan, grown
guessed, guest
heal, he'll
hear, here
heard, herd
higher, hire
hoarse, horse
hole, whole
hours, ours
incite, insight
knew, new
know, no
lead, led
leased, least
lesson, lessen
made, maid
marshal, martial
meat, meet
morning, mourning
one, won
pact, packed
pail, pale
passed, past
patience, patients
pause, paws
peace, piece
plain, plane
poor, pour
rain, reign
raise, rays
rap, wrap
right, write
road, rode
roll, role
sale, sail
scene, seen
see, sea
soar, sore
stair, stare
steel, steal
sun, son
sweet, suite
tents, tense
their, there, they're
threw, through
throne, thrown
tide, tied
to, too, two
trooper, trouper
vary, very
wade, weighed
ware, wear, where
weight, wait
weather, whether
wood, would
your, you're

▶ Spelling

Generally, spelling tests are in a multiple-choice format. You will be given several possible spellings for a word and asked to identify the one that is correct. Thus, you must be able to see very fine differences between word spellings. The best way to prepare for a spelling test is to have a good grasp of the spelling fundamentals and be able to recognize when those rules don't apply. Remember that English is full of exceptions in spelling. You have to develop a good eye to spot the errors.

Even though there are so many variant spellings for words in English, police officer exams generally are looking to make sure that you know and can apply the basic rules. Here are some of those rules to review:

- *i* before *e*, except after *c*, or when *ei* sounds like *a*.
  Examples: piece, receive, neighbor
- *gh* can replace *f* or be silent.
  Examples: enough, night
- Double the consonant when you add an ending.
  Examples: forget/forgettable, shop/shopping
- Drop the *e* when you add *-ing*.
  Example: hope/hoping
- The spelling of prefixes and suffixes generally doesn't change.
  Examples: project, propel, proactive

Spelling Practice

Here are some examples of how spelling questions might appear on a police officer exam. Choose the word that is spelled correctly in the following sentences. There's no answer key for this section. Instead, use your dictionary to find the right answers.

27. We went to an ____________________ of early Greek art.

a. exibition
b. exhibition
c. excibition
d. exebition

28. We will ________________ go to the movies tonight.

a. probly
b. probbaly
c. probely
d. probably

29. We took ________________ of pictures on our vacation.

a. allot
b. alot
c. a lot
d. alott

30. The sharpshooter had the greatest number of ______________ target shots.

a. accurate
b. acurate
c. accuret
d. acccurit

31. He was warned not to use ______________ force.

a. exessive
b. excesive
c. excessive
d. excesive

Answers

27. b.
28. d.
29. c.
30. a.
31. c.

Using Spelling Lists

Some test makers will give you a list of words to study before you take the test. If you have a list to work with, here are some suggestions.

- Divide the list into groups of three, five, or seven words to study. Consider making flash cards of the words you don't know.
- Highlight or circle the tricky elements in each word.
- Cross out or discard any words that you already know for certain. Don't let them get in the way of the ones you need to study.
- Say the words as you read them. Spell them out in your mind so you can hear the spelling.

Here's a sample spelling list. These words are typical of the words that appear on exams. If you are not given a list by the agency that's testing you, study this one.

Ways to Improve Your Vocabulary

- Learn groups of synonyms for words.
- Learn new words in context.
- Memorize common word roots, prefixes, and suffixes.
- Create and use flashcards regularly.

achievement
allege
anxiety
appreciate
asthma
arraignment
autonomous
auxiliary
brief
ballistics
barricade
beauty
beige
business
bureau
calm
cashier
capacity
cancel
circuit
colonel
comparatively
courteous
criticism
custody
cyclical
debt
definitely
descend
doubtful
eligible
enough
enthusiasm
equipped
exception
fascinate
fatigue
forfeit
gauge
grieve
guilt
guarantee
harass
hazard
height
incident
indict
initial
innocent
irreverent
jeopardy
knowledge
leisure
license
lieutenant
maintenance
mathematics
mortgage
ninety
noticeable
occasionally
occurred
offense
official
pamphlet
parallel
personnel
physician
politics
possess
privilege
psychology
recommend
referral
recidivism
salary
schedule
seize
separate
specific
statute
surveillance
suspicious
tentative
thorough
transferred
warrant

How to Answer Spelling Questions

- Sound out the word in your mind. Remember that long vowels inside words usually are followed by single consonants: *sofa*, *total*, *crime*. Short vowels inside words usually are followed by double consonants: *dribble*, *scissors*, *toddler*.
- Give yourself auditory (listening) clues when you learn words. Say *Wed-nes-day* or *lis-ten* or *bus-i-ness* to yourself so that you remember to add the letters you do not hear.
- Look at each part of a word. See if there is a root, prefix, or suffix that will always be spelled the same way. For example, in *uninhabitable*, *un-*, *in-*, and *-able* are always spelled the same. What's left is *habit*, a self-contained root word that's pretty easy to spell.

More Practice in Vocabulary and Spelling

Here is a second set of practice exercises with samples of each kind of question covered in this chapter. Answers to all questions except spelling questions are at the end of the test. For spelling questions, use a dictionary.

Synonyms

Circle the word that means the *same* or nearly the same as the underlined word.

32. <u>convivial</u> company
- **a.** lively
- **b.** dull
- **c.** tiresome
- **d.** dreary

33. <u>conspicuous</u> behavior
- **a.** secret
- **b.** notable
- **c.** visible
- **d.** boorish

34. <u>meticulous</u> record-keeping
- **a.** dishonest
- **b.** casual
- **c.** painstaking
- **d.** careless

35. <u>superficial</u> wounds
- **a.** life-threatening
- **b.** bloody
- **c.** severe
- **d.** shallow

36. <u>impulsive</u> actions
- **a.** cautious
- **b.** imprudent
- **c.** courageous
- **d.** cowardly

Antonyms

Circle the word that is most nearly *opposite* in meaning to the underlined word.

37. <u>amateur</u> athlete
- **a.** professional
- **b.** successful
- **c.** unrivaled
- **d.** former

38. <u>lucid</u> opinions
- **a.** clear
- **b.** strong
- **c.** hazy
- **d.** heartfelt

39. traveling <u>incognito</u>
- **a.** unrecognized
- **b.** alone
- **c.** by night
- **d.** publicly

40. <u>incisive</u> reporting
- **a.** mild
- **b.** sharp
- **c.** dangerous
- **d.** insightful

41. <u>tactful</u> comments
- **a.** rude
- **b.** pleasant
- **c.** complimentary
- **d.** sociable

Synonyms

Using the context, choose the word that means the *same* or nearly the same as the underlined word.

42. Though he had little time, the student took <u>copious</u> notes in preparation for the test.
- **a.** limited
- **b.** plentiful
- **c.** illegible
- **d.** careless

43. Although she was flexible about homework, the teacher was adamant that papers be in on time.
  a. liberal
  b. casual
  c. strict
  d. pliable

44. The suspect's living conditions were deplorable.
  a. regrettable
  b. pristine
  c. festive
  d. tidy

Complete the Sentences

Choose the word that best completes the following sentences.

45. Her position as a(n) ____________________ teacher took her all over the city.
  a. primary
  b. secondary
  c. itinerant
  d. permanent

46. Despite the witness's promise to stay in town, she remained ____________________ and difficult to locate.
  a. steadfast
  b. stubborn
  c. dishonest
  d. elusive

Word Roots, Prefixes, and Suffixes

Choose the word or phrase closest in meaning to the underlined part of the word.

47. universe
  a. one
  b. three
  c. under
  d. opposite

48. reentry
  a. back
  b. push
  c. against
  d. forward

49. benefit
  a. bad
  b. suitable
  c. beauty
  d. good

50. education
  a. something like
  b. state of
  c. to increase
  d. unlike

51. urbanite
  a. resident of
  b. relating to
  c. that which is
  d. possessing

Spelling

Circle the correct spelling of the word that fits in the blank.

52. The information was __________________ to the action.

a. irelevent
b. irrevelent
c. irrelevant
d. irrevelent

53. She made no __________________ to take the job.

a. comittment
b. commitment
c. comitment
d. comittmint

54. He made an income __________________ to meet his needs.

a. adaquate
b. adequate
c. adiquate
d. adequet

55. We were assigned to stake out the _________.

a. restarant
b. restaraunt
c. restaurant
d. resteraunt

56. The vote was __________________ to elect the chairperson.

a. unannimous
b. unanimous
c. unanimus
d. unaminous

Answers

32. a.
33. c.
34. c.
35. d.
36. b.
37. a.
38. c.
39. d.
40. a.
41. a.
42. b.
43. c.
44. a.
45. c.
46. d.
47. a.
48. a.
49. d.
50. b.
51. a.

▶ Additional Resources

One of the best resources for any adult student is the public library. Many libraries have sections for adult learners or for those preparing to enter or change careers. Those sections contain skill books and review books on a number of subjects, including spelling and vocabulary. Here are some books you might consult to improve your vocabulary and spelling skills.

Books

- *Goof-Proof Spelling* (LearningExpress)
- *Practical Spelling, 2nd Edition* (LearningExpress)
- *Practical Vocabulary, 2nd Edition* (LearningExpress)
- *Thirty Days to a More Powerful Vocabulary* by Wilfred John Funk (Pocket Books)
- *Vocabulary and Spelling Success in 20 Minutes a Day, 4th Edition* (LearningExpress)
- *Word Watcher's Handbook: A Deletionary of the Most Abused and Misused Words* by Phyllis Martin (St. Martin's Press)
- *Spelling Made Simple* by Sheila Henderson (Made Simple)
- *Word Smart II, 2nd Edition* by Adam Robinson (The Princeton Review)
- *1001 Vocabulary and Spelling Questions* (LearningExpress)

Websites

- Vocabulary Exercises and Games
  www.vocabulary.com
- 5,000 Words & Definitions to Improve Your Vocabulary
  www.freevocabulary.com
- Daily Vocabulary Quiz
  www.zdaily.com/word.shtml
- Online Dictionary and Spelling Quizzes
  www.merriam-webster.com
- Online Dictionary, Word Games, and Crosswords
  www.dictionary.com
- Online Thesaurus and Word Games
  www.thesaurus.com

CHAPTER

10 Math

CHAPTER SUMMARY

A basic understanding of math will be tested on some police officer exams. This chapter reviews the common types of math questions found on these tests and provides tips and exercises to improve your skills in this area.

As a law enforcement officer, it is not likely that you will be doing complex mathematical formulas, but some basic math skills will most certainly be needed. Adding up the value of stolen property and computing the price of street drugs are just a couple of examples of the type of math problems you will need to be able to solve on the job. Use this chapter to brush up on your basic math skills, especially if it has been a while since you have taken a math course or if you suffer from math anxiety.

▶ Math Strategies

- **Don't work in your head! Use your test book or scratch paper to take notes, draw pictures, and calculate.** Although you might think that you can solve math questions more quickly in your head, that's a good way to make mistakes. Write out each step.
- **Read a math question in chunks rather than straight through from beginning to end.** As you read each chunk, stop to think about what it means and make notes or draw a picture to represent that chunk.
- **When you get to the actual question, circle it.** This will keep you more focused as you solve the problem.
- **Glance at the answer choices for clues.** For example, if they're all fractions, you probably should do your work in fractions; if they're decimals, you should probably work in decimals.
- **Make a plan of attack** to help you solve the problem.
- **If a question stumps you, try one of the backdoor approaches** explained in the next section. These are particularly useful for solving word problems.
- **When you get your answer, reread the circled question to make sure you've answered it.** This helps avoid the careless mistake of answering the wrong question.
- **Check your work after you get an answer.** Test takers get a false sense of security when they get an answer that matches one of the multiple-choice answers. Here are some good ways to check your work if you have time:
  - Ask yourself if your answer is reasonable. Does it make sense?
  - Plug your answer back into the problem to make sure the problem holds together.
  - Do the question a second time, but use a different method.
- **Approximate when appropriate.** For example:
  - \$5.98 + \$8.97 is a little less than \$15. (Add: \$6 + \$9)
  - .9876 × 5.0342 is close to 5. (Multiply: 1 × 5)
- **Skip hard questions and come back to them later.** Mark them in your test book so you can find them quickly.

Backdoor Approaches for Answering Questions that Puzzle You

Remember those word problems you dreaded in high school? Many of them are actually easier to solve by backdoor approaches. The two techniques that follow are terrific ways to solve multiple-choice word problems that you don't know how to solve with a straightforward approach. The first technique, *nice numbers*, is useful when there are unknowns (like x) in the text of the word problem, making the problem too abstract for you. The second technique, *working backward*, presents a quick way to substitute numeric answer choices back into the problem to see which one works.

Nice Numbers

1. When a question contains unknowns, like x, plug nice numbers in for the unknowns. A nice number is easy to calculate with and makes sense in the problem.
2. Read the question with the nice numbers in place. Then solve it.
3. If the answer choices are all numbers, the choice that matches your answer is the correct one.

4. If the answer choices contain unknowns, substitute the same nice numbers into *all* the answer choices. The choice that matches your answer is the right one. If more than one answer matches, do the problem again with different nice numbers. You'll have to check only the answer choices that have already matched.

Example: Judi went shopping with p dollars in her pocket. If the price of shirts was s shirts for d dollars, what is the maximum number of shirts Judi could buy with the money in her pocket?

a. psd **b.** $\frac{ps}{d}$ **c.** $\frac{pd}{s}$ **d.** $\frac{ds}{p}$

To solve this problem, let's try these nice numbers: $p = \$100$, $s = 2$; $d = \$25$. Now reread it with the numbers in place:

Judi went shopping with ***$100*** in her pocket. If the price of shirts was ***2*** shirts for ***$25***, what is the maximum number of shirts Judi could buy with the money in her pocket?

Since 2 shirts cost $25, that means that 4 shirts cost $50, and 8 shirts cost $100. So our answer is ***8***. Let's substitute the nice numbers into all 4 answers:

a. $100 \times 2 \times 25 = 5{,}000$ **b.** $\frac{100 \times 2}{25} = 8$ **c.** $\frac{100 \times 25}{2} = 1{,}250$ **d.** $\frac{25 \times 2}{100} = \frac{1}{2}$

The answer is choice **b** because it is the only one that matches our answer of **8**.

Working Backward

You can frequently solve a word problem by plugging the answer choices back into the text of the problem to see which one fits all the facts stated in the problem. The process is faster than you think because you will probably only have to substitute one or two answers to find the right one.

This approach works only when

- all of the answer choices are numbers, and
- you're asked to find a simple number, not a sum, product, difference, or ratio.

Here's what to do:

1. Look at all the answer choices and begin with the one in the middle of the range. For example, if the answers are 14, 8, 2, 20, and 25, begin by plugging 14 into the problem.
2. If your choice doesn't work, eliminate it. Determine whether you need a bigger or a smaller answer.
3. Plug in one of the remaining choices.
4. If none of the answers work, you may have made a careless error. Begin again or look for your mistake.

Example: Juan ate $\frac{1}{3}$ of the jelly beans. Maria then ate $\frac{3}{4}$ of the remaining jelly beans, which left 10 jelly beans. How many jelly beans were there to begin with?

a. 60 **b.** 80 **c.** 90 **d.** 120 **e.** 140

Starting with the middle answer, let's assume there were **90** jelly beans to begin with:

Since Juan ate $\frac{1}{3}$ of them, that means he ate 30 ($\frac{1}{3} \times 90 = 30$), leaving 60 of them ($90 - 30 = 60$). Maria then ate $\frac{3}{4}$ of the 60 jelly beans, or 45 of them ($\frac{3}{4} \times 60 = 45$). That leaves 15 jelly beans ($60 - 45 = 15$).

The problem states that there were **10** jelly beans left, and we wound up with **15** of them. That indicates that we started with too big a number. Thus, 90, 120, and 140 are all wrong. With only two choices left, let's use common sense to decide which one to try. The next lower answer is only a little smaller than 90 and may not be small enough. So, let's try **60**:

Since Juan ate $\frac{1}{3}$ of them, that means he ate 20 ($\frac{1}{3} \times 60 = 20$), leaving 40 of them ($60 - 20 = 40$). Maria then ate $\frac{3}{4}$ of the 40 jelly beans, or 30 of them ($\frac{3}{4} \times 40 = 30$). That leaves 10 jelly beans ($40 - 30 = 10$).

Because this result of **10** jelly beans agrees with the problem, the right answer is choice **a**.

► Glossary of Terms

Denominator The bottom number in a fraction. **Example:** 2 is the denominator in $\frac{1}{2}$.

Difference Subtract. The difference of two numbers means subtract one number from the other.

Divisible by A number is divisible by a second number if that second number divides *evenly* into the original number. **Example:** 10 is divisible by 5 ($10 \div 5 = 2$, with no remainder). However, 10 is not divisible by 3. (See *multiple of*)

Even integer Integers that are divisible by 2, like . . . −4, −2, 0, 2, 4. . . . (See *integer*)

Integer Numbers along the number line, like . . . −3, −2, −1, 0, 1, 2, 3. . . . Integers include the whole numbers and their opposites. (See *whole number*)

Multiple of A number is a multiple of a second number if that second number can be multiplied by an integer to get the original number. **Example:** 10 is a multiple of 5 ($10 = 5 \times 2$); however, 10 is not a multiple of 3. (See *divisible by*)

Negative number A number that is less than zero, like −1, −18.6, $-\frac{3}{4}$.

Numerator The top part of a fraction. **Example:** 1 is the numerator of $\frac{1}{2}$.

Odd integer Integers that aren't divisible by 2, like . . . −5, −3, −1, 1, 3. . . .

Positive number A number that is greater than zero, like 2, 42, $\frac{1}{2}$, 4.63.

Prime number Integers that are divisible only by 1 and themselves, like 2, 3, 5, 7, 11. . . . All prime numbers are odd, except for 2. The number 1 is not considered prime.

Product Multiply. The product of 2 numbers means the numbers are multiplied together.

Quotient The answer you get when you divide. **Example:** 10 divided by 5 is 2; the quotient is 2.

Real number All the numbers you can think of, like 17, −5, $\frac{1}{2}$, −23.6, 3.4329, 0. Real numbers include integers, fractions, and decimals. (See *integer*)

Remainder The number left over after division. **Example:** 11 divided by 2 is 5, with a remainder of 1.

Sum Add. The sum of two numbers means the numbers are added together.

Whole number Numbers you can count on your fingers, like 1, 2, 3. . . . All whole numbers are positive.

▶ Word Problems

Many of the math problems on tests are word problems. A word problem can include any kind of math, including simple arithmetic, fractions, decimals, percentages, and even algebra and geometry.

The hardest part of any word problem is translating English into math. When you read a problem, you can frequently translate it word for word from English statements into mathematical statements. At other times, however, a key word in the word problem hints at the mathematical operation to be performed. Here are the translation rules:

EQUALS key words: is, are, has

English	*Math*
The rookie **is** 20 years old.	$R = 20$
There **are** 7 hats.	$H = 7$
Officer Judi **has** commendations.	$J = 5$

ADDITION key words: sum; more, greater, or older than; total; all together

English	*Math*
The **sum** of two numbers is 10.	$X + Y = 10$
Karen has $5 **more than** Sam.	$K = 5 + S$
The base is 3″ **greater than** the height.	$B = 3 + H$
Judi is 2 years **older than** Tony.	$J = 2 + T$
The **total** of three numbers is 25.	$A + B + C = 25$
How much do Joan and Tom have **all together**?	$J + T = ?$

SUBTRACTION key words: difference, less or younger than, fewer, remain, left over

English	*Math*
The **difference** between two numbers is 17.	$X - Y = 17$
Mike has 5 **fewer** cats **than** twice the number Jan has.	$M = 2J - 5$
Jay is 2 years **younger than** Brett.	$J = B - 2$
After Carol ate 3 apples, *R* apples **remained.**	$R = A - 3$

MULTIPLICATION key words: of, product, times

English	*Math*
20% **of** the stolen radios	$.20 \times R$
Half **of** the recruits	$\frac{1}{2} \times R$
The **product** of two numbers is 12.	$A \times B = 12$

DIVISION key word: per

English	*Math*
15 drops **per** teaspoon	$\frac{\text{15 drops}}{\text{teaspoon}}$
22 miles **per** gallon	$\frac{\text{22 miles}}{\text{gallon}}$

Distance Formula: Distance = Rate × Time

The key words are movement words like *plane, train, boat, car, walk, run, climb, travel,* and *swim.*

- How far did the **plane travel** in 4 hours if it averaged 300 miles per hour?

  $D = 300 \times 4$

  $D = 1{,}200$ miles
- Ben **walked** 20 miles in 4 hours. What was his average speed?

  $20 = r \times 4$

  5 miles per hour $= r$

Solving a Word Problem Using the Translation Table

Remember the problem at the beginning of this chapter about the jelly beans?

Juan ate $\frac{1}{3}$ of the jelly beans. Maria then ate $\frac{3}{4}$ of the remaining jelly beans, which left 10 jelly beans. How many jelly beans were there to begin with?

a. 60 **b.** 80 **c.** 90 **d.** 120 **e.** 140

We solved it by *working backward.* Now let's solve it using our translation rules.

Assume Juan started with J jelly beans. Eating $\frac{1}{3}$ **of** them means eating $\frac{1}{3} \times J$ jelly beans. Maria ate a fraction of the **remaining** jelly beans, which means we must **subtract** to find out how many are left: $J - \frac{1}{3} \times J = \frac{2}{3} \times J$. Maria then ate $\frac{3}{4}$, leaving $\frac{1}{4}$ **of** the $\frac{2}{3} \times J$ jelly beans, or $\frac{1}{4} \times \frac{2}{3} \times J$ jelly beans. Multiplying out $\frac{1}{4} \times \frac{2}{3} \times J$ gives $\frac{1}{6}J$ as the number of jelly beans left. The problem states that there were **10 jelly beans left**, meaning that we set $\frac{1}{6} \times J$ **equal** to 10:

$$\frac{1}{6} \times J = 10$$

Solving this equation for J gives $J = 60$. Thus, the correct answer is choice **a** (the same answer we got when we *worked backward*). As you can see, both methods—working backward and translating from English to math—work. You should use whichever method is more comfortable for you.

Practice Word Problems

You will find word problems using fractions, decimals, and percentages in those sections of this chapter. For now, practice using the translation table on problems that just require you to work with basic arithmetic.

_____ **1.** Officer Miller pledged three dollars for every mile his son walked in the Police Athletic League walk-a-thon. His son walked nine miles. How much does Officer Miller owe?

a. $3.00 **b.** $12.00 **c.** $18.00 **d.** $27.00 **e.** $36.00

_____ **2.** Officer Brown writes six speeding tickets every week . At this rate, how long will it take for her to write 21 citations?

a. 3 weeks **b.** 4 weeks **c.** 3.5 weeks **d.** 4.75 weeks **e.** 5.5 weeks

3. The precinct clerk can type 80 words per minute. How many minutes will it take him to type a report containing 760 words?

a. 8 **b.** $8\frac{1}{2}$ **c.** 9 **d.** $9\frac{1}{2}$ **e.** 10

4. Chief Wallace is writing a budget request to upgrade his personal computer system. He wants to purchase 4gb of RAM, which will cost $100, two new software programs at $350 each, an external hard drive for $249, and printer ink for $25. What is the total amount Chief Wallace should write on his budget request?

a. $724 **b.** $974 **c.** $1,049 **d.** $1,064 **e.** $1,074

Answers

1. d.
2. c.
3. d.
4. e.

▶ Fraction Review

Problems involving fractions may be straightforward calculation questions, or they may be word problems. Typically, they ask you to add, subtract, multiply, divide, or compare fractions.

Working with Fractions

A fraction is a part of something.

Example: Let's say that a pizza was cut into 8 equal slices and you ate 3 of them. The fraction $\frac{3}{8}$ tells you what part of the pizza you ate. The pizza below shows this: 3 of the 8 pieces (the ones you ate) are shaded.

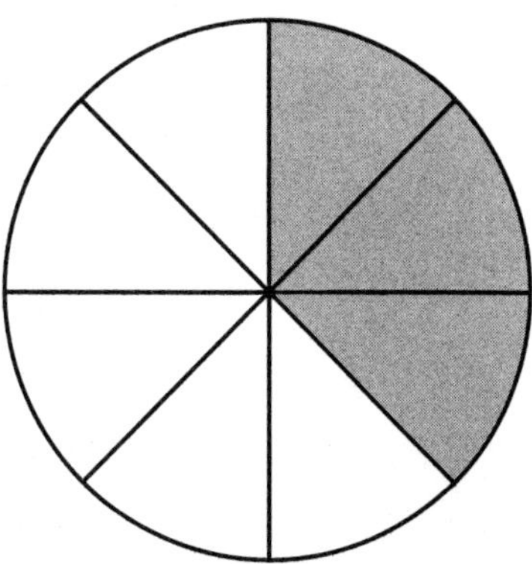

Three Kinds of Fractions

Proper fraction: The top number is less than the bottom number:

$\frac{1}{2}$; $\frac{2}{3}$; $\frac{4}{9}$; $\frac{8}{13}$

The value of a proper fraction is less than 1.

Improper fraction: The top number is greater than or equal to the bottom number:

$\frac{3}{2}$; $\frac{5}{3}$; $\frac{14}{9}$; $\frac{12}{12}$

The value of an improper fraction is 1 or more.

Mixed number: A fraction is written to the right of a whole number:

$3\frac{1}{2}$; $4\frac{2}{3}$; $12\frac{3}{4}$; $24\frac{3}{4}$

The value of a mixed number is more than 1: It is the sum of the whole number plus the fraction.

Changing Improper Fractions into Mixed or Whole Numbers

It's easier to add and subtract fractions that are mixed numbers than those in the form of improper fractions. To change an improper fraction, say $\frac{13}{2}$, into a mixed number, follow these steps:

1. Divide the bottom number (2) into the top number (13) to get the whole number portion (6) of the mixed number:

$$\begin{array}{r} 6 \\ 2\,\overline{)13} \\ -12 \\ \hline 1 \end{array}$$

2. Write the remainder of the division (1) over the old bottom number (2): $6\frac{1}{2}$
3. Check: Change the mixed number back into an improper fraction. (See the following steps.)

Changing Mixed Numbers into Improper Fractions

It's easier to multiply and divide fractions when you are working with improper fractions than with mixed numbers. To change a mixed number, say $2\frac{3}{4}$, into an improper fraction, follow these steps:

1. Multiply the whole number (2) by the bottom number (4): $2 \times 4 = 8$
2. Add the result (8) to the top number (3): $8 + 3 = 11$
3. Put the total (11) over the bottom number (4): $\frac{11}{4}$
4. Check: Reverse the process by changing the improper fraction into a mixed number. If you get back the number you started with, your answer is correct.

Reducing Fractions

Reducing a fraction means writing it in lowest terms, that is, with smaller numbers. For instance, 50¢ is $\frac{50}{100}$ of a dollar, or $\frac{1}{2}$ of a dollar. In fact, if you have a 50¢ piece in your pocket, you say that you have a half dollar. Reducing a fraction does not change its value.

Follow these steps to reduce a fraction:

1. Find a whole number that divides *evenly* into both numbers that make up the fraction (the numerator and the denominator).
2. Divide that number into the top of the fraction, and replace the top of the fraction with the quotient (the answer you got when you divided).
3. Do the same thing to the bottom number.
4. Repeat the first 3 steps until you can't find a number that divides evenly into both numbers of the fraction.

For example, let's reduce $\frac{8}{24}$. We could do it in 2 steps: $\frac{8 \div 4}{24 \div 4} = \frac{2}{6}$; then $\frac{2 \div 2}{6 \div 2} = \frac{1}{3}$. Or we could do it in a single step: $\frac{8 \div 8}{24 \div 8} = \frac{1}{3}$.

Shortcut: When the top and bottom numbers both end in zeros, cross out the same number of zeros in both numbers to begin the reducing process. For example, $\frac{300}{4,000}$ reduces to $\frac{3}{40}$ when you cross out 2 zeros in both numbers.

Whenever you do arithmetic with fractions, reduce your answer. On a multiple-choice test, don't panic if your answer isn't listed. It may mean that you need to reduce it. So try to reduce it and then compare it to the choices.

Reduce the following fractions to lowest terms.

1/6 **5.** $\frac{6}{36}$

6/11 **6.** $\frac{18}{33}$

7/10 **7.** $\frac{35}{50}$

1/6 **8.** $\frac{9}{54}$

2/3 **9.** $\frac{16}{24}$

29/33 **10.** $\frac{58}{66}$

Raising Fractions to Higher Terms

Before you can add and subtract fractions, you have to know how to raise a fraction to higher terms. This is actually the opposite of reducing a fraction.

Follow these steps to raise $\frac{2}{3}$ to 24ths:

1. Divide the old bottom number (3) into the new one (24): $3\overline{)24} = 8$
2. Multiply the answer (8) by the old top number (2): $2 \times 8 = 16$
3. Put the answer (16) over the new bottom number (24): $\frac{16}{24}$
4. Check: Reduce the new fraction to see if you get the original one: $\frac{16 \div 8}{24 \div 8}$

Raise these fractions to higher terms:

______ **11.** $\frac{3}{8} = \frac{}{32}$

______ **12.** $\frac{1}{5} = \frac{}{25}$

______ **13.** $\frac{7}{9} = \frac{}{36}$

______ **14.** $\frac{5}{13} = \frac{}{39}$

______ **15.** $\frac{7}{26} = \frac{}{130}$

______ **16.** $\frac{7}{37} = \frac{}{296}$

Adding Fractions

If the fractions have the same bottom numbers, just add the top numbers together and write the total over the bottom number.

Examples: $\frac{2}{9} + \frac{4}{9} = \frac{2+4}{9} = \frac{6}{9}$ Reduce the sum: $\frac{2}{3}$

$\frac{5}{8} + \frac{7}{8} = \frac{12}{8}$ Change the sum to a mixed number: $1\frac{4}{8}$; then reduce: $1\frac{1}{2}$

There are a few extra steps to add mixed numbers with the same bottom numbers, say $2\frac{3}{5} + 1\frac{4}{5}$:

1. Add the fractions: $\frac{3}{5} + \frac{4}{5} = \frac{7}{5}$
2. Change the improper fraction into a mixed number: $\frac{7}{5} = 1\frac{2}{5}$
3. Add the whole numbers: $2 + 1 = 3$
4. Add the results of steps 2 and 3: $1\frac{2}{5} + 3 = 4\frac{2}{5}$

Finding the Least Common Denominator

If the fractions you want to add don't have the same bottom number, you will have to raise some or all of the fractions to higher terms so that they all have the same bottom number, called the **common denominator**. All of the original bottom numbers divide evenly into the common denominator. If it is the smallest number that they all divide evenly into, it is called the **least common denominator (LCD)**.

Here are a few tips for finding the LCD, the smallest number that all the bottom numbers evenly divide into:

- See if all the bottom numbers divide evenly into the biggest bottom number.
- Check out the multiplication table of the largest bottom number until you find a number that all the other bottom numbers evenly divide into.
- When all else fails, multiply all the bottom numbers together.

Example: $\frac{2}{3} + \frac{4}{5}$

1. Find the LCD. Multiply the bottom numbers: $3 \times 5 = 15$
2. Raise each fraction to 15ths: $\frac{2}{3} = \frac{10}{15}$, $+\ \frac{4}{5} = \frac{12}{15}$
3. Add as usual: $\frac{22}{15}$

Try these addition problems:

______ **17.** $\frac{1}{4} + \frac{1}{3} =$

______ **18.** $\frac{1}{3} + \frac{1}{6} =$

______ **19.** $\frac{1}{4} + \frac{1}{5} + \frac{1}{20} =$

______ **20.** $3\frac{4}{5} + 2\frac{7}{8} =$

______ **21.** $5\frac{2}{7} + 3\frac{5}{8} =$

______ **22.** $3\frac{1}{7} + 5\frac{2}{3} =$

Subtracting Fractions

If the fractions have the same bottom numbers, just subtract the top numbers and write the difference over the bottom number.

Example: $\frac{4}{9} - \frac{3}{9} = \frac{4-3}{9} = \frac{1}{9}$

If the fractions you want to subtract don't have the same bottom number, you will have to raise some or all of the fractions to higher terms so that they all have the same bottom number, or LCD. If you forgot how to find the LCD, just read the section on adding fractions with different bottom numbers.

Example: $\frac{5}{6} - \frac{3}{4}$

1. Raise each fraction to 12ths because 12 is the LCD, the smallest number that 6 and 4 both divide into evenly: $\frac{5}{6} = \frac{10}{12}$
2. Subtract as usual: $-\ \frac{3}{4} = \frac{9}{12}$

$$\frac{1}{12}$$

Subtracting mixed numbers with the same bottom number is similar to adding mixed numbers.

Example: $4\frac{3}{5} - 1\frac{2}{5}$

1. Subtract the fractions: $\frac{3}{5} - \frac{2}{5} = \frac{1}{5}$
2. Subtract the whole numbers: $4 - 1 = 3$
3. Add the results of steps 1 and 2: $\frac{1}{5} + 3 = 3\frac{1}{5}$

Sometimes, there is an extra borrowing step when you subtract mixed numbers with the same bottom numbers, say $7\frac{3}{5} - 2\frac{4}{5}$:

1. You can't subtract the fractions the way they are because $\frac{4}{5}$ is bigger than $\frac{3}{5}$. So you borrow 1 from the 7, making it 6, and change that 1 to $\frac{5}{5}$ because 5 is the bottom number: $7\frac{3}{5} = 6\frac{5}{5} + \frac{3}{5}$
2. Add the numbers from step 1: $6\frac{5}{5} + \frac{3}{5} = 6\frac{8}{5}$
3. Now you have a different version of the original problem: $6\frac{8}{5} - 2\frac{4}{5}$
4. Subtract the fractional parts of the two mixed numbers: $\frac{8}{5} - \frac{4}{5} = \frac{4}{5}$

5. Subtract the whole number parts of the two mixed numbers: $6 - 2 = 4$
6. Add the results of the last two steps together: $4 + \frac{4}{5} = 4\frac{4}{5}$

Try these subtraction problems:

_____ 23. $\frac{1}{4} - \frac{1}{8} =$

_____ 24. $\frac{1}{3} - \frac{1}{9} =$

_____ 25. $\frac{1}{2} - \frac{1}{5} =$

_____ 26. $3\frac{1}{3} - 1\frac{5}{8} =$

_____ 27. $5\frac{4}{9} - 2\frac{2}{3} =$

_____ 28. $4\frac{3}{5} - 2\frac{3}{8} =$

Now let's put what you've learned about adding and subtracting fractions to work in some real-life problems.

_____ 29. To train for her physical ability test, Lori ran $5\frac{1}{2}$ miles on Monday, $6\frac{1}{4}$ miles on Tuesday, $4\frac{1}{2}$ miles on Wednesday, and $2\frac{3}{4}$ miles on Thursday. What is the average number of miles Lori ran each day?

a. 5 b. $4\frac{1}{2}$ c. 4 d. $4\frac{3}{4}$ e. $5\frac{1}{4}$

_____ 30. Officers Perez and Staub are transporting a prisoner from the courthouse to the county jail. The total trip is $54\frac{2}{3}$ miles. If they have completed $23\frac{1}{5}$ miles, how many miles do they have to go?

a. $31\frac{7}{15}$ b. $31\frac{13}{15}$ c. $21\frac{4}{15}$ d. $31\frac{1}{2}$ e. $31\frac{4}{15}$

_____ 31. The precinct is on $1\frac{3}{4}$ acres of land. To expand the precinct, the county plans to buy the adjoining property, which is $2\frac{3}{4}$ acres. How many acres will the precinct sit on after the purchase?

a. $5\frac{1}{4}$ b. $3\frac{3}{4}$ c. $3\frac{1}{2}$ d. $4\frac{1}{2}$ e. $5\frac{1}{2}$

_____ 32. Officer DeRosa kept track of how many overtime hours she worked during the month of August. The first week she worked $4\frac{1}{2}$ hours, the second week $3\frac{3}{4}$ hours, the third week $8\frac{1}{5}$ hours, and the fourth week $1\frac{1}{3}$ hours. How many hours of overtime did she work altogether in the month of August?

a. $17\frac{47}{60}$ b. 16 c. $16\frac{1}{8}$ d. $18\frac{2}{15}$

Multiplying Fractions

Multiplying fractions is actually easier than adding them. All you do is multiply the top numbers and then multiply the bottom numbers.

Examples: $\frac{2}{3} \times \frac{5}{7} = \frac{2 \times 5}{3 \times 7} = \frac{10}{21}$ $\quad \frac{1}{2} \times \frac{3}{5} \times \frac{7}{4} = \frac{1 \times 3 \times 7}{2 \times 5 \times 4} = \frac{21}{40}$

Shortcut: Sometimes you can *cancel* before multiplying. Cancelling is a shortcut that makes the multiplication go faster because you're multiplying with smaller numbers. It's very similar to reducing: If there is a number that divides evenly into both a top number and a bottom number, do that division before multiplying. If you forget to cancel, you will still get the right answer, but you will have to reduce it.

Example: $\frac{5}{6} \times \frac{9}{20}$

1. Cancel the 6 and the 9 by dividing 3 into both of them: $6 \div 3 = 2$ and $9 \div 3 = 3$. Cross out the 6 and the 9: $\frac{5}{\cancel{6}_2} \times \frac{\cancel{9}^3}{20}$
2. Cancel the 5 and the 20 by dividing 5 into both of them: $5 \div 5 = 1$ and $20 \div 5 = 4$. Cross out the 5 and the 20: $\frac{\cancel{5}^1}{\cancel{6}_2} \times \frac{\cancel{9}^3}{\cancel{20}_4}$
3. Multiply across the new top numbers and the new bottom numbers: $\frac{1 \times 3}{2 \times 4} = \frac{3}{8}$

Try these multiplication problems:

______ **33.** $\frac{4}{5} \times \frac{1}{2} =$	______ **36.** $\frac{8}{9} \times \frac{3}{4} =$
______ **34.** $\frac{9}{10} \times \frac{1}{8} =$	______ **37.** $\frac{5}{6} \times \frac{4}{5} =$
______ **35.** $\frac{5}{7} \times \frac{2}{3} =$	______ **38.** $\frac{3}{8} \times \frac{4}{9} =$

To multiply a fraction by a whole number, first rewrite the whole number as a fraction with a bottom number of 1:

Example: $5 \times \frac{2}{3} = \frac{5}{1} \times \frac{2}{3} = \frac{10}{3}$ (Optional: convert $\frac{10}{3}$ to a mixed number: $3\frac{1}{3}$)

To multiply with mixed numbers, it's easier to change them to improper fractions before multiplying.

Example: $4\frac{2}{3} \times 5\frac{1}{2}$

1. Convert $4\frac{2}{3}$ to an improper fraction: $4\frac{2}{3} = \frac{4 \times 3 + 2}{3} = \frac{14}{3}$
2. Convert $5\frac{1}{2}$ to an improper fraction: $5\frac{1}{2} = \frac{5 \times 2 + 1}{2} = \frac{11}{2}$
3. Cancel and multiply the fractions: $\frac{\cancel{14}^7}{3} \times \frac{11}{\cancel{2}_1} = \frac{77}{3}$
4. Optional: Convert the improper fraction to a mixed number: $\frac{77}{3} = 25\frac{2}{3}$

Now try these multiplication problems with mixed numbers and whole numbers:

______ **39.** $4\frac{1}{3} \times \frac{2}{5} =$

______ **40.** $2\frac{1}{2} \times 6 =$

______ **41.** $3\frac{3}{4} \times 4\frac{2}{5} =$

______ **42.** $3\frac{4}{5} \times 3 =$

______ **43.** $5\frac{1}{7} \times 3\frac{2}{5} =$

______ **44.** $6\frac{1}{4} \times \frac{2}{7} =$

Here are a few more real-life problems to test your skills:

______ **45.** After driving $\frac{1}{4}$ of the 27 miles to work, Officer Hamm stopped to get a cup of coffee. How many miles had she driven when she stopped?

a. $6\frac{3}{4}$ **b.** $6\frac{1}{2}$ **c.** $5\frac{3}{4}$ **d.** 7 **e.** $7\frac{1}{4}$

______ **46.** Officer Henry worked a 66-hour work week, of which $\frac{1}{3}$ of the hours were overtime. How many hours of overtime did Officer Henry work?

a. 6 **b.** 11 **c.** 20 **d.** $20\frac{1}{2}$ **e.** 22

______ **47.** In 2004, there were 715 auto thefts in Rose County. In 2005, there were only $\frac{2}{5}$ as many. How many auto thefts were there in Rose County in 2005?

a. 143 **b.** 286 **c.** 385 **d.** 429 **e.** 485

______ **48.** Officer Amis worked $\frac{4}{5}$ of the days last year. How many days did he work? (1 year = 365 days)

a. 273 **b.** 281 **c.** 292 **d.** 300 **e.** 312

Dividing Fractions

To divide one fraction by a second fraction, invert the second fraction (that is, flip the top and bottom numbers) and then multiply. That's all there is to it!

Example: $\frac{1}{2} \div \frac{3}{5}$

1. Invert the second fraction ($\frac{3}{5}$): $\frac{5}{3}$
2. Change the division sign (÷) to a multiplication sign (×): $\frac{1}{2} \times \frac{5}{3}$
3. Multiply the first fraction by the new second fraction: $\frac{1}{2} \times \frac{5}{3} = \frac{1 \times 5}{2 \times 3} = \frac{5}{6}$

To divide a fraction by a whole number, first change the whole number to a fraction by putting it over 1. Then follow the division steps above.

Example: $\frac{3}{5} \div 2 = \frac{3}{5} \div \frac{2}{1} = \frac{3}{5} \times \frac{1}{2} = \frac{3 \times 1}{5 \times 2} = \frac{3}{10}$

When the division problem has a mixed number, convert it to an improper fraction and then divide as usual.

Example: $2\frac{3}{4} \div \frac{1}{6}$

1. Convert $2\frac{3}{4}$ to an improper fraction: $2\frac{3}{4} = \frac{2 \times 4 + 3}{4} = \frac{11}{4}$

2. Divide $\frac{11}{4}$ by $\frac{1}{6}$: $\frac{11}{4} \div \frac{1}{6} = \frac{11}{4} \times \frac{6}{1}$

3. Flip $\frac{1}{6}$ to $\frac{6}{1}$, change ÷ to ×, cancel and multiply: $\frac{11}{\cancel{4}_2} \times \frac{\cancel{6}^3}{1} = \frac{11 \times 3}{2 \times 1} = \frac{33}{2}$

Here are some division problems to try:

_____ **49.** $\frac{3}{4} \div \frac{2}{3} =$

_____ **50.** $4\frac{1}{4} \div \frac{1}{3} =$

_____ **51.** $\frac{2}{3} \div 5 =$

_____ **52.** $6\frac{6}{11} \div 1\frac{1}{5} =$

_____ **53.** $\frac{5}{8} \div \frac{5}{8} =$

_____ **54.** $5\frac{1}{6} \div \frac{2}{3} =$

Let's wrap this up with some real-life problems.

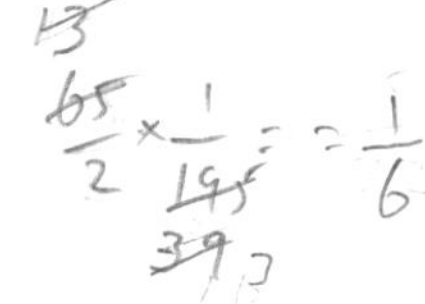

_____ **55.** Lucy worked $32\frac{1}{2}$ hours last week and earned \$195. What is her hourly wage?
a. \$5.00 **b.** \$6.00 **c.** \$6.09 **d.** \$7.00 **e.** \$7.35

_____ **56.** Officers Feliciano and Wolny arrested George Rodney for possession of 28 ounces of marijuana, separated into a number of $3\frac{1}{2}$-ounce packages. How many packages of marijuana were in Rodney's possession?
a. 2 **b.** 4 **c.** 6 **d.** 8 **e.** 10

_____ **57.** Officer Talis has the flu. If four officers evenly split his $6\frac{1}{2}$ hours of work to cover for him, how many extra hours must each officer work?
a. $\frac{8}{13}$ **b.** $1\frac{5}{8}$ **c.** $1\frac{1}{2}$ **d.** $1\frac{5}{13}$ **e.** 4

_____ **58.** The Police Athletic League is hosting a bingo night fundraiser and will give away \$2,400 in prize money. The first winner of the night will receive $\frac{1}{3}$ of the money. The next ten winners will each receive $\frac{1}{10}$ of the remaining amount. How much prize money will each of the ten winners receive?
a. \$160 **b.** \$200 **c.** \$240 **d.** \$700 **e.** \$800

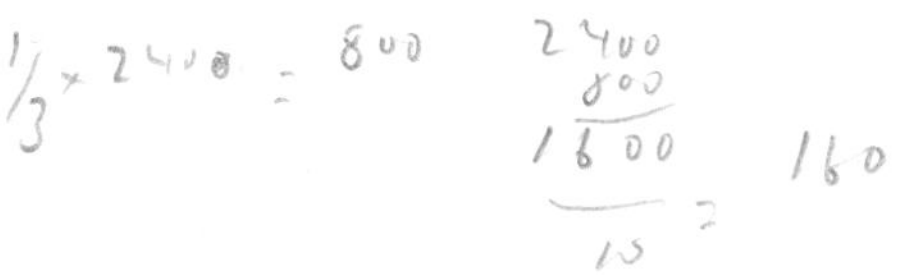

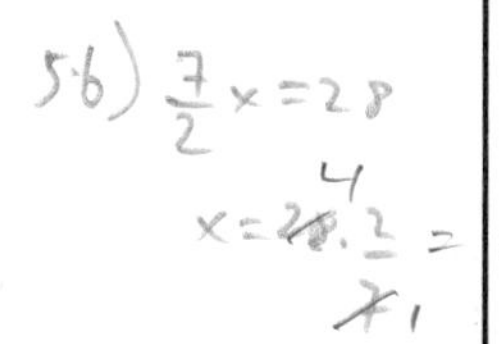

Answers

5. $\frac{1}{6}$
6. $\frac{6}{11}$
7. $\frac{7}{10}$
8. $\frac{1}{6}$
9. $\frac{2}{3}$
10. $\frac{29}{33}$
11. 12
12. 5
13. 28
14. 15
15. 35
16. 56
17. $\frac{7}{12}$
18. $\frac{1}{2}$
19. $\frac{1}{2}$
20. $6\frac{27}{40}$
21. $8\frac{51}{56}$
22. $8\frac{17}{21}$
23. $\frac{1}{8}$
24. $\frac{2}{9}$
25. $\frac{3}{10}$
26. $1\frac{17}{24}$
27. $2\frac{7}{9}$
28. $2\frac{9}{40}$
29. d.
30. a.
31. d.
32. a.
33. $\frac{2}{5}$
34. $\frac{9}{80}$
35. $\frac{10}{21}$
36. $\frac{2}{3}$
37. $\frac{2}{3}$
38. $\frac{1}{6}$
39. $\frac{26}{15}$ or $1\frac{11}{15}$
40. 15
41. $\frac{33}{2}$ or $\frac{16}{2}$
42. $\frac{57}{5}$ or $11\frac{2}{5}$
43. $6\frac{12}{35}$ or $17\frac{17}{35}$
44. $\frac{25}{14}$ or $1\frac{11}{14}$
45. a.
46. e.
47. b.
48. c.
49. $\frac{9}{8}$ or $1\frac{1}{8}$
50. $\frac{51}{4}$ or $12\frac{3}{4}$
51. $\frac{10}{3}$ or $3\frac{1}{3}$
52. $\frac{60}{11}$ or $5\frac{5}{11}$
53. $\frac{1}{1}$ or 1
54. $\frac{31}{4}$ or $7\frac{3}{4}$
55. b.

▶ Decimals

What Is a Decimal?

A decimal is a special kind of fraction. You use decimals every day when you deal with money—\$10.35 is a decimal that represents 10 dollars and 35 cents. The decimal point separates the dollars from the cents. Because there are 100 cents in one dollar, 1¢ is $\frac{1}{100}$ of a dollar, or \$.01.

Each decimal place to the right of the decimal point has a name:

Example: .1 = 1 tenth = $\frac{1}{10}$
.02 = 2 hundredths = $\frac{2}{100}$
.003 = 3 thousandths = $\frac{3}{1{,}000}$
.0004 = 4 ten-thousandths = $\frac{4}{10{,}000}$

When you add zeros after the rightmost decimal place, you don't change the value of the decimal. For example, 6.17 is the same as all of these:

6.170
6.1700
6.17000000000000000

If there are digits on both sides of the decimal point (such as 10.35), the number is called a *mixed decimal.* If there are digits only to the right of the decimal point (such as .53), the number is simply called a *decimal.* A whole number (such as 15) is understood to have a decimal point at its right (15.). Thus, 15 is the same as 15.0, 15.00, 15.000, and so on.

Changing Fractions to Decimals

To change a fraction to a decimal, divide the bottom number into the top number after you put a decimal point and a few zeros on the right of the top number. When you divide, bring the decimal point up into your answer.

Example: Change $\frac{3}{4}$ to a decimal.

1. Add a decimal point and 2 zeros to the top number (3): 3.00
2. Divide the bottom number (4) into 3.00:
   Bring the decimal point up into the answer:

$$\begin{array}{r} .75 \\ 4\overline{)3.00} \\ \underline{2\,8} \\ 20 \\ \underline{20} \\ 0 \end{array}$$

3. The quotient (result of the division) is the answer: .75

Some fractions may require you to add many decimal zeros in order for the division to come out evenly. In fact, when you convert a fraction like $\frac{2}{3}$ to a decimal, you can keep adding decimal zeros to the top number forever because the division will never come out evenly. As you divide 3 into 2, you will keep getting 6's:

$$2 \div 3 = .6666666666\ldots$$

This is called a **repeating decimal** and it can be written as $.66\overline{6}$ or as $.66\frac{2}{3}$. You can approximate it as .67, .667, .6667, and so on.

Changing Decimals to Fractions

To change a decimal to a fraction, write the digits of the decimal as the top number of a fraction and write the decimal's name as the bottom number of the fraction. Then reduce the fraction, if possible.

Example: .018

1. Write 18 as the top of the fraction: $\frac{18}{}$
2. Three places to the right of the decimal means *thousandths,* so write 1000 as the bottom number: $\frac{18}{1000}$
3. Reduce by dividing 2 into the top and bottom numbers: $\frac{18 \div 2}{1000 \div 2} = \frac{9}{500}$

Change the following decimals or mixed decimals to fractions. The answers can be found at the end of this section on page 198

_____**59.** .008

_____**60.** 2.58

_____**61.** 127.586

_____**62.** .090

_____**63.** .0006

_____**64.** 1.00

Comparing Decimals

Because decimals are easier to compare when they have the same number of digits after the decimal point, tack zeros onto the end of the shorter decimals. Then all you have to do is compare the numbers as if the decimal points weren't there.

Example: Compare .08 and .1

1. Tack one zero at the end of .1: .10
2. To compare .10 to .08, just compare 10 to 8.
3. Since 10 is larger than 8, .1 is larger than .08.

Adding and Subtracting Decimals

To add or subtract decimals, line them up so their decimal points are aligned. You may want to tack on zeros at the ends of shorter decimals so you can keep all your digits evenly lined up. Remember, if a number doesn't have a decimal point, then put one at the end of the number.

Example: 1.23 + 57 + .038

1. Line up the numbers like this:

```
    1.230
   57.000
 +   .038
 --------
```

2. Add: 58.268

Example: 1.23 − .038

1. Line up the numbers like this:

```
   1.230
 -  .038
 -------
```

2. Subtract: 1.192

Try these addition and subtraction problems:

_____**65.** .326 + .57 + 96.08

_____**66.** .009 + 15 + .7

_____**67.** .015 +3.49 + 8 + .07

_____**68.** 4.33 − 2.56

_____**69.** 30.41 − 19.73

_____**70.** 121.06 − 98.34

71. Officer Peterson drove 6.3 miles to the state park. He then walked .8 miles around the park to make sure everything was all right. He got back into the car, drove 4.33 miles to check on a broken traffic light, and then drove 3 miles back to the police station. How many miles did he drive in total?

a. 14.03 **b.** 13.43 **c.** 14.43 **d.** 15 **e.** 15.43

72. The average number of burglaries in Millbrook fell from 63.7 per week to 59.5 per week. By how many burglaries per week did the average fall?

a. 4.2 **b.** 3.3 **c.** 4.1 **d.** 5.2 **e.** 4.9

Multiplying Decimals

To multiply decimals, ignore the decimal points and just multiply the numbers. Then count the total number of decimal digits (the digits to the right of the decimal point) in the numbers you are multiplying. Count off that number of digits in your answer beginning at the right side and put the decimal point to the left of those digits.

Example: 215.7 × 2.4

1. Multiply 2157 times 24:

$$\begin{array}{r} 2157 \\ \times\ 24 \\ \hline 8628 \\ 4314 \\ \hline 51768 \end{array}$$

2. Because there are a total of 2 decimal digits in 215.7 and 2.4, count off 2 places from the right in 51768, placing the decimal point to the *left* of the last 2 digits: 517.68

If your answer doesn't have enough digits, tack zeros on to the left of the answer.

Example: .03 × .006

1. Multiply 3 times 6: 3 × 6 = 18
2. You need 5 decimal digits in your answer, so tack on 3 zeros: 00018
3. Put the decimal point at the front of the number (which is 5 digits in from the right): .00018

You can practice multiplying decimals with the following problems.

______ **73** .17 × .39

______ **74.** 1.4 × 6.92

______ **75.** 192 × .46

______ **76.** Officer Joe earns $14.50 per hour. Last week, he worked 37.5 hours. How much money did he earn that week?

a. $518.00 **b.** $518.50 **c.** $525.00 **d.** $536.50 **e.** $543.75

______ **77.** Officer Jay bought 25 $0.39 stamps. How much did he spend?

a. $7.45 **b.** $7.95 **c.** $8.55 **d.** $9.75 **e.** $10.15

______ **78.** A full box of bullets costs $7.50. Approximately how much will 5.25 boxes of bullets cost?

a. $38.00 **b.** $38.50 **c.** $39.00 **d.** $39.38 **e.** $41.00

Dividing Decimals

To divide a decimal by a whole number, set up the division ($8\overline{).256}$) and immediately bring the decimal point straight up into the answer ($8\overline{)\dot{.}256}$). Then divide as you would normally divide whole numbers:

Example:

$$
\begin{array}{r}
.032 \\
8\overline{)\,.256} \\
-0 \\
\hline
25 \\
-24 \\
\hline
16 \\
-16 \\
\hline
0
\end{array}
$$

To divide any number by a decimal, you must perform an extra step before you can divide. Move the decimal point to the very right of the number you are dividing by, counting the number of places you are moving it. Then move the decimal point the same number of places to the right in the number you are dividing into. In other words, first change the problem to one in which you are dividing by a whole number.

Example: $.06\overline{)1.218}$

1. Because there are two decimal digits in .06, move the decimal point two places to the right in both numbers and move the decimal point straight up into the answer: .06.)1.21.8
2. Divide using the new numbers:

$$\begin{array}{r} 20.3 \\ 6\overline{)121.8} \\ -12 \\ \hline 01 \\ -00 \\ \hline 18 \\ -18 \\ \hline 0 \end{array}$$

Under certain conditions, you have to add zeros to the right of the last decimal digit in a number you are dividing into:

- if there aren't enough digits for you to move the decimal point to the right
- if the answer doesn't come out evenly when you do the division
- if you are dividing a whole number by a decimal, you will have to tack on the decimal point as well as some zeros

Try your skills on these division problems:

____ **79.** .5)10

____ **80.** .19)3.61

____ **81.** .06)0.9636

____ **82.** .42)1.3734

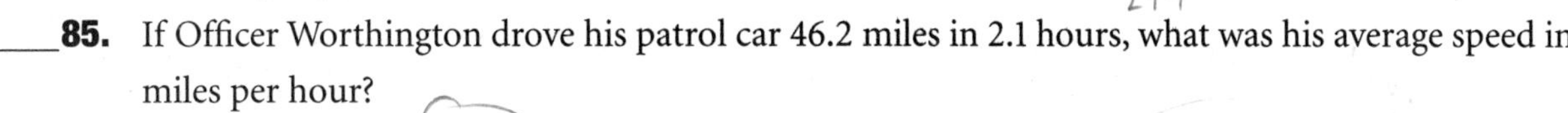

____ **85.** If Officer Worthington drove his patrol car 46.2 miles in 2.1 hours, what was his average speed in miles per hour?

a. 21 **b.** 22 **c.** 44.1 **d.** 48.3 **e.** 97.02

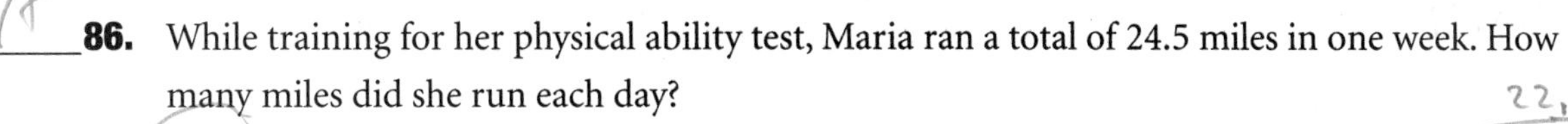

____ **86.** While training for her physical ability test, Maria ran a total of 24.5 miles in one week. How many miles did she run each day?

a. 3.5 **b.** 3.75 **c.** 4.5 **d.** 17.5 **e.** 31.5

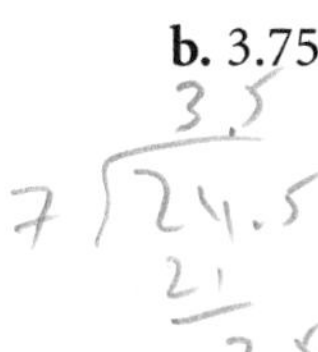

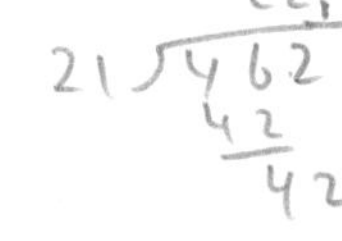

Answers

59. $\frac{8}{1,000}$ or $\frac{1}{125}$
60. $2\frac{58}{100}$ or $2\frac{29}{50}$
61. $127\frac{586}{1,000}$ or $127\frac{293}{500}$
62. $\frac{9}{100}$
63. $\frac{6}{10,000}$ or $\frac{3}{5,000}$
64. $\frac{1}{1}$
65. 96.976
66. 15.709
67. 11.575
68. 1.77
69. 10.68
70. 22.72
71. c.
72. a.
73. 0.0663
74. 9.688
75. 88.32
76. e.
77. d.
78. d.
79. 20
80. 19
81. 16.06
82. 3.27
83. 3.4
84. 10,400
85. b.
86. a.

▶ Percents

What Is a Percent?

A percent is a special kind of fraction. The denominator is always 100. For example, 17% is the same as $\frac{17}{100}$. Literally, the word *percent* means *per 100 parts*. The root cent means 100: A century is 100 years, there are 100 cents in a dollar, etc. Thus, 17% means 17 parts out of 100. Because fractions can also be expressed as decimals, 17% is also equivalent to .17, which is 17 hundredths.

You come into contact with percents every day. Sales tax, interest, and discounts are just a few common examples.

If you are shaky on fractions, you may want to review the fraction section before reading further.

Changing a Decimal to a Percent and Vice Versa

To change a decimal to a percent, move the decimal point two places to the **right** and add a percent sign (%) at the end. If the decimal point moves to the very right of the number, you don't have to write the decimal point. If there aren't enough places to move the decimal point, add zeros on the **right** before moving the decimal point.

To change a percent to a decimal, drop off the percent sign and move the decimal point two places to the left. If there aren't enough places to move the decimal point, add zeros on the **left** before moving the decimal point.

Try changing the following decimals to percents. The answers can be found at the end of this section on page 203

_____ **87.** .31

_____ **88.** .005

_____ **89.** $.13\frac{4}{5}$

_____ **90.** 2.25

Now change these percents to decimals:

_____ **91.** 32%

_____ **92.** $53\frac{1}{4}\%$

_____ **93.** 420%

_____ **94.** .33%

Changing a Fraction to a Percent and Vice Versa

To change a fraction to a percent, there are two techniques. Each is illustrated by changing the fraction $\frac{1}{4}$ to a percent:

Technique 1: Multiply the fraction by 100%.
Multiply $\frac{1}{4}$ by 100%:

$$\frac{1}{\cancel{4}_{1}} \times \frac{\overset{25}{\cancel{100\%}}}{1} = 25\%$$

Technique 2: Divide the fraction's bottom number into the top number; then move the decimal point two places to the **right** and tack on a percent sign (%).
Divide 4 into 1 and move the decimal point 2 places to the right:

$$4\overline{)1.00}^{\,.25} \quad .25 = 25\%$$

To change a percent to a fraction, remove the percent sign and write the number over 100. Then reduce if possible.

Example: Change 4% to a fraction.

1. Remove the % and write the fraction 4 over 100: $\frac{4}{100}$
2. Reduce: $\frac{4 \div 4}{100 \div 4} = \frac{1}{25}$

Here's a more complicated example: Change $16\frac{2}{3}\%$ to a fraction.

1. Remove the % and write the fraction $16\frac{2}{3}$ over 100: $\frac{16\frac{2}{3}}{100}$
2. Since a fraction means "top number divided by bottom number," rewrite the fraction as a division problem: $16\frac{2}{3} \div 100$
3. Change the mixed number ($16\frac{2}{3}$) to an improper fraction ($\frac{50}{3}$): $\frac{50}{3} \div \frac{100}{1}$
4. Flip the second fraction ($\frac{100}{1}$) and multiply: $\frac{\overset{1}{\cancel{50}}}{3} \times \frac{1}{\cancel{100}_{2}} = \frac{1}{6}$

Try changing these fractions to percents:

______ **95.** $\frac{6}{50}$

______ **96.** $\frac{9}{20}$

______ **97.** $\frac{8}{10}$

______ **98.** $\frac{3}{25}$

Now change these percents to fractions:

______ **99.** 47%

______ **100.** 10%

______ **101.** 0.8%

______ **102.** 73.5%

Sometimes, it is more convenient to work with a percentage as a fraction or a decimal. Rather than having to calculate the equivalent fraction or decimal, consider memorizing the following conversion table. Not only will this increase your efficiency on the math section of your written exam, but it will also be practical for reallife situations.

CONVERSION TABLE

DECIMAL	%	FRACTION
.25	25%	$\frac{1}{4}$
.50	50%	$\frac{1}{2}$
.75	75%	$\frac{3}{4}$
.10	10%	$\frac{1}{10}$
.20	20%	$\frac{1}{5}$
.40	40%	$\frac{2}{5}$
.60	60%	$\frac{3}{5}$
.80	80%	$\frac{4}{5}$
$.3\overline{33}$	$33\frac{1}{3}\%$	$\frac{1}{3}$
$.6\overline{66}$	$66\frac{2}{3}\%$	$\frac{2}{3}$

Percent Word Problems

Word problems involving percents come in three main varieties:

- Find a percent of a whole.
  Example: What is 30% of 40?
- Find what percent one number is of another number.
  Example: 12 is what percent of 40?
- Find the whole when the percent of it is given.
  Example: 12 is 30% of what number?

While each variety has its own approach, there is a single shortcut formula you can use to solve each of these:

$$\frac{is}{of} = \frac{\%}{100}$$

The ***is*** is the number that usually follows, or is just before, the word ***is*** in the question.
The ***of*** is the number that usually follows the word ***of*** in the question.
The **%** is the number that is in front of the **%** or ***percent*** in the question.

Or you may think of the shortcut formula as:

$$\frac{part}{whole} = \frac{\%}{100}$$

To solve each of the three varieties, we are going to use the fact that the **cross products** are equal. The cross products are the products of the numbers diagonally across from each other. Remembering that *product* means *multiply*, here's how to create the cross products for the percent shortcut:

$$\frac{part}{whole} = \frac{\%}{100}$$

$$part \times 100 = whole \times \%$$

Here's how to use the shortcut with cross products:

- Find a percent of a whole.

  What is 30% of 40?

  30 is the % and 40 is the *of* number: $\frac{is}{40} = \frac{30}{100}$

  Cross-multiply and solve for *is*:

  $is \times 100 = 40 \times 30$

  $is \times 100 = 1200$

  $\mathbf{12} \times 100 = 1{,}200$

  Thus, **12 *is*** 30% of 40.

- Find what percent one number is of another number.

  12 is what percent of 40?

  12 is the *is* number and 40 is the *of* number: $\frac{12}{40} = \frac{\%}{100}$

  Cross-multiply and solve for %:

  $12 \times 100 = 40 \times \%$

  $1{,}200 = 40 \times \%$

  $1{,}200 = 40 \times \mathbf{30}$

  Thus, 12 is **30%** of 40.

- Find the whole when the percent of it is given.

  12 is 30% of what number?

  12 is the *is* number and 30 is the %: $\frac{12}{\textit{of}} = \frac{30}{100}$

  Cross-multiply and solve for the *of* number: $12 \times 100 = \textit{of} \times 30$

  $1{,}200 = \textit{of} \times 30$

  $1{,}200 = \mathbf{40} \times 30$

  Thus, 12 is 30% ***of* 40**.

You can use the same technique to find the percent increase or decrease. The *is* number is the actual increase or decrease, and the *of* number is the original amount.

Example: If a uniform supply store put its $20 hats on sale for $15, by what percent does the selling price decrease?

1. Calculate the decrease, the *is* number: $\$20 - \$15 = \$5$
2. The *of* number is the original amount, $20:
3. Set up the equation and solve for *of* by cross-multiplying: $\frac{5}{20} = \frac{\%}{100}$

   $5 \times 100 = 20 \times \%$

   $500 = 20 \times \%$

   $500 = 20 \times \mathbf{25}$
4. Thus, the selling price is decreased by **25%**.

   If the store later raises the price of the hats from $15 back to $20, don't be fooled into thinking that the percent increase is also 25%! It's actually more, because the increase amount of $5 is now based on a lower original price of only $15:

   $\frac{5}{15} = \frac{\%}{100}$

   $5 \times 100 = 15 \times \%$

   $500 = 15 \times \%$

   $500 = 15 \times \mathbf{33\frac{1}{3}}$

   Thus, the selling price is increased by $33\frac{1}{3}$%.

Find a percent of a whole:

______**103.** 1% of 50

______**104.** 17% of 150

______**105.** $32\frac{1}{4}$% of 200

______**106.** 78.2% of 1,745

Find what percent one number is of another number:

_____ **107.** 12 is what % of 40?

_____ **108.** 3 is what % of 12?

_____ **109.** 12 is what % of 3?

_____ **110.** 7 is what % of 35?

Find the whole when the percent of it is given:

_____ **111.** 20% of what number is 12?

_____ **112.** $32\frac{1}{2}$% of what number is 19.5?

_____ **113.** 400% of what number is 40?

_____ **114.** 75% of what number is $67\frac{1}{2}$?

Now try your percent skills on some real-life problems.

_____ **115.** Last Monday, 15% of the 200-member police department was absent. How many staff members were absent that day?

a. 15 **b.** 20 **c.** 30 **d.** 185 **e.** 215

_____ **116.** 30% of Cape Rose's police department employees are women. If there are 90 women in Cape Rose's police department, how many men are employed there?

a. 27 **b.** 60 **c.** 120 **d.** 210 **e.** 300

_____ **117.** Of the 760 crimes committed last month, 76 involved petty theft. What percent of the crimes involved petty theft?

a. .01% **b.** 1% **c.** 10% **d.** 76% **e.** .76%

Answers

87. 31%
88. 0.5%
89. 13.8% or $13\frac{4}{5}$%
90. 225%
91. 0.32
92. 0.5325
93. 4.2%
94. .0033
95. 12%
96. 45%
97. 80%
98. 12%
99. $\frac{47}{100}$
100. $\frac{1}{10}$
101. $\frac{1}{125}$
102. $\frac{147}{200}$
103. $\frac{1}{2}$ or .5
104. 25.5
105. 64.5
106. 1,364.59
107. 30%
108. 25%
109. 400%
110. 20%
111. 60
112. 60
113. 10
114. 90
115. c.
116. d.
117. c.

▶ Averages

What Is an Average?

An average, also called an *arithmetic mean,* is a number that typifies a group of numbers, and is a measure of central tendency. You come into contact with averages on a regular basis: your bowling average, the average grade on a test, the average number of hours you work per week.

To calculate an average, add up each item being averaged and divide by the total number of items.

Example: What is the average of 6, 10, and 20?

Solution: Add the three numbers together and divide by 3: $\frac{6 + 10 + 20}{3} = 12$

Shortcut

Here's a neat shortcut for some average problems.

- Look at the numbers being averaged. If they are equally spaced, like 5, 10, 15, 20, and 25, then the average is the number in the middle, or 15 in this case.
- If there are an even number of such numbers, say 10, 20, 30, and 40, then there is no middle number. In this case, the average is halfway between the two middle numbers. In this case, the average is halfway between 20 and 30, or 25.
- If the numbers are almost evenly spaced, you can probably estimate the average without going to the trouble of actually computing it. For example, the average of 10, 20, and 32 is just a little more than 20, the middle number.

Try these average questions:

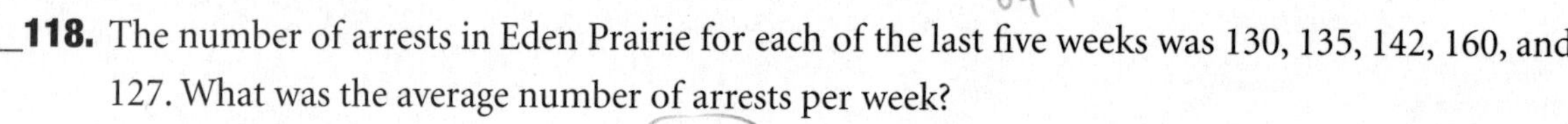

_____ **118.** The number of arrests in Eden Prairie for each of the last five weeks was 130, 135, 142, 160, and 127. What was the average number of arrests per week?

a. 127 **b.** 135 **c.** 139 **d.** 140 **e.** 160

_____ **119.** Officer Bellini averaged 45 miles an hour for the three hours she drove in town and 55 miles an hour for the three hours she drove on the highway. What was her average speed in miles per hour?

a. 30 **b.** 45 **c.** 49 **d.** 50 **e.** 100

_____ **120.** There are 10 females and 20 males in the academy first aid course. If the females achieved an average score of 85 and the males achieved an average score of 95, what was the academy average? (Hint: Don't fall for the trap of taking the average of 85 and 95; there are more 95s being averaged than 85s, so the average is closer to 95.)

a. $90\frac{2}{3}$ **b.** $91\frac{2}{3}$ **c.** 92 **d.** $92\frac{2}{3}$ **e.** 95

B **121.** A national park keeps track of how many people enter the park in each car. Today, 57 cars had 4 people, 61 cars had 2 people, 9 cars had 1 person, and 5 cars had 5 people. What is the average number of people per car? Round to the nearest person.

a. 2 **b.** 3 **c.** 4 **d.** 5 **e.** 6

57 – 4 = 228
61 – 2 = 122
9 – 1 = 9
5 – 5 = 25
132 132/384

Answers

118. c.
119. d.
120. b.
121. e.

▶ Additional Resources

If you feel that you need a more in-depth review of math, you can get a private tutor, take classes at your local community college, obtain a math book or two to review on your own, or visit websites that offer math practice exercises. Call your community's high school for their list of qualified math tutors, or check with local colleges for the names of professional tutors and advanced math students who can help you. Don't forget to ask the schools you call for their adult education schedule. The yellow pages and the classified section of your city's newspaper are other excellent sources for locating tutors, learning centers, and educational consultants.

If you'd rather work on your own, you'll find many superb math review books at your local bookstore or library. You can also find plenty of math-related websites to help improve your math skills.

Books

- *501 Algebra Questions, 2nd Edition* (LearningExpress)
- *501 Geometry Questions* (LearningExpress)
- *501 Math Word Problems* (LearningExpress)
- *Algebra Success in 20 Minutes a Day, 2nd Edition* (LearningExpress)
  Covers all the basics of algebra, including easy-to-follow examples and practice exercises.
- *Math Essentials, 3rd Edition* (LearningExpress)
  If you have trouble with fractions, decimals, or percents, this book offers an easy, step-by-step review.
- *1,001 Math Problems, 2nd Edition* (LearningExpress)
  Offers readers 1,001 practice problems to help improve basic math skills.
- *Practical Math Success in 20 Minutes a Day, 3rd Edition* (LearningExpress)
  Provides review of basic math skills and easy-to-follow examples with opportunities for practice.

Websites

- The Math Forum
  http://mathforum.org/
- Professor Freedman's Math Help
  www.mathpower.com
- Solving Math Word Problems
  www.studygs.net/mathproblems
- Advice about Taking Math Exams
  www.studygs.net/
- Math Reference Tables
  www.math.com/tables/index.html
- Practice Math Problems Online
  www.mathbiz.com

CHAPTER

11 Judgment

CHAPTER SUMMARY

This chapter shows you how to deal with exam questions that test your judgment and common sense. Reading carefully and learning to think like a police officer are the keys to doing well on these types of questions.

Walk into any police academy around the country and you are likely to see the following words emblazoned across a wall: "Common Sense and Good Judgment." While it might seem obvious that a police officer needs common sense and good judgment, not everyone has these traits, and some people who do have them need to be reminded to use them. Police agencies need to have some way of determining who has these traits. Therefore, you will probably encounter questions that test your judgment either on a multiple-choice exam or on a situational video exam. On a written exam, judgment questions are designed to see if you can make a sound decision—pick the right multiple-choice answer—based on the information given to you. To come to the right conclusion, you will need your common sense, good judgment, and good reading skills.

Most judgment questions on written exams fall into three categories: situational judgment, application of rules and procedures, and judgment based on eyewitness accounts. This chapter will look at each category, take apart an example of each type of judgment question, and then identify the best approach to answering the question. There are also tips on what is most likely to trip up the unwary test taker.

In addition to judgment questions on multiple-choice exams, you may encounter a video exam that shows you a situation and asks you to use your judgment skills when responding to it. This chapter will explain this type of video exam and provide tips on how to do your best on the exam.

▶ Situational Judgment Questions

Situational judgment questions ask you to climb inside the mind of a police officer and make decisions from this viewpoint. It isn't necessary for you to know the laws of any state or the policies and procedures of any law enforcement agency. The test itself will give you the information you need to answer the question.

Some exams put you right into the hot seat with language such as, "You are on patrol in a high-crime area. . ." while other exams use a more subtle approach: "Officer Jones is on patrol when she sees a man breaking into a car." Although the approach is different, both test makers are asking you to look at their questions from the same viewpoint—a police officer's view.

The structure of situational judgment questions is quite simple. You will be given a situation, and then you will be asked to choose how you would handle the situation if you were the police officer responding to that call. The nice part is that you don't have to come up with your own plan. You get to choose the best answer from four multiple-choice options that follow the question. Keep in mind that there is only *one* best answer.

Here's an example:

1. Officer Granderson is directing traffic at a busy intersection after the end of a baseball game near the stadium. A small car stalls and the driver can't restart the engine. He is blocking the one lane of traffic leading out of the stadium area. There is a shoulder next to each lane of traffic on this flat roadway. What should Officer Granderson do?

a. Call for a tow truck to move the vehicle.
b. Push the car onto the shoulder of the road so that the other traffic may proceed.
c. Tell the driver to keep trying to start the engine with the hope that the car will start after a brief wait.
d. Direct traffic around the stalled vehicle by having the cars drive on the shoulder of the road.

In this situation, all of the options could conceivably happen, but only one choice is the best answer. The best way to approach this type of question is to start by eliminating the choices that you know aren't going to work. Choice **a** is not as appealing as some of the other choices because traffic would be snarled until the tow truck arrived to clear the lane. Choice **c** is not much of an option for the same reason: The idea here is to keep traffic moving safely. Now we've narrowed the choices down to two, which makes the odds of getting this question right much better. If you compare the two, choice **d** is not as good as choice **b** because it is not as practical or as safe as simply pushing the small car several feet until it is on the shoulder of the road. The shoulder of the road is intended for this sort of emergency. Also, this option should appeal to your good judgment and common sense: You want to remove the problem (the stalled vehicle) in the safest, most effective manner.

The temptation with situational judgment questions is to project your own thoughts and feelings into the scenario. You may catch yourself chewing on your pencil thinking, "Well, I'd have the driver behind the stalled vehicle get out and help the other driver push the car to the side of the road. That's what I would do." That may be how this situation would play out in real life if the other driver were amenable, but that's not one of your options, so this kind of thinking merely complicates the question and wastes valuable time.

Another temptation is to read more into the situation than is there. You may think, "Maybe the car is too heavy to push, or it won't roll right, or maybe this department doesn't allow its officers to push cars . . . ." The list goes on. Use the information you see on the page, not the information that could be there, to make your decision.

In some testing situations, you may be shown situations on a video and then asked to respond. These tests are a bit more nerve-racking because you might have to come up with your own options to the situations you see. Here, you will just have to think as much like a police officer as possible, watch the situation on the video monitor as closely as you can, and listen to what the actors are saying if the video has dialogue.

Whether the test is written or audiovisual, you will be required to exercise your good judgment and common sense.

Through Their Eyes

It's easy to "think like a cop" if you know how cops think. The ideal way to learn is to ride with officers in your area and ask lots of questions. See what type of situations officers handle on the job, find out how they feel about the calls they make, and ask them—in calmer moments, of course—what they were looking for when they handled specific calls. Do what you can to look at each situation through their eyes.

Unfortunately, police departments are growing more reluctant to take people out on ride-alongs, so you may not have this option. As an alternative, try one of these strategies: 1) Go to the police station and talk to the desk officers. You might have to ask them when a slow period is and come back, but they are very often glad to talk about their jobs. 2) Almost every police department has a community outreach program. Call and find out if your department has a community relations officer. Make an appointment to speak to that person. 3) Attend a neighborhood watch meeting or community meeting. You will get to see a police officer interacting with the community and probably be able to ask questions. These three strategies can help get you inside the mind of a police officer. Perhaps more importantly, you will have some great material when the oral board asks you, "What have you done to prepare yourself for the job of a police officer?"

Safety First

If you got tired of hearing your parents say, "Safety first!" when you were growing up, get ready for an exhausting experience. In every action an officer takes, the safety and well-being of everyone involved is the first priority. Even the suspect's safety is an issue. Protecting life is an officer's first responsibility.

When you look at a test question, remember that officers have the importance of safety drilled into them from day one at the academy. Is it safer to let the driver stand in the street while he tells you how the accident happened, or is it better to have him move onto the sidewalk? Is it safer for the accident victims if the patrol car is blocking this lane of traffic or that lane of traffic? Is it safer for you to stand in front of a door or to the side of a door before knocking? Is it safer for bystanders if you pursue the speeder through downtown traffic or let him go?

The safety issue may not surface in every judgment question, but when it does, be aware that safety is a police officer's highest priority. Remember that for a police officer, human life always takes precedent over property.

Use of Force

Police officers use force for two reasons: to overcome a suspect's resistance and to defend life. In both instances, the smallest amount possible is the right amount of force. You don't need to go through six months in a police academy to recognize that it's a monumental waste of effort to swat a fly with a ten-pound sledge-hammer when a one-ounce plastic fly-swatter will get the job done. Common sense comes into play heavily in this area. Expect to see test questions asking you what the proper amount of force is for an officer to use when physical control is necessary, and what kind of force is appropriate out of the choices you are given. When answering judgment questions, keep in mind that the test makers know that the best officers will use the least force possible in all situations.

The Choices: Lecture, Cite, or Arrest

Do you write a ticket, or are the law and the public better served with a warning and a brief lecture on good driving? Is every breach of the peace a signal to break out the handcuffs? Situational judgment questions on a written exam will demand that you know the answers. For example, you might see a question like this:

2. You are on foot patrol downtown when you see one man punch another man in the stomach. You separate the two men and find out that it was a minor disturbance. The two men are embarrassed that you witnessed the altercation because they are good friends. They assure you that no one is hurt. The victim laughs and says "no" when you ask if he wants to file assault charges. What should you do about this obvious breach of the peace that has occurred in your presence?

- **a.** Arrest the suspect anyway because the assault occurred in front of you.
- **b.** Arrest the suspect because the victim may change his mind later.
- **c.** Let the suspect go free because the victim does not want to file charges.
- **d.** Arrest the suspect because bystanders are watching to see what kind of action you will take.

Once again, the process of elimination can help you answer this question. After reading all of the options, you should reason immediately that choice **d** is not a good option. Police work, especially in a city, is rarely conducted in total privacy. The opinions of bystanders should not affect how you enforce the law. Choice **a** is not the best course of action either. It is not in the best interest of the public or the overcrowded justice system to take a person into custody each and every time a violation of the law occurs in your presence. Choice **b** is a bad option for the same reason. The victim obviously knows the suspect. In the unlikely event that he changes his mind later and wants to file charges, he knows the identity of his attacker and can contact the police department with that information. A warrant can always be issued for the suspect.

That leaves us with choice **c**, the best option. Maybe you've heard the expression "no victim, no crime." If the man who was assaulted did not consider himself a victim of a crime, then you have no need to arrest the suspect for assault. Arresting the suspect for any other violation in this situation would not be in the best interest of the law, the public, or the police department. Common sense should tell you that arrest is not warranted because the two men resolved the situation themselves, no one was hurt, no damage to property occurred, and no one else was affected by the altercation. And by not arresting this man, you remain available for more serious calls.

Tips for Answering Situational Judgment Questions

- Read carefully, but don't read anything into the situation that isn't there.
- Think like a cop: Safety first. Use the least possible force.
- Use your common sense.

Tips for Performing Well on Video Exams

- Be polite yet firm when dealing with the public. You don't want to appear harsh or overly controlling when talking to bystanders or witnesses.
- Don't be overly nice when dealing with rough suspects who are creating chaos. You want to show that you can take charge of stressful situations when needed.
- Always be honest, and remember the importance of ethical behavior, even if it means turning in a fellow police officer who is dishonest.
- Face the monitor when responding to each situation instead of looking at the video camera that is taping your response.
- Don't respond by saying what you "would do" in the situation; act as if you are actually the officer who is on the scene handling the call.

Using Your Judgment on Video Exams

Some police agencies now use one or more situational video exams called the Behavioral Personnel Assessment Device (B-PAD) to assess your judgment and interpersonal skills. If you are required to take a video exam in addition to or in place of a written exam, the same basic steps apply: Remember the importance of safety, use an appropriate amount of force, and take a common-sense approach.

During a B-PAD exam, you will be shown eight short situations that are typical in a police officer's line of duty. For example, you may be asked to defuse hostile domestic disputes, calm an angry motorist, or comfort a lost child. You will most likely see one-on-one situations and group problems with a mixture of ethnic groups and ages. After each one or two minute situation is shown, you will have 45 seconds to respond to the actors in the video as if you were the officer handling the situation. Your response is taped on a video camera, which is normally positioned right next to the video monitor. You will probably get to respond to a practice scene before beginning the actual test. The entire B-PAD takes about 20 minutes to complete.

You will not be scored on your knowledge of any policies, procedures, or law. Rather, you will be assessed for your judgment, problem-solving, and interpersonal skills in dealing with different types of people in different situations commonly found in police work.

▶ Application of Laws and Procedures

Your written exam may include questions that ask you to read rules, laws, policies, or procedures and then apply those guidelines to a hypothetical situation. You may still be able to use your good judgment and common sense in these questions, but even more important is your ability to read carefully and accurately.

These kinds of questions ask you to do something police officers do every day: Take their knowledge of the laws of their city and state, or of their department's procedures, and use that knowledge to decide what to do in a given situation. The questions don't expect you to know the laws or procedures; they're right there as part of the test question. That's why your reading skills really come into play.

Questions that ask you to apply rules and laws are a little different from ones that ask you to apply procedures, so each kind of question is treated separately in this chapter.

Application of Laws

Some questions will give you a definition of a crime and then ask you to apply that definition to hypothetical situations to see which situation matches the definition. Here's an example:

> **Shoplifting** is a theft of goods from a store, shop, or place of business during business hours where the suspect takes the good(s) past the last point of opportunity to pay for the merchandise without attempting to offer payment.

3. Which of the following is the best example of shoplifting?

- **a.** Terry walks into the Bag and Save grocery store and gets a piece of candy. He takes it to the counter and discovers he has no money. The clerk tells him to go ahead and keep the candy this time. Terry leaves the store eating the candy.
- **b.** Gloria walks into an electronics store to get a pack of triple-A batteries. She sticks the small package in her coat pocket while she looks at the computer display. After a few minutes, she turns to walk out. Before she reaches the door, she remembers the batteries and turns back to the counter to pay for them.
- **c.** Gail enters Philo's Pharmacy on 12th Street to pick up a prescription. After paying for the medicine, she walks over to the perfume counter, where she finds a small bottle of cologne she likes. She puts the cologne in her purse and walks out of the front door of the pharmacy.
- **d.** Pete and his mother, Abby, are grocery shopping. Pete picks up a candy bar, peels off the wrapper, and hands Abby the wrapper. When they reach the checkout counter, Pete walks out of the store while Abby puts the groceries, along with the candy wrapper, on the stand for checkout. The clerk rings up the price of the candy along with the groceries.

The best approach to application of law questions is to read each option carefully and decide whether or not it fits the definition. You have to rely on your good judgment, your careful reading skills, and your ability to put two and two together to reach a conclusion. The questions do not assume that you have any knowledge of the law or of police procedures; you are given all the information you need to reason out the best possible answer.

Let's look at the options in our example. Choice **a** is not an example of shoplifting because the clerk told Terry he did not have to pay for the candy. Terry did not hide the candy or try to leave the business without an attempt to pay. The clerk had the option of having Terry put back the candy, but he instead chose to give it away.

Choice **b** is not an example of shoplifting because Gloria did not pass the last point of opportunity to pay before leaving the store without making an attempt to pay for the batteries. In businesses where the checkout stands are located in the middle or toward the rear of the store, the benefit of the doubt goes to the shopper until he or she walks out the door.

Choice **c** *is* an example of shoplifting because Gail made no attempt to pay for the cologne before leaving the business.

Choice **d** is not an example of shoplifting because Abby paid for her son's candy, even though he ate the candy in the store and eventually walked out of the store.

Again, careful reading is the key to getting the application of law questions correct. You have to read exactly what is there, while not reading anything more into the situation than is actually written on the page. For example, if while reading choice **b**, you focus on Gloria putting the batteries in her pocket instead of whether or not she attempted to pay for the item, you may end up with an incorrect answer. Reread the definition and note that *where* someone carries goods while he or she is shopping has no bearing on the crime as defined.

Application of Procedures

Application of procedures questions are a lot like the previous type. You will be given information about police procedures and then asked to apply these procedures to a hypothetical situation. You might have to decide which step in a set of procedures is the next step to be taken in the situation, or you might have to decide whether a hypothetical officer followed the procedures properly in the situation given. In either case, you're being tested on your ability to follow directions and on your reading comprehension skills.

The question is usually preceded by a brief passage telling you about the procedure; for example:

When an officer handles found property—property that has been discovered by someone, but is not necessarily evidence from a crime scene—the officer should follow these procedures:

1. Write a report detailing who found the property, what the property is, where it was found, and where it is now located, and turn in the report before the end of his or her shift.
2. Attach a tag to the property.
3. Write the report number on the tag, along with the officer's name, badge number, and the date and time the property was turned in.
4. Turn the property into the Property Room before the end of his or her shift.

4. Officer Smith is on patrol when he is flagged down by a pedestrian on the northeast corner of Elm and St. John. The pedestrian, Carl Randal, tells Officer Smith that he found a gold watch on the sidewalk in the 200 block of Elm. The clasp is broken on the watch, and Randal tells the officer he believes the watch must have fallen off of someone without that person's knowledge. He gives the watch to the officer and provides his name and other information to the officer for the report. Officer Smith writes a found property report using all the details provided by Randal, places a tag on the property, and writes the report number, his name, his badge number, and the date and time the watch came into his possession. He then puts the watch in the glove box of the patrol car. He turns in his report an hour after writing it, and at the beginning of his next shift he takes the watch to the Property Room. In this situation, Officer Smith acted

a. improperly, because he should have let Carl Randal keep the watch until someone reported it as missing.
b. properly, because he turned in his report before the end of his shift.
c. improperly, because he failed to take the property to the Property Room before the end of his shift.
d. properly, because he wrote all of the pertinent information in his report.

What the test maker wants you to do is study how Officer Smith handled the found property case and see if he followed his department's rules on handling found property.

Each choice actually has two parts that require you to make two decisions. First, you have to decide if the officer acted properly or improperly, and then you have to decide if the reason stated in the choice is correct or incorrect. In this case, choice **c** is correct on both counts because the officer did not act properly, according to the procedures for turning in found property. He should have turned the watch in before the end of his shift (Step 4).

To help you choose the right choice, see if you can assign a step to the information in the option. For example, choice **a** states that Officer Smith should have let Randal, the man who found the watch, keep it until someone reported it stolen. If you look at the steps in the list of procedures, you will not see that action in any of the steps.

These questions can be tricky if you read too fast or read only part of the answer choices. Take your time and make sure both parts of the answer are correct. For example, in choice **b**, the second part of the answer is correct. That action, turning in the report in a timely manner, is what Officer Smith is supposed to do according to Step 1. However, if you look at the first part of the answer, it says Smith acted correctly in this situation because he turned in his report on time. This is not the best answer because Smith did not act properly, since he failed to turn in the found property before the end of his shift. Remember, there's only one best answer.

Tips for Answering Application Questions

- Read what's there, not what you think should have been there.
- Read through all the choices before you pick an answer.
- Find the exact spot in the law or the procedure that supports your answer.

▶ Judgment Questions Based on Eyewitness Accounts

You'll need a careful eye for detail for the kinds of judgment questions that ask you to choose among eyewitness accounts. The test maker is looking to see if you can pick out the common elements in the list of answer choices in order to arrive at the right answer. The test question usually will contain a description of suspects, vehicles, or license plates. Here's an example:

5. You are called to the scene of a gasoline theft at a neighborhood gas station. The station manager tells you that a woman in a green Chevrolet Cavalier pumped $20 of unleaded gasoline into her car and took off northbound on Elm St. He and three other witnesses tell you they saw the license plate on the vehicle. Which of the plates listed below, given to you by the witnesses, is most likely to be the correct plate?
a. PG-2889
b. PG-2089
c. PG-2880
d. PC-2889

In eyewitness account questions, the actual situation in the question has little bearing on what the test maker wants you to do. You are being asked to pick out which license plate is most likely to be the license plate for the suspect vehicle. The correct answer to this question lies in the answer choices themselves. The end result isn't focusing on the crime that took place so much as on your ability to take information, average it all up, and arrive at a conclusion.

Your best approach to this question is to start comparing the similarities in each answer. You will notice that all of the answers start with the letter "P." The second letter is the letter "G" in all of the answers except for choice **d**. The first number is the number 2 for all of the answers. Then you see that all of the answers except for choice **b** agree that the number 8 is the second number on the license plate. The third number of the plate is 8 in all of the answers. The final number of the plate is 9 in all of the answers except for **d**. You should have picked choice **a** as the right answer because the license plate that has the most common elements is PG-2889.

You will be asked to use the same kind of reasoning when you see a test question asking you to pick out a suspect description. Once again, the scenario described in the question is not going to carry as much weight as the answers themselves. Your task will be to find the common threads in each answer until you come up with the most likely description of the suspect.

Tips for Answering Eyewitness Account Questions

- Stay calm and work methodically.
- Compare each element of each answer choice until you find the ones that have the common elements.

▶ Improving Your Judgment Skills

You have more options than you may realize when it comes to honing your judgment skills—not only for the police exam, but also for your career as a police officer. There are some surprisingly simple exercises you can do in your everyday life that will sharpen your judgment skills.

What If...

There's a game most police officers play in their minds called "What if." You probably play it too, but you may not be aware of it. "What if I won the lottery tomorrow? If I did, I'd empty my desk drawers on top of my supervisor's desk and run screaming out of the building." Sound familiar?

Professional baseball players watch slow-motion videos of a batter with perfect form in the hope that by memorizing and studying his moves, they will be able to improve their own performance. And research shows that this works: In times of stress, people are more likely to succeed on a task if they've practiced it—either mentally or physically.

"What if" uses the same logic. If you've thought about a situation and you've arrived at a conclusion about what you would do under the given circumstances, then you've given your brain a plan for the situation if it actually comes up. Maybe you've heard someone say, "I didn't have any idea what to do. I just froze." That brain didn't have a plan to follow. Playing "What if" can give it a plan.

Train yourself to practice "What if" scenarios. Do it in the grocery store. You're standing in line behind a man in a heavy coat. Ask yourself "If I were a police officer, *what* would I do *if* I saw this man slip a package of batteries into his coat pocket and go through the checkout line and then out of the store without paying for them?" This could turn out to be one of the situational judgment questions you find on a police officer exam. Practice. At the very least, it might add a new dimension to your grocery shopping.

Self-Confidence Checks

Practice your self-confidence. Self-confidence is what makes most police officers able to make decisions with a minimum of confusion and self-doubt. Although you aren't a police officer yet, you need to develop the same self-confidence so that you will make the right decisions as a test taker. If you aren't confident about your judgment skills and your ability to decide what to do in a situation, then you are likely to torture yourself with every judgment question that appears on the exam.

Believe it or not, it is possible to practice self-confidence. Many people practice the opposite of self-confidence by thinking and saying negative things like, "I don't know if I can do that," or "What if I can't do that?"

Start listening to yourself to see if you talk like that. And then turn it around. Tell yourself and others,

"The police officer exam is coming up and I intend to ace it," and "I know I will make a good police officer. I know that when I read the test questions I can rely on my own good judgment to help me. My common sense will point me in the right direction."

This isn't bragging. It's how you set yourself up for success. You will start thinking of what you need to do to ace the test. You're practicing self-confidence right now by reading this book. You are getting the tools you need to do the job. Your self-confidence has no option but to shoot straight up—and your score along with it.

Read, Read, Read

Reading is as vital on judgment questions as it is on reading comprehension questions. This isn't the kind of reading you do when you are skimming a novel or skipping through articles in a newspaper. It's the kind where you not only have to pay attention to what the writer is telling you, but must make decisions based on the information you've received. There's a whole chapter in this book on reading. Check out the suggestions there, under Additional Resources, on ways to improve your reading skills.

CHAPTER

12 Map Reading

CHAPTER SUMMARY

Some police departments include a map reading section on their written exam. They want to find out whether you will be able to navigate through the streets of your jurisdiction. This chapter will explain the types of map reading questions you may encounter.

Have you ever been lost in an unfamiliar city? Have you ever driven up and down unknown streets, gone in circles, or come to a dead end? While these may be common occurrences for the average person, they can prove deadly to a police officer who needs to respond immediately to an urgent call. That is why you may be tested on your ability to read maps. Once you become a police officer, you may need to consult maps on a regular basis to become familiar with the different neighborhoods or key locations in your jurisdiction. If you don't know where an address is located when you get a call, you will need to be able to consult a map quickly and expertly to get directions.

Reading a map sounds simple enough, but in practice it can be quite a frustrating experience. And practice is the only way to get good at map reading.

Police officer exams have a method for testing your map reading skills. Typically, you will see a simple map with the north-south-east-west directions clearly marked, and a key explaining symbols. You will find instructions on which questions should be answered based on the map. Don't be surprised to find several different maps in one test.

A sentence or two is usually devoted to telling you that you can't make up your own traffic laws in order to get from Point A to Point B. You can't go up one-way streets the wrong way or choose paths that will have you driving through office buildings to get to the call. After that, you will find one or more questions about the map you're looking at. The questions may ask you which is the shortest route from Point A to Point B, or they may tell you to make a series of right and left turns and then ask you in which direction you're heading.

► Finding the Shortest Route

Questions that ask you to find the shortest legal route are based on a map like the one on the next page. A scenario follows the instructions, followed by a question asking for the shortest route and the answer choices.

The best approach to solving these puzzles is to first study the map for a minute to get your bearings. As you read the question, pay special attention to the two vital clues—your current location and where you must go. For example, think about going to the mall and shopping for shoes. You have no idea where the shoe store is located, so you walk up to the kiosk and look at the map. What is the first thing you try to find? The "you are here" symbol. That is because you cannot plan your trip without knowing your starting point.

The next thing you look for is shoe stores. Once you find them, you know where you are and where you want to go. This map reading puzzle is the same. Find the start point and the end point. Now, use a small object, like a penny, and pretend it is your police car. Move the penny around the map, paying special attention to the traffic symbols (like one-way streets), and find the quickest route.

Once you think you have the quickest route, check the answers and see if your solution is among the given answers. If it is, great! If your answer isn't there, start again by finding your start and end points, and then finding the best route.

Try this strategy on the sample question that follows.

Sample Shortest-Route Question

Here's a question that asks you to find the shortest route on the map on the next page.

Answer questions 1 through 3 based solely on the following map. You are required to follow traffic laws and the flow of traffic. A single arrow depicts one-way streets and two arrows pointing in opposite directions represent two-way streets.

1. Officer Nguyen is sitting at a red light at the intersection of Eighth Street and Carver Road facing southbound. The dispatcher sends him on a one-vehicle collision call. A motorist has run into the northwest corner of the Town Hall building. What is the quickest route for Officer Nguyen to take to Town Hall?

a. Turn west onto Carver Road, then south on Seventh Street, and then west on Grand Street to Temple Road.

b. Turn west onto Carver Road, then south onto Temple Road, and then east to Arnold Avenue.

c. Turn west onto Carver Road, south on Sixth Street, and then east onto Grand Street to Temple Road.

d. Turn west onto Carver Road, then south onto Temple Road, and then east onto Grand Street.

Strategy for Shortest-Route Questions

Here's how to apply this strategy to the question.

The situation tells you that Officer Nguyen needs to answer a collision call. You have an idea of a specific

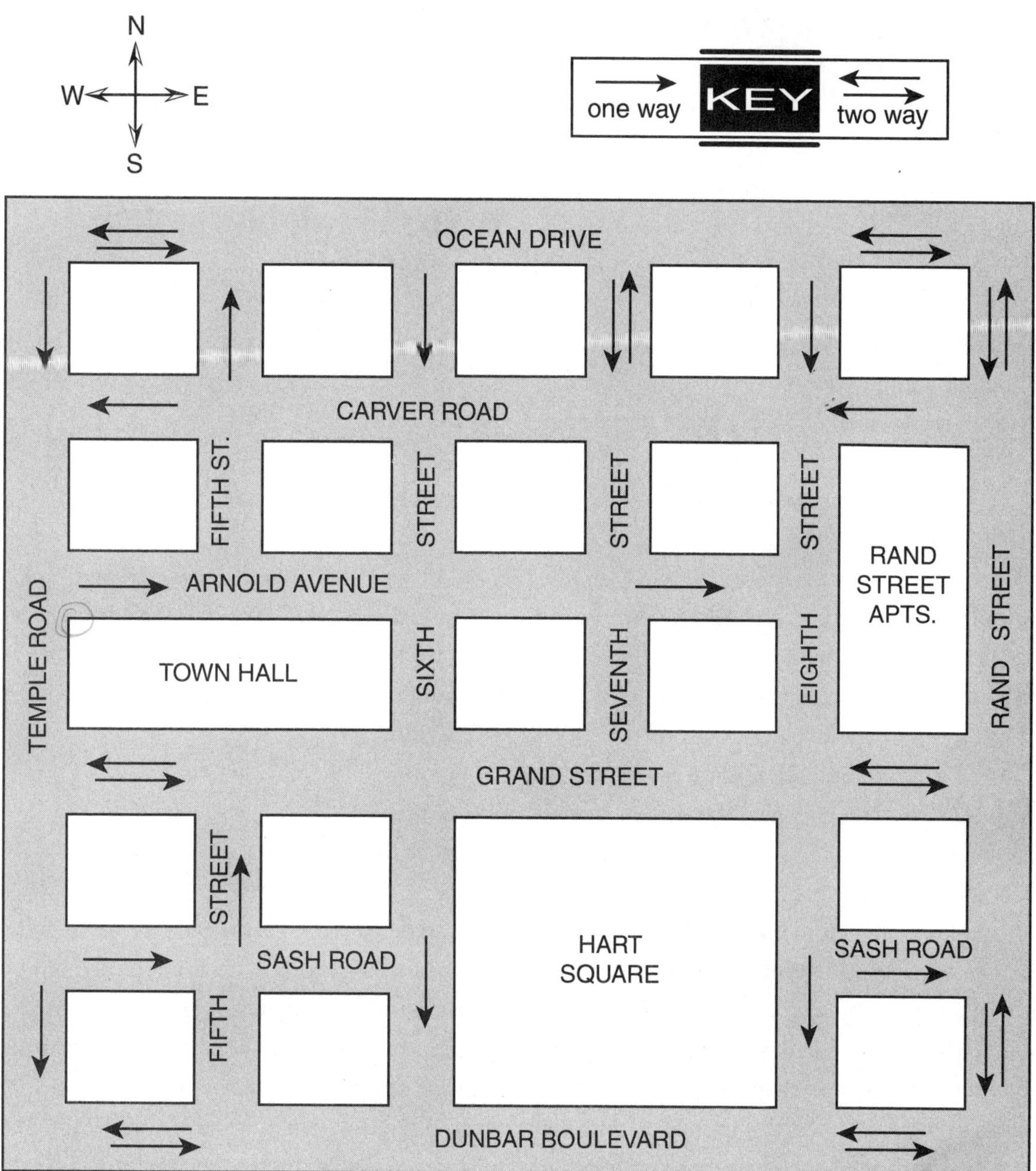

location when you read that a motorist has run into the northwest corner of Town Hall. As you can see by the map, the Town Hall building can be approached on four sides by four different streets. Because you'd like to be close to the northwest corner of the building, you should be considering a route that will put you on that side of Town Hall.

Your first step will be to study the map and pick out the quickest legal route to the collision. The arrows show you that Carver Road is a one-way street. Because Officer Nguyen is facing south on Eighth Street at Carver Road, his only option available is to turn west onto Carver Road. Notice that Carver Road runs parallel to Arnold Avenue, the street where Town Hall is located. Also notice that Arnold Avenue runs to the east and you want to end up on the northwest corner of the building. Now look at Town Hall. The northwest corner of this building is at the intersection of Temple Road and Arnold Avenue. (To determine the northwest corner of the building, it may be helpful to imagine that the north-south-east-west indicator is written in the middle of the words "Town Hall." That makes it easy to see where the northwest corner would be.) The quickest, easiest route appears to be west on Carver Road, south on Temple Road, and east on Arnold Avenue. You have your route, so now it's time to see if one of the multiple-choice options matches the route you determined.

When you first glance at the four choices, you see that they all start with a turn west onto Carver Road. Starting with choice **a**, we see that this option lists turning south onto Seventh Street and then west on Grand Street. Grand Street is one block south of the street you'd like to be on, so this option is not as efficient as the route you arrived at. Eliminate this option and go on to choice **b**.

In choice **b**, you see that the first turn after heading west on Carver Road is to turn south onto Temple Road, then east to Arnold Avenue, which will put the officer at the scene of the collision. This option matches the route you figured out before reading the answers, so choice **b** is more than likely right.

However, it's always best to continue reading the answers to make sure you don't pass up an option that turns out to be better than the one you figured out. Option **c** makes Officer Nguyen turn east on Grand Street, which is heading away from the call and does not end up at Temple Road. Choice **d** is not the best answer because the corner of Temple Road and Grand Street is one block too far to the south. You'd only choose either of these options if you didn't know which was the northwest corner of Town Hall.

Remember, even when you feel like you already have the right answer, it is best to examine all of the answer choices to be on the safe side.

▶ Finding the Direction

Question 2 is based on the same map you used to answer Question 1, but is different because the test maker wants to know if you can figure out which direction you are facing.

Sample Direction Question

2. Officer Pitt is driving eastbound on Grand Street at Eighth Street. If she makes a U-turn on Grand Street, turns onto Seventh Street and then makes another U-turn, what direction will she be facing?

a. east
b. west
c. north
d. south

Strategy for Direction Questions

The best strategy for solving this type of question is the same one you used on Question 1. Trace out your path after reading the question, then look through the answers until you find the one that matches your decision. Obviously, you don't have much reading to do to pick out the right answer. You will mainly be looking to see which letter is in front of the answer you want.

In the case of Question 2, the answer you want is choice **d**. When you traced out your path on the map, you should have seen that if Officer Pitt is heading east on Grand Street and she makes a U-turn, she will be heading west. If she turns onto Seventh Street, the only way she can turn will have her heading north on Seventh Street. If she makes a second U-turn, she will now be facing south.

Tips for Map Reading Questions

- Read carefully and follow all directions.
- Feel free to move the map around during the test to face the direction you find comfortable.
- Find your starting point.
- Find your ending point.

▶ More Map Reading Practice

The key to answering map reading questions is to take your time. If you hurry through a question, you may misread the question or the answer choices, which will naturally cause you to choose the wrong answer.

Let's try a third question using the same sample map.

3. On a rainy, windy night Officers Magnani and Mays are dispatched to a burglar alarm at a business on Sash Road and Rand Street. They are driving north on Fifth Street and have just passed Carver Road. What is the quickest route they can take?

a. North on Fifth Street, west on Ocean Drive, then south on Temple Road, then east on Dunbar Boulevard, then north on Rand Street to Sash Road.

b. North on Fifth Street, then east on Ocean Drive, then south on Seventh Street, then east on Grand Street, then north on Rand Street to Sash Road.

c. North on Fifth Street, then east on Ocean Drive, then south on Rand Street to Sash Road.

d. North on Fifth Street, then west on Ocean Drive, then south on Temple Road, then east on Arnold Avenue, then south on Sixth Street, then east on Dunbar Boulevard, then north on Rand Street to Sash Road.

After reading the question, you are ready to trace your route. Keep in mind that you want to get to Sash Road and Rand Street in the quickest, easiest manner without going the wrong way on any one-way streets. Fifth Street is a one-way street going toward a two-way street, Ocean Drive. You have the option of heading east or west on Ocean Drive. East makes more sense because it is in the direction of Rand Street. The most direct route appears to be east on Ocean Drive to Rand Street, then south on Rand Street to Sash Road.

Now it's time to check your answer against the options. Choice **a** has you turning west on Fifth Street, and you've already determined that west is not the most efficient direction to turn. Choice **b** suggests that you turn east on Ocean Drive, then south on Seventh Street, then east on Grand Street, and then north on Rand Street. You should turn south on Rand Street to get to Sash Road, not north. You already have too many turns for this to be an efficient route in any event. Time to look at choice **c**. Choice **c** directs you east on Ocean Drive, then south on Rand Street—and there you are at Sash Road. This route matches the route we had in mind. Choice **d** has too many turns (like choice **b**), in addition to involving a west turn onto Ocean Drive, which we already decided was inefficient.

Now that you're becoming an expert in map reading—be sure to make up your own questions to test your growing skills. Or better yet, take a map, get in your car, and try to locate places in unfamiliar neighborhoods. As an alternative exercise, use websites like www.mapquest.com, http://maps.yahoo.com, or http://maps.google.com to improve your skills. Every day, you drive to different locations, but do you always use the best route? These sites can be used to simulate your test-taking strategy by entering your home address (where you are on the map) and your destination (where you want to go). Look at the maps they provide. Are you taking the best route? Can you work out alternative routes if there is a traffic problem?

There's nothing like hands-on practice to improve your map reading skills.

CHAPTER

13 Memory and Observation

CHAPTER SUMMARY

This chapter contains hints and tips to help you answer questions that test your memory skills. Memory questions can be based on pictures or on written materials; you may get the materials ahead of time or on test day. However the memory questions are structured, this chapter will help you deal with them.

It's amazing what your mind will file away in that cabinet we call memory. You may remember every snippet of dialogue uttered by Clint Eastwood in his first *Dirty Harry* movie from years ago, but you can't remember which bus route you used yesterday to get to the dentist. Some people remember names well, but can't put them with the right faces. Others forget names quickly, but know exactly when, where, and why they met the person whose name they've forgotten. There are a few lucky individuals who have what is commonly referred to as a photographic memory or total recall. And then there are those of us who wake up every morning to a radio alarm so we can find out what day of the week it is. Fortunately, a good memory is actually a skill that can be developed and improved.

Written exams for police officers may test your ability to memorize material using different techniques. You may have to read passages of various lengths or look at a sketch of a street scene; drawings of men and women with differing facial features, weapons, and other characteristics; or photographs. Usually, you will be given a set amount of time (anywhere from 5 to 25 minutes) to look at the material, and then you will be asked to answer test questions about what you saw. Your goal is to memorize as much of that material as you can in the allotted time.

Other police departments are more interested in longer-term memory skills. They may send you a study booklet a few weeks in advance of the test and ask you to memorize material in the booklet. In that case, you will answer questions based on what you've been memorizing from the study booklet.

This chapter will help you improve your ability to memorize material from written passages, wanted poster drawings with accompanying text, and pictures of street scenes.

▶ Memorizing and Applying Police Information

Questions Based on Written Passages

We've all watched police dramas on television where the gruff sergeant tells the assembled troops which criminals are running amock in the city and then hands out paperwork that our heroes, more often than not, leave on their desks on their way out the door. That scenario is not too far removed from reality. Police officers receive a lot of information in a short length of time and are expected to remember most of it. And of course someone has come up with a way to test your ability to accomplish this task.

You will be given a set time to read one or more written passages and study several drawings of people or places, sometimes with accompanying text. Then you will have to answer questions based on what you learned and observed, without being able to refer back to the material.

The written passages are not usually more than 500–600 words long. The subject matter will have something to do with criminal law, police procedures, or police techniques. The passage will not assume you have any previous knowledge about police techniques, but it will assume that you can read to learn information and then apply that knowledge. Because you don't have much time to absorb the material, it's best to focus on what you feel will be the most important facts. The questions will most likely ask you to recall the details your common sense will lead you to believe to be most important. For example, here's a short piece on handcuffing techniques. Read it and then answer the questions that follow *without* looking back at the text.

> Proper handcuffing technique is an essential part of officer safety. A suspect cannot easily pick up a weapon or hit an officer when his or her hands are firmly secured. When an officer makes the decision to place handcuffs on an individual, departmental policy states that the officer must always handcuff the individual's hands behind his or her back. The only exception to this rule is when the individual has a physical disability which makes this position impossible. A broken arm set in a cast is an example of such a situation.

Officers will handcuff suspects using the following technique:

1. Instruct the suspect to turn around, putting his or her back to you.
2. Instruct the suspect to place both hands behind his or her back.
3. Grab the suspect's wrist firmly with one hand and secure one ring of the handcuff around the wrist.
4. Grab the remaining wrist firmly and secure the other ring of the handcuff to that wrist.
5. Make sure the handcuffs are loose enough to allow for normal circulation.
6. Lock each side of the handcuff to prevent them from tightening accidentally.
7. Place the suspect inside the patrol car.

Answer the following questions without referring back to the handcuffing piece.

1. The passage on proper handcuffing technique says the suspect's hands should always be handcuffed
   a. behind the suspect.
   b. in front of the suspect.
   c. to the officer.
   d. to a hook in the patrol car.

2. The passage on proper handcuffing technique says the first step the officer should take when the decision to handcuff a suspect has been made is to
   a. allow the suspect to telephone a lawyer.
   b. instruct the suspect to place both hands behind his or her back.
   c. instruct the suspect to turn around, placing his or her back to the officer.
   d. lock the handcuffs firmly in place.

Remember, all you have to do to answer questions like this successfully is to remember and apply what you've learned. In the case of question 1, you're applying what you learned about handcuffing if you picked choice **a** as the right answer. In question 2, your common sense should tell you that now is not the time to have the suspect call a lawyer, so choice **a** is not likely to be the answer. Combine your reasoning skills with your ability to remember what you've read, and you should come up with choice **c** as the right answer.

It's also important to pay attention to hints from the author—and this applies both to learning and to memorization. If you see a phrase such as "The most important point to remember," pay attention. The test questions are going to pick up on that kind of hint, so your chances of seeing that material again are really good.

What to Do

1. Visualize as you read. Keeping a movie of sorts running through your mind as you read is a helpful way to remember details. If you have a visual image of what the passage is describing, you are more likely to remember it.
2. Pay special attention to the first and last steps in a list of procedures.
3. Rely on your common sense and ability to reason to supplement your memorization skills. Sometimes, you will instinctively know which answer is right even though you cannot specifically recall the exact words in the passage.
4. When applicable, attach parts of the passage to a personal experience you have had. For example, let's say you once witnessed a person with a physical disability being handcuffed. This experience would help you remember the part of the passage that mentions the one exception to the handcuffing rule.

The passage on handcuffing techniques is approximately 200 words long. On the actual test, you should expect longer passages, perhaps more than one of them, and therefore you should expect more questions on the passages than the two given above.

If all this seems daunting, think about the times you've read a news article on, say, a grisly murder. You're talking to a friend later that evening and you say, "Did you read in the paper this morning about that guy who got stabbed with an ice pick? Yeah, some guy in a trench coat stabbed him right in the forehead with an ice pick while they were on the ferry to Martha's Vineyard. He jumped overboard right after that." This example may be a little dramatic, but you get the point. It probably takes only a minute or so to read a news article, but the information stays with you much longer than a minute. Face the memory portion of your exam with the expectation that you will remember what you read.

What Not to Do

- **Do not** draw conclusions or waste time thinking of ways a procedure really should be done. For instance, while reading the article about handcuffing techniques, don't waste time thinking of alternative methods of handcuffing. You're being tested on your ability to remember what you've read, not on your knowledge of the subject matter or your creativity.
- **Do not** add elements to the written passage that weren't originally there. If the author didn't mention the advantages of using hinge cuffs over chain cuffs, then there's no reason for you to add this information to the situation.
- **Do not** spend too much of your allotted time on one written passage if your test also includes more passages or drawings. Be sure to leave time for all of the memory material.

Questions Based on Wanted Posters

Many police departments use mock wanted posters to test memorization skills. Some departments send this material out in study guides to be memorized weeks in advance, and some ask you to memorize the material right then and there during the test, within a set period of time. Either way, you will be asking yourself the same question, "How am I going to remember all of this?" The answer is, the same way you'll one day recognize and remember facts about the criminals in your jurisdiction when you've become an officer. The technique you will learn here works in real life as well as in test situations.

Memorization, as you know by now, relies heavily on solid reading comprehension and observation skills. The wanted poster sets you are given to memorize will most likely contain line drawings of adult males, females, and juveniles. Next to the drawings, you will see the text that tells each person's story.

For example, suppose you have a drawing of an adult white male with shoulder-length hair parted down the middle. He is clean-shaven, has large eyes, and has a mole in the middle of his chin. Next to it, you see the following text.

WANTED
Rodney Jones Walker

ALIASES: Rod Jones
WANTED BY: Los Angeles Police Department
CHARGES: Assault
DESCRIPTION:

Age: 37
Race: White
Height: 5′8″
Weight: 190
Hair: Black
Eyes: Green

REMARKS: Has relatives in the Fresno area and is believed to be headed for San Diego. Was last seen with a white cast on his left wrist.
CAUTION: Switchblade hidden in the suspect's left boot. Known to carry brass knuckles.

Your task is to remember enough details about this person to correctly answer questions about him on the exam. This isn't much to ask until you consider that you will see more than one poster with accompanying text *and* be asked to remember information from written passages. Don't panic, though. Just take the posters one at a time, and remember that there are tricks you can use to improve your memory skills.

Which Comes First, Drawing or Text?

If you're like most people, your eyes will gravitate to the drawing first. That's fine, because you want to make this work as easy on your brain as possible. Start with the top of the head and work your way down. Try holding a conversation in your head to help you memorize the person's features. For example, if you were looking at a drawing of our suspect, you might think to yourself, "Oh, his hair touches his shoulders just the way my Aunt Joan's does. In fact, he has beady eyes like Aunt Joan's. His nose is sort of crooked like hers, and his head is shaped the same way. She doesn't have a mole on her chin like he does, but if she did they'd look like twins." Of course this is outlandish, but when you see the name Rodney Jones Walker, you'll remember exactly what he looks like. What you are doing is creating links between your long-term memory and your short-term memory. This is one of the best ways to improve your short-term memory skills.

While you look at each face, look for jewelry, scars, facial hair (or lack of it), facial shape, size of facial features, and teeth, if the subject is shown smiling. When you eventually get to the text, you will want to tie in such details. For example, suppose Walker is shown wearing a cross on a chain around his neck. After you read the text, you could tie lots of information together by thinking, "Now what is a guy named Rodney Jones Walker, who looks like Aunt Joan and keeps a switchblade in his boot, doing wearing a cross? I wear a cross, and I would not even think about assaulting another person." Your brain has locked in the suspect's name, his weapon, what he looks like, what he's charged with, and a distinctive piece of jewelry all in one thought.

Once you are ready to study the text, you will be using the same technique you used for studying the drawing. Read slowly from top to bottom. As you read, carry on your mental conversation. It may sound something like this: "Rodney James Walker. I used to watch the TV show *Walker, Texas Ranger* with my old college buddy Rodney Jones. Bet I don't forget the name Rodney Jones Walker. And he uses Rod Jones as an alias. My friend Rodney *hates* the nickname 'Rod' because he says it reminds him of the 1980s. Hmm. He's wanted by LAPD for assault. Hey, the actor who plays Walker probably actually lives in Los Angeles. This guy is 37? That's how old Aunt Joan is. This is getting spooky. Hmm, he's white, just like the actor on *Walker, Texas Ranger,* and he's my height and I weigh 190 also. He's ugly, but he's strong."

You get the picture. Your goal is to find a way to make the information you see mean something to you. Your mental conversation may not turn out to be as elaborate or outlandish as the one described above, but you will be far more likely to remember the details when you make them come alive and relate them to something or someone familiar.

Look at the information on the previous page again, make up your own mental conversation, and then see how easy it is to answer the following questions.

3. What is Walker wanted for?
   a. homicide
   b. burglary
   c. assault
   d. theft

4. How old is Walker?
   a. 30
   b. 33
   c. 37
   d. 27

5. What kind of weapon is Walker known to carry?
   a. boot knife
   b. diving knife
   c. brass knuckles
   d. boot razor blade

Check your answers by glancing back at the description. These questions should have seemed pretty simple. However, because this isn't a perfect world for the test taker, keep in mind that you'll be seeing questions containing information from other wanted posters. You may be asked to look at six or more posters and memorize them all. For example, in question 3 above, the right answer is choice **c**, but choices **a**, **b**, and **d** are likely to be crimes committed by some of the other suspects you've memorized for the same test. In other words, don't count on picking the most familiar answer—chances are, the choices will *all* look familiar. Instead, rely on the little conversation you had with yourself about a given suspect; that way you're less likely to confuse the various criminals.

This technique of associating the new and unfamiliar with something old and familiar works well for almost any type of memorization. Practice this technique for this test, and then use it again when you get your patrol car.

What to Do

1. Divide the number of minutes you have for memorizing the wanted posters by the number of posters, and then spend only that number of minutes on each poster.
2. Proceed methodically, top to bottom, with both the picture and the text.
3. Have a conversation with yourself; tell yourself a story about the suspect. Associate the unfamiliar picture and description with people you know.

What Not to Do

- **Do not** choose an answer just because it looks familiar. It might be related to the wrong suspect.
- **Do not** try to memorize all the wanted posters at once. Work on one at a time.

Questions Based on Street Scenes

Another way police departments test your memory skills is to let you study a drawing or photograph of a scene for a certain amount of time—either as part of a packet that include passages and wanted posters or by itself—and then ask you questions about the scene.

The picture will usually be a scene of a busy city street with plenty of details for you to memorize: store names, buses, taxis, people, clothing, action scenes (a mugging or maybe someone changing a flat tire on a car), and street signs.

At the end of this chapter, you will find a street scene and several related questions that you can use to practice.

What to Do

Use a methodical approach to studying what you see. When you read sentences on a page, you read from left to right. This skill is as automatic as breathing for most English-language readers. Approach memorizing a picture the same way you read, taking in the information from left to right. Instead of staring at the street scene with the whole picture in focus, make yourself start at the left and work your way across the page until you get to the right.

What Not to Do

- **Do not** let yourself get overwhelmed when you first see the busy street scene. Take a deep breath and decide to be methodical.
- **Do not** try to start memorizing with a shotgun approach, letting your eyes roam all over the page without really taking in the details.

Questions Based on a Video

Some departments will show you a video and then have you answer questions about what you have observed. This test is not widely used, but it is a method you may encounter. Your best bet is to relax, study the situation on the screen carefully and with confidence that you will remember what you see, and then tackle the questions.

▶ Using a Study Guide

Instead of making you memorize material right there during the test, some departments send out a study booklet a few weeks in advance of the test. The booklet contains detailed instructions on what you will be expected to know for the test. The expectation is that you will have plenty of time to memorize the information and that you will be able to answer questions based on what you have memorized.

For example, you may see several pictures of items stolen in a burglary—maybe a wristwatch or a crown inlaid with six rubies. On test day, you may see a question like this:

6. In the study booklet provided to you, there are several drawings of items taken in a burglary. One of the items was a crown. How many jewels did you see on the crown?
a. three
b. four
c. none
d. six

The questions are simple. No tricks here. You just have to be able to recall details.

What to Do

If you get material to study in advance, study it *in advance.* Don't start the day before the test. Spend a little time on your study booklet every day from the day you get it until the day before the test.

What Not to Do

Do not read the questions too quickly. If you're having trouble remembering the details, going with what initially feels like the correct answer is usually a good idea—but you must make sure you're answering the right question. If you were reading quickly and didn't look at the last sentence in the example above, you might anticipate that the question asks you how many crowns you saw in the drawing, not how many jewels were on the crown. Haste can produce easily avoidable errors.

▶ Memorization Tips

Memorization is much easier if you approach the task with the expectation that you *will* remember what you see. Call it positive thinking, self-hypnosis, or concentration—it doesn't really matter as long as you get results. When you run through the practice questions in this book, prepare your mind before you start. Tell yourself over and over that you will remember what you see as you study the images. Your performance level will rise to meet your expectations.

Yes, it's easy for your brain to freeze up when you see a drawing filled with details, a test section full of questions, and a test proctor standing above you with a stopwatch in one hand intoning, "You have five minutes to study this drawing. You may begin." But if you've programmed yourself to stay calm, stay alert, and execute your plan, you will be much more likely to remember the details when you need them.

Plan? Yes, you need a plan. If you have a method for memorizing, say, a busy urban street scene—like the left-to-right scheme we just outlined—then you will be more likely to relax and allow yourself to retain what you've seen long enough to answer the test questions. Keep in mind that you aren't trying to memorize the scene forever; you are merely doing it to retain the information long enough to answer the test questions.

Salon & Spa
212-555-1605
SALON & SPA
212-555-1605
Salon & Spa
212–555–1605
ENTRANCE
Messenger Service
Rush Trucking
PHOTO
Joe's
DISCOUNT
PHOTO
CIGARETTES
MAGAZINES
COLD DRINKS
PHONE CARDS
2 CORTLANDT ST.
PHOTO
SHOP
COLOR FILM
PROCESSING
FREE
FILM
FREE
2nd SET

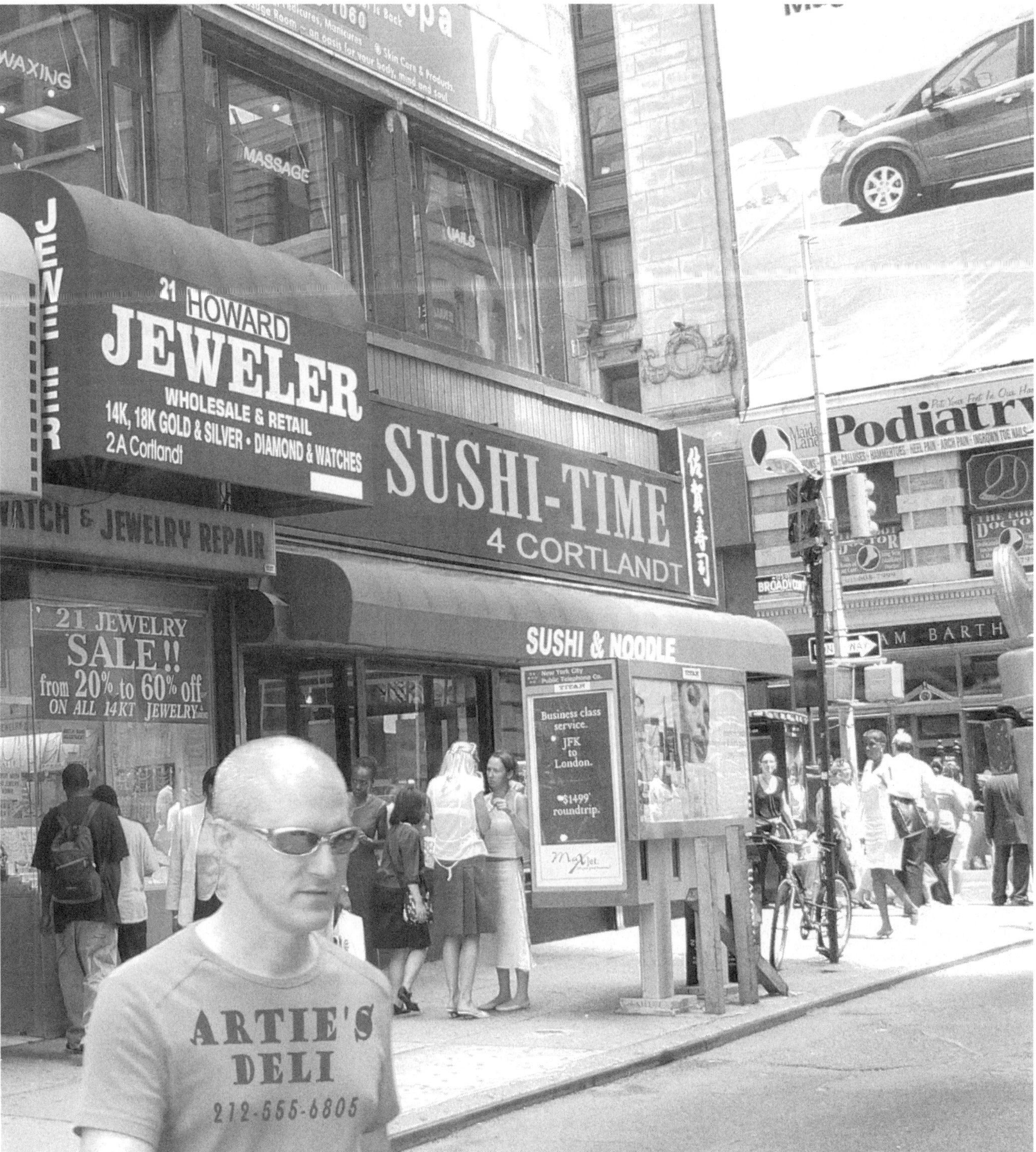
WAXING
MASSAGE
JEWELER
21 HOWARD
JEWELER
WHOLESALE & RETAIL
14K, 18K GOLD & SILVER • DIAMOND & WATCHES
2A Cortlandt
WATCH & JEWELRY REPAIR
SUSHI-TIME
4 CORTLANDT
21 JEWELRY
SALE!!
from 20% to 60% off
ON ALL 14KT JEWELRY
SUSHI & NOODLE
Business class
service.
JFK
to
London.
$1499
roundtrip.
Podiatry
ARTIE'S
DELI
212-555-6805

▶ Observation Tips

It's almost impossible to talk about memorization without bringing up observation. Some people are naturally observant. Some drift off frequently and have no awareness of the world around them. Whatever category you think you are in, it's never too late to sharpen, or to acquire, strong observation skills. How? Practice, of course.

Newspaper photos make great practice tools. News photos are action-oriented and usually have more than one person in the scenes. Sit down in a quiet place, clear your mind, remind yourself for several minutes that you will retain all the details you need when you study the picture, and then turn to a picture and study it for about five minutes. At the end of the time, turn the picture over, get a piece of paper and a pencil, then write down all the details you can think of in the picture. Make yourself do this as often as possible before the test.

You can practice your observation skills on the way to work or school, too. Instead of sitting in your car waiting for the light to change with a blank stare on your face, look around you and say out loud what you see. "I'm at the corner of 12th and Walnut. I see a man in a black, full-length raincoat standing on the northeast corner looking in the display window of Hank's Motorcycle Shop. There's a black Subaru station wagon parked at a meter near the motorcycle shop. The license plate is . . ." (If you ride to work on a bus or train, you can say these things silently to yourself.) Not only are you practicing a basic skill that you will need to become an excellent police officer, you are training your mind to succeed at whatever memory questions the test maker throws your way.

▶ Memory and Observation Practice

On the previous page is a street scene like those found on some police exams. Following are several questions about details of the scene. Use this scene to practice your memory skills. Take exactly five minutes to study the picture and then answer the questions that follow, without looking back at the picture.

Then check your answers by looking back at the scene. If you get all the questions right, you know you're well prepared for memory questions. If you miss a few, you know you need to spend more time practicing, using the tips outlined above. Remember, you *can* improve your memory with practice.

7. What type of sale is advertised at Howard Jeweler?
- **a.** 50% off
- **b.** 2 for 1
- **c.** Going out of Business
- **d.** 20% to 60% off

8. Which of the following is true about the man wearing the Artie's Deli shirt?
- **a.** His sunglasses are black.
- **b.** He has a shaved head.
- **c.** He has a tattoo on his right arm.
- **d.** He wears an earring in his right ear.

9. What is the complete name of the store located directly to the left of Howard Jeweler?
- **a.** Photo by Joe
- **b.** Photo Discount
- **c.** Joe's Photo
- **d.** Joe's Discount Photo

Tips for Memory and Observation Questions

- Use a methodical approach to memorization.
- Find ways to create links between your long-term memory and short-term memory.
- For questions based on pictures, "read" the picture from top to bottom or left to right.
- For questions based on materials you receive in advance, study the materials for a few minutes every day before the test.
- Visualize as you read passages, forming the words into a moving picture in your mind.
- Read the questions carefully; make sure you're answering the question that's being asked.
- Practice your memory and observation skills in your daily routine.

10. What is Howard Jeweler's address?

a. 2 Cortlandt
b. 2A Cortlandt
c. 3 Cortlandt
d. 3A Cortlandt

11. What is Salon & Spa's phone number?

a. 212-555-1605
b. 212-555-1606
c. 212-555-1506
d. 212-555-1505

12. How many bicycles are there in the photograph?

a. 0
b. 1
c. 2
d. 3

13. There are two young women talking to each other in the photo. Where are they standing?

a. at a payphone kiosk
b. next to a rack of sunglasses
c. near a bicycle rack
d. outside the Salon & Spa entrance

14. What phrase is written on Sushi-Time's awning?

a. Sushi & Noodle Restaurant
b. Sushi & Noodle
c. Sushi
d. Sushi Restaurant

15. What is the man wearing the backpack doing in the photograph?

a. talking on a cell phone
b. looking at the Howard Jeweler window display
c. crossing the street
d. exiting from Salon & Spa

▶ Additional Resources

To help you improve your memory and observation skills, take advantage of one or more of the following resources.

Books

- *The Memory Book* by Harry Lorayne and Jerry Lucas (Ballantine Books)
- *Learn to Remember: Practical Techniques and Exercises to Improve Your Memory* by Dominic O'Brien (Chronicle Books)
- *Improve Your Memory* by Ron Fry (Career Press)
- *The Complete Idiot's Guide to Improving Your Memory* by Michael Kurland (Alpha Books)

Websites

- www.memoryzine.com/games.html
  If you'd like to get some practice and help improving your memory skills, this site has some memory games developed by the Practical Memory Institute (PMI) that are designed to improve spatial memory and focus.
- www.mindtools.com/memory.html
  This website's explanations are particularly helpful in studying for exams or in situations in which you need to remember detailed, structured information. They also make things like learning foreign languages and remembering people's names much easier.

CHAPTER

14 Number and Letter Recall

CHAPTER SUMMARY

If you are going to take the Law Enforcement Candidate Record (LECR) written exam, then you will need to complete a section on the exam that asks you to match up number and letter combinations. This chapter will help you practice the format of this type of question.

When you encountered the recall questions in Exam 3 of this book, you probably thought, "What in the world does this have to do with law enforcement work? This looks like a test for clerical workers!" On the face of it, being able to match number combinations to letter combinations doesn't look like something police officers have to do every day—and it isn't. But this portion of the exam is testing two important skills: your visual perception and your short-term memory. Indirectly, the recall portion also tests your ability to keep your cool under pressure. You have a short amount of time to answer a lot of questions. If you can keep your head and work methodically through the task, you demonstrate your capacity to maintain composure under fire—a vital ability for any police officer.

You can't really study for this portion of the exam. What you can do is familiarize yourself with the recall question format and practice with it. If you know what to expect, you will have an edge over candidates who arrive on test day unfamiliar with this unusual type of question.

▶ What Recall Questions Are Like

If you're following the plan outlined in this book, you've already seen number and letter recall questions in the third practice exam. The recall portion of the test gives you a key consisting of combinations of three letters, each of which is paired with a two-digit number. Each question consists of one of the three-letter combinations from the key, followed by five two-digit numbers, one of which is the number that matches the letter combination in the key. Your task is simply to choose the matching number combination and fill in the appropriate circle on your answer sheet. You will have the key in front of you as you work. Here's a brief example:

KEY

SWO	BDT	MUB	LIH	R I Z
84	28	42	48	24

		a	b	c	d	e
1.	MUB	28	48	24	42	84
2.	SWO	48	24	84	28	42
3.	RIZ	24	84	42	48	28
4.	BDT	42	28	48	84	24

The first question asks you which number combination goes with MUB. The correct number is 42, so you would fill in the **d** circle on your answer sheet. The number that goes with SWO in question 2 is 84, so you'd fill in circle **c**. The answer for question 3 is **a**, and the answer for question 4 is **b**.

Looks simple, right? The task itself *is* simple and doesn't require a lot of brain power. But there's a catch: The key will be longer than this, including more letter/number combinations, and you will have to answer 100 questions like this in only nine minutes.

The Purpose of Recall Questions

The time limit is the point of this portion of the exam. Any reasonably intelligent eight-year-old could find the appropriate number to go with the letter combination, given enough time. But you *aren't* given enough time. You have 100 questions to answer in nine minutes. That averages out to 5.4 seconds per question, in which time you have to

1. Look at the question to identify the letter combination you have to find in the key.
2. Find that letter combination in the key and identify the number that goes with it.
3. Go back to the question to see which choice that number is.
4. Fill in your answer choice on the answer sheet.

Why is the hiring agency putting you through this? Because there is a demonstrable correlation between candidates' ability to do well on this test and their success in training and on the job. This portion of the test sorts out people who have

- good perceptual skills
- a reliable short-term memory
- the ability to work quickly without sacrificing accuracy
- the ability to work well under pressure

If you can find the appropriate letter/number combinations in the allotted time, you have the ability to focus your attention and pick out details. If you happen to remember some of the letter/number combinations as you work, you won't have to consult the key as often and will move more quickly through the questions. Because points are subtracted for wrong answers, your test score will show when you guessed or chose the wrong number. Finally, if you can work methodically through this portion of the test, knowing that you have only nine minutes, you show your ability to keep your cool under high-pressure conditions.

► How to Deal with Recall Questions

There's just one secret to doing well on this portion of the test: Focus and stay calm. You may think, "That's easier said than done." Of course it is. But you can do it. By the time you finish this chapter and the second practice test, not only will you know what to expect, but you will also have practiced this odd type of question—and that's probably more than the other candidates taking the test will have done.

Here are some calming facts about the recall portion of the exam:

- The task itself is really quite simple: to match letter and number combinations.
- You're not expected to get through all 100 questions. If you do, great, but you can do well without finishing the entire section.

Armed with those facts, here's your strategy:

- Plan ahead for success. Remind yourself of how simple this task really is. Build a reservoir of self-confidence for exam day.
- When you hit the recall section, focus and stay calm. Take three deep breaths and then turn to the first letter combination.
- Don't bother scanning the key before you start, unless it's very short. Start with the first question.
- Do one question at a time. Trying to pick up the numbers for several letter combinations at a time will just confuse you.
- Say the letter combination you're looking for silently to yourself. Move your lips if you want; the other test takers will not be looking at you. When you find the number you're looking for, say it silently too. This tactic helps fix the letters or number in your mind.
- Once you've decided on your answer, *go with it.* Don't waste time checking back to the key to make sure your answer is right.
- If you can't find the letter combination you're looking for on the key, or if the number you've chosen isn't one of the answer choices, just skip that question and move to the next one.
- Try to keep one finger on your place on the answer sheet at all times, and check frequently to make sure that you're filling in the circle of the number that corresponds with the question number you're answering.

Try these tactics on the following practice set. Find a watch with a second hand and recruit a friend to time you. You have two minutes to do this practice set.

KEY

REC	DBE	HRA	OLB	RAQ	ONK	POH	GKI
48	87	98	75	27	45	79	29
MAQ	BLD	RIW	HOK	GEB	WOL	INB	PAH
57	28	94	78	92	84	47	95
DNI	PKI	LAR	RIK	KIG	HMA	LIN	ODB
82	42	59	49	97	24	72	74

		a	b	c	d	e
1.	HMA	24	98	27	74	72
2.	OLB	27	45	75	94	57
3.	HOK	92	45	24	78	87
4.	POH	29	79	84	78	95
5.	KIG	97	49	79	92	29
6.	DNI	57	28	87	47	82
7.	LAR	42	72	47	94	59
8.	INB	84	59	47	95	72
9.	DBE	98	87	28	48	78
10.	GKI	79	97	29	92	47
11.	RIK	49	59	94	82	97

		a	b	c	d	e
12.	LIN	24	49	75	72	47
13.	BLD	48	75	94	28	42
14.	WOL	72	24	95	79	84
15.	HRA	98	87	59	75	24
16.	ONK	28	45	79	27	97
17.	RIW	27	78	94	28	75
18.	PKI	28	42	59	29	49
19.	ODB	72	95	45	75	74
20.	REC	84	87	48	74	42
21.	RAQ	57	95	28	27	45
22.	GEB	92	95	48	95	74

Now that your two minutes are up, you can go back and check your answers with the key. Did you manage to do most of the 22 questions in two minutes? If so, you will do fine on the real test. If you got just one or two questions wrong, don't worry about them. You're not expected to finish all the questions, and you don't need a perfect score to get the job.

If you got only halfway through the set, or if you got more than three questions wrong, the problem is probably that you lost your cool. Your own confidence in your ability to do this test is the most important factor in your success. Review the strategy tips, and practice improving your self-confidence.

Say these words to yourself three times a day between now and exam day: *I can do this test. It's really quite simple. I just need to focus on doing one step at a time, and then I know I'll do well.* Armed with that kind of self-confidence, you're on your way to a high score.

Tips for Answering Number and Letter Recall Questions

- Focus and stay calm.
- Work methodically on one question at a time.
- Say the letter and number combinations to yourself silently as you look for them.
- Skip any questions you find difficult.
- Don't expect to finish all the questions.

► Extra Practice with Recall Questions

There's no way you can really study for the recall section of the test, but you can practice. So here's an extra bonus section: a complete recall section of 100 questions so you can practice. There's an answer sheet on the opposite page—tear it out of the book so you can use it with the test. If you do not own this book, use a piece of scrap paper.

To review: You'll be given a key; in this case, each key has 27 letter-number combinations. The questions consist of one of the three-letter combinations from the key, followed by 5 two-digit numbers. Your job is to find the number combination that goes with the given three-letter combination and mark the corresponding circle on the answer sheet.

Remember, time is of the essence. Before you do this practice section, review the strategy tips in this chapter. Then get prepared: Tear out the answer sheet or get a piece of scrap paper, get a couple of pencils, and situate yourself at a table or desk where you can work undisturbed. Then set a timer for nine minutes, which is the amount of time you'll be allowed for this section on the real test. And then begin. Remember the key to success: Focus and stay calm.

When you've finished this practice section, check your answers against the answer key that follows. You'll probably find you did better than in the practice exam in Chapter 6. And you'll have another chance to improve your recall skills when you take the second practice exam of this type in Chapter 18.

Number and Letter Recall Practice

1.	ⓐ	ⓑ	ⓒ	ⓓ	ⓔ
2.	ⓐ	ⓑ	ⓒ	ⓓ	ⓔ
3.	ⓐ	ⓑ	ⓒ	ⓓ	ⓔ
4.	ⓐ	ⓑ	ⓒ	ⓓ	ⓔ
5.	ⓐ	ⓑ	ⓒ	ⓓ	ⓔ
6.	ⓐ	ⓑ	ⓒ	ⓓ	ⓔ
7.	ⓐ	ⓑ	ⓒ	ⓓ	ⓔ
8.	ⓐ	ⓑ	ⓒ	ⓓ	ⓔ
9.	ⓐ	ⓑ	ⓒ	ⓓ	ⓔ
10.	ⓐ	ⓑ	ⓒ	ⓓ	ⓔ
11.	ⓐ	ⓑ	ⓒ	ⓓ	ⓔ
12.	ⓐ	ⓑ	ⓒ	ⓓ	ⓔ
13.	ⓐ	ⓑ	ⓒ	ⓓ	ⓔ
14.	ⓐ	ⓑ	ⓒ	ⓓ	ⓔ
15.	ⓐ	ⓑ	ⓒ	ⓓ	ⓔ
16.	ⓐ	ⓑ	ⓒ	ⓓ	ⓔ
17.	ⓐ	ⓑ	ⓒ	ⓓ	ⓔ
18.	ⓐ	ⓑ	ⓒ	ⓓ	ⓔ
19.	ⓐ	ⓑ	ⓒ	ⓓ	ⓔ
20.	ⓐ	ⓑ	ⓒ	ⓓ	ⓔ
21.	ⓐ	ⓑ	ⓒ	ⓓ	ⓔ
22.	ⓐ	ⓑ	ⓒ	ⓓ	ⓔ
23.	ⓐ	ⓑ	ⓒ	ⓓ	ⓔ
24.	ⓐ	ⓑ	ⓒ	ⓓ	ⓔ
25.	ⓐ	ⓑ	ⓒ	ⓓ	ⓔ
26.	ⓐ	ⓑ	ⓒ	ⓓ	ⓔ
27.	ⓐ	ⓑ	ⓒ	ⓓ	ⓔ
28.	ⓐ	ⓑ	ⓒ	ⓓ	ⓔ
29.	ⓐ	ⓑ	ⓒ	ⓓ	ⓔ
30.	ⓐ	ⓑ	ⓒ	ⓓ	ⓔ
31.	ⓐ	ⓑ	ⓒ	ⓓ	ⓔ
32.	ⓐ	ⓑ	ⓒ	ⓓ	ⓔ
33.	ⓐ	ⓑ	ⓒ	ⓓ	ⓔ
34.	ⓐ	ⓑ	ⓒ	ⓓ	ⓔ
35.	ⓐ	ⓑ	ⓒ	ⓓ	ⓔ
36.	ⓐ	ⓑ	ⓒ	ⓓ	ⓔ
37.	ⓐ	ⓑ	ⓒ	ⓓ	ⓔ
38.	ⓐ	ⓑ	ⓒ	ⓓ	ⓔ
39.	ⓐ	ⓑ	ⓒ	ⓓ	ⓔ
40.	ⓐ	ⓑ	ⓒ	ⓓ	ⓔ
41.	ⓐ	ⓑ	ⓒ	ⓓ	ⓔ
42.	ⓐ	ⓑ	ⓒ	ⓓ	ⓔ
43.	ⓐ	ⓑ	ⓒ	ⓓ	ⓔ
44.	ⓐ	ⓑ	ⓒ	ⓓ	ⓔ
45.	ⓐ	ⓑ	ⓒ	ⓓ	ⓔ
46.	ⓐ	ⓑ	ⓒ	ⓓ	ⓔ
47.	ⓐ	ⓑ	ⓒ	ⓓ	ⓔ
48.	ⓐ	ⓑ	ⓒ	ⓓ	ⓔ
49.	ⓐ	ⓑ	ⓒ	ⓓ	ⓔ
50.	ⓐ	ⓑ	ⓒ	ⓓ	ⓔ
51.	ⓐ	ⓑ	ⓒ	ⓓ	ⓔ
52.	ⓐ	ⓑ	ⓒ	ⓓ	ⓔ
53.	ⓐ	ⓑ	ⓒ	ⓓ	ⓔ
54.	ⓐ	ⓑ	ⓒ	ⓓ	ⓔ
55.	ⓐ	ⓑ	ⓒ	ⓓ	ⓔ
56.	ⓐ	ⓑ	ⓒ	ⓓ	ⓔ
57.	ⓐ	ⓑ	ⓒ	ⓓ	ⓔ
58.	ⓐ	ⓑ	ⓒ	ⓓ	ⓔ
59.	ⓐ	ⓑ	ⓒ	ⓓ	ⓔ
60.	ⓐ	ⓑ	ⓒ	ⓓ	ⓔ
61.	ⓐ	ⓑ	ⓒ	ⓓ	ⓔ
62.	ⓐ	ⓑ	ⓒ	ⓓ	ⓔ
63.	ⓐ	ⓑ	ⓒ	ⓓ	ⓔ
64.	ⓐ	ⓑ	ⓒ	ⓓ	ⓔ
65.	ⓐ	ⓑ	ⓒ	ⓓ	ⓔ
66.	ⓐ	ⓑ	ⓒ	ⓓ	ⓔ
67.	ⓐ	ⓑ	ⓒ	ⓓ	ⓔ
68.	ⓐ	ⓑ	ⓒ	ⓓ	ⓔ
69.	ⓐ	ⓑ	ⓒ	ⓓ	ⓔ
70.	ⓐ	ⓑ	ⓒ	ⓓ	ⓔ
71.	ⓐ	ⓑ	ⓒ	ⓓ	ⓔ
72.	ⓐ	ⓑ	ⓒ	ⓓ	ⓔ
73.	ⓐ	ⓑ	ⓒ	ⓓ	ⓔ
74.	ⓐ	ⓑ	ⓒ	ⓓ	ⓔ
75.	ⓐ	ⓑ	ⓒ	ⓓ	ⓔ
76.	ⓐ	ⓑ	ⓒ	ⓓ	ⓔ
77.	ⓐ	ⓑ	ⓒ	ⓓ	ⓔ
78.	ⓐ	ⓑ	ⓒ	ⓓ	ⓔ
79.	ⓐ	ⓑ	ⓒ	ⓓ	ⓔ
80.	ⓐ	ⓑ	ⓒ	ⓓ	ⓔ
81.	ⓐ	ⓑ	ⓒ	ⓓ	ⓔ
82.	ⓐ	ⓑ	ⓒ	ⓓ	ⓔ
83.	ⓐ	ⓑ	ⓒ	ⓓ	ⓔ
84.	ⓐ	ⓑ	ⓒ	ⓓ	ⓔ
85.	ⓐ	ⓑ	ⓒ	ⓓ	ⓔ
86.	ⓐ	ⓑ	ⓒ	ⓓ	ⓔ
87.	ⓐ	ⓑ	ⓒ	ⓓ	ⓔ
88.	ⓐ	ⓑ	ⓒ	ⓓ	ⓔ
89.	ⓐ	ⓑ	ⓒ	ⓓ	ⓔ
90.	ⓐ	ⓑ	ⓒ	ⓓ	ⓔ
91.	ⓐ	ⓑ	ⓒ	ⓓ	ⓔ
92.	ⓐ	ⓑ	ⓒ	ⓓ	ⓔ
93.	ⓐ	ⓑ	ⓒ	ⓓ	ⓔ
94.	ⓐ	ⓑ	ⓒ	ⓓ	ⓔ
95.	ⓐ	ⓑ	ⓒ	ⓓ	ⓔ
96.	ⓐ	ⓑ	ⓒ	ⓓ	ⓔ
97.	ⓐ	ⓑ	ⓒ	ⓓ	ⓔ
98.	ⓐ	ⓑ	ⓒ	ⓓ	ⓔ
99.	ⓐ	ⓑ	ⓒ	ⓓ	ⓔ
100.	ⓐ	ⓑ	ⓒ	ⓓ	ⓔ

KEY 1

BNB	FDE	RST	XAZ	JKI	DEB	FIV	ABS	QBN
21	29	44	42	61	55	63	99	62
GFL	BVG	POQ	GAQ	BXC	WGL	YIR	RJC	BAZ
23	88	13	71	87	72	16	32	54
MHY	KVT	NOP	SEF	LQG	GEX	HIK	DTE	MUQ
42	86	47	12	19	65	11	98	33

		a	b	c	d	e
1.	MHY	62	78	99	42	33
2.	FIV	81	44	47	98	63
3.	WGL	72	71	55	23	17
4.	POQ	36	22	47	13	95
5.	LQG	91	43	52	27	19
6.	NOP	12	11	35	47	70
7.	SEF	51	37	39	54	12
8.	GEX	37	44	41	65	95
9.	FDE	29	12	88	35	63
10.	BVG	65	88	23	49	11
11.	MUQ	75	91	55	33	87
12.	HIK	32	11	95	94	88
13.	HIK	63	14	65	93	42
14.	GFL	75	23	93	45	83
15.	RST	91	44	19	31	13
16.	JKI	55	42	46	61	93
17.	DTE	11	98	53	25	16
18.	KVT	65	32	86	23	13
19.	BXC	36	87	18	14	98
20.	BAZ	54	81	23	12	11
21.	GAQ	17	63	71	29	30
22.	DEB	55	29	23	82	91
23.	BNB	87	21	47	19	62
24.	RJC	61	32	93	24	36
25.	QBN	34	72	45	62	95

KEY 2

GOF	EOG	JKO	DAJ	XOE	KGO	OIG	JIX	ANA
32	88	42	54	86	53	41	23	14
FNO	FDE	IHG	ASA	BVI	GDO	IAF	OXW	LDO
34	39	74	63	57	11	52	37	55
GYH	MAE	TGN	AFH	JTG	XEH	IQF	PAH	QFA
13	85	45	43	49	51	44	38	20

		a	b	c	d	e
26.	JTG	35	49	11	23	55
27.	KGO	68	47	53	83	35
28.	GOF	35	58	33	45	32
29.	JKO	42	54	12	23	50
30.	EOG	15	88	23	34	94
31.	ASA	44	63	88	12	25
32.	GYH	47	52	13	41	24
33.	OXW	62	33	54	24	37
34.	FDE	52	43	47	39	63
35.	DAJ	43	24	68	53	54
36.	TGN	11	36	45	48	23
37.	FNO	34	88	13	43	86
38.	MAE	52	46	85	23	33

		a	b	c	d	e
39.	AFH	61	22	43	14	28
40.	QFA	51	32	45	20	24
41.	XEH	51	43	11	23	58
42.	XOE	24	86	21	14	54
43.	PAH	32	47	38	62	24
44.	IQF	52	44	84	47	83
45.	ANA	35	48	23	34	14
46.	GDO	93	11	23	43	52
47.	IAF	52	25	90	31	28
48.	IHG	42	36	74	42	13
49.	BVI	31	57	23	38	75
50.	LDO	98	35	55	64	37

KEY 3

KAM	LAE	YAN	MFD	JAD	XYD	IEN	DBF	MFB
15	85	45	49	47	51	44	58	22
ABK	ENA	LNF	DPB	ATR	KXJ	ANI	IDB	BGN
72	88	42	59	81	19	41	25	14
DAF	QEF	MNI	BYX	XIC	DNH	IYU	LMQ	JFD
54	16	34	51	53	11	52	53	55

		a	b	c	d	e
51.	LAE	68	34	45	85	58
52.	MFB	58	74	12	22	59
53.	DPB	55	58	19	95	59
54.	BGN	55	54	14	52	99
55.	ABK	15	58	25	51	72
56.	QEF	62	16	54	24	15
57.	KXJ	52	45	43	69	19
58.	JAD	44	64	88	47	25
59.	DNH	43	85	25	11	24
60.	BYX	45	24	18	51	45
61.	LNF	42	11	58	25	58
62.	ENA	52	88	51	42	86
63.	MFD	78	49	95	46	56

		a	b	c	d	e
64.	MNI	11	96	94	48	34
65.	YAN	51	45	43	48	24
66.	KAM	42	56	15	42	17
67.	JFD	27	55	21	94	54
68.	ATR	81	34	45	83	24
69.	IYU	29	47	84	52	58
70.	IEN	15	84	52	49	44
71.	DAF	75	65	25	54	52
72.	IDB	25	52	70	15	82
73.	XYD	61	82	51	14	28
74.	DBF	51	60	25	58	35
75.	XIC	53	46	15	25	99

KEY 4

GHT	JAV	DRT	SLV	HMZ	DTA	AGB	PDL	GRX
45	75	43	56	35	11	25	35	55
HGF	**RTS**	**LQC**	**DZB**	**ALW**	**CWK**	**PTF**	**MKS**	**WER**
51	58	54	94	74	15	44	85	22
VAF	**CXR**	**YEG**	**KUB**	**JMT**	**SQN**	**ZKD**	**RTF**	**ZOT**
27	88	24	95	18	59	14	52	41

		a	b	c	d	e
76.	DZB	26	78	94	42	33
77.	KUB	95	44	74	98	63
78.	SLV	72	71	56	23	17
79.	CXR	36	22	88	13	95
80.	HGF	51	73	39	45	12
81.	DTA	12	11	35	47	70
82.	VAF	19	43	25	27	19
83.	DRT	37	43	41	65	95
84.	ZOT	29	41	88	53	36
85.	HMZ	35	88	23	49	11
86.	WER	75	91	55	22	78
87.	JAV	32	11	75	49	88
88.	LQC	63	14	54	93	42

		a	b	c	d	e
89.	YEG	75	24	93	45	83
90.	CWK	15	44	91	31	13
91.	ALW	75	42	46	61	93
92.	ZKD	11	98	53	14	16
93.	JMT	65	32	80	23	18
94.	RTF	36	52	18	14	89
95.	PDL	54	81	35	12	11
96.	GHT	71	36	45	92	30
97.	PTF	44	92	23	28	19
98.	GRX	87	12	47	55	26
99.	AGB	16	25	39	24	63
100.	SQN	34	27	54	26	59

Answers

1. d.
2. e.
3. a.
4. d.
5. e.
6. d.
7. e.
8. d.
9. a.
10. b.
11. d.
12. b.
13. d.
14. b.
15. b.
16. d.
17. b.
18. c.
19. b.
20. a.
21. c.
22. a.
23. b.
24. b.
25. d.
26. b.
27. c.
28. e.
29. a.
30. b.
31. b.
32. c.
33. e.
34. d.
35. e.
36. c.
37. a.
38. c.
39. c.
40. d.
41. a.
42. b.
43. c.
44. b.
45. e.
46. b.
47. a.
48. c.
49. b.
50. c.
51. d.
52. d.
53. e.
54. c.
55. e.
56. b.
57. e.
58. d.
59. d.
60. d.
61. a.
62. b.
63. b.
64. e.
65. b.
66. c.
67. b.
68. a.
69. d.
70. e.
71. d.
72. a.
73. c.
74. d.
75. a.
76. c.
77. a.
78. c.
79. c.
80. a.
81. b.
82. d.
83. b.
84. b.
85. a.
86. d.
87. c.
88. c.
89. b.
90. a.
91. a.
92. d.
93. e.
94. b.
95. c.
96. c.
97. a.
98. d.
99. b.
100. e.

CHAPTER

15 Personal Background

CHAPTER SUMMARY

This chapter describes the personal background section of the police officer exam, and explains why honesty is the best policy when responding to questions on this part of the exam.

Virtually every police department conducts a background investigation of its candidates. If you get far enough in the selection process, you can expect to fill out a traditional background form and to be investigated.

If the police department to which you are applying uses the Law Enforcement Candidate Record (LECR) as their written exam to screen candidates, then you will need to answer several questions about your personal background as a part of the exam. This chapter will help you become familiar with this portion of the exam.

The personal background section of the police officer exam allows the hiring agency to evaluate the kind of person you are, using a method that is easy for the department to assess—a multiple-choice exam.

You may see questions on the personal background section of the exam that usually aren't included in a traditional background investigation. For instance, you might be asked what kinds of books you like to read or whether you've spent time with a group of friends in the past two weeks. Such questions have nothing to do with your personal integrity and other such issues that are the purpose of the background investigation. Instead, they yield a statistical profile of the kind of person you are.

That profile can then be matched with the profiles of successful police officers. A statistical comparison suggests who is likely to become a good officer and who isn't. While it's possible that your answers to some of the questions will be checked in a background investigation later in the selection process, the real function of this section of the exam is to establish that statistical match-up.

▶ What the Personal Background Section Is Like

The personal background section of the exam consists of 185 multiple-choice questions. You will be given as much time as you need to complete these questions, which will be a refreshing break after the timed verbal and recall sections. Most people take two to four hours to complete the personal background section.

The questions cover your personal experience: your education, your work history and work habits, your relationships with family and friends, and your feelings or attitudes about any of those aspects of your life. Here's an example of a question that asks you about your relationship with your family:

1. Other than the people I live with, I get together with family
- **a.** at least once a year.
- **b.** every few months.
- **c.** monthly.
- **d.** at least weekly.
- **e.** at holiday times only.
- **f.** never.

All you have to do is answer the question honestly. There are no correct or incorrect answers to these questions. The correct answer is the one that's most true to your own experience.

In addition to questions that ask for more or less factual information, you may encounter questions that ask about your feelings or attitudes:

2. If I were passed over for a promotion, my main reaction would be one of
- **a.** bitterness.
- **b.** despair.
- **c.** happiness for the person who was promoted.
- **d.** determination to earn the next promotion.

Notice that there are fewer answer choices for this question than for the previous one. There may be as few as two or as many as ten answer choices for each question.

▶ How to Answer Personal Background Questions

There are no tricks to answering personal background questions. You simply choose the answer that best describes you or your experience.

Questions with More Than One Answer Choice

One thing that's a little unusual about this section of the test is that some questions allow you to choose more than one answer. Such questions are clearly marked:

3. If given the opportunity to volunteer, I would enjoy working with (Mark all that apply)
- **a.** children.
- **b.** older individuals.
- **c.** disabled individuals.
- **d.** homeless individuals.
- **e.** a cultural organization.
- **f.** a religious organization.
- **g.** I don't have time for volunteer activities.

In this example, you could mark only one choice, or you could mark all seven of them—though at that point someone might start wondering how honest you are. Questions that allow more than one answer choice are always clearly identified as such. For all other questions, you should mark only one answer.

Honesty is the Best Policy

It's impossible to stress the point too much: *You must answer all the questions honestly.* For one thing, this is a police officer exam, and police departments do have officers whose job is to investigate potential recruits. You wouldn't want to mark anything on your answer sheet that could later be shown to be untrue.

You might think that a question that asks about your feelings and attitudes would be tough to check on. In a sense that's true, in that a background investigator wouldn't be likely to find out that your real reaction to being passed over for a promotion would be one of bitterness. However, a test like this is constructed so that one answer checks against another in ways that are impossible for the test taker to detect. The test itself may be able to show when you haven't been completely truthful.

That being the case, even if you think your honest answer is not the one that would make your profile match that of successful police officers, you're better off marking that honest answer anyway. Your guess about what successful police officers would answer might well be wrong.

Here's an example:

4. I consider taking a few sheets of copier paper home from work to be
- **a.** employee theft.
- **b.** a trivial matter.
- **c.** acceptable behavior.
- **d.** okay, if done only once or twice.

Now, lots of people have taken copier paper home from work. Whether or not you're one of them yourself, you may think it's no big deal, choice **b**, or all right as long as one doesn't make a habit of it, choice **d**. Maybe you even think it's acceptable behavior (choice **c**) under some circumstances. But choice **a** leaps out at you—shouldn't a person who wants to be a law enforcement officer say that taking copier paper is employee theft? And so your impulse is to fill in choice **a**.

Don't do it—unless that answer is true. Fill in the answer that really reflects how you feel. It's impossible to tell what this question is getting at. Is the "correct" answer the one that seems to reflect a law-abiding personality—choice **a**? Or is it one of the ones that actually reflects how most people feel, thereby showing that you are answering this question honestly? The point is that you can't tell. The only safe course of action is to choose the honest answer, the one that truly reflects your own attitudes.

That's why this section of the exam is nothing to worry about. Now that you know what to expect, you've done everything you can or need to do to get ready. Just go in there and answer each question as honestly as you can.

CHAPTER

16 Police Officer Practice Exam 4

CHAPTER SUMMARY

This fourth exam tests your basic reading and writing skills. Comparing your performance on this exam with your performance on the first exam in this book will help you see how much you've improved.

Like the first exam in this book, Exam 4 is an example of the basic reading and writing skills that show up on police officer exams administered by many cities across the country. If you've already taken Exam 1 in Chapter 4, you've probably studied the areas where you needed the most work, and now you're ready to tackle the same kinds of questions with a little more authority.

There are 105 questions on this test: 65 in Book One and 40 in Book Two. Book One covers clarity of expression (grammar), vocabulary, spelling, and reading comprehension. Book Two is a different kind of reading test that requires you to fill in the missing words in a passage. The directions for each type of question are included in the test. The answer sheet you should use to mark your answers comes before the test, and the answer key and an explanation of how to score your test results come after.

One of the keys to doing well on any exam is simply knowing what to expect. While there's no substitute for having the skills the exam is testing, the experience of taking similar exams goes a long way toward enhancing your self-confidence—and self-confidence is key to doing well.

On the real test, you will have an enforced time limit to answer all the questions, but for now, don't worry about timing. Just take the test in as relaxed a manner as you can. Make sure you have enough time, however, to do the whole test at a sitting. Find a quiet spot where you won't be interrupted, and turn off the radio and TV. When you've finished, turn to the answer key to see how you did.

Police Officer Practice Exam Book One

1.	ⓐ	ⓑ	ⓒ	ⓓ	**26.**	ⓐ	ⓑ	ⓒ	ⓓ	**51.**	ⓐ	ⓑ	ⓒ	ⓓ
2.	ⓐ	ⓑ	ⓒ	ⓓ	**27.**	ⓐ	ⓑ	ⓒ	ⓓ	**52.**	ⓐ	ⓑ	ⓒ	ⓓ
3.	ⓐ	ⓑ	ⓒ	ⓓ	**28.**	ⓐ	ⓑ	ⓒ	ⓓ	**53.**	ⓐ	ⓑ	ⓒ	ⓓ
4.	ⓐ	ⓑ	ⓒ	ⓓ	**29.**	ⓐ	ⓑ	ⓒ	ⓓ	**54.**	ⓐ	ⓑ	ⓒ	ⓓ
5.	ⓐ	ⓑ	ⓒ	ⓓ	**30.**	ⓐ	ⓑ	ⓒ	ⓓ	**55.**	ⓐ	ⓑ	ⓒ	ⓓ
6.	ⓐ	ⓑ	ⓒ	ⓓ	**31.**	ⓐ	ⓑ	ⓒ	ⓓ	**56.**	ⓐ	ⓑ	ⓒ	ⓓ
7.	ⓐ	ⓑ	ⓒ	ⓓ	**32.**	ⓐ	ⓑ	ⓒ	ⓓ	**57.**	ⓐ	ⓑ	ⓒ	ⓓ
8.	ⓐ	ⓑ	ⓒ	ⓓ	**33.**	ⓐ	ⓑ	ⓒ	ⓓ	**58.**	ⓐ	ⓑ	ⓒ	ⓓ
9.	ⓐ	ⓑ	ⓒ	ⓓ	**34.**	ⓐ	ⓑ	ⓒ	ⓓ	**59.**	ⓐ	ⓑ	ⓒ	ⓓ
10.	ⓐ	ⓑ	ⓒ	ⓓ	**35.**	ⓐ	ⓑ	ⓒ	ⓓ	**60.**	ⓐ	ⓑ	ⓒ	ⓓ
11.	ⓐ	ⓑ	ⓒ	ⓓ	**36.**	ⓐ	ⓑ	ⓒ	ⓓ	**61.**	ⓐ	ⓑ	ⓒ	ⓓ
12.	ⓐ	ⓑ	ⓒ	ⓓ	**37.**	ⓐ	ⓑ	ⓒ	ⓓ	**62.**	ⓐ	ⓑ	ⓒ	ⓓ
13.	ⓐ	ⓑ	ⓒ	ⓓ	**38.**	ⓐ	ⓑ	ⓒ	ⓓ	**63.**	ⓐ	ⓑ	ⓒ	ⓓ
14.	ⓐ	ⓑ	ⓒ	ⓓ	**39.**	ⓐ	ⓑ	ⓒ	ⓓ	**64.**	ⓐ	ⓑ	ⓒ	ⓓ
15.	ⓐ	ⓑ	ⓒ	ⓓ	**40.**	ⓐ	ⓑ	ⓒ	ⓓ	**65.**	ⓐ	ⓑ	ⓒ	ⓓ
16.	ⓐ	ⓑ	ⓒ	ⓓ	**41.**	ⓐ	ⓑ	ⓒ	ⓓ					
17.	ⓐ	ⓑ	ⓒ	ⓓ	**42.**	ⓐ	ⓑ	ⓒ	ⓓ					
18.	ⓐ	ⓑ	ⓒ	ⓓ	**43.**	ⓐ	ⓑ	ⓒ	ⓓ					
19.	ⓐ	ⓑ	ⓒ	ⓓ	**44.**	ⓐ	ⓑ	ⓒ	ⓓ					
20.	ⓐ	ⓑ	ⓒ	ⓓ	**45.**	ⓐ	ⓑ	ⓒ	ⓓ					
21.	ⓐ	ⓑ	ⓒ	ⓓ	**46.**	ⓐ	ⓑ	ⓒ	ⓓ					
22.	ⓐ	ⓑ	ⓒ	ⓓ	**47.**	ⓐ	ⓑ	ⓒ	ⓓ					
23.	ⓐ	ⓑ	ⓒ	ⓓ	**48.**	ⓐ	ⓑ	ⓒ	ⓓ					
24.	ⓐ	ⓑ	ⓒ	ⓓ	**49.**	ⓐ	ⓑ	ⓒ	ⓓ					
25.	ⓐ	ⓑ	ⓒ	ⓓ	**50.**	ⓐ	ⓑ	ⓒ	ⓓ					

Police Officer Practice Exam Book Two

WRITE 1ST LETTER OF WORD HERE

CODE LETTERS HERE

1	2	3	4	5	6	7	8	9	10
A	A	A	A	A	A	A	A	A	A
B	B	B	B	B	B	B	B	B	B
C	C	C	C	C	C	C	C	C	C
D	D	D	D	D	D	D	D	D	D
E	E	E	E	E	E	E	E	E	E
F	F	F	F	F	F	F	F	F	F
G	G	G	G	G	G	G	G	G	G
H	H	H	H	H	H	H	H	H	H
I	I	I	I	I	I	I	I	I	I
J	J	J	J	J	J	J	J	J	J
K	K	K	K	K	K	K	K	K	K
L	L	L	L	L	L	L	L	L	L
M	M	M	M	M	M	M	M	M	M
N	N	N	N	N	N	N	N	N	N
O	O	O	O	O	O	O	O	O	O
P	P	P	P	P	P	P	P	P	P
Q	Q	Q	Q	Q	Q	Q	Q	Q	Q
R	R	R	R	R	R	R	R	R	R
S	S	S	S	S	S	S	S	S	S
T	T	T	T	T	T	T	T	T	T
U	U	U	U	U	U	U	U	U	U
V	V	V	V	V	V	V	V	V	V
W	W	W	W	W	W	W	W	W	W
X	X	X	X	X	X	X	X	X	X
Y	Y	Y	Y	Y	Y	Y	Y	Y	Y
Z	Z	Z	Z	Z	Z	Z	Z	Z	Z

11	12	13	14	15	16	17	18	19	20
A	A	A	A	A	A	A	A	A	A
B	B	B	B	B	B	B	B	B	B
C	C	C	C	C	C	C	C	C	C
D	D	D	D	D	D	D	D	D	D
E	E	E	E	E	E	E	E	E	E
F	F	F	F	F	F	F	F	F	F
G	G	G	G	G	G	G	G	G	G
H	H	H	H	H	H	H	H	H	H
I	I	I	I	I	I	I	I	I	I
J	J	J	J	J	J	J	J	J	J
K	K	K	K	K	K	K	K	K	K
L	L	L	L	L	L	L	L	L	L
M	M	M	M	M	M	M	M	M	M
N	N	N	N	N	N	N	N	N	N
O	O	O	O	O	O	O	O	O	O
P	P	P	P	P	P	P	P	P	P
Q	Q	Q	Q	Q	Q	Q	Q	Q	Q
R	R	R	R	R	R	R	R	R	R
S	S	S	S	S	S	S	S	S	S
T	T	T	T	T	T	T	T	T	T
U	U	U	U	U	U	U	U	U	U
V	V	V	V	V	V	V	V	V	V
W	W	W	W	W	W	W	W	W	W
X	X	X	X	X	X	X	X	X	X
Y	Y	Y	Y	Y	Y	Y	Y	Y	Y
Z	Z	Z	Z	Z	Z	Z	Z	Z	Z

21	22	23	24	25	26	27	28	29	30
A	A	A	A	A	A	A	A	A	A
B	B	B	B	B	B	B	B	B	B
C	C	C	C	C	C	C	C	C	C
D	D	D	D	D	D	D	D	D	D
E	E	E	E	E	E	E	E	E	E
F	F	F	F	F	F	F	F	F	F
G	G	G	G	G	G	G	G	G	G
H	H	H	H	H	H	H	H	H	H
I	I	I	I	I	I	I	I	I	I
J	J	J	J	J	J	J	J	J	J
K	K	K	K	K	K	K	K	K	K
L	L	L	L	L	L	L	L	L	L
M	M	M	M	M	M	M	M	M	M
N	N	N	N	N	N	N	N	N	N
O	O	O	O	O	O	O	O	O	O
P	P	P	P	P	P	P	P	P	P
Q	Q	Q	Q	Q	Q	Q	Q	Q	Q
R	R	R	R	R	R	R	R	R	R
S	S	S	S	S	S	S	S	S	S
T	T	T	T	T	T	T	T	T	T
U	U	U	U	U	U	U	U	U	U
V	V	V	V	V	V	V	V	V	V
W	W	W	W	W	W	W	W	W	W
X	X	X	X	X	X	X	X	X	X
Y	Y	Y	Y	Y	Y	Y	Y	Y	Y
Z	Z	Z	Z	Z	Z	Z	Z	Z	Z

31	32	33	34	35	36	37	38	39	40
A	A	A	A	A	A	A	A	A	A
B	B	B	B	B	B	B	B	B	B
C	C	C	C	C	C	C	C	C	C
D	D	D	D	D	D	D	D	D	D
E	E	E	E	E	E	E	E	E	E
F	F	F	F	F	F	F	F	F	F
G	G	G	G	G	G	G	G	G	G
H	H	H	H	H	H	H	H	H	H
I	I	I	I	I	I	I	I	I	I
J	J	J	J	J	J	J	J	J	J
K	K	K	K	K	K	K	K	K	K
L	L	L	L	L	L	L	L	L	L
M	M	M	M	M	M	M	M	M	M
N	N	N	N	N	N	N	N	N	N
O	O	O	O	O	O	O	O	O	O
P	P	P	P	P	P	P	P	P	P
Q	Q	Q	Q	Q	Q	Q	Q	Q	Q
R	R	R	R	R	R	R	R	R	R
S	S	S	S	S	S	S	S	S	S
T	T	T	T	T	T	T	T	T	T
U	U	U	U	U	U	U	U	U	U
V	V	V	V	V	V	V	V	V	V
W	W	W	W	W	W	W	W	W	W
X	X	X	X	X	X	X	X	X	X
Y	Y	Y	Y	Y	Y	Y	Y	Y	Y
Z	Z	Z	Z	Z	Z	Z	Z	Z	Z

▶ Police Officer Practice Exam 4 Book One

Part One: Clarity

In the following sets of sentences, choose the sentence that is most clearly written.

1. **a.** The words *Equal Justice under Law* is carved above the main entrance to the Supreme Court.
b. The words *Equal Justice under Law* has been carved above the main entrance to the Supreme Court.
c. The words *Equal Justice under Law* carved above the main entrance to the Supreme Court.
d. The words *Equal Justice under Law* are carved above the main entrance to the Supreme Court.

2. **a.** I ordered the suspect to hand over his weapon to Officer Smith and I.
b. To Officer Smith and I, I ordered that the suspect hand over his weapon.
c. I ordered the suspect to hand over his weapon to Officer Smith and me.
d. I ordered the suspect that he hand over his weapon to Officer Smith and me.

3. **a.** Both the weather and the time of year influences the crime rate in New York City.
b. Both the weather and the time of year influence the crime rate in New York City.
c. Either the weather and the time of year influences the crime rate in New York City.
d. Both the weather and the time of year influencing the crime rate in New York City.

4. **a.** Neither Jim Green nor Carla McKenzie was granted parole.
b. Neither Jim Green or Carla McKenzie were granted parole.
c. Neither Jim Green nor Carla McKenzie were granted parole.
d. Neither Jim Green or Carla McKenzie was granted parole.

5. **a.** Officer Williams arrived on the scene first, moreover Officer Jenkins arrived 15 minutes later.
b. Officer Williams arrived on the scene first, Officer Jenkins arrived 15 minutes later.
c. Officer Williams arrived on the scene first, and Officer Jenkins arrived 15 minutes later.
d. Officer Williams arrived on the scene first, next officer Jenkins arrived 15 minutes later.

6. **a.** For a variety of many reasons, more people applied to the police academy this year than ever before.
b. More people, for various different reasons, applied to the police academy this year than ever before.
c. For a number of reasons, more people applied to the police academy this year than ever before.
d. For a wide variety of different reasons, more and more people applied to the police academy this year than ever before.

7. **a.** The firefighters sold less raffle tickets than they sold last year.
b. The firefighters sold fewer raffle tickets than they sold last year.
c. The firefighters sold fewer raffle tickets than they sell last year.
d. The firefighters sell less raffle tickets than they sold last year.

8. **a.** When the police arrived, they saw the gun laid on the bed.
b. When the police arrived, they saw the gun lieing on the bed.
c. When the police arrived, they saw the gun lying on the bed.
d. When the police arrived, they saw the gun laying on the bed.

9. **a.** Sandra Day O'Connor, the first woman to serve on the Supreme Court, she appointed by President Ronald Reagan in 1981.
b. Sandra Day O'Connor, the first woman to serve on the Supreme Court, and appointed by President Ronald Reagan in 1981.
c. Sandra Day O'Connor, the first woman to serve on the Supreme Court, then appointed by President Ronald Reagan in 1981.
d. Sandra Day O'Connor, the first woman to serve on the Supreme Court, was appointed by President Ronald Reagan in 1981.

10. **a.** Patrol effectiveness is often measured in response time.
b. Patrol effectiveness are often measured in response time.
c. Patrols effectiveness is often measured in response time.
d. Patrol's effectiveness are often measured in response time.

11. **a.** Some people say jury duty is a nuisance that just takes up their precious time and that we don't get paid enough.
b. Some people say jury duty is a nuisance that just takes up your precious time and that one doesn't get paid enough.
c. Some people say jury duty is a nuisance that just takes up one's precious time and that one doesn't get paid enough.
d. Some people say jury duty is a nuisance that just takes up our precious time and that they don't get paid enough.

12. **a.** Sergeant Bradford retired on May 22 2006.
b. Sergeant Bradford retired on May 22, 2006.
c. Sergeant bradford retired on May 22, 2006.
d. Sergeant Bradford retired on May, 22 2006.

13. a. Opposite to what Officer Yu had suspected, the DNA samples were not a match.
b. Contrary to what Officer Yu had suspected, the DNA samples were not a match.
c. Contrary with what Officer Yu had suspected, the DNA samples were not a match.
d. Opposite from what Officer Yu had suspected, the DNA samples were not a match.

14. **a.** An abused woman's cries for help were sometimes ignored, and she is advised to go back to her abuser.
b. An abused woman's cries for help were sometimes ignored, and she will be advised to go back to her abuser.
c. An abused woman's cries for help are sometimes ignored, and she is advised to go back to her abuser.
d. An abused woman's cries for help are sometimes ignored, and she was advised to go back to her abuser.

15. **a.** Sergeant Ahlamady often bought pizza for herself and I.
b. Sergeant Ahlamady often bought pizza for herself and me.
c. Sergeant Ahlamady often bought pizza for her and me.
d. Sergeant Ahlamady often bought pizza for herself and myself.

Part Two: Vocabulary

In each of the following sentences, choose the word or phrase that most nearly expresses the same meaning as the underlined word.

16. The sergeant emphasized the use-of-force continuum.
a. collection
b. scale
c. prohibition
d. training

17. Under the agency's arrest policy, police officers have more discretion with infractions and some misdemeanors than with more serious offenses.
a. choice
b. limits
c. responsibility
d. aptitude

18. The evidence kit was running low on disposable gloves.
a. irreplaceable
b. authorized
c. synthetic
d. throwaway

19. He based his conclusion on what he inferred from the evidence, not on what he actually observed.
a. intuited
b. imagined
c. surmised
d. implied

20. The police officer used the pretext of a traffic violation to investigate the gang activity.
a. example
b. idea
c. literature
d. excuse

21. For health reasons, the evidence lab is required to sanitize the work area after each analysis.
a. photograph
b. inventory
c. purify
d. contaminate

22. Officer Green was thought to be one of the most astute officers on the force.
a. perceptive
b. inattentive
c. stubborn
d. studious

23. The judge ruled that the evidence was immaterial, which angered the defense team.
a. appropriate
b. germane
c. considerable
d. irrelevant

24. The matter reached its conclusion only after diplomatic efforts by both sides.
a. tactful
b. delaying
c. elaborate
d. combative

25. The suspect refused to show remorse for his flagrant disregard for the law.
a. immoral
b. malicious
c. callous
d. outright

26. Sergeant Williams gave the young deputy some sage advice.
a. wise
b. unwanted
c. foolish
d. redundant

27. The witness described the mugger as a tall, gangly man with dark hair and glasses.
a. ugly
b. lanky
c. rowdy
d. ferocious

28. There was palpable tension in the courtroom.
a. rising
b. understated
c. nervous
d. tangible

29. The suspect stoically answered Officer Levine's questions.
a. impassively
b. loudly
c. angrily
d. sarcastically

30. The witness's account of the robbery was characterized by hyperbole.
a. sincerity
b. mistakes
c. exaggeration
d. honesty

Part Three: Spelling

In each of the following sentences, choose the correct spelling of the missing word.

31. Bodily ________ are often the best source of DNA evidence at crime scenes.
a. flueds
b. fluids
c. fluedes
d. fluides

32. It is my ______ that the police officers in this county do a fine job.
a. beleif
b. bilief
c. belief
d. beleaf

33. An officer must be ______ to the distress of a crime victim.
a. sinsitive
b. sensitive
c. sensative
d. sinsative

34. Most local police officers work for a __________ police department.
a. municipal
b. municiple
c. municepal
d. municeple

35. The District Attorney announced his intention to ______ the suspected drug smugglers.
a. prosecute
b. prossecute
c. prosacute
d. prosecuute

36. Officer Brady found herself in a very dangerous ________.
a. sittuation
b. situation
c. situachun
d. situacion

37. An _______ donor contributed $10,000 to the police officers' fundraiser for the children's hospital.
a. annonimous
b. anonimous
c. annonymous
d. anonymous

38. The deputy gave his _____ that the report would be completed on time.
a. asurrance
b. assurance
c. assurence
d. assureance

39. To maintain peak physical condition, a police officer must eat well and get plenty of _______.
a. excercise
b. exercise
c. exersize
d. exercize

40. Officer Forster immediately reported the problem to her ________.
a. superviser
b. supervizer
c. supervizor
d. supervisor

41. The members of the jury listened carefully as the suspect gave his ______.
a. testamony
b. testimony
c. testamoany
d. testemony

42. Officer Chang expressed her _____ to the civilian who helped her foil the robbery.
a. graditude
b. gradatude
c. gratatude
d. gratitude

43. Due to his hard work and ______, John graduated from the police academy at the top of his class.
a. discipline
b. disapline
c. discapline
d. dissaplin

44. The attorney was confident she could prove her client's __________.

a. inosence
b. innosence
c. innocence
d. innosince

45. The information was certainly___________, but it was not criminal.

a. imbarassing
b. imbarrasing
c. embarassing
d. embarrassing

Part Four: Reading Comprehension

Several reading passages, each accompanied by three or more questions, follow. Answer each question based on what is stated or implied in the preceding passage.

Criminology researchers who take a normative view on crime define crime as a behavior that deviates from established norms, culture, and values. In this view, what is criminal is that which is not normally engaged in or sanctified by society at large. The laws regarding the use of marijuana provide a good lens with which to understand the normative view. Prior to the twentieth century, it was not illegal to use or possess marijuana. In 1915, Utah passed the first law against marijuana use, and through the years the laws became more widespread and serious. In the 1950s, the Boggs Act and the Narcotics Control Act set mandatory sentences for drug crimes, including marijuana, which had a first offense penalty of two to ten years in prison and a $20,000 fine. However, by the early 1970s, views on the use of marijuana were beginning to change. Many researchers attribute the change in views not to an increase in the medical or scientific understanding of the drug, but to the increased use of the drug for recreational and medicinal purposes by a larger segment of society. During this time, many states began to significantly decriminalize their marijuana laws, and by the late 1980s, individual states began to legalize the use of marijuana for certain medical conditions.

46. In what year did Utah pass a law against marijuana?

a. 1970
b. 1915
c. 1956
d. 1941

47. According to the passage, the view that crime is a behavior that deviates from established norms, culture, and values is the

a. police view.
b. criminology view.
c. normative view.
d. Boggs view.

48. Based on the passage, which of the following phrases best sums up the normative view's reason for the recent decriminalization of marijuana?

a. societal acceptance
b. moral depravity
c. prison overcrowding
d. gang violence

49. Based on the passage, which of the following is NOT correct?

a. Societal views on marijuana began to change in the 1970s.
b. Marijuana is often used for medicinal purposes.
c. It is now legal to possess marijuana for recreational use.
d. The Boggs Act set mandatory sentences for the possession of marijuana.

Hearsay evidence, which is the secondhand reporting of a statement, is allowed in court only when the truth of the statement is irrelevant. Hearsay that depends on the statement's truthfulness is inadmissible because the witness does not appear in court and swear an oath to tell the truth; his or her demeanor when making the statement is not visible to the jury; the accuracy of the statement cannot be tested under cross-examination; and to introduce it would be to deprive the accused of the constitutional right to confront the accuser. Hearsay is admissible, however, when the truth of the statement is unimportant. If, for example, a defendant claims to have been unconscious at a certain time, and a witness claims that the defendant actually spoke to her at that time, this evidence would be admissible because the truth of what the defendant actually said is irrelevant.

50. The main purpose of the passage is to

a. explain why hearsay evidence abridges the rights of the accused.

b. question the truth of hearsay evidence.

c. argue that rules about the admissibility of hearsay evidence should be changed.

d. specify which use of hearsay evidence is inadmissible, and why.

51. Which of the following is NOT a reason given in the passage for the inadmissibility of hearsay evidence?

a. Rumors are not necessarily credible.

b. The person making the original statement was not under oath.

c. The jury should be able to watch the gestures and facial expressions of the person making the statement.

d. The person making the statement cannot be cross-examined.

52. How does the passage explain the proper use of hearsay evidence?

a. by listing a set of criteria

b. by providing a hypothetical example

c. by referring to the Constitution

d. by citing case law

A good police officer realizes that a crime scene is not just the location where a crime was committed, but also any location where evidence of a crime may be contained. Evidence is often located great distances away from where the crime was committed. As an example, an offender might kidnap a victim; transport the victim to another location and murder the victim; dump the victim's body at a third location; then go home and change clothing.

In this example, there are four crime scenes, of which two were not the location in which the primary crimes were committed. Even though the offender did not commit the murder at the body dump, nor in the home where he or she changed clothing, the offender did leave trace evidence of the crime at all four locations. Moreover, the vehicle with which the offender transported the victim is a fifth crime scene.

The idea of multiple crime scenes can be traced back to a critical theory in forensic science called transfer theory. Transfer theory was developed in the 1800s by the French scientist Henry Locard. Locard theorized that whenever two objects come into contact, they transfer some evidence or trace of that contact with each other. Consider that as you touch this book you are leaving your fingerprints, which are trace evidence that you came into contact with the book. As you touch the pages, some of the ink and fibers from the pages are transferred onto your fingers.

The first police officer at a crime scene should try to limit the number of people and objects who enter the scene until after a forensic examination. This is because the officer knows that as people enter the crime scene they will leave evidence of their presence. Also, as people enter and leave the crime scene, they may inadvertently take other critical trace evidence, like hair and fibers, from the scene on the bottom of their shoes.

53. According to the passage, a crime scene is
  a. any location where a crime may have occurred.
  b. any location wherein evidence of a crime may be located.
  c. any location where a crime has occurred.
  d. any location wherein evidence of a crime is located.

54. Based on the passage, which of the following is true?
  a. Henry Locard invented the theory of crime scenes.
  b. Whenever two objects come into contact, they leave some trace of that contact with each other.
  c. Police officers discovering a crime scene should wait for the arrival of detectives before securing the scene.
  d. A vehicle cannot be a crime scene.

55. Which of the following would be the best title for the passage?
  a. Locard's Theory
  b. Forensic Science and Crime Scenes
  c. Multiple Crime Scene Theory
  d. Protection of Crime Scenes

56. Based on the passage, which of the following is NOT true?
  a. A vehicle can be a crime scene.
  b. A police officer wants to limit the number of people and objects that enter a crime scene.
  c. A police officer's sole purpose in securing a crime scene is to prevent people from contaminating the scene on purpose.
  d. Locard's transfer theory concerns trace evidence.

57. Based on the passage, which of the following is NOT trace evidence?
  a. fingerprints
  b. hair
  c. vehicles
  d. ink

At 9:30 P.M., while parked at 916 Woodward Avenue, Officers Whitebear and Morgan were asked to respond to an anonymous complaint of a disturbance at 826 Rosemary Lane. When they arrived, they found the back door open and the jamb splintered. They drew their weapons, identified themselves, and entered the dwelling, where they found Mr. Darrell Hensley, of 1917 Roosevelt Avenue, sitting on the couch. Mr. Hensley calmly stated he was waiting for his wife. At that point, two children emerged from a hallway: Dustin Hensley, age 7, who lives in the dwelling, and Kirstin Jackson, age 14, Dustin's babysitter, who lives at 916 Ambrose Street. Kirstin stated she and Dustin had been sitting at the kitchen table when the back door was kicked in and Mr. Hensley entered, shouting obscenities and calling for Karen Hensley, Dustin's mother. Kirstin then hid with Dustin in a hallway storage closet. The officers contacted Mrs. Hensley at her place of employment at O'Reilley's Restaurant at 415 Ralston. At 9:55, she returned home and showed an Order of Protection stating Mr. Hensley was not to have contact with his wife or child. Mr. Hensley was placed under arrest and taken in handcuffs to the station house.

58. Based on Darrell Hensley's behavior when he first arrived at his wife's house, what was his most likely motivation for being there?
- **a.** to see his child for a scheduled visitation
- **b.** to provoke a confrontation with his wife
- **c.** to have a place to stay that night
- **d.** to peacefully reconcile with his family

59. Who called the police to investigate the disturbance described in the passage?
- **a.** the babysitter
- **b.** the arrestee's wife
- **c.** a neighbor
- **d.** an unknown person

60. Based on the information in the passage, what is the most likely reason the officers drew their weapons before entering the Hensley home?
- **a.** There were signs of forced entry into the house.
- **b.** There was an Order of Protection against Mr. Hensley.
- **c.** Children were in danger inside the premises.
- **d.** They knew Mr. Hensley to be a violent man.

61. Based on the information in the passage, what was Mr. Hensley's demeanor when the police first spoke to him?
- **a.** He was enraged.
- **b.** He was remorseful.
- **c.** He was matter-of-fact.
- **d.** He was confused.

Use the following information to answer questions 62–65.

Police officers are occasionally called upon to use force to overcome a suspect's resistance and gain compliance. Many police agencies are using hand-held devices to deliver an electrical shock. Typically, these devices fire darts that are connected to the device by a thin wire. When the darts strike the suspect, an electrical charge flows from the device through the thin wires into the suspect's body.

1. Only trained personnel are allowed to carry and use the device. In addition to an initial training, police officers must receive annual updated training on the use of the device. Training shall be conducted by a certified trainer.
2. If the device is carried, it must be on the opposite side of the body from the police officer's firearm.
3. An officer should never hold both a firearm and the device at the same time.
4. Unless it would endanger an officer or is impractical, a verbal warning should be given before the device is used.
5. The device should never be aimed at a suspect's eyes.
6. The device may be used to control a violent or physically resisting suspect. The device may also be used on a potentially violent or potentially resistant suspect if the officer has given a verbal warning and the suspect has clearly demonstrated that he or she is potentially violent or intends to resist, and other means of control appear unreasonable.
7. Although it is not absolutely prohibited, police officers should strongly consider other options if the suspect is pregnant, is elderly, is a young juvenile, has recently been sprayed with an

alcohol-based pepper spray or other flammable substance, or is in a position wherein his or her collapse might cause injury (such as a falling from a high place).

8. All suspects who have been subject to an electrical discharge shall receive immediate medical care.
9. All discharges of the device, except during training, must be reported.

62. Which of the following would be an improper way of carrying the device?

a. on the side of your equipment belt that is opposite your firearm
b. in your left hand, with your flashlight in your right hand
c. in your right hand, with your flashlight in your left hand
d. in your left hand, with your firearm in your right hand

63. Based on the passage, for which of the following suspects should a police officer strongly consider a use of force option other than the device?

a. a 17-year-old female inside a local church
b. a 32-year-old male standing on a two-foot step stool
c. a 75-year-old male on a city bus
d. a 22-year-old female in the shower

64. Based on the passage, under what circumstances shall an officer give a warning before using the device?

a. a potentially violent suspect
b. any circumstance in which the device is about to be used
c. before using it on a person who has been sprayed with an alcohol-based pepper spray
d. during a training exercise

65. Based on the passage, which of the following is NOT true?

a. Training must be conducted by a certified trainer.
b. An officer who received training 14 months ago is not certified.
c. Training discharges of the device need not be reported.
d. The suspect's eyes are a good aiming point.

▶ Book Two

This is a test of your reading ability. In the following passages, words have been omitted. Each numbered set of dashed blank lines indicates where a word is left out; each dash represents one letter of the missing word. The correct word should not only make sense in the sentence but also have the number of letters indicated by the dashes.

Read through the whole passage, and then begin filling in the missing words. Fill in as many missing words as possible. If you aren't sure of the answer, take a guess.

Then mark your answers on the answer sheet on page 254 as follows: Write the **first letter** of the word you have chosen in the square under the number of the word. Then blacken the circle of that letter of the alphabet under the square.

Only the blackened alphabet circles will be scored. The words you write on this page and the letters you write at the top of the column on the answer sheet **will not be scored.** Make sure that you blacken the appropriate circle in each column.

Many people become angry when they hear that prison inmates have the opportunity to study for their **1**) _ _ _ _ school equivalency diplomas, take college courses, and even earn **2**) _ _ _ _ _ _ _ degrees while they are serving **3**) _ _ _ _. Such educational services are often provided at **4**) _ _ charge to the inmates, which means that the **5**) _ _ _ _ _ are borne by taxpayers. Many people see these **6**) _ _ _ _ educational services as coddling criminals, and providing rewards for lawbreakers. Higher education is **7**) _ _ _ _ _ _ _ _ _ and it is frustrating to many people to see convicted criminals **8**) _ _ _ for free what working people have to struggle so hard to **9**) _ _ _ _ _ _ _ for their children. On the other hand, those **10**) _ _ _ support educational services for inmates argue that it is in society's **11**) _ _ _ _ interest to provide such services. Rather **12**) _ _ _ _ being seen as a reward for **13**) _ _ _ _ _ _ _ _ _, education should be viewed as an investment in social order. A decent **14**) _ _ _ _ _ _ _ _ _ will make the ex-offender **15**) _ _ _ _ employable, and that, in turn, should remove one **16**) _ _ _ _ _ _ for repeat offenses—the inability to earn a living in a socially acceptable **17**) _ _ _. We should not **18**) _ _ _ _ educational opportunities to those in **19**) _ _ _ _ _ _ if we expect them to become useful citizens when **20**) _ _ _ _ leave.

Members for high-risk occupations like law enforcement and fire fighting form tightly knit groups. The dangers they share naturally **21**) _ _ _ _ _ them close, as does the knowledge that their **22**) _ _ _ _ _ are sometimes in one another's hands. The bonds of loyalty and trust help police **23**) _ _ _ _ _ _ _ _ work more effectively. However, the sense **24**) _ _ loyalty can be taken to **25**) _ _ _ _ _ _ _ _. Sometimes officers believe that they always must defend their comrades' actions. What happens though, **26**) _ _ _ _ those actions are wrong? Frank Serpico found a disturbing **27**) _ _ _ _ _ _ to that question. Serpico **28**) _ _ _ _ _ _ the New York City Police Department assuming **29**) _ _ _ _ high moral standards were typical of his fellow officers. When he **30**) _ _ _ _ _ out otherwise, he was faced with a dilemma: **31**) _ _ _ _ _ _ he violate the trust of his fellow officers by exposing the corruption, **32**) _ _ should he close his **33**) _ _ _ _ because loyalty to his **34**) _ _ _ _ _ _ officers outweighed all other moral (and legal) considerations? Serpico made his **35**) _ _ _ _ _ _. Public attention was focused on police **36**) _ _ _ _ _ _ _ _ _ _ and the NYPD was improved as a **37**) _ _ _ _ _ _, but those improvements came at a tremendous personal **38**) _ _ _ _ to Serpico. Ostracized and reviled by other officers, who felt **39**) _ _ _ _ _ _ _ _, Serpico eventually left the **40**) _ _ _ _ _.

▶ Answer Key Book One

Part One: Clarity

1. d. This is the only choice that is a complete sentence and has subject-verb agreement. In choices **a** and **b**, the subject *words* is plural and does not agree with the singular verb. Choice **c** is a sentence fragment.

2. c. In choices **a** and **b**, the pronoun *I* is incorrect. Choice **d** is an awkward construction.

3. b. Choice **a** is wrong because the plural subject does not agree with the singular verb. Choice **c** is poorly written; the sentence should read, *Either the weather or the time of year…* Choice **d** is a sentence fragment.

4. a. When using *neither . . . nor*, also use a singular verb. Choice **c** is incorrect because it uses a plural verb. Choice **d** is incorrect because *neither* is always used with *nor*. In choice **b**, both the use of *neither* with *or* and the plural verb are incorrect.

5. c. The other choices are comma splices or run-on sentences.

6. c. This is the only choice that avoids wordiness or redundancies. In choice **a**, the phrase *variety of many* is redundant. In choice **b**, *various different* is redundant. In choice **d**, *variety of different reasons, more and more* is both wordy and redundant.

7. b. Choices **a** and **d** are incorrect because *less* is used with quantities that cannot be counted, e.g. *less* power, *less* risk. Use *fewer* with nouns that can be counted, e.g. *fewer* cars, *fewer* raffle tickets. In choice **c**, *fewer* is correct, but there is an unnecessary shift in verb tense—from past to present.

8. d. The simplest rule to remember is that things *lay* and people *lie*. If the sentence involved a person, it would be *they saw Thelma lying on the bed.*

9. d. This is the only choice that does not contain faulty subordination.

10. a. Choices **b** and **d** are not correct because they lack subject-verb agreement. Choice **c** is incorrect because *patrol* requires an apostrophe.

11. c. The other choices contain unnecessary shifts in person, from *people* to *their* and *we* in choice **a**, to *your* and *one* in choice **b**, and to *our* and *they* in choice **d**.

12. b. *Bradford* is a proper name and should be capitalized, and there should be a comma after the number of the day in the date.

13. b. This is the only choice that uses the standard convention of written English. The other choices—*opposite to*, *contrary with*, and *opposite from*—are idiomatically incorrect.

14. c. There is no unnecessary shift in tense between *are* in the first half of the sentence and *is* in the second half; in the other choices, there are unnecessary shifts in tense.

15. b. *Herself* is the proper pronoun because it refers to something Sergeant Ahlamady does *for herself*, but there is no reason for the speaker to refer to *myself*. Incorrect pronouns are used in the other choices.

Part Two: Vocabulary

Consult a dictionary if you're not sure why the answers for the vocabulary and spelling questions are correct.

16. b.
17. a.
18. d.
19. c.
20. d.
21. c.

22. a.
23. d.
24. a.
25. d.
26. a.
27. b.
28. d.
29. a.
30. c.

Part Three: Spelling

31. b.
32. c.
33. b.
34. a.
35. a.
36. b.
37. d.
38. b.
39. b.
40. d.
41. b.
42. d.
43. a.
44. c.
45. d.

Part Four: Reading Comprehension

46. **b.** The answer is found in the fifth sentence.

47. **c.** This is the main idea of the entire passage, and is explicitly stated in the first sentence.

48. **d.** The passage mentions *increased use of the drug for recreational and medicinal purposes by a larger segment of society.*

49. **c.** The passage states that *by the late 1980s, individual states began to legalize the use of marijuana for certain medical conditions.*

50. **d.** Although the last sentence expands on the main point, the rest of the passage explains why hearsay evidence is only admissible when it doesn't matter whether or not the statement is true.

51. **a.** This statement may be true, but it isn't in the passage.

52. **b.** See the last sentence of the passage.

53. **b.** The idea that a crime scene is any location wherein evidence may be located permeates the passage. With small trace evidence, for example, officers would not know whether or not the scene contained evidence until after close, often specialized, analysis. Therefore, for the purposes of securing a crime scene, it is best to operate under the principle that evidence may be there.

54. **b.** The idea for the correct answer is presented in the third paragraph. Choice **a** is incorrect because Locard developed the transfer theory. Choice **c** is incorrect because the passage emphasizes that the first police officers discovering the scene should secure it. Choice **d** is incorrect because a vehicle is used in the passage as an example of a potential crime scene.

55. **d.** Although all the subjects are broached within the passage, the overall idea is the protection of crime scenes.

56. **c.** While police officers do not want people to contaminate a crime scene on purpose, they are primarily concerned with accidental contamination.

57. **c.** A vehicle may be a crime scene that contains trace evidence, but it is not itself trace evidence. All of the other items are specifically mentioned in the passage.

58. **b.** Mr. Hensley has forced open the door and has told police he is waiting for his wife. Choice **a** is incorrect; Mr. Hensley's child hid from him in a closet, and he evidently didn't try to get the child to come out. Choice **c** is incorrect, because Mr. Hensley has a residence of his own at 1917 Roosevelt. Mr. Hensley evidently didn't intend peaceful reconciliation (choice **d**), since he kicked the door in.

59. **d.** The first sentence of the passage states that the complaint was anonymous.

60. **a.** The door had been kicked in. The officers didn't know any of the other facts until after they were inside the house.

61. **c.** Mr. Hensley spoke to the police *calmly*, and he made a seemingly matter-of-fact statement. There is no indication in the passage that Mr. Hensley was enraged at police or that he was remorseful or confused.

62. **d.** Neither choice **b** nor choice **c** is mentioned in the passage. Item three clearly prohibits the conduct.

63. **c.** Based on item seven, only the 75-year-old male is *elderly*.

64. **a.** Based on item six, a police officer should give a verbal warning before using it on a potentially violent suspect.

65. **d.** Item five says that the device should never be aimed at a suspect's eyes.

▶ Book Two

1. high
2. college
3. time
4. no
5. costs
6. free
7. expensive
8. get
9. provide
10. who
11. best
12. than
13. lawbreakers
14. education
15. more
16. reason
17. way
18. deny
19. prison
20. they
21. bring
22. lives
23. officers
24. of
25. extremes
26. when
27. answer
28. joined
29. that
30. found
31. should
32. or
33. eyes
34. fellow
35. choice
36. corruption
37. result
38. cost
39. betrayed
40. force

▶ Scoring

Most cities require a score of at least 70% to pass a police officer exam. But a score of 70 doesn't necessarily mean that you got 70 questions correct. The number of correct answers you need for a score of 70 changes each time the test is given. A good estimate of a passing score is 70%, or 74 questions correct.

But your total score isn't really the main point right now. What's more important is to note how you've improved since you took the first exam in Chapter 4. Once again, take a subscore of each of the categories of questions. Did you do better on the reading questions than on the clarity questions, or vice versa? You should spend more of your review time on the area in which you scored lower, and less time on the area in which you scored well.

If you didn't improve much since the first exam, your overall reading skills could be one reason. Lots of challenging reading between now and the time of the exam can make a real difference in your score. You might also consider having a smart friend or former teacher help you with the areas that give you the most trouble.

On the other hand, if you scored pretty well, you can feel confident as you continue your review. (Having a good score does not mean you shouldn't continue studying. It means you don't have to review as much.) You probably just need to brush up on a few things and continue to familiarize yourself with what's likely to be on the exam.

A table follows that will show you which of the instructional chapters correspond to the different parts of the exam. Your best bet is to review all of the chapters carefully, but you will want to spend the most time on the chapters that correspond to the kind of questions that gave you the most trouble. See which exam questions were most challenging to you, and study the corresponding chapter(s).

EXAM PART	CHAPTER
One	8
Two	9
Three	9
Four	7
Book Two	7

Remember, reading and writing skills are important not only for the exam, but also for your job as a police officer. So the time you spend improving those skills will pay off—not only in higher exam scores, but also for success in your career.

CHAPTER

17 Police Officer Practice Exam 5

CHAPTER SUMMARY

This fifth exam is representative of the job-related police officer exams used by many cities throughout the United States. It tests map reading, memory, judgment, and common sense, as well as basic skills like math and reading.

This practice exam, like Exam 2 in Chapter 5, is an example of the type of police officer exam that tests job-related skills. Though the official exam you eventually take may not look exactly like the one in this chapter, many police exams test the same skills, so the following exam provides vital practice. If you've already taken Exam 2 in Chapter 5, you should have pinpointed your weak areas and worked on the appropriate study chapters in this book. Having strengthened these areas, you're going into this practice test ready to improve your score.

For this exam, simulate the actual test-taking experience as much as possible. In addition to your number 2 pencils, get a timer or stopwatch. Set your timer for 15 minutes, and use that time to study the memory materials that come right after the answer sheet. Then reset the timer for two and a half hours, which is the amount of time you have to answer the 100 questions on the exam. When time is up, stop. You won't have a true feel for how well you will do on the real exam if you exceed the time limit.

When you're done, check your answers against the answer key on the pages following the exam. An explanation of how to score your exam comes after that.

Police Officer Practice Exam 5

1.	ⓐ	ⓑ	ⓒ	ⓓ	36.	ⓐ	ⓑ	ⓒ	ⓓ	71.	ⓐ	ⓑ	ⓒ	ⓓ
2.	ⓐ	ⓑ	ⓒ	ⓓ	37.	ⓐ	ⓑ	ⓒ	ⓓ	72.	ⓐ	ⓑ	ⓒ	ⓓ
3.	ⓐ	ⓑ	ⓒ	ⓓ	38.	ⓐ	ⓑ	ⓒ	ⓓ	73.	ⓐ	ⓑ	ⓒ	ⓓ
4.	ⓐ	ⓑ	ⓒ	ⓓ	39.	ⓐ	ⓑ	ⓒ	ⓓ	74.	ⓐ	ⓑ	ⓒ	ⓓ
5.	ⓐ	ⓑ	ⓒ	ⓓ	40.	ⓐ	ⓑ	ⓒ	ⓓ	75.	ⓐ	ⓑ	ⓒ	ⓓ
6.	ⓐ	ⓑ	ⓒ	ⓓ	41.	ⓐ	ⓑ	ⓒ	ⓓ	76.	ⓐ	ⓑ	ⓒ	ⓓ
7.	ⓐ	ⓑ	ⓒ	ⓓ	42.	ⓐ	ⓑ	ⓒ	ⓓ	77.	ⓐ	ⓑ	ⓒ	ⓓ
8.	ⓐ	ⓑ	ⓒ	ⓓ	43.	ⓐ	ⓑ	ⓒ	ⓓ	78.	ⓐ	ⓑ	ⓒ	ⓓ
9.	ⓐ	ⓑ	ⓒ	ⓓ	44.	ⓐ	ⓑ	ⓒ	ⓓ	79.	ⓐ	ⓑ	ⓒ	ⓓ
10.	ⓐ	ⓑ	ⓒ	ⓓ	45.	ⓐ	ⓑ	ⓒ	ⓓ	80.	ⓐ	ⓑ	ⓒ	ⓓ
11.	ⓐ	ⓑ	ⓒ	ⓓ	46.	ⓐ	ⓑ	ⓒ	ⓓ	81.	ⓐ	ⓑ	ⓒ	ⓓ
12.	ⓐ	ⓑ	ⓒ	ⓓ	47.	ⓐ	ⓑ	ⓒ	ⓓ	82.	ⓐ	ⓑ	ⓒ	ⓓ
13.	ⓐ	ⓑ	ⓒ	ⓓ	48.	ⓐ	ⓑ	ⓒ	ⓓ	83.	ⓐ	ⓑ	ⓒ	ⓓ
14.	ⓐ	ⓑ	ⓒ	ⓓ	49.	ⓐ	ⓑ	ⓒ	ⓓ	84.	ⓐ	ⓑ	ⓒ	ⓓ
15.	ⓐ	ⓑ	ⓒ	ⓓ	50.	ⓐ	ⓑ	ⓒ	ⓓ	85.	ⓐ	ⓑ	ⓒ	ⓓ
16.	ⓐ	ⓑ	ⓒ	ⓓ	51.	ⓐ	ⓑ	ⓒ	ⓓ	86.	ⓐ	ⓑ	ⓒ	ⓓ
17.	ⓐ	ⓑ	ⓒ	ⓓ	52.	ⓐ	ⓑ	ⓒ	ⓓ	87.	ⓐ	ⓑ	ⓒ	ⓓ
18.	ⓐ	ⓑ	ⓒ	ⓓ	53.	ⓐ	ⓑ	ⓒ	ⓓ	88.	ⓐ	ⓑ	ⓒ	ⓓ
19.	ⓐ	ⓑ	ⓒ	ⓓ	54.	ⓐ	ⓑ	ⓒ	ⓓ	89.	ⓐ	ⓑ	ⓒ	ⓓ
20.	ⓐ	ⓑ	ⓒ	ⓓ	55.	ⓐ	ⓑ	ⓒ	ⓓ	90.	ⓐ	ⓑ	ⓒ	ⓓ
21.	ⓐ	ⓑ	ⓒ	ⓓ	56.	ⓐ	ⓑ	ⓒ	ⓓ	91.	ⓐ	ⓑ	ⓒ	ⓓ
22.	ⓐ	ⓑ	ⓒ	ⓓ	57.	ⓐ	ⓑ	ⓒ	ⓓ	92.	ⓐ	ⓑ	ⓒ	ⓓ
23.	ⓐ	ⓑ	ⓒ	ⓓ	58.	ⓐ	ⓑ	ⓒ	ⓓ	93.	ⓐ	ⓑ	ⓒ	ⓓ
24.	ⓐ	ⓑ	ⓒ	ⓓ	59.	ⓐ	ⓑ	ⓒ	ⓓ	94.	ⓐ	ⓑ	ⓒ	ⓓ
25.	ⓐ	ⓑ	ⓒ	ⓓ	60.	ⓐ	ⓑ	ⓒ	ⓓ	95.	ⓐ	ⓑ	ⓒ	ⓓ
26.	ⓐ	ⓑ	ⓒ	ⓓ	61.	ⓐ	ⓑ	ⓒ	ⓓ	96.	ⓐ	ⓑ	ⓒ	ⓓ
27.	ⓐ	ⓑ	ⓒ	ⓓ	62.	ⓐ	ⓑ	ⓒ	ⓓ	97.	ⓐ	ⓑ	ⓒ	ⓓ
28.	ⓐ	ⓑ	ⓒ	ⓓ	63.	ⓐ	ⓑ	ⓒ	ⓓ	98.	ⓐ	ⓑ	ⓒ	ⓓ
29.	ⓐ	ⓑ	ⓒ	ⓓ	64.	ⓐ	ⓑ	ⓒ	ⓓ	99.	ⓐ	ⓑ	ⓒ	ⓓ
30.	ⓐ	ⓑ	ⓒ	ⓓ	65.	ⓐ	ⓑ	ⓒ	ⓓ	100.	ⓐ	ⓑ	ⓒ	ⓓ
31.	ⓐ	ⓑ	ⓒ	ⓓ	66.	ⓐ	ⓑ	ⓒ	ⓓ					
32.	ⓐ	ⓑ	ⓒ	ⓓ	67.	ⓐ	ⓑ	ⓒ	ⓓ					
33.	ⓐ	ⓑ	ⓒ	ⓓ	68.	ⓐ	ⓑ	ⓒ	ⓓ					
34.	ⓐ	ⓑ	ⓒ	ⓓ	69.	ⓐ	ⓑ	ⓒ	ⓓ					
35.	ⓐ	ⓑ	ⓒ	ⓓ	70.	ⓐ	ⓑ	ⓒ	ⓓ					

▶ Police Officer Practic Exam 5

Study Booklet

You have 15 minutes to study the following wanted posters and to read the article on police procedure. After 15 minutes are up, turn the page and go on to answer the test questions, beginning with questions about the study material. **Do not refer to this study section to answer the questions.** When you have finished Part One: Memorization and Visualization, you may continue with the rest of the exam.

MISSING
Fabian Rollo Vernon

DESCRIPTION:

Age: 47
Race: White
Height:: 6′1″
Weight: 200 lbs.
Hair: Bald
Eyes: Blue

REMARKS: Schizophrenic patient last seen in lobby of Red Hook Psychiatric Center on Thanksgiving Day. Has been found wandering in Red Hook Park on other occasions.

IF LOCATED: Call Red Hook Police Department, Red Hook, Kentucky, at 508-555-8000.

WANTED
Patrice Dwyer

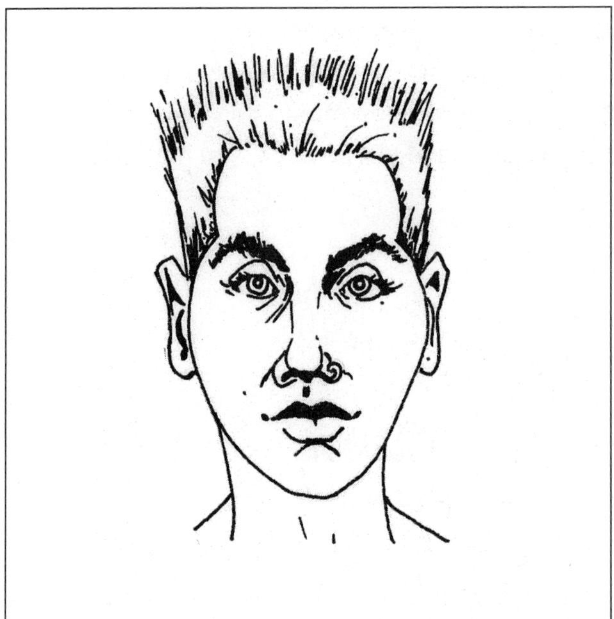

ALIASES: Patty Dwyer; Pat Dwy
WANTED BY: Fox County Parole Board
CHARGES: Violation of Parole
DESCRIPTION:
Age: 22
Race: White
Height: 5′2″
Weight: 100 lbs.
Hair: Blond
Eyes: Hazel

IDENTIFYING SCARS OR MARKS: Six-inch surgical scar on left shoulder blade; needle marks on inner right arm.
REMARKS: Known prostitute. Frequents Sandy Grove area. Is thought to be active heroin addict. Last seen with short, purple-tinted hair. May head for sister's home in Bangor, Maine.
CAUTION: Has been known to carry knives and will fight police. Approach with caution.

WANTED
Ali Jamal

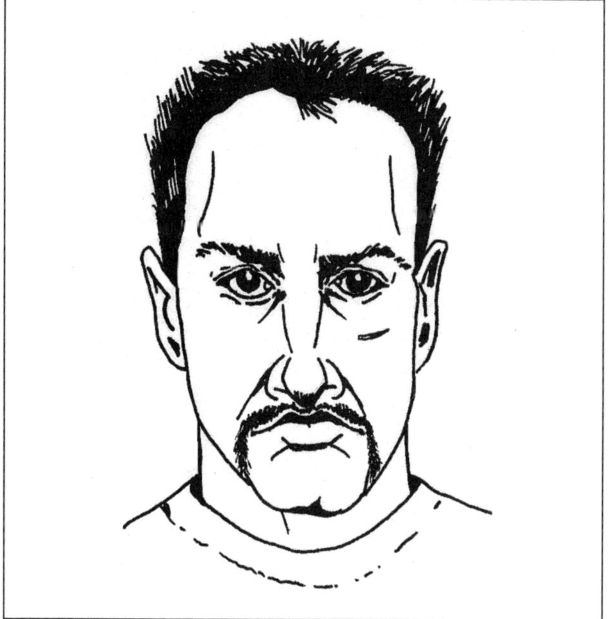

ALIASES: Al Jam
WANTED BY: FBI
CHARGES: Conspiracy to commit murder
DESCRIPTION:

Age: 27
Race: Middle Eastern
Height: 5′10″
Weight: 165 lbs.
Hair: Black
Eyes: Black

IDENTIFYING SCARS OR MARKS: Thin scar along left cheek.
REMARKS: Last known employer, Lenny's Limo Service in Atlantic City, New Jersey. Frequently seen with full black beard and mustache. Speaks with thick Middle Eastern accent.
CAUTION: Jamal is known to carry a .45 mm Browning.

WANTED

Michael Adam Rosen

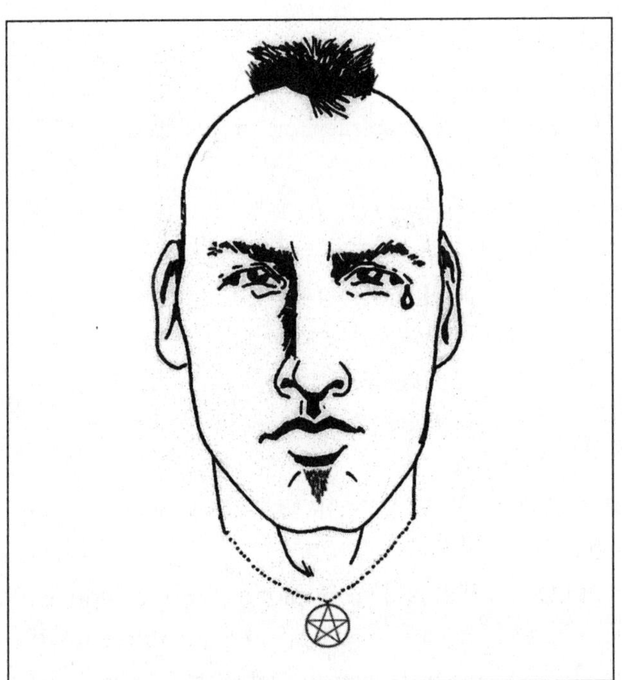

ALIASES: Adam Rose
WANTED BY: Ann Arbor Police Department
CHARGES: Assault
DESCRIPTION:

Age: 17
Race: White
Height: 5′8″
Weight: 160 lbs.
Hair: Black
Eyes: Black

IDENTIFYING SCARS OR MARKS: Tattoos of a tear drop at base of left eye, "Kim" on right upper shoulder, and tiger curling around left wrist.
REMARKS: Satan's Riders gang member. Limps heavily on left leg.

WANTED

Kathleen Lisa Eglund

ALIASES: Katie England
WANTED BY: Coal County Sheriff's Department
CHARGES: Abuse of the Disabled
DESCRIPTION:

Age: 38
Race: White
Height: 5′7″
Weight: 230 lbs.
Hair: Brunette
Eyes: Green

IDENTIFYING SCARS OR MARKS: Burn scars along top of right hand.
REMARKS: Frequently works as an orderly. Last seen in Nogales, New Mexico, but is believed to be en route to San Diego, California.

Roadblock Guidelines

The Advisory Committee of the State Police has issued the following guidelines for establishing a roadblock in order to identify and apprehend drunk drivers:

1. **Selecting the location.** The roadblock must be established in a location that affords motorists a clear view of the stop. It cannot be established, for example, just over a hill or around a curve. Motorists must be able to see that a roadblock is ahead and that cars are being stopped.

2. **Staffing the location.** A roadblock must display visible signs of police authority. Therefore, uniformed officers in marked patrol cars should primarily staff the roadblock. Plainclothes officers may supplement the staff at a roadblock, but the initial stop and questioning of motorists should be conducted by uniformed officers. In addition to the officers conducting the motorist stops, officers should be present to conduct field sobriety tests on suspect drivers. A command observation officer must also be present to coordinate the roadblock.

3. **Operation of the roadblock.** All cars passing through the roadblock must be stopped. It should not appear to an approaching motorist that some cars are being singled while others are not stopped, as this will generate unnecessary fear on the part of the motorist. The observation vehicle that is present at the roadblock will be able to pursue any motorists who refuse to stop.

4. **Questioning the drivers.** Each motorist stopped by the roadblock should be questioned only briefly. In most cases, an officer should ask directly if the driver has been drinking. In suspicious cases, an officer may engage in some further questioning to allow him or her to evaluate the driver's sobriety. A driver who appears to have been drinking should be directed to the side of the road, out of the line of traffic, where other officers may conduct a field sobriety test. Each nonsuspicious driver should be stopped only briefly, for approximately a minute or less.

5. **Duration of operation.** No drunk-driving roadblock should be in operation for more than two hours. Roadblocks in place for longer periods lose their effectiveness as word spreads as to the location of the roadblock, and motorists who have been drinking will avoid the area. In addition, on average only about one percent of all the drivers who pass through a roadblock will be arrested for drunk driving, and, after a short period of time, officers can be used more efficiently elsewhere.

6. **Charges other than drunk driving.** A roadblock may only be established for a single purpose—in this case, detecting drunk drivers—and should not be seen as an opportunity to check for a variety of motorist offenses. However, officers are not required to ignore what is plainly obvious. For example, motorists and passengers who are not wearing seat belts should be verbally warned that failure to do so is against the law. Detaining and ticketing such drivers is not the purpose of the roadblock and would unduly slow down the stops of other cars. An officer who spots a situation that presents a clear and present danger should follow through by directing the motorist to the side of the road where the officers are conducting field sobriety tests. These officers can then follow through on investigating the driver for crimes other than drunk driving.

Part One: Memorization and Visualization

Answer the following 30 questions based on the wanted posters and police procedure article you have just studied. **Do not refer to the study material to answer these questions.**

1. Patrice Dwyer is wanted for
- **a.** armed robbery.
- **b.** fraud.
- **c.** sexual assault.
- **d.** violation of parole.

2. Fabian Rollo Vernon is
- **a.** Middle Eastern.
- **b.** white.
- **c.** Hispanic.
- **d.** African American.

3. Fabian Rollo Vernon has
- **a.** a mostly bald head.
- **b.** a tattoo near his eye.
- **c.** missing front teeth.
- **d.** a scar on his cheek.

4. Michael Adam Rosen also goes by the name
- **a.** Adam Rosenberg.
- **b.** Mike Adams.
- **c.** Adam Rose.
- **d.** M.A. Rosen.

5. Ali Jamal's last known employer was
- **a.** L.J.'s Limo Service.
- **b.** Lenny's Limo Service.
- **c.** Smith's Limo Service.
- **d.** Red Hook Limo Service.

6. Kathleen Lisa Eglund is wanted for
- **a.** conspiracy.
- **b.** violation of parole.
- **c.** abuse of the disabled.
- **d.** assault.

7. Patrice Dwyer's hair is
- **a.** spiked on top.
- **b.** curly.
- **c.** dyed blond.
- **d.** wavy.

8. Michael Adam Rosen's tiger tattoo is located on his
- **a.** right shoulder.
- **b.** chest.
- **c.** forehead.
- **d.** left wrist.

9. Kathleen Lisa Eglund is believed to be en route to
- **a.** Atlantic City, New Jersey.
- **b.** Nogales, New Mexico.
- **c.** Red Hook, Kentucky.
- **d.** San Diego, California.

10. Ali Jamal's scar runs
- **a.** vertically down his chin.
- **b.** vertically down his right cheek.
- **c.** horizontally along his left cheek.
- **d.** horizontally along his forehead.

11. Which of the following is true of Fabian Rollo Vernon?
- **a.** He is wanted for violation of parole.
- **b.** He has schizophrenia.
- **c.** He is armed and dangerous.
- **d.** He is a former nursing home employee.

12. Michael Adam Rosen has been seen wearing
- **a.** a scarf around his head.
- **b.** a T-shirt.
- **c.** a heavy jacket.
- **d.** a pentacle around his neck.

13. Which two suspects are known to carry weapons?
- **a.** Jamal and Eglund
- **b.** Dwyer and Rosen
- **c.** Rosen and Eglund
- **d.** Dwyer and Jamal

14. Which suspect walks with a limp?
- **a.** Vernon
- **b.** Jamal
- **c.** Rosen
- **d.** Eglund

15. Which two suspects are in their twenties?
- **a.** Vernon and Jamal
- **b.** Dwyer and Jamal
- **c.** Eglund and Jamal
- **d.** Dwyer and Eglund

16. Which two suspects have black hair and black eyes?
- **a.** Dwyer and Eglund
- **b.** Jamal and Eglund
- **c.** Rosen and Dwyer
- **d.** Jamal and Rosen

17. Of the people listed below, which is tallest?
- **a.** Vernon
- **b.** Jamal
- **c.** England
- **d.** Rosen

18. Which suspect is known to carry a gun?
- **a.** Rosen
- **b.** Dwyer
- **c.** Jamal
- **d.** Eglund

19. Based on the information in the wanted posters, which of the following is true?
- **a.** Eglund is the only suspect with green eyes.
- **b.** Rosen is the only suspect with brown eyes.
- **c.** Eglund and Dwyer both have green eyes.
- **d.** Vernon and Dwyer both have hazel eyes.

20. Based on the information in the wanted posters, which of the following is false?
- **a.** Dwyer wears a nose ring.
- **b.** Rosen has a tattoo of the name "Kim."
- **c.** Rosen and Jamal both have full beards.
- **d.** Eglund wears glasses.

21. According to the Roadblock Guidelines, officers must make sure they set up a drunk-driving roadblock that
- **a.** can be seen by motorists from a distance.
- **b.** provides a well-hidden place for officers to park their cars.
- **c.** is near a bar or tavern.
- **d.** is near a busy street or highway.

22. While questioning motorists at a drunk-driving roadblock, Officer Firth notices that, although the driver of a particular car appears to be sober, the passenger in that car seems extremely nervous and has bruises on his face. She asks the passenger if he is all right and, after glancing at the driver, the passenger nods, *yes*. According to the guidelines, Officer Firth should
- **a.** let the car pass through, because the driver is not drunk.
- **b.** question the passenger and driver further about the passenger's condition.
- **c.** arrest the driver on suspicion of assault.
- **d.** direct the driver to pull to the side of the road where other officers can investigate further.

23. Officers have been conducting a drunk-driving roadblock since 7:00 P.M. and have made 35 drunk-driving arrests, which is one-quarter of all cars stopped. It is now 9:00 P.M. According to the guidelines, the officers should

a. continue the roadblock because they are making a high percentage of arrests.
b. reestablish the roadblock one-quarter mile down the road.
c. ask the Advisory Committee for permission to operate the roadblock longer.
d. dismantle the roadblock, because it has been in operation for two hours.

24. Officers have been directed to operate a drunk-driving roadblock from 6:00 P.M. to 8:00 P.M. at the corner of Greene and First. At 6:45, the unusually heavy traffic begins to back up. According to the guidelines, officers should NOT

a. dismantle the roadblock early.
b. begin stopping only every third car.
c. move the roadblock to a quieter intersection.
d. ask for extra officers to help staff the roadblock.

25. According to the guidelines, the officers stopping and questioning motorists at a drunk-driving roadblock should be in uniform so that motorists

a. will take the roadblock more seriously.
b. will answer their questions more truthfully.
c. can identify which agency they are from.
d. can tell from a distance that this is an official activity.

26. Officer Robb is stopping and questioning eastbound cars at the drunk-driving roadblock on Highway 7. He asks one driver if she has been drinking. The driver says, "No, Officer, I haven't," but she slurs her words. According to the guidelines, Officer Robb should

a. ask the driver a couple more questions.
b. arrest the driver for drunk driving.
c. ask the driver to take a breathalyzer test.
d. pass the driver through with a warning.

27. A car approaching a drunk-driving roadblock slows down, then at the last minute speeds up and passes through the roadblock without stopping. According to the guidelines,

a. the officers should note the car's license number and radio headquarters.
b. the officers should request backup to pursue the car.
c. the officers conducting field sobriety tests should pursue the vehicle.
d. the officer in the command observation vehicle should pursue the motorist.

28. Based on the guidelines, which of the following statements is true?

a. Guidelines for drunk-driving roadblocks are determined by the State Police.
b. Guidelines for drunk-driving roadblocks are determined by local police departments.
c. Guidelines for drunk-driving roadblocks are determined by the State Legislature.
d. Guidelines for drunk-driving roadblocks are determined by the County Sheriff.

29. According to the guidelines, officers operating a drunk-driving roadblock can expect
- **a.** cooperation from most drivers.
- **b.** to arrest only about one percent of the drivers stopped.
- **c.** to issue several tickets for failure to wear a seat belt.
- **d.** that many cars will refuse to stop.

30. According to the guidelines, the main role of the command observation officer at a drunk-driving roadblock is to
- **a.** conduct field sobriety tests.
- **b.** establish the official police presence.
- **c.** determine when to dismantle the roadblock.
- **d.** coordinate the roadblock.

Part Two: Reading Skills

Answer questions 31–34 solely on the basis of the information in following passage.

In order for evidence to be admissible and therefore introduced into court, it must conform to many rules and restrictions. A court can rule that evidence is inadmissible if it is irrelevant, confusing, unfairly prejudicial, or cumulative. For police officers, another key element of introducing evidence at a trial is maintaining the chain of custody.

By ensuring the chain of custody, the judge is trying to ensure that evidence presented in court is in nearly the same condition as it was found at the crime scene. Typically, the chain of custody begins with the person who found the evidence and culminates with the person who brings the evidence before the court. Chain of custody is proven by people testifying as to where and how evidence was maintained from its first finding until its ultimate presentation in court.

31. Which of the following is a reason a judge may NOT allow evidence into court?
- **a.** It may prove the defendant guilty.
- **b.** It may prove the defendant not guilty.
- **c.** The witness knows the defendant.
- **d.** It doesn't prove any facts related to the case.

32. It can be inferred that the chain of custody probably ends with
- **a.** the judge presiding over the trial.
- **b.** the defendant.
- **c.** the defendant or plaintiff's trial attorney.
- **d.** the jury.

33. Where does the chain of custody begin?
- **a.** when the crime is committed
- **b.** when the trial begins
- **c.** when the jury returns a verdict
- **d.** when the evidence is found

34. Which of the following is NOT true?
- **a.** Evidence must be relevant.
- **b.** Evidence must be prejudicial.
- **c.** Judges and juries use evidence.
- **d.** Evidence must be admissible.

Answer questions 35–37 solely on the basis of the map below. The arrows indicate traffic flow; one arrow indicates a one-way street going in the direction of the arrow: two arrows represent a two-way street. You are not allowed to go the wrong way on a one-way street.

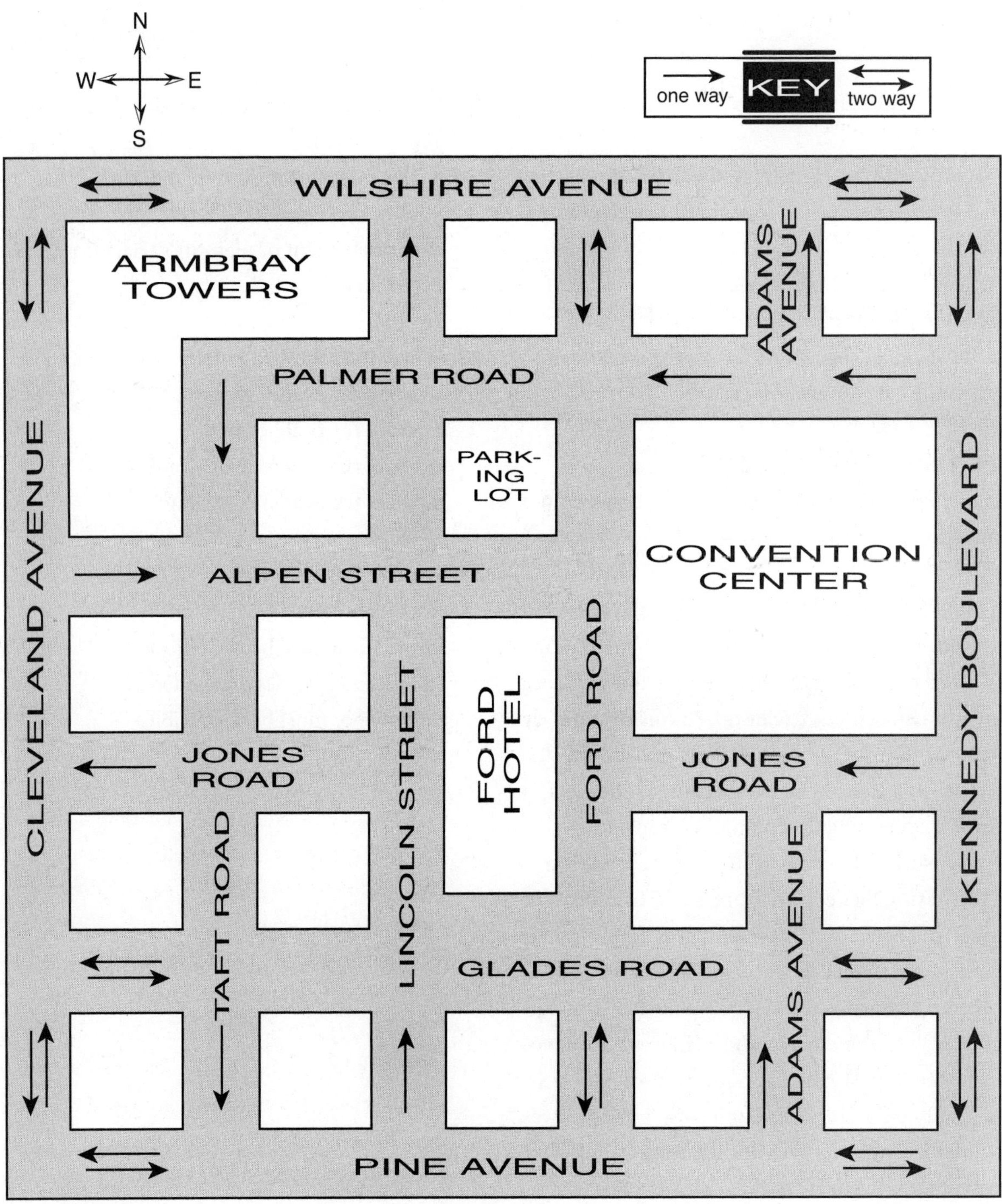

35. Officers Muldoon and Chavez are eating at Al's Cafe, which faces Jones Road. They get a call of a suspicious person at the Cleveland Avenue entrance to the Armbray Towers. What is their most direct route to the Armbray Towers?

a. Go east on Jones Road, then south on Kennedy Boulevard, then west on Glade Road, and then north on Cleveland Avenue to the Armbray Towers.

b. Go west on Jones Road to Cleveland Avenue and then north on Cleveland to the Armbray Towers.

c. Go west on Jones Road, then south on Ford Road, then west on Glade Road, and then north on Cleveland Avenue to the Armbray Towers.

d. Go west on Jones Road, then north on Ford Road, then west on Palmer Road, then south on Taft Road, then west on Jones Road, and then north on Cleveland Avenue to the Armbray Towers.

36. Officers Chang and Parker are northbound on Lincoln Street and have just crossed Alpen Street. They receive a call about a two-car, injury collision on Adams Avenue at Pine Avenue. What is their most direct route to the accident scene?

a. Continue north on Lincoln Street, then east on Wilshire Avenue, then south on Ford Road, then east on Glade Road, and then south on Adams Avenue to the accident scene.

b. Continue north on Lincoln Street, then west on Palmer Road, then south on Taft Road, and then east on Pine Avenue to the accident scene.

c. Make a U-turn on Lincoln Street, and then go south on Lincoln Street and then east on Pine Avenue to the accident scene.

d. Continue north on Lincoln Street, then east on Wilshire Avenue, then south on Kennedy Boulevard, and then west on Pine Avenue to the accident scene.

37. Officer Tananga is southbound on Kennedy Boulevard. He makes a right turn onto Glade Road, then a left onto Taft Road, a right onto Pine Avenue, another right onto Cleveland Avenue, and then a right onto Wilshire Avenue. Which direction is he facing?

a. west

b. south

c. east

d. north

Answer questions 38–41 solely on the basis of the following passage.

As early as 1880, it was suspected, and later confirmed, that no two individuals' fingerprints are alike. While the basic pattern for human fingerprints comes from their genetic encoding, fingerprints are also affected during development by the conditions in the womb, including the position of the fetus, condition of the amniotic fluid in the womb, and other environmental factors. The combination of the vast number of possible genetic patterns and the environmental factors means that no two individuals have the same fingerprints, not even twins.

Once they had been found to be a reliable way to identify individuals, fingerprints had a number of uses in the police service. Fingerprints can be described as visible, plastic, or latent. Visible prints would be those left by touching a substance before touching a surface, like a bloody fingerprint. Plastic would be prints left in a soft substance like wood putty or clay. Latent means hidden. Latent fingerprints are left behind by the natural oils from our hands. These oils remain on an object even if they are not visible.

38. According to the passage, which of the following is true?
a. Identical twins have identical fingerprints.
b. An individual's genetic code provides the basic pattern for his or her fingerprints.
c. Environmental conditions have no impact on the development of fingerprints.
d. Few genetic combinations of fingerprints are possible.

39. Which of the following is an example of plastic fingerprints?
a. an ink thumbprint left on a piece of paper
b. a fingerprint on a doorknob
c. a fingerprint found in tar
d. a fingerprint found on a glass door

40. According to the passage, which of the following is NOT a type of fingerprint?
a. latent
b. visible
c. amniotic
d. plastic

41. What causes latent fingerprints when a suspect touches an object?
a. the suspect's genetic code
b. the wet objects the suspect touched earlier
c. the secretion of amniotic fluid
d. the oil on the suspect's fingers

Answer questions 42–46 based on the map on the opposite page and the following information.

A police officer is often required to assist civilians who seek travel directions or referral to city agencies and facilities.

The map is a section of the city where some public buildings are located. Each of the squares represents one city block. Street names are as shown. If there is an arrow next to the street name, it means the street is one way only in the direction of the arrow. If there is no arrow next to the street name, two-way traffic is allowed.

42. You arrive at the scene of a vehicular accident at the corner of Brown Street and 9th Avenue to find gasoline leaking from one of the cars. What is the most direct legal way for the fire engine to travel to the scene of the accident?
a. east on Maple Street and north on 9th Avenue to the accident
b. west on Maple Street, north on 12th Avenue, and east on Brown Street to the accident
c. east on Maple Street and north on 11th Avenue to the accident
d. west on Maple Street, north on 11th Avenue, and east on Brown Street to the accident

43. What streets cross at the southeast corner of the park?
a. Park Street and 10th Avenue
b. Park Street and 9th Avenue
c. Brown Street and 10th Avenue
d. Brown Street and 9th Avenue

44. A civilian leaving the clinic needs to drive to the drugstore. If you were giving her directions from the clinic, what would be the most direct, legal route?
a. east on Maple Street, north on 9th Avenue, and west on Brown Street to the store entrance
b. west on Maple Street, north on 10th Avenue, and west on Brown Street to the store entrance
c. west on Green Street, north on 12th Avenue, and east on Brown Street to the store entrance
d. east on Oak Street, north on 11th Avenue, and east on Brown Street to the store entrance

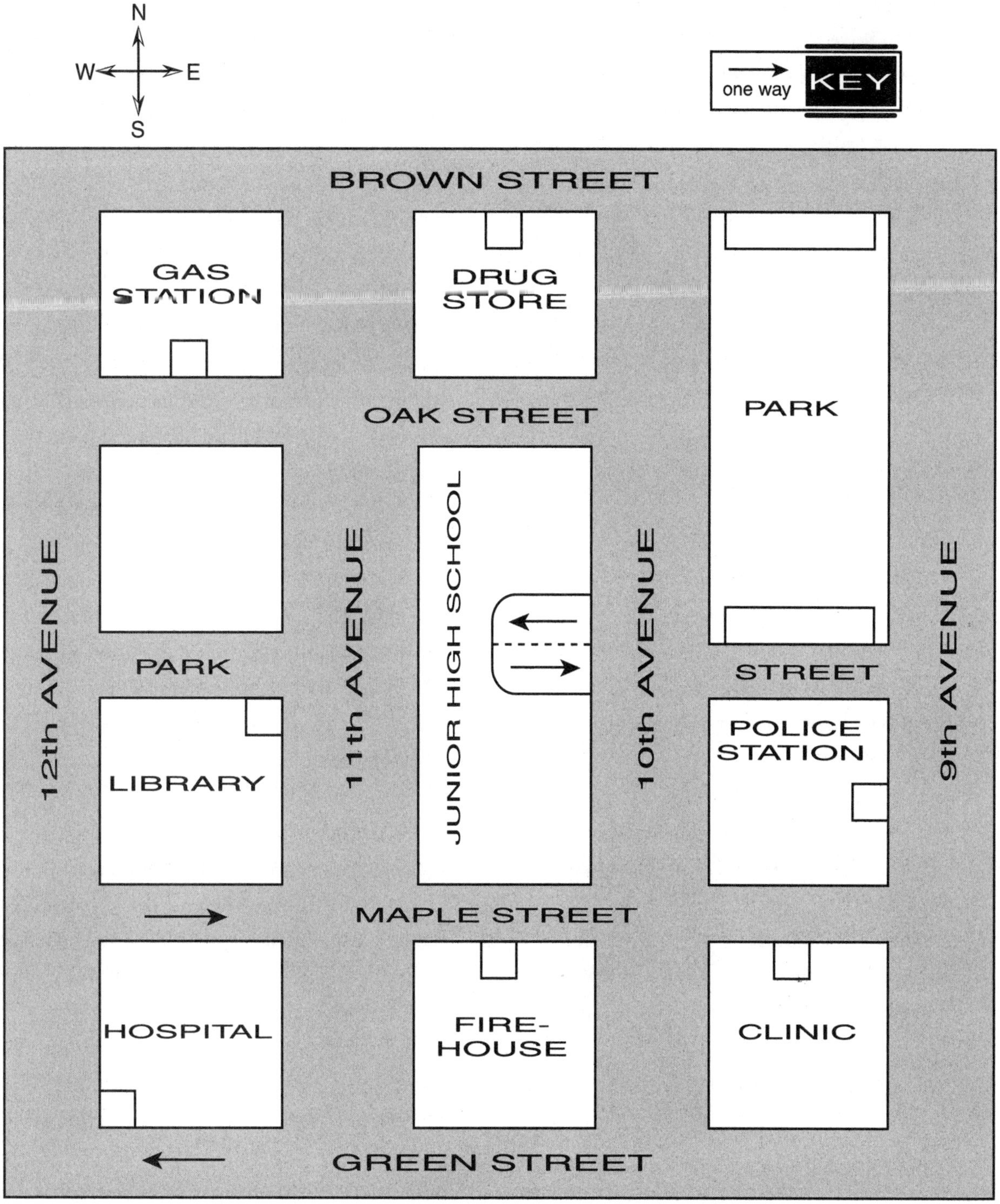

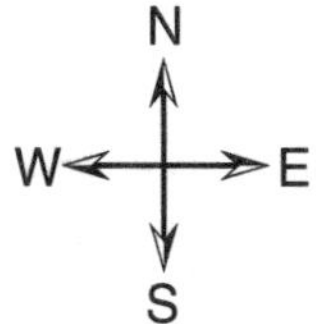

BROWN STREET

GAS STATION

DRUG STORE

PARK

OAK STREET

JUNIOR HIGH SCHOOL

12th AVENUE

11th AVENUE

10th AVENUE

9th AVENUE

PARK

STREET

LIBRARY

POLICE STATION

MAPLE STREET

HOSPITAL

FIRE-HOUSE

CLINIC

GREEN STREET

45. Someone at the junior high school has been injured and needs to go to the hospital. What directions from the junior high school would you give to the ambulance driver?

a. north on 10th Avenue, west on Brown Street, and south on 12th Avenue to the hospital entrance
b. south on 10th Avenue and west on Green Street to the hospital entrance
c. north on 10th Avenue and south on Brown Street to the hospital entrance
d. south on 10th Avenue, west on Maple Street, and west on Green Street to the hospital entrance

46. You are leaving work at the police station and need to fill your gas tank before you go home. What is the quickest legal route to the gas station?

a. south on 9th Avenue, west on Maple Street, north on 11th Avenue, and west on Oak Street to the entrance
b. east on Maple Street, north on 10th Avenue, and west on Oak Street to the entrance
c. north on 9th Avenue and west on Brown Street to the entrance
d. north on 9th Avenue, west on Park Street, north on 10th Avenue, and west on Oak Street to the entrance

Answer questions 47–51 solely on the basis of the following passage.

In police work, a procedure is a set of step-by-step directions that tells a police officer what to do, how to do it, and in what order it should be done. As an example, many police departments have a booking procedure for when an offender is officially recorded as being arrested. Having a booking procedure makes sense because it is something that is done with relatively few changes and under generally controlled conditions. With these types of procedures, a police officer has very little discretion. Discretion is a police officer's ability to act or decide based on his or her own judgment.

Police departments use policies to limit discretion in situations with a large number of variables. In the instance of using force, a police department's policy may dictate that an officer must use the minimum amount of force necessary to overcome resistance. How much force is the minimum will be determined by the situation and the officer's judgment. In addition to procedures and policies, departments use rules and regulations to further limit a police officer's discretion. Rules are primarily concerned with limiting an officer's individual behavior, such as ensuring that officers show up for work on time or are prohibited from drinking alcohol while on duty.

While rules limit and dictate individual behavior, regulations are designed to standardize equipment and therefore limit choice. Many police departments have regulations that determine the type of handguns officers can carry, the uniforms they wear, or the type of shoes they must have. Just as there would be a penalty for violating a rule, there is often a penalty for violating a regulation. While police officers still have a tremendous amount of discretion and, therefore, must exercise proper judgment, police departments use policies, procedures, rules, and regulations to limit discretion and control behavior.

47. According to the passage, which of the following is a set of step-by-step instructions?
- **a.** policy
- **b.** procedure
- **c.** rule
- **d.** regulation

48. Based on information from the passage, which of the following police activities is best covered by a policy?
- **a.** vehicle pursuits
- **b.** vacation schedule
- **c.** shoulder patch design
- **d.** telephone etiquette

49. According to the passage, which of the following is true?
- **a.** Police officers have the least amount of discretion with policies.
- **b.** Police officers have the most amount of discretion with rules.
- **c.** Police officers have the most amount of discretion with policies.
- **d.** Police officers have the most amount of discretion with regulations.

50. What is the main idea of the passage?
- **a.** Police officers are guided by many different rules.
- **b.** Police officers are guided by few rules.
- **c.** Police departments have little control over the discretion used by police officers in the field.
- **d.** Police departments use policies, procedures, rules, and regulations to control individual discretion.

51. According to the passage, which of the following is NOT true?
- **a.** Police officers have a tremendous amount of discretion.
- **b.** There are penalties for violating rules but not regulations.
- **c.** Rules are concerned with controlling individual behavior.
- **d.** Polices are used in situations wherein police officers have a lot of discretion.

Answer questions 52–54 solely on the basis of the following map. The arrows indicate traffic flow; one arrow indicates a one-way street going in the direction of the arrow; two arrows represent a two-way street. You are not allowed to go the wrong way on a one-way street.

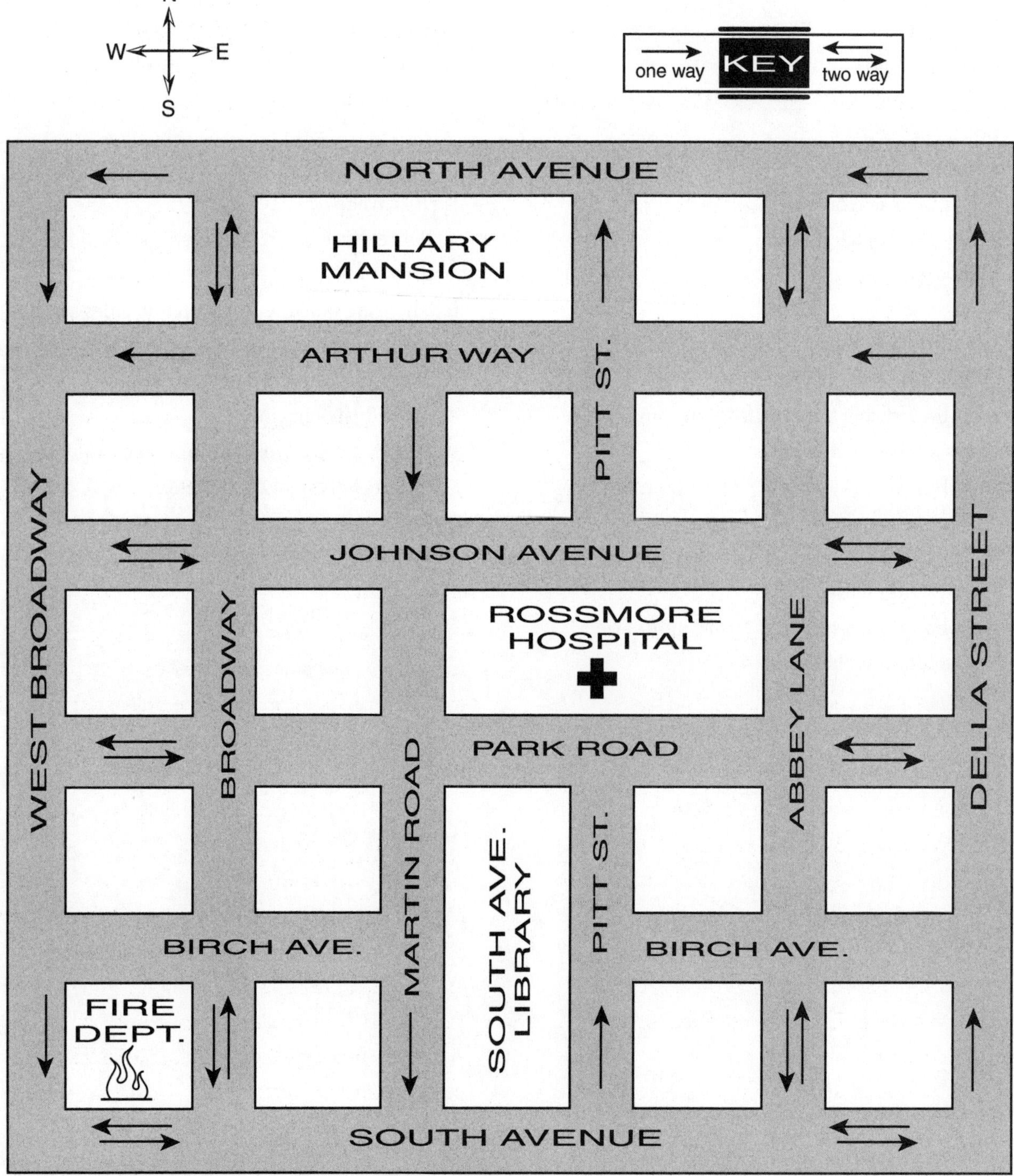

52. Officer Lazere is spending his lunch break at the South Avenue Library, which faces South Avenue. He gets a call of a burglary at the Hillary Mansion, the entrance to which faces North Avenue. What is Officer Lazere's most direct route to the Hillary Mansion?

a. Go east on South Avenue, then north on Abbey Lane to North Avenue, and then west on North Avenue to the Hillary Mansion.

b. Go east on South Avenue, then north on Pitt Street, and then west on North Avenue to the Hillary Mansion.

c. Go west on South Avenue, then north on West Broadway, and then east on North Avenue to the Hillary Mansion.

d. Go west on South Avenue, then north on Broadway to North Avenue, and then east on North Avenue to the Hillary Mansion.

53. Officer Lew is southbound on Martin Road, and has just crossed Park Road. Dispatch assigns a family disturbance call to him and sends him to a residence at the corner of Arthur Way and Della Street. What is Officer Lew's most direct route to the residence?

a. Make a U-turn on Martin Road and go north on Martin Road to Arthur Way and then east on Arthur Way to the residence.

b. Continue south on Martin Road and then go east on South Avenue, then north on Pitt Street, then east on Park Road, then north on Abbey Lane, and then east on Arthur Way to the residence.

c. Continue south on Martin Road and then go east on South Avenue and then north on Della Street to the residence.

d. Continue south on Martin Road and then go east on Birch Avenue and then north on Della Street to the residence.

54. Officer Berger is heading west on Johnson Avenue. She makes a right turn on Broadway, a left turn on Arthur Way, a left turn onto West Broadway, and finally a left turn onto Birch Avenue. Which direction is Officer Berger facing?

a. east

b. south

c. west

d. north

Answer questions 55–60 solely on the basis of the following passage.

Identify theft comes in many forms. It is the act of stealing someone's unique, personal identifying information to commit crimes such as stealing funds out of bank or financial accounts, or to completely assume someone else's identity to run up debts while fraudulently using that victim's name. The effects on these victims may not be only financial; they often extend deeper into victims' reputations and personal lives.

One of the newer and more notorious forms of identity theft is known as phishing. To commit this crime, identity thieves create e-mails and websites that mimic those of well-known organizations such as banks, corporations, and government agencies to trick users into believing they are disclosing their personal information for legitimate purposes.

There is no one law enforcement agency responsible for investigating identity theft crimes, and because identity theft is constantly evolving and is still considered by many to be a nontraditional crime, the lack of proper training and knowledge of the subject have created serious obstacles to law enforcement agencies in fighting identity theft and prosecuting its perpetrators.

55. According to the passage, which of the following is true?
- **a.** Phishers use fingerprints to commit crimes.
- **b.** Identity theft is a traditional crime.
- **c.** Many victims suffer more than just financial expenses.
- **d.** Identity theft is not a crime.

56. Which of the following is identified by the passage as a challenge for law enforcement officials?
- **a.** Identify theft perpetrators are extremely difficult to apprehend.
- **b.** Many law enforcement agencies lack training in identity theft crimes.
- **c.** Many identity theft victims fail to come forward.
- **d.** Businesses tend to cover up identity theft crimes.

57. Based on the passage, which of the following is something an identity thief would NOT be interested in?
- **a.** bank account number
- **b.** full name
- **c.** Social Security number
- **d.** credit card number

58. According to details from the passage, which of the following would be an example of identity theft?
- **a.** taking out a loan in another person's name
- **b.** stealing a wallet that contains another person's personal identification
- **c.** using an alias
- **d.** any nontraditional crime

59. According to the passage, which of the following is NOT true?
- **a.** There is not one specific law enforcement agency responsible for investigating identity theft.
- **b.** Phishers use information for criminal purposes, such as identity theft and fraud.
- **c.** Phishing is the most common form of identity theft.
- **d.** Identity theft is still considered a nontraditional crime.

60. What would be the best title for this passage?
- **a.** Identity Theft: A Modern Crime
- **b.** Phishers and Fraud
- **c.** Identity Theft: Causes and Prevention
- **d.** Information Super-Highway Fraud

Part Three: Judgment and Problem Solving

Use good judgment and common sense, as well as the information provided in the question, to answer the following questions.

61. The new governor has decreed that one quarter of all inmates in the state prison system must be released, due to overcrowding. She has directed police officials to release the inmates who have been held the longest. Weston has been in prison longer than Papak, but not as long as Gomez. Rashad has been in prison less time than Weston, but more time than Papak. Which one prisoner should be released?
- **a.** Gomez
- **b.** Weston
- **c.** Papak
- **d.** Rashad

Use the following information to answer questions 62–64.

The use of warnings may sometimes provide a satisfactory solution to a problem and may enhance the public perception of the department. Normally, the use of a warning occurs in traffic offenses, but warnings may occasionally be applied to misdemeanor criminal offenses. In determining whether a warning should be issued, the officer should consider:

1. the seriousness of the offense
2. the likelihood that the violator will heed the warning
3. the reputation of the violator, (i.e., known repeat offender, has received previous warnings, etc.)

62. Which of the following is the best example of a situation in which a police officer might issue a warning?

a. a city councilperson who has been stopped for drunk driving
b. a known heroin addict who is trespassing in an abandoned building
c. a group of 14-year-old boys who are throwing rocks at each other
d. a 35-year-old woman on probation for shoplifting who has been detained for stealing $2 from a local store

63. Which of the following is a situation where a police officer could NOT issue a warning?

a. a minor traffic violation
b. a ten-year-old who shoplifted a candy bar
c. a felony assault
d. a city councilperson accused of trespassing

64. Which of the following is the best situation for a police officer to issue a warning?

a. a foreign tourist accused of stealing $500
b. a 22-year-old soldier, home on leave, who is drunk in public
c. an offender who has a warrant for failing to appear in court
d. a 35-year-old man with an out-of-state driver's license who is accused of fraud

65. Officer Yang has noticed an increase in gang graffiti in his area. Store owners are complaining about the damage and have asked him to keep a closer eye out for this problem. Which situation below should Officer Yang investigate?

a. Two teenagers are leaning against a park wall completely covered with gang-related graffiti.
b. Four teenagers are leaning against the clean white wall of a neighborhood grocery store. One teenager has a spray paint can hanging out of the rear pocket of his pants.
c. Three teenagers are riding bicycles in a grocery store parking lot late at night.
d. Six teenagers are walking along the sidewalk bouncing a basketball and yelling at passing cars while making gang signs with their hands.

66. Last month, Officer Meadows had more arrests than Officer Ash. Officer Ash had more arrests than Officer Westerman, but fewer than Officer Governale. Which officer had the fewest arrests?

a. Officer Ash
b. Officer Governale
c. Officer Meadows
d. Officer Westerman

67. Merchants in the South Oaks Shopping Mall are upset by a recent rash of purse snatchings in their parking lot. Officer Crandall is closely patrolling the mall area, including the vacant lot behind the stores. Which situation below would Officer Crandall most likely investigate?

a. a car horn honking continuously in the mall parking lot
b. a car in the mall parking lot with four flat tires and a broken windshield
c. a woman's voice raised in anger in the mall parking lot
d. a man running through the vacant lot with a bulky object under his sweatshirt

68. Taylor, Hudson, Xavier, and Muller are on the security detail for the governor's visit. Taylor is in front of the stage, Hudson is behind the stage, Xavier is near the exit door, and Muller is at the back of the auditorium. If Hudson switches places with Xavier and Xavier then switches places with Muller, where is Muller?

a. near the exit
b. in front of the stage
c. at the back of the auditorium
d. behind the stage

69. Drug addicts often try to pass fake prescriptions at pharmacies in order to get drugs illegally. Which situation below would lead an officer to investigate a possible forgery at the City Drugstore?

a. a prescription written on a piece of notebook paper
b. a written prescription covered with coffee stains
c. a prescription called in by a doctor
d. a prescription for painkillers with a date showing it was written the day before

70. Ronald is serving one more year in the state penitentiary than Parisi. Donofrio is serving one year less than Parisi and one year more than Yardley. Parisi is serving nine years. How many years is Yardley serving?

a. seven
b. eight
c. nine
d. ten

71. Officer Rannick is meeting his girlfriend at the mall to see a movie. He is running late and is afraid she may have left the theater thinking he was not going to show up. As he enters the mall, he sees a man about 10 yards away grab a woman's purse, push her down, and take off running through the mall. What should Officer Rannick do?

a. Walk away because he is not on duty.
b. Have a store manager call mall security and then hurry on his way.
c. Chase the suspect.
d. Find mall security himself.

Use the following information to answer questions 72–74.

To pick up a motorcycle without help after it has fallen, motorcycle officers should do the following:

1. Turn the ignition switch to off.
2. Place both hands on the handlebars.
3. Position the motorcycle so that both tires are touching the ground.
4. Rock the motorcycle back and forth on the metal engine guards until momentum is built up.
5. Stand the bike upright using the momentum from the rocking motion.
6. Rest the bike on its kickstand.

72. Officer Greene has completed a radar assignment in the school zone near West High School. Before he starts his motorcycle, his foot slips on the kick-stand, and the motorcycle falls over onto its left side. Officer Greene sees that both tires are on the ground, so he places both hands on the handle bars. What should the officer do now?
- **a.** Turn the ignition switch to off.
- **b.** Rock the bike on its engine guards.
- **c.** Position the bike so that the tires are touching the ground.
- **d.** Stand the bike upright.

73. The streets are slick following a brief rain. Officer Woodrow rolls her motorcycle to a stop at a red light. Her right foot slips, and she drops the motorcycle onto its right side. She turns the engine off at the ignition switch. What should she do next?
- **a.** Put the kickstand down so the bike can rest on it.
- **b.** Rock the bike on its engine guards to build momentum.
- **c.** Place both hands on the handlebars.
- **d.** Position the bike so that both tires are touching the ground.

74. Officer Wilson is on a motorcycle in pursuit of a vehicle that has refused to pull over for him. As the suspect and Officer Wilson reach Anderson Lane, the suspect makes a sharp left turn. Officer Wilson makes the turn too fast, and the motorcycle slides out from under him. He runs to the bike. What should he do next?
- **a.** Quickly stand the motorcycle upright and continue the pursuit.
- **b.** Turn off the ignition.
- **c.** Radio a description of the suspect vehicle, and then rock the bike on the engine guards.
- **d.** Put the kickstand down so that the bike will have something to rest on when he stands it up.

75. Officer North has been a police officer for 15 years, which is six years fewer than Officer Wilson but seven more than Officer Trainor. Officer Sanchez has been a police officer for five years more than Officer Trainor. How many years has Officer Sanchez been a police officer?
- **a.** 15
- **b.** 13
- **c.** 9
- **d.** 5

76. Officer Bettis has arrived at the scene of a family disturbance. Two other officers are in the front yard of the residence fighting with family members. Officer Bettis pulls out her departmentally approved nightstick and runs up to help one of the officers. A man steps up and swings a broken beer bottle at Officer Bettis's head. What should she do next?
- **a.** Try to snatch the beer bottle out of his hand and hope she doesn't get cut.
- **b.** Strike him in a departmentally approved target area so he will drop the bottle.
- **c.** Immediately call for more backup.
- **d.** Dodge his blows and continue on to help the officer being attacked.

77. While operating a speed trap on the interstate, Officer Hamin is running the radar in the eastbound lane, and Officer Firth is posted further down that lane to pursue speeders that Officer Hamin identifies. Officer Wong is running the radar in the westbound lane, and Officer Kelly is further down that lane to pursue speeders. If Officer Kelly switches with Officer Wong, who then switches with Officer Hamin, where is Wong now posted?

a. running the radar in the westbound lane
b. pursuing speeders in the eastbound lane
c. running the radar in the eastbound lane
d. pursuing speeders in the westbound lane

78. Fred is a business owner downtown who makes it well known that he hates the police and thinks they are all corrupt. Fred runs a red light downtown, almost causing a van to hit him, and then pulls over in front of his store, cursing loudly about the other driver's driving skills. Officer Martinez was standing on the corner and watched Fred run the light. What should he do?

a. Write Fred a citation for running a red light.
b. Warn Fred not to run red lights and hope this improves Fred's opinion of police.
c. Suggest to Fred that he take defensive driving classes.
d. Look into having someone check the timing of the lights in the downtown area.

79. Extortion is a less serious crime than burglary. Breaking and entering is more serious than extortion, but less serious than assault. Assault is more serious than burglary. Which crime is the most serious?

a. burglary
b. breaking and entering
c. assault
d. extortion

Use the following information to answer questions 80–82.

After arresting a suspect, officers should conduct a search for weapons and contraband by doing the following:

1. Make sure the prisoner's hands are handcuffed securely behind his or her back.
2. Check the waistband and area within reach of the prisoner's handcuffed hands.
3. Check the prisoner's cap or hat.
4. Check the neck area and both arms.
5. Check the prisoner's front pockets.
6. Check the inseam of the pants and crotch area.
7. Check the legs and ankles.
8. Check the prisoner's shoes.

80. Officer Linder arrests a man wearing a baseball cap, a T-shirt, blue jeans, and lace-up work boots. She checks to make sure the handcuffs are secure. She notices a bulge in his cap. What should Officer Linder do next?

a. Check his front pockets.
b. Check the cap for weapons.
c. Check the prisoner's waistband.
d. Check the area near his neck.

81. Officer Petrochowsky arrests a man for public intoxication. The man is wearing a cowboy hat, a long-sleeved shirt, dress slacks, and cowboy boots. The officer checks the prisoner's handcuffs and checks to make sure the waistband and back pocket area are clear of weapons. Suddenly, the prisoner sits down on the curb and refuses to stand up. Two other officers help get the prisoner to his feet. What should Officer Petrochowsky do next?

a. Check the prisoner's cowboy hat.
b. Check the prisoner's boots.
c. Check the prisoner's waistband and back pocket area.
d. Take the prisoner straight to jail before he tries to sit back down.

82. Officer Chastaine has a woman under arrest for possession of cocaine. She is wearing a scarf, a long dress, stockings, and high heels. He checks to make sure the handcuffs are secure on the woman. What should he do next?

a. Check the suspect's scarf.
b. Check the waistline of the suspect's dress and any pockets near her hands.
c. Check the suspect's neck area.
d. Check the suspect's shoes, which are partially hidden by her skirt.

83. The owner of the Sun Times Chevrolet dealership tells Officer Chervenack that someone is stealing running boards and other parts from the vans he has parked in the south lot sometime after 10:30 P.M. Officer Chervenack decides to patrol the area carefully. Which of the following situations should she investigate?

a. After midnight, a male in his early twenties is walking up and down rows of new pickups parked near the edge of the dealership.
b. After midnight, a panel truck pulls out of the vacant lot next to the dealership near where the vans are lined up.
c. After midnight, two teenagers in baggy pants and T-shirts are rollerblading around the new cars on the Sun Times lot.
d. After midnight, a station wagon drives into the lot and stops near the door to the main show room. A man gets out and unloads a mop, a bucket, and a broom.

84. Officer Walters is on foot patrol three blocks south of the precinct and two blocks east of Officer Polovich, who is on bicycle patrol. Sergeant Rooney is in her squad car one block north of Officer Walters, radioing Officer Hampton, who is located two blocks north of Sergeant Rooney. Officer Hampton is probably

a. in the squad car with Rooney.
b. at the precinct.
c. on foot patrol with Walters.
d. on bike patrol with Polovich.

85. Winslow Elementary School is having a criminal mischief problem: Windows are being broken at the school between 7:00 P.M. and 6:00 A.M. Officer Link has talked to the school principal and is keeping a closer eye on the school. Which of the following situations should he investigate?

a. At 1:00 A.M., Officer Link watches a man carrying a grocery sack cut through the school yard and come out on the other side of the school grounds. The officer can see a loaf of bread protruding out of the sack.
b. At 11:00 P.M., a car pulls up in the school parking lot. Officer Link sees the driver turn on the cabin light and unfold a map.
c. Around 11:30 P.M., Officer Link passes the school and sees two figures come out from behind one of the classroom buildings. They stop when they see him and then start walking, each in a different direction.
d. At 9:00 P.M., several teenagers skateboard into the parking lot, set up a small wooden ramp, and practice skateboarding tricks.

86. In the K-9 Corps, Officer Thomas is partnered with Ranger, Officer Cain is partnered with Scout, Officer Stern is partnered with Laddie, and Officer Walker is partnered with Astro. If Officer Thomas switches partners with Officer Stern and Officer Stern then switches with Officer Cain, who is Officer Stern's new partner?

a. Ranger
b. Scout
c. Laddie
d. Astro

87. Officers aren't always required to make a custody arrest the very moment a law has been broken. A warrant can always be issued at a later date for the suspect if the person can be identified. Which of the following situations best illustrates this point?

a. Jeremy is well-known in his community for his appearance at political demonstrations. Police are called to the scene of a massive riot where Jeremy has incited over 100 college students to throw rocks and attack the outnumbered police force.
b. Melody is walking along the street when a man jumps out from the shadows, grabs her purse, and takes off running. Officer Bentley catches him one block later.
c. Antonio tells Officer DiAngelo that his cousin has been threatening to burn his house down. While Antonio is telling this story, a gasoline can comes crashing through the living room window.
d. Rachel, dragging a teenager by the jacket, walks up to Officer Xavier. She tells the officer that she caught the young man putting his hand into her coat pocket when she was waiting at the bus stop.

88. Four people saw Ramirez snatch a woman's purse. Which description of Ramirez is probably correct?

a. He wore blue pants and an orange sweatshirt.
b. He wore blue pants and a red sweatshirt.
c. He wore black pants and an orange sweatshirt.
d. He wore blue pants and an orange jacket.

Use the following information to answer questions 89–91.

Police officers are required to give out physical descriptions of suspects over police radios for other officers to assist in locating the person. A description should be given out in the following order:

1. race and sex
2. weapons the suspect may be carrying
3. approximate height and weight
4. color and length of hair
5. baseball cap or other headgear
6. coat, jacket, or shirt
7. long or short pants
8. footwear

89. Officer Lundy was on patrol when she saw a man on a sidewalk waving wildly at her. The man told her he'd been robbed about one block away by a white male carrying a lock-blade knife. The suspect has on white tennis shoes, olive drab fatigue pants, a black turtleneck, and a black baseball cap. He's about 6 feet tall and weighs about 180 pounds. What is the first thing Officer Lundy should put out over the radio when she begins describing the suspect?

a. a description of the suspect's knife
b. a description of the suspect's race and sex
c. a description of the suspect's pants
d. a description of the suspect's speaking voice

90. While investigating a possible burglary in progress, Officer Risher sees the burglar dart out the back door of the house and run through the backyard. Other officers are en route to help. He picks up his radio to put out a description of the suspect. He couldn't tell the race or sex of the suspect, but guessed the height to be 5′8″ and the weight about 140 pounds. He also couldn't tell if the suspect carried a weapon. He did see black pants, white high-top tennis shoes, a dark windbreaker, and a red baseball cap. What is the first thing Officer Risher should put out on the radio when he begins to give the description?

a. a description of the suspect's race and sex
b. a description of the suspect's pants
c. a description of the suspect's shoes
d. a description of the suspect's height and weight

91. Officer Scott is taking a report of a purse snatching at the mall. The victim says the thief was 5′10″ tall, weighed about 160 pounds, had short red hair, and was wearing a New York Yankees baseball cap with gray warm-up pants and a gray sweatshirt. He was wearing black jogging shoes, was a white male, and appeared to be without weapons. Officer Scott begins her description with the race and sex of the suspect, but is interrupted by the victim. When she resumes her description, Officer Scott should begin with the

a. suspect's footwear.
b. suspect's headgear.
c. suspect's height and weight.
d. suspect's weapon.

92. Officer Mattox is listening to Claude, an angry citizen. Claude is furious with Officer Mattox because he feels that he doesn't deserve a ticket for running a stop sign. At what point should the officer consider physically arresting Claude?

a. Claude is seated in his automobile shouting, "Why aren't you out catching real crooks?" while the officer opens his ticket book.

b. Claude is standing beside his car on the sidewalk holding his arms out, with palms up, at passing cars while the officer writes the ticket.

c. Claude points his pen at Officer Mattox and says, "I want your name and badge number because I'm calling your supervisor."

d. Claude pokes his forefinger in Officer Mattox's chest and tells him he doesn't know what he's talking about.

93. During the graduation ceremony at the police academy, Cadet Jurgens is standing immediately to Cadet Shirley's left. Cadet Shirley is immediately to the left of Cadet Davis. Cadet Riley is to the right of Cadet Shirley. There are no other cadets in this row. In what order are the cadets standing?

a. Riley, Jurgens, Shirley, Davis

b. Shirley, Davis, Riley, Jurgens

c. Davis, Riley, Jurgens, Shirley

d. Jurgens, Shirley, Davis, Riley

Use the following information to answer question 94.

When an officer goes to a business to pick up a shoplifter who is already in the custody of private security guards, the officer should take the following steps in the order listed:

1. Check with store security personnel to verify that the circumstances fit the criteria for shoplifting.
2. Have store personnel fill out witness statements and a complaint form for shoplifting.
3. Take a photograph of the evidence and return the evidence to the store.
4. Search the suspect for weapons or contraband.
5. Place the suspect in the patrol car, and seat belt him or her securely.
6. Transport the suspect directly to jail.

94. Officer O'Brien is dispatched to the Blue Moon Art Gallery to pick up a shoplifter. When she arrives, she talks to Jeffrey, the store security guard, who tells her that he watched a man pick up a five-inch-long statue, stuff it in his coat pocket, and walk out the front door of the shop. He chased the man down and brought him back to the store. Jeffrey takes Officer O'Brien into the back room where he gives her a photograph of the statue for her to turn in as evidence. Officer O'Brien searches the prisoner for weapons and then places him in the patrol car, seat belting him in securely. They drive straight to the jail, where O'Brien books the suspect for shoplifting. Officer O'Brien's actions were

a. proper, because the incident was obviously a shoplifting.

b. improper, because she did not take the statue itself in as evidence.

c. proper, because the security guard watched the man carefully before accusing him of anything.

d. improper, because she did not have the guard fill out a witness statement or complaint form.

95. The police department is staking out a warehouse. Officer Walters is stationed north of Officer Smits. Officer Foster is stationed north of Officer Walters. Officer Balboa is stationed south of Officer Foster. Given these facts, which of the following statements is definitely true?

a. Officer Walters is the farthest north of all the officers.
b. Officer Balboa is the farthest south of all the officers.
c. Officer Smits is stationed south of Officer Foster.
d. Officer Balboa is stationed south of Officer Walters.

Use the following information to answer question 96.

In many smaller police departments, the first officer to arrive at the scene of a homicide is often the same officer who will be responsible for taking photographs to preserve the scene. That officer should take the following steps in the order listed:

1. Make sure the crime scene is secure and assign another officer to be responsible for monitoring who comes in and out of the area.
2. Leave the crime scene as it is, not moving any objects or specific items of evidence until photos can be taken of the scene as it first appears to the officer.
3. Take a picture of the overall crime scene area, then take a more specific photo of the area where the body is, and then take photos of specific pieces of evidence.
4. After the first set of photographs is taken, shoot another set and put in an object such as a ruler that will give the pictures a sense of perspective.
5. Place the film in a container and write on the container the case number, the photographer's name and employee number, the date, and the location where the photographs were taken.
6. Take the film to the department photo lab to be developed.

96. Officer Scales received a call at 8:00 A.M. about a headless body found in a trash bin in an alley behind 4501 West Thompson Street. He arrives on scene and secures the area by having everyone step away from the trash bin and by assigning backup Officer Angel to keep onlookers away from the scene. He reaches inside the trash bin and moves a cardboard box so that he can see the body better. He steps back, takes an overall shot of the scene, then moves in closer and takes specific shots of the body and then of all items that appear to be potential evidence. He takes a second set of photographs of the scene using a ruler for a marker. He then places the film in an evidence container and writes his case number, name and employee number, the date, and the location of where the photos were taken. He takes the film to the department photo lab. Based on the information in the passage, Officer Scales's actions were

a. improper, because he needed a flash unit given that the inside of the trash bin is dark.
b. improper, because he didn't witness the development of the film himself to protect the chain of evidence.
c. improper, because he moved the cardboard box before taking photographs of the scene as it first appeared.
d. proper, because he fulfilled all the duties as outlined in the procedures.

97. The police department files information on crimes by date committed. Baker robbed a bank before Mitchell assaulted a police officer, but after Nelson stole a car. Edgar burgled a warehouse before Nelson committed his crime. In what order do these files appear at the police department?

a. Nelson, Baker, Mitchell, Edgar
b. Edgar, Nelson, Baker, Mitchell
c. Baker, Mitchell, Edgar, Nelson
d. Edgar, Mitchell, Nelson, Baker

Use the following information to answer question 98.

When called upon to work a collision scene, a police officer should do the following:

1. Have all drivers move all vehicles not in need of a tow truck out of the roadway.
2. Position the patrol car behind disabled vehicles to keep other traffic from becoming involved.
3. Turn on emergency lights so other traffic is warned of the problem.
4. Call tow trucks if needed.
5. Put on a reflective traffic vest if traffic direction becomes necessary.
6. Have the drivers, passengers, and witnesses step out of the roadway.
7. Collect information from drivers, passengers, and witnesses.

98. Officer Gofort has been dispatched to a four-car collision at Maple and Walnut. When he arrives, he notices that all four cars are in the same lane of traffic and have apparently run into the backs of each other. What is the first thing he should do?

a. Call for four tow trucks to come to his location.
b. Have the drivers move all driveable cars into a nearby parking lot.
c. Put on his reflective vest.
d. Collect information from all drivers, passengers, and witnesses.

99. Officer Littmar is driving by a mall when she is flagged down by four men at a bus stop. They tell her that they just watched a man jump out of a yellow taxicab and force a woman at gunpoint to get inside the cab with him. They drove away northbound on Exeter Street. All four witnesses say they saw the number painted on the side of the cab and give Officer Littmar the numbers. Which of the numbers below is most likely to be the true number painted on the side of the taxi?

a. 9266
b. 9336
c. 9268
d. 8266

100. Officer Manley is called to the scene of a theft of auto parts at Lucky Lube Auto Parts. The store manager, Alfonso, tells the officer that while he was waiting on another customer, a woman came inside the store, picked up a pen-shaped tire gauge, and ran out of the store without paying. He shouted at her to stop, but she kept running. Alfonso says he thinks this is the same woman who has been shoplifting up and down the strip mall for the past two weeks. Alfonso describes the woman as white, 5′2″, 105 pounds, with light brown hair touching the tops of her shoulders, dark navy-blue wire rimmed glasses, and a pale blue dress. Officer Manley looks at four other reports to see if the same woman fits as a suspect in the other four thefts.

Suspect in Theft #1: Female, white, 5′2″, 105 lbs., shoulder-length brownish hair, glasses, white sandals, stained pale-colored dress.
Suspect in Theft #2: Female, white, 5′3″, 110 lbs., shoulder-length brown hair and wire-rimmed glasses, wearing a green dress.
Suspect in Theft #3: Female, white, 5′5″, 125 lbs., dyed light blond hair, blue dress, bare feet.
Suspect in Theft #4: Female, white, 5′2″, 112 lbs., light hair worn slightly below the shoulder, thin-framed metal glasses, light colored sandals, black dress.

Which of the suspects is the most likely culprit?

a. 2, 3, 4
b. 1, 2, 4
c. 1, 2, 3
d. 1, 3, 4

► Answer Key

Part One: Memorization and Visualization

1. **d.** Refer to the Charges section on Dwyer.
2. **b.** Refer to the Description section on Vernon.
3. **a.** Refer to the drawing of Vernon.
4. **c.** Refer to the Aliases section on Rosen.
5. **b.** Refer to the Remarks section on Jamal.
6. **c.** Refer to the Charges section on Eglund.
7. **a.** Refer to the drawing of Dwyer.
8. **d.** Refer to the Identifying Scars or Marks section on Rosen.
9. **d.** Refer to the Remarks section on Eglund.
10. **c.** Refer to the drawing of Jamal, as well as to the Identifying Scars or Marks section.
11. **b.** Refer to the Remarks section on Vernon.
12. **d.** Refer to the drawing of Rosen.
13. **d.** Refer to the Caution section on both Dwyer and Jamal.
14. **c.** Refer to the Remarks section on Rosen.
15. **b.** Refer to the Description section of Dwyer and Jamal.
16. **d.** Refer to the Description section of Jamal and Rosen.
17. **a.** The Description section on Vernon notes that he is over six feet tall; thus, he is taller than any of the other persons depicted on the posters.
18. **c.** Refer to the Caution section on Jamal.
19. **a.** Refer to the Description sections for all persons depicted on the posters.
20. **c.** Both Rosen and Jamal have some facial hair but neither has a full beard. It is important not to miss the part of this question that asks you which statement is *false.*
21. **a.** See guideline 1, the fourth sentence.
22. **d.** See guideline 6, the sixth sentence.
23. **d.** See the second sentence of guideline 5.
24. **b.** See guideline 3.
25. **d.** See the first sentence of guideline 2.
26. **a.** See guideline 4, the fourth sentence.
27. **d.** See guideline 3, the fourth sentence.
28. **a.** See the first paragraph of the passage.
29. **b.** See the fourth sentence of guideline 5.
30. **d.** See guideline 2, the sixth sentence.

Part Two: Reading Skill

31. **d.** The passage states that *a court can rule that evidence is inadmissible if it is not relevant.* If evidence doesn't prove any facts related to the case, it may not be relevant to the matter before the court and the judge may not allow the evidence.
32. **c.** The passage states that the chain of custody *culminates with the person who brings the evidence before the court.* It makes sense that this would be a trial attorney for either the defendant or the plaintiff.
33. **d.** The passage states that the *chain of custody begins with the person who found the evidence.*
34. **b.** The paragraph states that evidence may be excluded if it is unfairly prejudicial. All evidence that would tend to convict a person of a crime would be prejudicial against that person, however, evidence that is unfairly so could be excluded.
35. **c.** This is the quickest way around the Ford Hotel and then to Cleveland Avenue. Choice **a** is not correct because it requires the officers to go the wrong way on Jones, a one-way street. Choice **b** would require the officers to drive through the Ford Hotel. Choice **d** has too many turns to be the most direct.
36. **b.** This choice is correct because it is the quickest and most direct route. Choice **a** has too

many turns and takes the officers the wrong way on Adams Avenue. Lincoln Street is a one-way street going north, so choice **c** is wrong. Choice **d** takes the officers several blocks out of their way and so is not the most direct.

37. c. A right turn onto Glade Road turns Officer Tananga west. The left onto Taft Road turns him south; the right onto Pine Avenue turns him west, the right onto Cleveland Avenue turns him back north, and the right onto Wilshire Avenue turns him east.

38. b. The passage states that *the basic pattern for human fingerprints comes from their genetic encoding.*

39. c. According to the passage, plastic fingerprints *would be prints left in a soft substance like wood putty or clay.* Tar would fit this description. You could also answer this question by eliminating the other choices.

40. c. The types of fingerprints are stated in the last paragraph.

41. d. The last sentence in the passage states, *Latent fingerprints are left behind by the natural oils from our hands.*

42. a. The other routes are impossible or illegal.

43. b. Park Street crosses 9th Avenue at the southeast corner of the park.

44. a. The other routes are impossible or illegal.

45. b. The other routes are impossible (choices **c** and **d**) or circuitous (choice **a**).

46. d. Choice **a** takes you the wrong way on Maple Street. Choice **b** starts from the firehouse, not the police station. Choice **c** will not get you to the entrance of the gas station.

47. b. This is stated in the first sentence of the passage.

48. a. The second paragraph states that policies *limit discretion in situations with a large number of variables.* Of all the choices, a police vehicle pursuit has the most unknown factors and, therefore, is best covered by a policy.

49. c. As stated in the passage, policies are used to guide behavior in situations in which police officers are using the most amount of discretion. These are situations in which all of the factors and variables cannot be known beforehand

50. d. The final sentence of the passage expresses the main idea of the passage, and is best summed up by choice **d**.

51. b. The final paragraph states that *there is often a penalty for violating a regulation.*

52. a. This the most direct route to the Hillary Mansion, requiring the fewest changes in direction. Choice **b** requires the officer to drive through the Rossmore Hospital. Choice **c** takes the officer the wrong way up West Broadway. Choice **d** takes the officer the wrong way on North Avenue.

53. c. This route requires the fewest number of turns. Choice **a** is wrong because Martin Road is a one-way street. Choice **b** requires a number of turns and goes the wrong way on Arthur Way. Choice **d** requires the officer to drive through the South Avenue Library.

54. a. A right turn onto Broadway turns Officer Berger north. The left turn onto Arthur Way turns her back west, the left turn onto West Broadway turns her south, and the left turn onto Birch Avenue turns her east.

55. c. The passage states that the *effects on these victims may not only be financial; they often extend deeper into victims' reputations and personal lives.*

56. b. Do not be fooled by choice **a**: This may be true in many cases, but the passage explicitly states that *prosecuting its perpetrators* is more of a problem.

57. b. The first sentence of the passage states that identity theft *is the act of stealing someone's unique, personal identifying information.* Choices **a**, **c**, and **d** all meet that criteria. You may feel like your full name is unique, but is not uncommon for many people to have the same name. It is the combination of the name and other information that is unique.

58. a. The crux of identity theft is the misuse of personal information for financial gain.

59. d. Nowhere in the passage is it stated that phishing is the most common form of identity theft.

60. a. A question that asks for a title usually deals with a main idea. The title that best sums up what this passage is about is choice **a**.

Part Three: Judgment and Problem Solving

61. a. Gomez has been in prison longer than Weston, who has been in longer than Rashad, who has been in longer than Papak.

62. c. Choice **a** is not a strong choice because a person's reputation has more to do with criminal history, or lack thereof, than his or her standing in the community. Moreover, if the city councilperson were warned about drunk driving, there is nothing to indicate that he or she would not continue the behavior. Both the known heroin addict and the woman on probation have reputations, like a criminal history, that run counter to giving warnings.

63. c. Of all the situations, only the case of the felony crime clearly prohibits the issuance of a warning.

64. b. Generally, stealing over $500 (choice **a**) and most frauds (choice **d**) are felony crimes. Beyond that, the two offenders lack direct ties to the community that would indicate that a warning would be sufficient. Finally, a person with a warrant is generally not a good candidate for a warning because he or she has already failed to appear in court on a previous charge.

65. b. Seeing a teenager with a spray paint can is the most suspicious of the incidents described since Officer Yang is looking for graffiti artists. Spray paint is not an item most people carry around with them, and is suspicious given the circumstances.

66. d. From most arrests to fewest, either Meadows or Governale had the highest number of arrests, followed by Ash and then Westerman, who had the fewest.

67. d. Seeing a man running through the vacant lot with a bulky item under his shirt should make the officer suspicious. A purse snatcher would very likely choose to run through the vacant lot to get away from the area and would want to hide an object as obvious as a stolen purse from view. Choice **a** is not particularly suspicious, given that most car alarms activate the car horn and that car alarms frequently go off in parking lots. In choice **b**, a car with flat tires and a broken windshield may indicate criminal mischief, but it isn't necessarily linked to the purse snatchings. In choice **c**, a woman's voice raised in anger would be a plausible thing to hear following a purse snatching, but it's not nearly as suspicious as the situation in choice **d**.

68. d. After all the switches are made, Muller is behind the stage, Hudson is near the exit, Xavier is at the back of the auditorium, and Taylor is still in front of the stage.

69. a. Prescriptions are usually written on standardized prescription pads recognized by pharmacists. A prescription written on any other kind of paper would be suspect. In choice **b**, the doctor or the patient could be responsible for the coffee stains. It has no apparent bearing on the validity of the prescription. Choice **c** is incorrect because doctors frequently phone in prescriptions. In choice **d**, it may be odd that the patient is just now getting around to filling a prescription for pain killers, but the fact that it took a day to do so does not necessarily suggest forgery.

70. a. Start with Parisi; you are given that he is serving nine years. If Ronald is serving one more year than Parisi, Ronald is serving ten years. If Donofrio is serving one less year than Parisi, he is therefore serving eight years. Donofrio is serving one more year than Yardley; therefore, Yardley is serving seven years.

71. c. Officer Rannick is obligated to fulfill his duties as a police officer. He cannot allow a crime to occur in his presence.

72. b. The ignition is off because the bike has not been started. The officer has placed both hands on the handlebars and has seen that both tires are already positioned on the ground. Thus, the next thing he should do is to perform step 4 in the procedure, rock the bike on its engine guards.

73. c. The officer should place both hands on the handle bars after she has turned off the ignition. The other choices are correct steps but are out of order for this scenario.

74. b. The first step is always to turn the engine off. In the heat of the moment, it may seem reasonable to do what is listed in the other choices, but this would not be correct according to the procedures list.

75. b. Start with what is known: North has been a police officer for 15 years, which is six years fewer than Wilson, who therefore has 21 years. North's 15 years are seven more than Trainor's, so North has been an officer for eight years. If Sanchez has been a police officer for five more years than Trainor, then Sanchez has 13 years on the police force.

76. b. Police officers are required to subdue combative suspects as quickly and safely as possible. If Officer Bettis is in a situation where the nightstick is an approved weapon and she or other officers are in physical danger, she should use her nightstick. No other option is safe or feasible.

77. c. After all the switches were made, Officer Wong was running the radar in the eastbound lane. Officer Firth was pursuing speeders in the eastbound lane, Officer Kelly was running the radar in the westbound lane, and Officer Hamin was pursuing speeders in the westbound lane.

78. a. Fred's opinion of police has nothing to do with the situation. Officer Martinez should write the ticket because the situation was dangerous, and that is what he would do under normal circumstances. A warning is not appropriate because a collision was narrowly averted.

79. c. Assault is the most serious crime, followed, in descending order, by burglary, breaking and entering, and extortion.

80. c. The officer has already performed step 1 by making sure the handcuffs are secure. Checking the suspect's waistband and back pocket area is step 2, which she should perform next. She should not be distracted by the bulge in the cap, so choice **b** is not correct.

81. **a.** The officer should check the arrestee's hat because that is the next step after checking the waistband and back pocket area. The officer should not be distracted from the proper procedures because the intoxicated man is difficult to control. The other officers are there to assist, and he should be able to safely conduct his search.

82. **b.** The officer should check the waistband area and the area near the arrestee's hands, because that is the next step on the list of procedures. That the arrestee is a woman and is wearing a dress should not distract the officer from following procedure, since dresses may have pockets and waistbands.

83. **b.** A panel truck pulling out of a vacant lot near a car dealership that has suffered a rash of theft of auto parts is suspicious. The truck would be able to hold plenty of auto parts. The two rollerbladers in choice **c** aren't likely to be able to carry off a new running board without attracting attention. The male in his early twenties in choice **a** appears to be doing what a lot of people do at night, which is look at new cars without having to worry about sales personnel. It is not unusual for cleanup crews to arrive late at night after everyone has gone, as in choice **d**.

84. **b.** Officer Hampton is probably at the precinct. Officer Walters is three blocks south of the precinct. If Sergeant Rooney is one block north of Walters, that puts Rooney two blocks south of the precinct. If Officer Hampton is two blocks north of Rooney, that puts Hampton at the precinct.

85. **c.** The odd behavior and the location of the two figures should cause the officer to investigate, given the problems the school has been having.

86. **b.** After all the switches were made, Officer Stern's partner was Scout. Officer Thomas's partner was Laddie, Officer Cain's was Ranger, and Officer Walker's was Astro.

87. **a.** Outnumbered officers attempting to control a hostile crowd may not be able to arrest the instigator safely; however, according to the situation they will likely be able to find him later, since they are aware of his identity. In the other situations, custody arrests are appropriate and more easily accomplished. Although in choice **c** it seems apparent that Antonio knows his cousin's identity, and therefore a warrant could be issued at a later date, the violence of the situation makes immediate action necessary.

88. **a.** Blue pants, sweatshirt, and the color orange are the elements repeated most often by the eyewitnesses and are therefore most likely correct.

89. **b.** The first step is to give the race and sex of the suspect. In this case, the victim has provided that information.

90. **d.** The officer can't give information he doesn't have. The first step he will be able to follow is to give the height and weight description.

91. **c.** The next information the officer can give out is a height and weight description. Since no weapon was seen, choice **d** is not possible.

92. **d.** Claude has just assaulted Officer Mattox by poking him in the chest. This is a safety issue for the officer, and he should not allow contact of this nature. Allowing an angry citizen to vent and release a certain amount of frustration, as in the other options, is appropriate in many situations.

93. **d.** The order of the cadets is Jurgens, Shirley, Davis, Riley. Jurgens is on Shirley's immediate left, and Davis is on Shirley's immediate right. Riley is therefore on Davis' immediate right.

94. **d.** Step 2 says the officer should have asked the security guard to fill out a witness statement and a complaint form.

95. **c.** Officer Smits is stationed south of Officer Foster. Officer Walters cannot be farthest north, because Foster is north of Walters. Balboa is south of Foster, but may or may not be south of Walters; therefore Balboa may not be farthest south, nor definitely south of Walters.

96. **c.** Step 2 instructs the officer not to move any objects until photos are taken of them as they first appeared when the officer arrived.

97. **b.** Edgar burgled a warehouse before Nelson stole a car. Baker robbed a bank after Nelson stole a car; Mitchell assaulted a police officer after Baker robbed a bank and Nelson stole a car. The order is Edgar, Nelson, Baker, Mitchell.

98. **b.** The first step in the procedure is to move all driveable vehicles, and that should be Officer Gofort's first move.

99. **a.** Three of the witnesses agree that the first number is 9. Three agree that the second number is 2. Three witnesses agree that the third number is 6, and three others agree that the fourth number is also 6. Choice **a** is the best choice because it is made up of the numbers that most of the witnesses agree that they saw.

100. **b.** The suspect described in theft 3 does not match Alfonso's suspect description very closely. The women in 1, 2, and 4 all appear to be the same woman Alfonso saw because of the similarities in height, weight, hair, and eyewear.

▶ Scoring

When you compare your scores from the exam you just took to Police Officer Practice Exam 2, you should see improvement. Once again, it's important that you use this exam as a means of figuring out where your strengths and weaknesses lie. To help you see where your trouble spots are again, break down your scores according to the three sections below:

Part One: _____ questions correct
Part Two: _____ questions correct
Part Three: _____ questions correct

Write down the number of correct answers for each section, and then add up all three numbers for your overall score. Each question is worth one point and the total you arrive at after adding all the numbers is also the percentage of questions that you got correct on the test. Remember, you need a score of at least 70 to pass, but in order to get near the top of the eligibility list, you need a much higher score than that. Every point counts.

If your score wasn't as high as you expected, then analyze the reasons:

- **If you ran out of time before finishing the test,** reread Chapter 3, The LearningExpress Test Preparation System, for tips on timing. Make sure you followed the rules, too. Did you take the full two and a half hours allotted? Did you read the directions and the questions carefully?
- **If your score on Part One was low,** review Chapters 7 and 13. Practice your memory and observation skills as suggested in Chapter 13.
- **If you didn't score as well as you'd like on Part Two,** reread Chapters 7 and 12, perhaps focusing on either reading comprehension or map reading, depending on which skill gave you the most trouble.
- **If you had trouble with Part Three,** review Chapter 11 and follow the suggestions there for working on your judgment skills in your daily life.

What comes next? If you got a high score on this practice exam, you might not need much more preparation. However, anyone can benefit from a little more study and practice. Use the following table to help you decide what do to next, based on your score.

YOUR SCORE:	YOUR STRATEGY:
69 or below	Consider looking for a private tutor or continuing education class to help you with your reading skills. Look back over Chapters 7, 11, 12, and 13 to see how to handle the questions.
70–89	Continue to study Chapters 7, 11, 12, and 13 and pay close attention to the tips and resources for further improvement. Identify and concentrate on what made you miss the questions you did.
90 or above	Maintain that edge. Keep this book handy and study it right up to the day you take the test.

If, as recommended in The LearningExpress Test Preparation System, you got a copy of the exam announcement and found out what will be on your exam, you may have more work ahead of you. If there are any skills tested on your exam that aren't on the exam you just took, you should spend some time working on those skills as well.

A key element to your success is self-confidence. The more comfortable you are with your ability to perform, the more likely you are to do well on the exam. You know what to expect, you know your strengths and weaknesses, and you can work to turn those weaknesses into strengths before the actual exam. Your preparedness should give you the confidence that you will need to do well on exam day.

CHAPTER

18 Police Officer Practice Exam 6

CHAPTER SUMMARY

This practice exam is similar in format to the practice exam in Chapter 6. It tests vocabulary, number and letter recall, and your personal background.

The first part of the exam in this chapter includes verbal comprehension and recall questions. You are given ten minutes to answer 50 vocabulary questions and nine minutes to answer 100 recall questions. Before you take those two sections, set a timer or stopwatch, so that you can time the sections exactly. Your main task in both of these sections is simply not to get flustered. If you stay calm and focused, you *can* get the right answers to these questions.

The second part of the official exam consists of 185 personal background questions, which you can take as much time as you need to answer. There's not much you can or need to do to prepare for these questions, since they're all about you, your experiences, your attitudes. The practice exam in this chapter includes 20 personal background questions that will help you get familiar with the format.

After the exam is an answer key for the first part of the exam, the verbal and number and letter recall questions. There is no answer key for the second part, the personal background questions, because those questions have no correct or incorrect answers.

Police Officer Practice Exam 6 Part One

Verbal Section

1. (a) (b) (c) (d)
2. (a) (b) (c) (d)
3. (a) (b) (c) (d)
4. (a) (b) (c) (d)
5. (a) (b) (c) (d)
6. (a) (b) (c) (d)
7. (a) (b) (c) (d)
8. (a) (b) (c) (d)
9. (a) (b) (c) (d)
10. (a) (b) (c) (d)
11. (a) (b) (c) (d)
12. (a) (b) (c) (d)
13. (a) (b) (c) (d)
14. (a) (b) (c) (d)
15. (a) (b) (c) (d)
16. (a) (b) (c) (d)
17. (a) (b) (c) (d)
18. (a) (b) (c) (d)
19. (a) (b) (c) (d)
20. (a) (b) (c) (d)
21. (a) (b) (c) (d)
22. (a) (b) (c) (d)
23. (a) (b) (c) (d)
24. (a) (b) (c) (d)
25. (a) (b) (c) (d)
26. (a) (b) (c) (d)
27. (a) (b) (c) (d)
28. (a) (b) (c) (d)
29. (a) (b) (c) (d)
30. (a) (b) (c) (d)
31. (a) (b) (c) (d)
32. (a) (b) (c) (d)
33. (a) (b) (c) (d)
34. (a) (b) (c) (d)
35. (a) (b) (c) (d)
36. (a) (b) (c) (d)
37. (a) (b) (c) (d)
38. (a) (b) (c) (d)
39. (a) (b) (c) (d)
40. (a) (b) (c) (d)
41. (a) (b) (c) (d)
42. (a) (b) (c) (d)
43. (a) (b) (c) (d)
44. (a) (b) (c) (d)
45. (a) (b) (c) (d)
46. (a) (b) (c) (d)
47. (a) (b) (c) (d)
48. (a) (b) (c) (d)
49. (a) (b) (c) (d)
50. (a) (b) (c) (d)

Number and Letter Recall Section

1. (a) (b) (c) (d) (e)
2. (a) (b) (c) (d) (e)
3. (a) (b) (c) (d) (e)
4. (a) (b) (c) (d) (e)
5. (a) (b) (c) (d) (e)
6. (a) (b) (c) (d) (e)
7. (a) (b) (c) (d) (e)
8. (a) (b) (c) (d) (e)
9. (a) (b) (c) (d) (e)
10. (a) (b) (c) (d) (e)
11. (a) (b) (c) (d) (e)
12. (a) (b) (c) (d) (e)
13. (a) (b) (c) (d) (e)
14. (a) (b) (c) (d) (e)
15. (a) (b) (c) (d) (e)
16. (a) (b) (c) (d) (e)
17. (a) (b) (c) (d) (e)
18. (a) (b) (c) (d) (e)
19. (a) (b) (c) (d) (e)
20. (a) (b) (c) (d) (e)
21. (a) (b) (c) (d) (e)
22. (a) (b) (c) (d) (e)
23. (a) (b) (c) (d) (e)
24. (a) (b) (c) (d) (e)
25. (a) (b) (c) (d) (e)
26. (a) (b) (c) (d) (e)
27. (a) (b) (c) (d) (e)
28. (a) (b) (c) (d) (e)
29. (a) (b) (c) (d) (e)
30. (a) (b) (c) (d) (e)
31. (a) (b) (c) (d) (e)
32. (a) (b) (c) (d) (e)
33. (a) (b) (c) (d) (e)
34. (a) (b) (c) (d) (e)
35. (a) (b) (c) (d) (e)
36. (a) (b) (c) (d) (e)
37. (a) (b) (c) (d) (e)
38. (a) (b) (c) (d) (e)
39. (a) (b) (c) (d) (e)
40. (a) (b) (c) (d) (e)
41. (a) (b) (c) (d) (e)
42. (a) (b) (c) (d) (e)
43. (a) (b) (c) (d) (e)
44. (a) (b) (c) (d) (e)
45. (a) (b) (c) (d) (e)
46. (a) (b) (c) (d) (e)
47. (a) (b) (c) (d) (e)
48. (a) (b) (c) (d) (e)
49. (a) (b) (c) (d) (e)
50. (a) (b) (c) (d) (e)
51. (a) (b) (c) (d) (e)
52. (a) (b) (c) (d) (e)
53. (a) (b) (c) (d) (e)
54. (a) (b) (c) (d) (e)
55. (a) (b) (c) (d) (e)
56. (a) (b) (c) (d) (e)
57. (a) (b) (c) (d) (e)
58. (a) (b) (c) (d) (e)
59. (a) (b) (c) (d) (e)
60. (a) (b) (c) (d) (e)
61. (a) (b) (c) (d) (e)
62. (a) (b) (c) (d) (e)
63. (a) (b) (c) (d) (e)
64. (a) (b) (c) (d) (e)
65. (a) (b) (c) (d) (e)
66. (a) (b) (c) (d) (e)
67. (a) (b) (c) (d) (e)
68. (a) (b) (c) (d) (e)
69. (a) (b) (c) (d) (e)
70. (a) (b) (c) (d) (e)
71. (a) (b) (c) (d) (e)
72. (a) (b) (c) (d) (e)
73. (a) (b) (c) (d) (e)
74. (a) (b) (c) (d) (e)
75. (a) (b) (c) (d) (e)

Number and Letter Recall Section (continued)

76. ⓐ ⓑ ⓒ ⓓ ⓔ
77. ⓐ ⓑ ⓒ ⓓ ⓔ
78. ⓐ ⓑ ⓒ ⓓ ⓔ
79. ⓐ ⓑ ⓒ ⓓ ⓔ
80. ⓐ ⓑ ⓒ ⓓ ⓔ
81. ⓐ ⓑ ⓒ ⓓ ⓔ
82. ⓐ ⓑ ⓒ ⓓ ⓔ
83. ⓐ ⓑ ⓒ ⓓ ⓔ
84. ⓐ ⓑ ⓒ ⓓ ⓔ
85. ⓐ ⓑ ⓒ ⓓ ⓔ
86. ⓐ ⓑ ⓒ ⓓ ⓔ
87. ⓐ ⓑ ⓒ ⓓ ⓔ
88. ⓐ ⓑ ⓒ ⓓ ⓔ
89. ⓐ ⓑ ⓒ ⓓ ⓔ
90. ⓐ ⓑ ⓒ ⓓ ⓔ
91. ⓐ ⓑ ⓒ ⓓ ⓔ
92. ⓐ ⓑ ⓒ ⓓ ⓔ
93. ⓐ ⓑ ⓒ ⓓ ⓔ
94. ⓐ ⓑ ⓒ ⓓ ⓔ
95. ⓐ ⓑ ⓒ ⓓ ⓔ
96. ⓐ ⓑ ⓒ ⓓ ⓔ
97. ⓐ ⓑ ⓒ ⓓ ⓔ
98. ⓐ ⓑ ⓒ ⓓ ⓔ
99. ⓐ ⓑ ⓒ ⓓ ⓔ
100. ⓐ ⓑ ⓒ ⓓ ⓔ

Part Two
Personal Background Section

1. ⓐ ⓑ ⓒ ⓓ ⓔ ⓕ
2. ⓐ ⓑ
3. ⓐ ⓑ ⓒ ⓓ ⓔ
4. ⓐ ⓑ ⓒ ⓓ ⓔ ⓕ
5. ⓐ ⓑ ⓒ ⓓ ⓔ ⓕ
6. ⓐ ⓑ ⓒ ⓓ ⓔ ⓕ
7. ⓐ ⓑ ⓒ ⓓ ⓔ
8. ⓐ ⓑ ⓒ ⓓ
9. ⓐ ⓑ ⓒ ⓓ
10. ⓐ ⓑ ⓒ ⓓ ⓔ ⓕ ⓖ ⓗ
11. ⓐ ⓑ ⓒ
12. ⓐ ⓑ ⓒ ⓓ
13. ⓐ ⓑ ⓒ ⓓ ⓔ ⓕ
14. ⓐ ⓑ ⓒ ⓓ

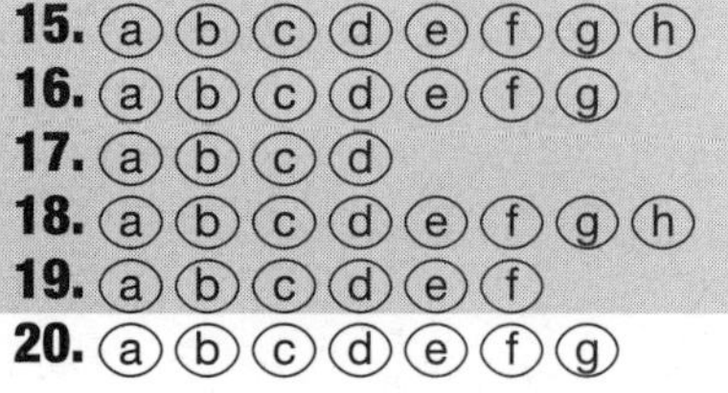

15. ⓐ ⓑ ⓒ ⓓ ⓔ ⓕ ⓖ ⓗ
16. ⓐ ⓑ ⓒ ⓓ ⓔ ⓕ ⓖ
17. ⓐ ⓑ ⓒ ⓓ
18. ⓐ ⓑ ⓒ ⓓ ⓔ ⓕ ⓖ ⓗ
19. ⓐ ⓑ ⓒ ⓓ ⓔ ⓕ
20. ⓐ ⓑ ⓒ ⓓ ⓔ ⓕ ⓖ

▶ Police Officer Practice Exam 6

Part One: Verbal Section

You have ten minutes for this section. Choose the correct answer for each question.

1. Which word means the *same* as ABSOLUTE?
  a. invalid
  b. complete
  c. hearsay
  d. partial

2. Which word means the *opposite* of ELOQUENT?
  a. shabby
  b. fluent
  c. inarticulate
  d. plain

3. Which word means the *opposite* of CONDITIONAL?
  a. unrestricted
  b. unclassified
  c. undeniable
  d. unsubstantiated

4. Which word means the *opposite* of ENHANCE?
  a. diminish
  b. improve
  c. digress
  d. deprive

5. Which word means the *same* as PROXY?
  a. authority
  b. prevent
  c. engage
  d. alternate

6. Which word means the *same* as MENIAL?
  a. lowly
  b. boring
  c. unpleasant
  d. unrewarding

7. Which word means the *opposite* of INTENTIONAL?
  a. premeditated
  b. accidental
  c. cognizant
  d. oblivious

8. Which word means the *same* as OBSTINATELY?
  a. repeatedly
  b. reluctantly
  c. foolishly
  d. stubbornly

9. Which word means the *same* as MALICIOUS?
  a. behaved
  b. methodical
  c. mean
  d. fashionable

10. Which word means the *opposite* of DISTINGUISHED?
  a. inflamed
  b. barbaric
  c. foolish
  d. inconspicuous

11. Which word means the *same* as PREDATOR?
  a. guardian
  b. hunter
  c. alien
  d. prey

12. Which word means the *opposite* of CANDID?
a. sincere
b. passive
c. dishonest
d. shy

13. Which word means the *same* as NEGLIGENCE?
a. prudence
b. pajamas
c. carelessness
d. criminality

14. Which word means the *same* as GRATUITY?
a. gift
b. receivable
c. grantor
d. annuity

15. Which word means the *same* as UNIVERSAL?
a. limited
b. syndicate
c. synthesized
d. widespread

16. Which word means the *same* as FORTIFIED?
a. reinforced
b. altered
c. disputed
d. developed

17. Which word means the *opposite* of COVERT?
a. loud
b. unguarded
c. public
d. colorful

18. Which word means the *opposite* of MALICE?
a. instinct
b. agitation
c. compassion
d. anger

19. Which word means the *opposite* of INCOMPETENCE?
a. ineffectiveness
b. ability
c. insane
d. average

20. Which word means the *same* as LIABILITY?
a. responsibility
b. slanderous
c. nuisance
d. reliability

21. Which word means the *same* as ACCOMMODATE?
a. constrain
b. disappoint
c. hinder
d. help

22. Which word means the *opposite* of NOVICE?
a. adversary
b. resident
c. expert
d. follower

23. Which word means the *same* as MINISCULE?
a. immense
b. tiny
c. long
d. short

24. Which word means the *opposite* of OBSOLETE?
a. contemporary
b. stubborn
c. perceptive
d. ancient

25. Which word means the *opposite* of IRRESISTIBLE?
a. unpredictable
b. unforseen
c. unappealing
d. unnecessary

26. Which word means the *same* as LIAISON?
a. silence
b. insult
c. conclusion
d. connection

27. Which word means the *same* as INOCULATE?
a. radiate
b. immunize
c. cut
d. brainwash

28. Which word means the *same* as CONSENT?
a. deny
b. challenge
c. consume
d. agree

29. Which word means the *opposite* of CONCURRENT?
a. separate
b. simultaneous
c. untethered
d. detached

30. Which word means the *opposite* of SKEPTICAL?
a. innovative
b. antagonistic
c. necessary
d. gullible

31. Which word means the *same* as ACQUIT?
a. sentence
b. exonerate
c. complain
d. surrender

32. Which word means the *same* as ANIMATED?
a. abbreviated
b. civil
c. secret
d. lively

33. Which word means the *same* as SUPERSEDE?
a. override
b. strengthen
c. rejuvenate
d. reorder

34. Which word means the *opposite* of PROMOTE?
a. explicate
b. curtail
c. concede
d. retain

35. Which word means the *opposite* of REASONABLE?
a. irrational
b. awkward
c. realistic
d. acceptable

36. Which word means the *same* as COMPLIANT?
- **a.** skeptical
- **b.** obedient
- **c.** forgetful
- **d.** appreciative

37. Which word means the *opposite* of SUSPEND?
- **a.** conceive
- **b.** trust
- **c.** delay
- **d.** sustain

38. Which word means the *opposite* of SCANT?
- **a.** invisible
- **b.** meager
- **c.** copious
- **d.** vocal

39. Which word means the *opposite* of WITHHOLD?
- **a.** deny
- **b.** bestow
- **c.** confer
- **d.** consummate

40. Which word means the *same* as AUGMENT?
- **a.** repeal
- **b.** evaluate
- **c.** expand
- **d.** criticize

41. Which word means the *same* as INDISPENSABLE?
- **a.** determined
- **b.** experienced
- **c.** essential
- **d.** creative

42. Which word means the *same* as DESICCATE?
- **a.** moisten
- **b.** dry
- **c.** cool
- **d.** warm

43. Which word means the *same* as EXPEDITE?
- **a.** accelerate
- **b.** evaluate
- **c.** reverse
- **d.** justify

44. Which word means the *opposite* of SUBJECTIVE?
- **a.** invective
- **b.** objectionable
- **c.** unbiased
- **d.** obedient

45. Which word means the *opposite* of SUCCINCT?
- **a.** distinct
- **b.** laconic
- **c.** unpersuasive
- **d.** verbose

46. Which word means the *opposite* of TEDIOUS?
- **a.** stimulating
- **b.** alarming
- **c.** intemperate
- **d.** tranquil

47. Which word means the *same* as PLAUSIBLE?
- **a.** unbelievable
- **b.** insufficient
- **c.** apologetic
- **d.** credible

48. Which word means the *opposite* of UNIFORM?
   a. dissembling
   b. diverse
   c. bizarre
   d. slovenly

49. Which word means the *same* as INFERRED?
   a. intuited
   b. imagined
   c. implied
   d. surmised

50. Which phrase means the *same* as ULTIMATUM?
   a. earnest plea
   b. formal petition
   c. solemn promise
   d. non-negotiable demand

Number and Letter Recall Section

In this section, each set of 25 questions is preceded by a key, which consists of letter sets and numbers. Each question consists of one of the letter sets followed by numbers. Use the key to pick the number that goes with each letter set, and then fill in the appropriate circle on the answer sheet. You have nine minutes for this section.

KEY 1

ABT	QXR	RLK	SAB	GTR	DBV	FRE	WRT	QGT
27	39	49	43	51	59	66	91	67
FTB	BEF	POM	QAW	BLU	XRK	YEG	RJT	BJI
29	82	17	70	82	71	19	37	58
NYH	TKG	NAP	ZEF	PTG	MAB	HTD	UGC	KGS
43	89	44	18	11	60	15	93	34

		a	b	c	d	e
1.	KGS	34	48	59	92	73
2.	ZEF	41	18	87	58	33
3.	FTB	62	41	65	13	29
4.	TKG	26	32	41	16	89
5.	QXR	92	47	39	77	10
6.	ABT	11	27	55	41	76
7.	MAB	60	57	49	56	13
8.	POM	75	17	55	33	87
9.	BLU	29	12	82	35	63
10.	RLK	63	14	41	93	49
11.	QGT	67	88	23	49	11
12.	NYH	37	43	65	82	95
13.	GTR	95	51	32	94	88
14.	NAP	85	33	44	55	93
15.	SAB	92	54	18	43	23
16.	DBV	52	56	71	59	97
17.	UGC	11	91	93	35	26
18.	BEF	75	82	96	33	13
19.	YEG	46	97	28	19	23
20.	PTG	44	71	23	11	17
21.	RJT	27	73	61	37	40
22.	XRK	65	39	33	92	71
23.	BJI	97	31	58	29	72
24.	FRE	71	42	13	34	66
25.	GTR	44	82	55	51	15

KEY 2

AOD	ROK	GKS	BRJ	ZQE	GDT	EIR	VID	ANB
10	80	41	55	87	57	47	26	16
RNY	GDJ	RHC	BSW	FVM	DYO	JAT	RXG	NDO
73	23	76	50	99	35	32	97	74
GPH	EAP	LGD	BGS	KRH	YFR	JWD	BFH	QFA
12	86	40	54	48	20	04	22	38

		a	b	c	d	e
26.	EAP	86	59	21	33	65
27.	DYO	78	35	73	93	45
28.	KRH	45	48	43	55	42
29.	QFA	52	64	12	23	38
30.	JWD	15	78	33	64	84
31.	GDJ	54	23	98	32	35
32.	ZQE	87	62	13	51	34
33.	AOD	72	43	10	24	37
34.	NDO	52	43	74	39	63
35.	GKS	41	24	68	53	54
36.	FVM	99	36	45	48	23
37.	BGS	54	88	13	43	86
38.	GPH	52	46	85	23	12

		a	b	c	d	e
39.	JAT	61	32	43	14	28
40.	EIR	51	32	47	20	24
41.	BFH	51	43	11	22	58
42.	ROK	24	80	21	14	54
43.	RNY	32	73	38	62	24
44.	VID	52	26	84	27	83
45.	ANB	35	48	23	34	16
46.	RHC	93	11	23	76	52
47.	BRJ	55	25	90	31	28
48.	YFR	42	36	74	42	20
49.	GDT	31	57	23	38	75
50.	RXG	98	35	55	64	97

KEY 3

UHJ	BKR	PJD	ABD	LBC	PRT	QAS	MNC	GKX
21	13	30	84	96	45	63	61	72
ASW	CPA	WQH	LDM	MAM	NAN	ANZ	IXD	BQC
88	90	42	62	81	77	53	79	10
DPB	QRT	MNA	UGL	XYZ	DAL	IYP	KUB	ASF
64	26	44	56	52	24	65	28	55

		a	b	c	d	e
51.	PJD	30	44	55	95	68
52.	QAS	63	84	22	12	69
53.	UHJ	65	68	21	15	69
54.	ABD	65	84	14	62	79
55.	GKX	25	68	35	61	72
56.	BKR	72	13	64	34	25
57.	MNC	61	35	53	79	29
58.	LBC	54	74	96	57	90
59.	ASF	55	95	35	21	14
60.	ASW	55	34	28	61	88
61.	PRT	45	21	68	35	24
62.	WQH	42	98	61	52	96
63.	LDM	18	59	85	62	76

		a	b	c	d	e
64.	ANZ	21	76	84	53	44
65.	NAN	41	77	63	58	14
66.	IXD	22	66	25	79	27
67.	MAM	37	65	81	84	34
68.	XYZ	52	54	35	93	14
69.	DPB	39	57	94	62	64
70.	IYP	25	65	62	59	54
71.	DAL	75	85	25	24	12
72.	BQC	15	62	10	25	92
73.	UGL	71	56	61	24	18
74.	MNA	61	70	35	18	44
75.	QRT	63	26	25	15	89

KEY 4

BGR	MDV	LRW	BLE	NRW	GBY	VDJ	XAQ	MUP
55	85	53	66	45	21	15	45	65

HTF	SQN	QLU	NHT	MJY	LOK	PLM	QAZ	WSX
61	68	64	84	94	25	54	95	12

CDE	VFR	BGR	NHT	MJY	XDW	CDM	OZP	QMI
37	98	34	85	19	69	24	62	51

		a	b	c	d	e
76.	QMI	36	88	14	51	43
77.	NHT	85	54	84	28	73
78.	BGR	82	81	55	33	27
79.	HTF	16	32	98	23	61
80.	PLM	61	83	49	54	22
81.	VDJ	15	12	45	57	80
82.	NRW	29	53	35	45	29
83.	LRW	47	53	51	75	85
84.	WSX	39	51	12	63	46
85.	QLU	64	98	43	59	12
86.	BGR	85	89	65	34	88
87.	CDE	37	21	85	59	98
88.	VFR	73	24	64	98	52

		a	b	c	d	e
89.	MJY	85	94	73	55	19
90.	MUP	17	47	71	41	65
91.	BLE	85	52	66	71	83
92.	MDV	12	85	43	24	36
93.	NHT	75	42	85	84	28
94.	GBY	46	62	28	21	99
95.	SQN	68	91	45	22	21
96.	OZP	81	46	55	62	40
97.	MJY	54	82	33	38	94
98.	XDW	97	32	69	65	36
99.	LOK	25	35	49	14	73
100.	QAZ	44	37	64	95	69

Part Two: Personal Background Section

Answer each question honestly. Mark only one answer unless the question states otherwise. There is no time limit for this section.

1. If I were struggling with a course in school, the last thing I would do would be to
a. put in extra time on my own.
b. seek help from the teacher.
c. do extra research in the library.
d. request a tutor.
e. seek help from family or friends.
f. drop the course.

2. At work, I prefer to
a. work on one project at a time.
b. work on many projects simultaneously.

3. I exercise strenuously
a. daily.
b. every other day.
c. two or three times a week.
d. whenever I can fit it into my schedule.
e. rarely or never.

4. In school, I learned the most from
a. lectures by teachers.
b. guest lectures.
c. field trips.
d. visual presentations.
e. independent research.
f. participation in class discussions.

5. The main reason I accepted my most recent employment position was because it
a. offered a challenge.
b. provided a good income and benefits.
c. offered career advancement.
d. gave me a lot of responsibility.
e. allowed me to provide for myself and/or my family.
f. was conveniently located.

6. I prefer to meet with my supervisor
a. daily.
b. weekly.
c. every other day.
d. every other week.
e. as often as problems materialize.
f. infrequently.

7. I work late
a. on a regular basis.
b. whenever I need to catch up.
c. in order to meet deadlines.
d. when asked to do so.
e. never.

8. I enjoy myself the most when I spend time
a. alone.
b. with one or two other people.
c. with a group of three or four people.
d. in larger groups of people.

9. I prefer tasks that are
a. physically demanding.
b. mentally demanding.
c. both physically and mentally demanding.
d. neither physically nor mentally demanding.

10. Of the following hobbies, the ones I engage in at least once a year are (Mark all that apply)
- **a.** reading a book.
- **b.** watching a movie.
- **c.** golfing.
- **d.** hunting.
- **e.** skiing (water or snow).
- **f.** home improvement projects.
- **g.** attending cultural events.
- **h.** hiking.

11. If I get lost while driving, I am most likely to
- **a.** ask for directions.
- **b.** refer to a map.
- **c.** continue driving until I find my way.

12. If my supervisor needs to discipline me at work, I would prefer that my supervisor
- **a.** speak with me directly.
- **b.** issue me a memo.
- **c.** show me what I should have done.
- **d.** call the staff together to discuss the problem.

13. I consider an appropriate length of commitment for a new professional position to be
- **a.** six months.
- **b.** one year.
- **c.** two years.
- **d.** three years.
- **e.** five years.
- **f.** more than five years.

14. I have shoplifted
- **a.** never.
- **b.** once or a few times, when I was young.
- **c.** once or a few times, but only inexpensive items.
- **d.** several times.

15. The most important consideration for me when I am deciding whether to take a new position is
- **a.** the hours.
- **b.** the pay.
- **c.** the health benefits.
- **d.** the retirement/investment benefits.
- **e.** my coworkers.
- **f.** my supervisor.
- **g.** the work itself.
- **h.** other.

16. The most important thing I have gained from my family is a sense of
- **a.** trust.
- **b.** cooperation.
- **c.** responsibility.
- **d.** caring.
- **e.** commitment.
- **f.** self-sufficiency.
- **g.** other.

17. My free time is mostly spent
- **a.** alone.
- **b.** with family.
- **c.** with friends.
- **d.** with colleagues from work.

18. My coworkers would describe me as (Mark all that apply)
- **a.** motivated.
- **b.** laid-back.
- **c.** professional.
- **d.** driven.
- **e.** intelligent.
- **f.** fearless.
- **g.** focused.
- **h.** flexible.

19. If criticized at work, my first reaction is to

a. use the criticism to improve my skills.
b. defend myself to the person making the critical comments.
c. consider the criticism irrelevant.
d. get upset with myself.
e. lose focus.
f. sharpen my focus.

20. The main reason I enjoy being with my friends is being able to

a. confide in them.
b. have fun times together.
c. engage in serious discussions.
d. learn from them.
e. take my mind off concerns I may have.
f. engage in activities I can't do alone.
g. some other reason.

▶ Answer Key

Verbal

1. b.
2. c.
3. a.
4. a.
5. d.
6. a.
7. a.
8. d.
9. c.
10. d.
11. b.
12. c.
13. c.
14. a.
15. d.
16. a.
17. c.
18. c.
19. b.
20. a.
21. d.
22. c.
23. b.
24. a.
25. c.
26. d.
27. b.
28. d.
29. a.
30. d.
31. b.
32. d.
33. a.
34. b.
35. a.
36. b.
37. d.
38. c.
39. a.
40. c.
41. c.
42. b.
43. a.
44. c.
45. d.
46. a.
47. d.
48. b.
49. d.
50. d.

Number and Letter Recall

1. a.
2. b.
3. e.
4. e.
5. c.
6. b.
7. a.
8. b.
9. c.
10. e.
11. a.
12. b.
13. b.
14. c.
15. d.
16. d.
17. c.
18. b.
19. d.
20. d.
21. d.
22. e.
23. c.
24. e.
25. d.
26. a.
27. b.
28. b.
29. e.
30. d.
31. b.
32. a.
33. c.
34. c.
35. a.
36. a.
37. a.
38. e.
39. b.
40. c.
41. d.
42. b.
43. b.
44. b.
45. e.
46. d.
47. a.
48. e.
49. b.
50. e.
51. a.
52. a.
53. c.
54. b.
55. e.
56. b.
57. a.
58. c.
59. a.
60. e.
61. a.
62. a.
63. d.
64. d.
65. b.
66. d.
67. c.
68. a.
69. e.
70. b.
71. d.
72. c.
73. b.
74. e.
75. b.
76. d.
77. a.
78. c.
79. e.
80. d.
81. a.
82. d.
83. b.
84. c.
85. a.
86. d.
87. a.
88. d.
89. b.
90. e.
91. c.
92. b.
93. c.
94. d.
95. a.
96. d.
97. e.
98. c.
99. a.
100. d.

▶ Scoring

The exam score is computed using a formula that subtracts for incorrect answers on Part One, the verbal and number and letter recall sections. Scoring on the personal background section varies by department, so there's no way to estimate how you would score on that section. Here's a method for computing a rough score for Part One.

Verbal Score

First, count the number of questions you answered correctly. Then, count the number of questions you answered incorrectly and divide by four. Subtract the results of the division from the number you got correct for your raw score. Questions you didn't answer don't count either way.

1. Number of questions correct:______
2. Number of questions incorrect:______
3. Divide number **2** by 4:______
4. Subtract number **3** from number **1**:______

The result of number **4** above is your raw score on the verbal section.

Number and Letter Recall Score

Count the number and letter recall questions you answered correctly. Then, count the number of questions you answered incorrectly and divide by five. Subtract the results of the division from the number you got correct, and that's your score. Questions you didn't answer don't count.

1. Number of questions correct:______
2. Number of questions incorrect:______
3. Divide number **2** by 5:______
4. Subtract number **3** from number **1**:______

The result of number **4** is your raw score on the number and letter recall section.

What the Scores Mean

In general, a score of at least 70% is enough to pass. That would mean a score of at least 35 on the verbal section and 70 on the recall section. The personal background section will also be factored into your final score, but you can't predict how that section will be scored.

Your goal is to score as high as possible on the written exam, because that score in part determines your rank on the eligibility list. You've probably already seen an improvement in your score between the exam in Chapter 6 and this exam. If you want to score even higher, the best place to put your energy is the vocabulary section, because that's the one part of the exam you can really study for. Use the tips in Chapter 9 to help you continue to improve your vocabulary.

As exam day draws near, the biggest thing you can do to continue to improve is to practice your self-confidence. Remember, the key to doing well on this exam, in which timing counts so much, is to stay calm and focus.

Practice your self-confidence in front of the mirror every morning. Say to yourself: *I can beat this exam. It's not really that hard. I just have to focus and answer one question at a time. I can find the right answer. I can score well.* Armed with self-confidence, and knowing that you've practiced the kinds of questions on the exam, you can do your best on exam day.

CHAPTER

19 The Physical Ability Test

CHAPTER SUMMARY

This chapter presents an overview of what to expect on the physical test that is required for future police officers. It also offers specific advice on how to get in shape for this often demanding exam—and how to stay in shape for continued success on the job.

Physical fitness testing, otherwise known as the physical ability or physical agility test, is a staple in the police officer selection process. In an attempt to measure your ability either to successfully perform the duties of a police officer or to complete the training to perform those duties, a department will probably require you to perform a test or series of tests that will physically challenge you. The timing and makeup of the test are dictated to a certain extent by legislation that protects against potentially discriminatory practices. The goal of this chapter is to identify the types of tests you are likely to encounter and to provide you with some instruction so that you can run, jump, push, and pull your way through the selection test.

Tests to measure your physical ability to be a police officer generally take one of two forms: job task simulation and physical fitness. Physical fitness tests are widely used and favored for their validity and predictability. A battery of tests measure your physiological parameters, such as body composition, aerobic capacity, muscular strength and endurance, and flexibility. Physical fitness tests also hint at your medical status and, perhaps more importantly, they reveal your ability to perform the potentially hundreds of physical tasks required of a police officer.

Job task simulation tests, on the other hand, while they may tax your physiological fitness, are designed for the most part to illustrate your ability in a handful of job areas. Typically, these tests also challenge your motor skills: balance, coordination, power, speed, reaction time, and agility.

▶ Getting Organized for the Test

You should receive a notice that states the time, date, and location of your physical ability test. Read this notification carefully to see if it details what you should bring with you to the testing site. If it doesn't specify, you may want to call the recruiting office to find out exactly what you will need. Here are some items that you may want or need to bring with you to the testing site:

- photo ID
- medical verification or clearance form signed by a medical doctor stating that you are physically able to take the test
- check or money order to pay for an exam fee
- extra set of athletic clothing
- fruit
- bagel or bread
- sports drink, juice, or water
- change of clothes and towel if locker rooms are available
- gloves, kneepads, or ankle braces (if they are allowed by your testing agency)
- writing paper and two black pens

Physical Fitness Tests

Physical fitness testing typically takes place in a group setting, most often in a gymnasium, field house, or athletic field—remember, these are field tests. Plan to wear a warm-up suit or sweatpants along with shorts and a T-shirt so you can shed layers if you get too warm. Also, wear sneakers or rubber soled shoes. The time between events and the duration of the test vary according to the number of candidates and the number of test events.

Physical fitness test events typically include an *aerobic capacity test*, which measures your cardiorespiratory system's ability to take in and use oxygen to sustain activity. A field test, such as a 1.5-mile run or a 12-minute run, gives an indication of your ability to participate in sustained activities such as walking a patrol, foot pursuits, and subject control and restraint. The most common standards are "time to complete the distance" and "distance covered in the allotted time."

Flexibility—the ability to freely use the range of motion available at a given joint in your body—is frequently tested because it impacts many movements and activities. Sitting for long periods at a dispatching center or behind the wheel of a patrol car, or bending over to lift a handcuffed subject—all will affect or be affected by your flexibility. *Sit and reach tests* to evaluate low back and hamstring flexibility require you to sit with straight legs extended and to reach as far forward as possible. The performance standard for this commonly used test is to touch or to go beyond your toes.

Another staple of fitness tests is muscular strength and endurance measures. Muscular strength—the ability to generate maximum force—is indicative of your potential in a use-of-force encounter, subject control, or other emergency situations. *Bench press* and *leg press* tests to measure upper and lower body strength are commonly used and require you to lift a percentage of your present body weight. A maximum effort is required after a warm-up on the testing machine or apparatus.

Dynamic muscular endurance, on the other hand, is the ability to sustain effort over time. This very common element of fitness tests is related to sitting or standing for long periods of time as well as to the incidence of low back pain and disability. *Sit-up* and *push-*

Sample Physical Fitness Exam

Here is an example of an actual physical fitness exam used by a police department to screen potential candidates.

1. Sit-ups. The candidate lies flat on the back, knees bent, heels flat on the floor, fingers interlaced and placed behind the head. The monitor holds the feet down firmly. In the up position, the candidate should touch elbows to knees and return with shoulder blades touching floor. A passing score depends on your age and gender. For example, a 21-year-old female must do 32 sit-ups in one minute to pass the test.
2. Flex. The candidate removes shoes, sits down with legs extended, and places the feet squarely against a box with feet no wider than eight inches apart. Toes are pointed directly toward ceiling; knees remain extended throughout the test. With hands placed one on top of the other, the candidate leans forward without lunging or bobbing and reaches as far forward as possible. The hands must stay together and the stretch must be held for one second. Three attempts are allowed with the best of the three recorded to the nearest $\frac{1}{4}$ inch to determine whether the candidate passed/failed.
3. Push-ups. The hands are placed slightly wider than shoulder width apart, with fingers pointing forward. The monitor places one fist on the floor below the candidate's chest. (If a male monitor is testing a female candidate, a 3-inch sponge will be placed under the sternum to substitute for the fist.) Starting from the up position (elbows extended), the candidate must keep the back straight at all times and lower the body to the floor until the chest touches the monitor's fist. The candidate then returns to the up position. This is one repetition. The candidate's score will consist of the number of correct repetitions performed without a break (i.e., failing to extend the elbows, one or both knees touching the floor, hitting the floor, remaining on the floor, or stopping). A 22-year-old male must do 29 push-ups in one minute to achieve a passing score.
4. One-and-a-Half-Mile Run. The 1.5-mile run will be administered on a track. The candidate will be informed of his/her lap time during the test. A 31-year-old female must be able to complete the 1.5-mile run within 15 minutes and 57 seconds to achieve a passing score.

up tests are frequently timed events lasting one to two minutes that involve military push-ups and traditional or hands-across-the-chest sit-ups.

Finally, it is not uncommon to encounter a test that estimates the amount of fat compared to lean tissue or total body weight. *Body composition* is an indication of health risk status, and the results are usually expressed as a percent. Normal ranges for healthy young adults are 18–24% for females and 12–18% for males. A skinfold technique that measures the thickness of the skin and subcutaneous fat at gender-specific sites is the most common field test to estimate overall percentage of body fat.

Job Task Simulation Tests

Job task simulation tests use a small sample of actual or simulated job tasks to evaluate your ability to do the job of a police officer. This type of test is used because of its realistic relationship to the job and police officer training and because of its defensibility as a fair measure of a candidate's physical abilities.

Because courts of law have found it unreasonable to evaluate skills that require prior training, general job-related skills are tested at the applicant level. It's unlikely that you will be required to demonstrate competency with a firearm, for example. But climbing through a window, over barriers, and up stairs, and

Important

Regardless of the type of physical test you take, you need to be reasonably fit to successfully complete the test. Because the selection process, the police academy training, and the lifestyle of police officers are all stressful, it is essential to achieve fitness early and to maintain it for the duration of your career as a police officer. You should consult a physician any time you begin, change, or increase your workout program.

simulating use-of-force situations, such as a takedown or application of handcuffs, are common tasks.

Simulation tests are often presented as obstacle courses, with the events performed one after another and linked by laps around the gymnasium or athletic field. Frequently, the requirement is to successfully complete the course or each event in a given amount of time. The test may be given on an individual or small group basis. Candidates performing a job task simulation test may be walked or talked through the first run or allowed to practice certain events prior to actual testing.

A job task simulation test is typically held during one of two periods, subject to labor and antidiscrimination legislation. Testing can legally occur at the very beginning of the process, alone or in combination with a written test, to establish an applicant's rank. Or it can take place after a written test but before a conditional offer of employment. In some cases, it may also occur following a conditional offer of employment. If this is the case, you can reasonably expect a medical examination prior to participating in the test, which may also serve as an academy selection test. Due to the variability in the timing of the test, it is advisable to ask about physical standards as early in the selection process as possible.

▶ Beginning an Exercise Program

In preparing for the physical ability test, you must plan ahead, taking into account both the timing and the content of the test. The short-term objective, of course, is to pass the test. But your greater goal is to integrate fitness into your lifestyle so that you can withstand the rigors of the career you want in law enforcement.

The first order of business is to determine the type of physical ability test you'll have to complete. What you have to accomplish on the test naturally will guide your exercise program. You can tailor your training to simulate the test and to train for the test events. Even if you're facing a job simulation task test, you may want to include physical fitness test events, such as push-ups and sit-ups, in your training regimen. It's unsafe and inadequate to use skill events as your only training mode. If you're unfit, it won't allow for a slow progression, and if you are fit, it may not represent enough of a challenge for you.

To avoid injury while achieving overall fitness, balance in fitness training is essential. Steady progress is the name of the game. Remember, you didn't get into or out of shape overnight, so you won't be able to change your condition overnight. Work opposing muscle groups when doing strength or flexibility training, and include aerobic conditioning, as well as proper nutrition, in your total fitness program.

To achieve continued growth in fitness, you must overload the body's systems. The body makes progress by adapting to increasing demands. With adaptation, your systems are able to overcome the physical challenge, resulting in a higher level of fitness. That means if you can do a 40-pound leg lift this week, aim to do a 45-pound leg lift next week or the week after.

Finally, don't forget rest. It will allow your body and your mind to recover from the challenges of training—and to prepare for another day. So try to get plenty of sleep.

Sample Job Task Simulation Exam

Here is an example of an actual job task simulation exam used by a police department to screen potential candidates.

1. Obstacle Course. This event simulates the actions necessary to pursue and take down a suspect. The event begins with an obstacle course where the candidate will be faced with climbing under an obstacle, climbing up and down steps, going through an open window, climbing over a wall, and negotiating a series of cones arranged in a zigzag pattern. At the end of the course, the candidate will be required to grab hold of a weighted bag attached to a pulley and touch it to the ground. The candidate will then immediately move around the Power Station to the handcuffing simulation, where he or she will be required to pull on two hand levers until the cable hits the stop. This completes the event. The time limit is 130.4 seconds.
2. The Trigger Pull Event. This event consists of raising a handgun and squeezing the trigger six times with each hand. The time limit is 7.1 seconds.
3. The Separation Event. This event simulates tasks that require separating one party from another and controlling individuals, such as in crowd-control situations. The candidate will be required to pull a hanging bag backward, touching it to the ground across a marked line. Candidates will have to perform two pulls. The time limit is 14.2 seconds.
4. The Dummy Drag. This event simulates dragging an unconscious victim out of a burning vehicle. Candidates will be required to drag a dummy over a straight course. The time limit is 11 seconds.

► Get Active

Once you have decided to get into shape, the next step is to get active. Remember, you can do some things throughout your day to help increase your level of fitness. Take the stairs instead of the elevator, park your car in the furthest spot away from where you are going so you can walk, or do calf raises while standing in line at the grocery store. Granted, these things will not turn you into a fitness pro, but they can supplement your workouts.

As you probably know, the best frequency for workouts is three to five times per week. Since you are preparing for an important physical ability exam, however, you may need to exercise five or more days per week, depending on your current fitness level and the amount of time before your test. Here are some guidelines for getting active in an exercise program.

Warm-up

A warm-up phase should always precede strenuous activity. A warm-up is a gradual increase in intensity of physical activity that should last for five to ten minutes. During your warm-up, you can:

1. Increase your body temperature slowly.
2. Stretch your muscles and joints to avoid injury.
3. Gradually increase your heart rate and breathing.

Good warm-up activities include walking briskly, jogging slowly, or doing low-impact aerobic steps (such as the side to side step) followed by calisthenics and light stretching.

Stretching

You can do stretching exercises as a part of your warm-up, but only after you do some form of low intensity aerobic activity for at least five to ten minutes. Don't try to just jump into stretching when you are cold, or you could do some damage. If you don't want to stretch during your warm-up, you can include stretching exercises along with your calisthenics or as a part of your cooldown. Perform all stretching exercises slowly and gently, without any bouncing, bobbing, jerking, or lunging.

Calisthenics

You can perform calisthenics without using any equipment, although some people like to use hand or ankle weights. Calisthenics usually involve the repetitive lifting and lowering of a body segment as in push-ups, squats, or arm circles. These types of exercises can be used to develop strength, muscular endurance, and flexibility. Here are some recommended calisthenics to help you get into shape:

- Side straddle hop (jumping jacks)
- Half squats
- Heel raises
- Push-ups
- Stomach crunches

And for the more advanced:

- Diamond push-ups
- Bent leg raises

It is very important to get the proper instruction when beginning a workout program that involves the use of weights. Not only will your safety increase, but a professional who is versed in the use of weights can maximize your gain and minimize your pain.

Weight Training

Weight training should be used to develop your strength, muscular endurance, and flexibility. You can use free weights (such as barbells or dumbbells) or weight machines in your weight-training program. Be careful if you are not familiar with free weights; they could cause injury if they fall on you or if you strain yourself by trying to control the weight to keep it from falling. For instance, if you try to lift a weight that is too heavy for you, it could fall on your foot. If you are new to weight lifting, you may want to stick to weight machines rather than trying to use free weights. If you really want to use free weights for weight training, then always have a spotter who can help work with you.

Aerobic Training

Aerobic training will improve your cardiovascular fitness. Examples of aerobic training are jogging, bicycling, climbing stairs, rowing, walking, swimming, hiking, cross country skiing, skating, and aerobic dancing. Try to sustain aerobic activity for at least 20 minutes.

Don't forget to work your legs! This is the most common mistake police applicants make in preparing for the physical ability test. Practical tests, such as dragging a weight or scaling a wall, actually involve the use of your legs much more than the use of your upper body. In addition, research indicates that working your legs will activate your body and actually maximize your upper body workouts.

Cooldown

Your cooldown phase is as critical as your warm-up, and it too should last at least five to ten minutes. Your cooldown will help you decrease your heart rate gradually and will help you avoid nausea after a strenuous workout. You should slow down your last workout activity, and then switch over to walking or doing light calisthenics and stretching to complete your cooldown.

▶ Scheduling Your Workouts

Depending on the amount of time before your physical ability test, you may be able to ease into an exercise program slowly—or you may need a crash course in

Staying "FITT"

FITT stands for Frequency, Intensity, Type, and Time. FITT simplifies your training by helping you plan what to do, when, how hard, and for how long. Because the four FITT variables are interrelated, you need to be careful in how you exercise. For example, intensity and time have an inverse relationship: As the intensity of your effort increases, the length of time you can maintain that effort decreases. A good rule of thumb when adjusting your workout variables to achieve optimum conditioning is to modify one at a time, increasing by five to ten percent. Be sure to allow your body time to adapt before adjusting up again.

The following presents some FITT guidelines to help you plan your training program.

Frequency

- 3-5 times a week

Intensity

- Aerobic training—60–85% of maximum effort
- Resistance training—8–12 repetitions
- Flexibility training—Just to slight tension

Type

- Aerobic—Bike, walk, jog, swim
- Resistance—Free weights, weight machines, calisthenics
- Flexibility—Static stretching

Time

- Aerobic—20–60 minutes
- Resistance—1–3 sets, 2–4 exercises/body part
- Flexibility—Hold stretched position 8–30 seconds

physical fitness. Here are some tips about how to schedule your workouts.

12 Weeks or Less to the Test Date

Your primary goal when faced with a short window of preparation is to meet a given standard, either physical fitness or job task simulation. Therefore, specificity of training—training for what you will actually be asked to do on the test—is important.

If you're training for a physical fitness test, then the performance standards are your training goals. You should make every attempt to use, or to build up to, the standards as the training intensity level. If you are unable to reach the standards right away, approximate them and increase the intensity by five percent each week until you achieve them.

If you're training for a pre-academy test, try to determine what the academy's curriculum entails, use these as your modes of training, and test yourself with the standards every two to three weeks.

On the other hand, if the short-term goal is to meet a job task simulation test standard, particularly one that is used for pre-academy selection, you should determine the content of the curriculum and use it as the training model. At the same time, practice the skills required on the test once every two weeks in lieu of a training day.

Six or More Months to Go

The training program, when there are six or more months to prepare, is essentially similar to the one previously described. However, the longer time frame means that your goal can become making permanent, positive changes in your lifestyle rather than simply applying training principles to pass a test. Reasonable and gradual changes in your lifestyle will help you ensure that the behavioral and physical changes are permanent.

This extended timetable also reduces the likelihood of injury and allows for more diversity and balance in your training program and lifestyle. If you're preparing for a physical fitness test, you have the opportunity to set (and meet) performance goals that may be 25–50% greater than the standards themselves. On the other hand, if you have more than six months to prepare for a job task simulation test, you may want to avoid practicing any of the skills required for the first three months to avoid injury. Instead, consider incorporating sports activities into your conditioning routine; this will provide an enjoyable opportunity to train the necessary motor skills. After three months, you could begin practicing the physical test skills one day every two to four weeks.

▶ Exercise at the Academy

All your hard work in creating and sticking to an exercise plan will pay off once you pass your physical ability test and enter the academy. Because, like it or not, your physical training program is not over yet. Indeed, you can expect a workout like the following one once you enter the academy.

Physical training begins with a warm-up to increase your core body temperature and to prepare you for the more intense conditioning to follow. Brisk walking or jogging, in place or around a gymnasium, or jumping rope are good start-up options and should be conducted for five minutes. This is followed immediately by a period of active head-to-toe stretching to prevent injury.

Basic conditioning in the academy frequently is achieved with calisthenic exercises. Beginners can do sets of ten on a two count and those of intermediate or advanced fitness can begin on a four count (1, 2, 3, 1; 1, 2, 3, 2; etc.). Running in formation typically follows calisthenics and is done at about a nine to ten minutes per mile pace. Marine Corps cadences played on an mp3 player may help to put you in the mood for academy runs! For those who are just beginning to prepare for the fitness test, 8 to 12 minutes of running is a safe start; those who are more fit may begin with 25 or more minutes. A three- to five-minute cool-down period to recover and some gentle, static stretching from the floor, focusing on the lower legs, will complete your workout and prepare you for the showers.

▶ Additional Resources

Websites

- Fitness Info Developed by the President's Council on Physical Fitness and Sports
  www.hoptechno.com/book11.htm
- Physical fitness: Phases, types, and evaluations
  www.fitness-training.net/introduction
- In-Depth Health and Fitness Site
  www.personalhealthzone.com/fitsports.html
- The National Association for Health and Fitness
  www.physicalfitness.org

Books

- *Body for Life: 12 Weeks to Mental and Physical Strength* by Bill Phillips (Harper Collins).
- *Fitness for Dummies* by Suzanne Schlosberg and Liz Neporent (Wiley Publishing).
- *Getting Stronger: Weight Training for Men and Women* by Bill Pearl (Shelter Publications).
- *Eat Smart, Play Hard: Customized Food Plans for All Your Sports and Fitness Pursuits* by Elizabeth Ann Applegate and Liz Applegate (Rodale Press).
- *Essentials of Strength Training and Conditioning* by Thomas R. Baechle and Roger W. Earle (Human Kinetics Pub).
- *Fit for Duty* by Robert Hoffman and Thomas R. Collingwood (Human Kinetics Pub).
- *Fitness and Health* by Brian J. Sharkey (Human Kinetics Publishers).

CHAPTER

20 The Personal History Statement

CHAPTER SUMMARY

This chapter explores the quirks, subtleties, and realities of filling out the lengthy personal history statement. Paperwork tells the tale in police work—you only get one shot at this document.

The personal history statement is exactly that—a detailed personal statement of your life history. You may hear it called many things—"application" and "the applicant history statement" are other common terms. Although the paperwork may go by different names, the reason for it is the same. The purpose of the statement is to provide law enforcement background investigators with the material for a panel, an individual, or a personnel department to make a sound decision about whether or not to hire you.

When you take your first look at the personal history statement, you might want to be sitting down. Or at least have a chair handy. This document can seem like a black hole to the unprepared. All of your precious time, energy, and resources can be sucked into the void if you aren't prepared to be asked about the tiniest details of your life. Although not all departments require the same level of detail, don't be surprised to find yourself madly hunting for the address of that kindergarten you once attended.

Some departments aren't so demanding. They will ask you to start out this tale of your life with your high school days and work forward. It's best to expect the worst, though.

▶ The Importance of the Personal History Statement

No matter where you choose to apply, this chapter may be the helping hand you need to make your background investigation go as smoothly as possible. It will serve as a guide to help you present an accurate, honest summary of your past and present life. After all, the personal history statement—how you complete it, what you reveal, and what you don't reveal—can determine whether or not you get the opportunity to convince an oral board you are worth hiring.

You may not make the connection between the oral interview board and the personal history statement at first, but the connection is there and it's strong. What you reveal—and what you fail to reveal—in your personal history statement will come back around to help or haunt you at your oral board. Background investigators will rustle around in your life's basement using this document as a flashlight. They will illuminate the good things and the bad things for all the oral board members to see and to use in their questioning. You're forewarned, however, and you are ready.

One of the more frustrating aspects of searching for that perfect law enforcement job is realizing that every department, even within the same state, has its own way of doing business. Yes, you may have applied yesterday to one police department 20 miles away from the one you are applying to today, but the process may be entirely different. Law enforcement agencies rarely have the same priorities, budgets, or staffing, so the process, right down to the people they may want to hire, won't match up.

Be flexible. No matter how the application process is designed, no matter in what order you handle each task given to you, the information you will need to supply each department remains the same. They all want to know about your past, present, and potential.

Finally, if you do apply to multiple departments or agencies, you should keep in mind that some states have law enforcement applicant databases. One of the first places your background investigator may check is a statewide database to see if you have applied elsewhere. With this information, the investigator can compare your applications and see if you have been consistent in the information you supplied.

▶ Preparation Is the Key

Even if you haven't decided which departments you will grace with your applications, you can start work now. Beginning with the day you were born (or for at least the past ten years), make a list of every address where you've lived up to the present. You should include contact information for any landlords or property management offices, if applicable. Make this list and keep plenty of copies. You will need to do this only once—instead of every time you apply to a different department—if you are careful to keep copies of your efforts. You never know; the CIA, FBI, or another agency may lure you from your dream department one day and you will wish you'd kept up the list.

Addresses aren't the only project you can work on ahead of time to prepare for completing the personal history statement. Create a list of every part-time, full-time, or volunteer job you've had since your working life began. Once again, not every department will use the same starting point to investigate your job history. Many forms ask you to list the jobs you've held during the past ten years, some during the past five years, and the others want your history from the moment you received your first paycheck.

As you gather the information for your personal history statement, begin to keep it in an organized notebook. Include original copies of your birth certificate, Social Security card, and other important documents. Write down the addresses of your employers, friends, and relatives, and take special care in noting the telephone numbers and zip codes. This notebook will make the application process much smoother for you, and when you decide to aim for a promotion to detective or sergeant, you will have all of your information in one place.

Your Driving Record

Here's yet another project to work on before applying to a police agency: Research your driving history. You will be asked by some departments to list every traffic ticket you've ever received in any state or country, whether on a military post or on civilian roadways. Some may ask you to list only the moving violations (these include speeding, running red lights, and unsafe lane changes), while other departments want to see moving violations and tickets for things like expired license plates, failure to wear seat belts, and expired automobile insurance.

One agency may ask for you to tell them about the tickets you've received in the past five years, while others want to know your driving history from the moment your foot first touched an accelerator. Do your homework. And don't leave off tickets you think they won't find out about, because tickets leave paper trails, and a paper trail is the easiest kind to follow.

Gathering Documents

Your pre-application preparations wouldn't be complete without a list of documents you will need to have handy. This list does not include every form you may have to have, but it's almost a dead certainty your department will want to see your

- birth certificate
- Social Security card
- DD 214 (if you are a veteran)
- naturalization papers (if applicable)
- high school diploma or GED certificate
- high school transcripts
- college transcripts
- current driver's license(s)
- current copies of driving records
- current consumer credit reports
- selective service card
- court orders, including marriage certificates, divorce papers, legal separation documents, and name change paperwork.

If you don't have certified copies of these documents, start calling or writing the proper authorities now to find out what you need to do to get them. If you've sucked your Social Security card up in the vacuum cleaner and haven't seen it since, visit the Social Security office in your community and arrange for a new one. Legal documents often take anywhere from six to eight weeks for delivery, but you probably won't be able to wait that long if you have already received and started on your personal history statement. Most departments have a deadline for filling out and returning personal history statements, so you will have to schedule your time carefully.

If time runs out and you realize you won't be able to turn the personal history statement in with all the required documents, ask the powers that be what you should do. Many departments will tell you to attach a memo to your application outlining your problem and what you have done about it. For example, you've ordered a copy of your birth certificate, but haven't yet received it. Attach a letter of explanation to your application detailing when you requested a copy of your birth certificate, where you asked for the copy to be sent, and when you expect to receive the document. If you have it, attach all copies of correspondence you sent out requesting a copy of your certificate. That will show that you are making all the right moves.

You may have a little homework to do before rounding up all of these documents. Check with as many departments as you can to find out what rules they have for how certain documents are submitted—like college transcripts, for instance. Departmental officials may require that the school send the documentation directly to their recruiting office instead of to you. The same goes for credit reports or copies of driving records. It's best to call the recruiting department, explain that you are trying to round up all of your documentation, and ask them how they accept these documents so you will know what to do.

Other questions you need to ask are

- Do you need photocopies or original documents?
- Will you return my original document if I send it?
- How recent does the credit history have to be?
- What's the most recent copy you will accept of my college transcript?

The answers to these questions can save you lots of time and money. You'd be surprised at the number of ways each department can come up with for you to chase paper.

You may also want to check online to see if your targeted police department has a copy of the personal history statement available at their website. You may find detailed instructions about how to submit each type of document at the beginning of the online personal history statement.

▶ Ready For Action

So, you are as prepared as you can be. You've made your decision on where you are applying, and let's even assume you are at the point in the application process where you've received the personal history statement. Before you set pen to paper, make a copy of the form. Do not write on it, breathe on it, or set it down on the coffee table without making a copy first. After you have a copy, then put away the original for now. (You will be using the photocopy as a working draft and a place to make mistakes.) Eventually you will transfer all the information you have on your practice copy onto the original. And then you'll be making a copy of your original. You may be spending lots of time on this project and using more than a few dimes in the copy machine before this is all over, but it will be time and money well spent. Especially if the unthinkable happens:

> Your phone rings. It's your recruiter. "Gee, this is Officer Jones at Friendly P.D. recruiting and I have a little bad news. We can't seem to find that application you sent. Could you make us a copy from the one you have at home and send it out right away?"

Be sure to make copies of your completed personal history statement and accompanying documentation you submit and keep them in a safe place. Hold on to these copies! You need to review this document before the oral board contacts you, not to mention the possibility that you may need this information to complete other applications years down the road.

Personal history statements may vary from department to department, but the questions most applicants ask about filling out these tedious documents have not changed over the years. The following are a few questions and comments made by actual applicants as they went through application processes across the United States. The responses to and comments about these questions will allow you to learn from someone else's mistakes, thereby giving you an advantage over the competition—and having an advantage in this highly competitive field can never hurt!

"What do you mean you don't accept resumes? It took me four hours to get this one done!"

A formal resume like the one you may prepare for a civilian job may not be much good to a law enforcement agency. Although criminal justice instructors in many colleges suggest that their students prepare a resume, it's always best to call and ask a recruiter whether or not to bother. Why go to the trouble if the agency is going to throw away the resume upon receipt? Most agencies rely upon their personal history statements to get the details of your life, education, and experience, so save yourself the time and money when you can. Some departments do, however, request that you submit a resume. They use it as an additional screening element. So it's always best to ask first.

"I didn't realize the personal history statement would take so long to complete, and the deadline for turning it in caught me by surprise. I got in a hurry and left some things blank."

The letter this applicant received in the mail disqualifying her from further consideration probably caught her by surprise as well. As you know from reading this chapter so far, a personal history statement requires planning, efficiency, and attention to detail. Most police departments demand accuracy, thoroughness, and timeliness. There are entirely too many applicants who have taken the necessary time to properly fill out an application for a busy background investigator to bother with an applicant who has left half of the form blank and isn't quite sure what should go in the other half. In fact, many departments will tell you in their application instructions that failing to respond to questions or failure to provide requested information will result in disqualification.

"I read *most* of the instructions. I didn't see the part that said I had to print."

Read all of the instructions. Every sentence. Every word. And do so before you begin filling out your practice copy of the personal history statement. In fact, you should read the entire document from the first page to the last page before you tackle this project. Have a notepad next to you, and as you read, make notes of everything you do not understand. You will be making a phone call to your recruiter after reading the entire document to ask questions. It's important to read the whole document because the questions on your pad may be answered as you read along.

"No one is going to follow up on all this stuff anyway. It'd take way too long and it's way too involved."

A good background investigator will be thorough in following up on the details of your life. That's his or her job. When all is said and done, the investigator must sign his or her name at the bottom of the report documenting the investigation. It's not wise to assume someone will put their career at risk by doing a sloppy job on your background investigation. A thorough investigator will take as much time as it takes to do a good job. The good news is that you can earn brownie points by making that investigator's job as simple as possible. Give as much information as you possibly can and make sure that information is correct. When you write down a phone number, make sure it's current. For example, if you used to work at Jumpin' Jack's Coffee Parlor four years ago and you still remember the phone number, call that number to make sure it's still in service before you write it down. Nothing is more irritating to a busy investigator than dialing wrong number after wrong number. If that's the only number you have and you discover it's no longer in service, make a note of this so the investigator doesn't assume you are being sloppy. Phone numbers get changed and businesses fail every day.

When you turn in a personal history statement, you are building on the reputation you began forming from the moment you first made contact with the recruiting staff. An application that is turned in on time, is filled out neatly and meticulously, and has correct, detailed information—that is easily verified—says a lot about the person who filled it out. Not only will an investigator have warm fuzzy thoughts for anyone who makes his or her job easier, he or she will come to the conclusion that you will probably carry over these same traits into your police work.

The investigator, the oral board, and the staff psychologist all will be looking at how you filled out the application as well as what information is contained in the application. Police officers will build a case for hiring you (or not hiring you) based on facts, impressions, and sometimes even intuition. With this in mind, every detail is worth a second look before you call your personal history statement complete. Ask yourself:

- Is my handwriting as neat as it can be?
- Did I leave off answers or skip items?
- Do my sentences make sense?
- Is my spelling accurate?
- Are my dates and times consistent?
- Did I double-check the telephone numbers?
- Did I double-check the ZIP codes?

"I figured you could find out that information more easily than I could. That's why I didn't look up that information. After all, you're the investigator."

And this applicant is probably still looking for a job. The personal history statement is a prime opportunity for you to showcase your superb organizational skills, attention to detail, and professionalism. Do as much of the work as you can for the background investigator. For example, let's say you worked for Grace's Record Store. The business went under after a few months, and you moved on to other employment. You're not sure what happened to Grace, your immediate supervisor and the owner of the business, but you do know a friend of hers. Contact that friend, find out Grace's address and phone number, and give this information to your investigator. Going the extra mile shows initiative, and you are going to get the extra credit points.

It's not uncommon for a major police department to get thousands of applications per year. Most of the applicants have the same credentials to offer as you do. Do all you can do to stand out from the crowd by showing your efficiency, professionalism, and accuracy.

"I know I got disqualified, but it's only because I misunderstood the question. I didn't want to ask about it because I didn't want to look dumb."

If you do not understand a question, ask someone. By not making sure you know how to properly answer a question, you run the risk of answering it incorrectly, incompletely, or not at all. Any one of these mistakes can lead to your disqualification if an investigator thinks that you are not telling the truth, or that you are unwilling to provide the information requested. Don't take chances when a simple question can clear up the problem.

"You know, I didn't have any idea what that question meant, so I just guessed."

Never guess. Never assume. This advice can never be repeated too often—if you don't know, find out. Answering your questions is part of the job for recruiters or background investigators.

"I lied because I thought if I told the truth, I'd look bad."

Never lie about anything. As far as police departments are concerned, there is no such thing as a harmless lie. Supervisors don't want people working for them who cannot tell the truth, other officers don't want to work with partners whom they can't trust, and communities expect criminals to lie, not police officers. Your credibility must be beyond reproach.

Let's look at an example. One applicant told his recruiter that the reason he didn't admit to getting a ticket for an unregistered car was because he thought the department would think he wasn't organized and couldn't take care of business. Which would you prefer for a potential employer to know about you—that you lie instead of admitting to mistakes, or that you make mistakes and admit to them readily? Telling the truth is crucial if you want to do police work.

"I listed John Doe as a personal reference because he's the mayor and I worked on his campaign. Why did my investigator call me and ask me to give him another reference?"

Choose your personal references carefully. Background investigators do not want to talk to people because they have impressive credentials. They want to talk to them so they can understand you are a little better. Investigators will know within minutes whether or not a reference knows you well. Personal references are important enough to warrant their own in-depth discussion later in this chapter, so read on.

How to Read and Answer Questions

Reading questions and instructions carefully is critical to successfully completing the personal history statement. Certain words should leap off the page at you. These are the words you should key in on:

- all
- every
- any
- each

If you see these words in a question, you are being asked to include all the information you know. For example, you may see the following set of instructions in your personal history statement:

> List **any** and **all** pending criminal charges against you.

This doesn't mean to list only the charges facing you in Arizona, but not the ones from that incident in Nevada last week. This department wants to know about every single criminal charge that may be pending against you, no matter what city, county, parish, village, country, or planet may be handling the case(s). Do not try to dodge instructions like these for any reason. If your fear is that the information you list might make you look bad, you may have some explaining to do. And you may have perfectly good explanations for your past and your present. If you lie to try to make yourself look good, chances are you'll be disqualified in short order and no one will get the opportunity to consider your explanations.

Another question you may see is:

> Have you **ever** been arrested or taken into police custody for **any** reason?

The key words here are *ever* and *any*. This department means at any time in your life. If you don't know what is meant by the word *arrested*, then call your recruiter or investigator and ask. When in doubt, list any situation you think has a ghost of a chance of falling into the category you are working on. The best advice, though, is to ask if you don't know.

Here's a request for information that includes several eye-catching words.

> List **all** traffic citations you received in the past five (5) years, in this or **any** other state (moving and nonmoving), **excluding** parking tickets.

In this example, the department leaves little doubt that what you should do here is make a complete list of every kind of violation you've been issued a citation for, no matter where you got it and no matter what the traffic violation was for, within the past five years. They even let you know the one kind of citation they don't need to know about—parking tickets. If you aren't sure what a moving violation is or what a nonmoving violation is, call the department and have them explain. Keep in mind that if an officer issued you a citation on a single piece of paper, you may have been cited for more than one violation. Most citations have space for at least three violations, sometimes more. For example, say that last year you were pulled over for speeding. The officer discovered you had no insurance and your license plates were expired. She told you she was writing you three tickets for these violations, but handed you only one piece of paper. Did you get one ticket or three? You got three.

Once again, ask if you don't know. No one will make fun of you if you are unfamiliar with terminology such as *moving violation*.

Here are some sample questions taken from actual personal history statements:

> List all traffic citations ever received, including the date, place, and full details of each incident.
>
> Submit seven-year driving history from each state in which you have ever held a driver's license.
>
> List all moving and nonmoving traffic citations, excluding parking tickets (e.g., speeding, running a red light, expired registration, no insurance), that you have received in the past five (5) years, starting with the most recent citation. List the month and year each was issued, the type of violation, and the issuing agency.

Personal References

Your personal references are the people who will be able to give the background investigator the best picture of you as a whole person. Some personal history statements ask you to list up to six people as references, and some ask for only three. You also may be given a specific time limit for how long you may have known these people before listing them. Your instructions may direct you to list only those individuals whom you've known for a minimum of two years, for example. Pay close attention to the instructions for this section, if there are any. Selecting the people for this section is not something you should take lightly for many reasons.

Earlier, you read that by making the investigator's job easier you make your investigation run smoother, you get brownie points, and your background is finished quickly. The personal references section is one area where you really want to make it easy. You'll want the investigator to talk to people who know you well, who can comment on your hobbies, interests, personality, and ability to interact with others. Try to choose friends who will be honest, open, and sincere. When an investigator calls a reference and figures out quickly that the person he or she is talking to barely has an idea of who you are, the red flags will come shooting up. The investigator will wonder why you listed someone who doesn't know you well. Are you trying to throw him or her off track? Are you afraid someone who knows you too well will let out information you don't want known? This is how an investigator will look at the situation. And, at the very least, you will get a phone call requesting another reference because the one you listed was unsatisfactory.

Most investigators expect that you will notify your personal references and tell them that they will be getting a phone call or a personal visit from the investigating agency. Get the right phone numbers, find out from your references what times they are most accessible, and especially find out if they have any objections to being contacted. You don't need a reluctant personal reference. He or she will probably do more harm than good.

Tell your references how important it is for them to be open and honest with the investigator. It's also wise to let them know that there are no right or wrong answers to most of these questions. Investigators do not want to have a conversation with someone who is terrified about saying the wrong thing. And that's what your personal references should expect to have with an investigator—a conversation, not an interrogation. Your goal here is to let the investigator see you as a person through the eyes of those who know you best.

Here are sample requests for references taken from actual personal history statements:

> CHARACTER REFERENCES (do not include relatives, former employers, or persons living outside the United States or its Territories). List only character references who have definite knowledge of your qualifications and fitness for the position for which you are applying. Do not repeat names of job supervisors. List a minimum of three (3) character references. Give each person's name, the number of years known, street address, and phone number.

> Provide three (3) references (not relatives, fellow employees, or school teachers) who are responsible adults of reputable standing in their communities, such as heads of households, property owners, business or professional men or women, who have known you well during the past five (5) years. List each one's name, home and business phone numbers, street address, and occupation.
>
> Additionally, provide three (3) social acquaintances who have known you well during the past five (5) years. (These must be different people from the three references listed above.)
>
> Additionally, provide contact information for three (3) of your neighbors.

▶ Before You Turn It In

You've filled out the practice copy you made of the personal history statement, made all your mistakes on that copy, answered all the questions, and filled in all the appropriate blanks. Now you're ready to make the final copy.

Part of the impression you will make on those who make the hiring and firing decisions will come from how your application looks. Is your handwriting so sloppy that investigators pass your work around to see who can read it? Did you follow the instructions directing you to print? Were you too lazy to attach an additional sheet of paper, and instead you wrote up and down the sides of the page? Did you spell words correctly? Do your sentences make sense to the reader? (A good tip here is to read your answers aloud to yourself. If it doesn't make sense to your ear, then you need to work on what you wrote.)

Every time you contact the hiring agency, you make an impression. The written impression you make when you turn in your personal history statement is one that can follow you through the entire process and into the academy. In fact, it can have a bearing on whether or not you even make it into the academy because most departments have a method of scoring you on the document's appearance.

Here are some items you might find useful as you work on your application and prepare it for submission.

- a dictionary
- a grammar handbook
- a good pen (or pencil—whatever the directions tell you to use)

Make sure that you check your work, check it again, and have someone you trust check it yet again before you make your final copy.

You now have the information you need to make the personal history statement a manageable task. This is not a document to take lightly, especially when you are now aware of the power this document has over your potential career as a police officer. Remember, it's important that you:

- follow instructions and directions
- be honest and open about your past and present
- provide accurate information
- choose excellent personal references
- turn in presentable, error-free documentation
- submit documents on time

A recruiting department can ask for nothing better than an applicant who takes this kind of care and interest in the application process.

CHAPTER

20 The Oral Interview

CHAPTER SUMMARY

This chapter is the next best thing to having someone do your oral interview for you. The oral interview is demystified in these pages with a down-to-earth look at the process. Read on for tips, suggestions, and instructions.

Municipal police departments nationwide depend on some form of oral interview to help them choose suitable police candidates. In Los Angeles, California, a panel of two civilians and one retired police officer questions applicants for 15 to 20 minutes about their qualifications. In Austin, Texas, applicants can expect to be grilled by a panel of five higher-ranking police officers and a civilian psychologist for over an hour—and that's if you keep your responses short and to the point.

The oral interview board, no matter what form it takes, is unlike any oral job interview you will ever experience. The questions are pointed, personal, and uncompromising. Vague responses will usually goad a panel of veteran police officers into rougher questioning techniques until they get an honest response. This chapter will show you how to prepare for the oral board from the moment you decide to apply to a department until the moment you walk into the interview.

▶ The Oral Board Members

If you are like most people, you've had some experience asking someone for a job. So, it's not unrealistic to expect that the police oral interview board will be similar to a civilian oral interview—is it? Yes and no. There are a few similarities: Both prospective civilian and police employers are looking for the most qualified person for the job—reliable, honest men and women who will work hard and be there when they are needed.

Civilian employers expect applicants to show up on time for their interviews, to dress professionally, and to show off their best manners, as do police employers. When you step into a police oral interview board, however, you will realize that the people who are interviewing you have more than a surface interest in you and your past experiences. And the board will have more than a one- or two-page resume in their hands when the interview begins.

Exactly who is going to be using the details of your personal and professional life to interview you? More than likely it will be a panel of two or more individuals with one purpose in mind: to get to know you well. The board members will most likely be supervisory-level police officers who have several years' experience on the force. Some departments use civilian personnel specialists to sit on their boards, but most interview boards will be made up of experienced police officers.

These board members will be using information you have provided on your personal history statement and information investigators discovered during your background investigation. Investigators will provide board members with a detailed report on your past and present life history. Yes, you will be asked questions when board members already know the answers and when they don't know the answers. You will be asked to explain why you've made the decisions you've made in your life—both personal and professional. You will also be asked questions that don't have correct or incorrect answers. In short, you can expect an intense grilling from men and women who don't have the time or patience for applicants who walk into their interviews unprepared.

▶ The Importance of the Personal History Statement

Before you reach the oral interview board stage of the application process, you will have had to fill out a detailed personal history statement often referred to as the applicant history statement, the personal history statement, or simply the application. Terminology differs from department to department. Unless you are skipping around in this book, you have probably read about it by now. Call it what you want—just do not underestimate its role in the oral interview.

The personal history statement guides the oral board through your past and present life. You must be willing to open your life up to the board by giving them an informative, accurate picture of where you have been in your life and who you are.

Because the personal history statement is what background investigators use to conduct investigations and what a final report to the board is built on, it follows that you should make that document the most important thing in your life when you are filling it out. Members of the oral board generally are given a copy of your personal history statement and then a copy of the investigators' final report on you. While you are answering questions for the board, most board members will be shuffling through the pages of your life—checking what you say against what they see on paper. Naturally, you will want to remember what information you gave them. Instead of tossing and turning the night before your interview, your time will be well spent reading and rereading your personal history statement so that you know what they know about you.

How much effort you put into the personal history statement will have a direct impact on how difficult your oral interview will be. If board members have an accurate, detailed picture of you as a whole person from the information you have supplied, your time under the microscope will be less than the applicant who turned in a vague, mistake-laden account of his or her past and present life. If the thought of the oral interview board makes your palms sweat, then pay close attention to the chapter on how to handle the personal history statement. You will feel better knowing that you are well prepared.

▶ Preparing for Your Interview

Preparation for the oral interview board begins when you make the decision to apply. From the moment you first make contact with a police department, everything you say and do will be potential fuel for the oral interview board. Just walking through the doors of the recruiting office to pick up an application gives you the opportunity to make a lasting impression. You are dealing with professionals who are trained to notice and remember people and details.

If you show up to pick up an application wearing your favorite cutoff blue jeans and stained T-shirt, you may be in for a shock several months later when a board member asks you why you chose to make that particular fashion statement. Dress neatly and as professionally as possible each and every time you make contact with the department where you want to work.

The same goes for telephone contacts—if you call a department to request an application you will make an impression on the person who answers the phone. If all you want is an information packet or application and you do not have any specific questions to ask, do not take this opportunity to tell the recruiter your entire life story.

Not only are you probably the hundredth person to request an application that day, but also the recruiter has no way, or reason, to remember the details of your life at this stage of the process. Remember, though, you have to give your name and address to this person who will be responsible for mailing your application, so the potential for connecting your name to the impression you make on the phone is high.

Self-Awareness—Don't Show Up without It!

You would not want to show up for a car race on a tricycle any more than you would want to try putting out a fire with gasoline. Using this same logic, it's safe to say you would never want to sit down in front of a panel of professionals—who have the power to offer you a career dealing with people—without a good measure of self-awareness.

Self-awareness is knowing yourself—being aware of what you do and why you do it. Many of the questions you will hear from the board are designed to reveal how well you know yourself and how honest you can be about your talents and your shortcomings.

Do not pay any attention to advice suggesting that you downplay, or do not admit to, weaknesses. If an oral board member asks you to list the weaknesses you believe you have and you can't think of any, they will be more than happy to bring up a few instances in your life to illustrate the weaknesses you are not able to identify.

You should be able to list your weaknesses in the same unhesitating manner in which you list your strengths. And you should be able to tell the board what you are doing to correct or compensate for your weaknesses. If you truly aren't aware of your failings, ask trusted friends and relatives for their input. Write down what you think your weaknesses are and then compare your list with what your friends and family have said. Don't forget to ask your friends about your strengths as well. Some applicants find talking about strengths as difficult as talking about weaknesses. You must be able to do both.

Part of being self-aware is knowing what others know about you. Hardly any of the questions during your oral board interview should come as a surprise to you if you have studied a copy of your application.

Before showing up for the board, you must take the time to go back over your application and carefully think about each piece of information in this document. The questions put to you by the board are generated mostly from the information you write in the personal history statement. As you review your copy of the statement, think about the type of questions such information could generate.

For example, if one of the questions on the application directed you to list any instances where you've been fired from a job, think about how you would answer the question, "Can you tell the board why you got fired from Tread Lightly Tire Shop in 1993?" Although you may have told the investigator why you were fired during an earlier conversation, the board will want to hear it for themselves.

Practice Speaking in Front of Others

Being interviewed by a group of people is a lot like having one of those dreams in which you show up to work in nothing but a pair of socks. You may experience anxiety, sweaty palms, and a burning desire to be some place else. Public speaking classes will go a long way toward easing your fear of talking to groups.

Strongly consider taking a speech class at a nearby community college or through an adult education course. At the very least, have friends ask you questions about yourself and have them take notes about any mannerisms you may exhibit while speaking. Then practice speaking and learn to control those mannerisms.

Practice is one of the keys to success on an oral board. If you've ever truly practiced something—batting a ball, for instance—you know that once you have the motion down, you can rely on your muscles to remember what to do when it comes time to play the game. The same rationale holds true for practicing oral board answers.

One effective technique is to mentally place yourself in a situation and visualize how you want to act or respond when the pressure is on. Some police officers call this mental exercise "What if..." and they use it to formulate a plan of action for those times when split-second decisions rule the moment. Visualizing a successful performance ahead of time can help trigger that response once you're in the actual situation. This technique will work for you if you practice, practice, practice.

Dress Like a Professional

You may feel like you don't have much control over what happens to you in an oral interview setting, but this is one area in which you have total control. The initial impression you make on board members is up to you and this is the perfect opportunity to score points without ever opening your mouth. The way you dress sends a signal to the people who are watching you walk into the room.

All human beings, including the oral board, make snap judgments and tend to stereotype people. If you walk in looking like a well-groomed and well-dressed professional, that is what the board is going to presume. However, if you are less than professional in your grooming and clothing, you are going to have to work harder during the interview to convince the board you are a professional. Remember, the oral board is your first step in a long career. That new suit of clothing is an investment in your future.

Appearance goes beyond your clothing. Make sure your haircut is conservative and well kept, your fingernails are clean, and your shoes are shined. Com-

Arrive Early

Show the board how much you want this job. They will check to see when you arrived for your board. An early arrival means you planned ahead for emergencies (flat tires, wrong turns, and so on), that you arrived in enough time to prepare yourself mentally for what you are about to do, and that you place a value on other people's time as well as your own.

petition for law enforcement jobs can be fierce; some candidates even get their teeth cleaned for the oral! Take every advantage your appearance can give you.

Practice Your Manners

After you've earned bonus points with your professional appearance, it's time to earn more with your manners. Most law enforcement agencies are paramilitary organizations—your first clue should be the uniforms and the rank structure. In the military, it's customary to address higher-ranking men and women with courtesy and respect. "Yes, ma'am" or "yes, sir" or "no, ma'am" or "no, sir" is expected from military personnel. If you have military experience, you will be ahead in this area.

If you are not accustomed to using these terms of courtesy, practice them! Make a conscious effort to use them. It's rarely considered rude to simply respond "yes" or "no" to a question, but you'll always be on shaky ground if "yeah" or "uh-huh" are your customary responses. You won't go wrong with "yes, sir" instead of "yeah," or "Could you repeat the question?" instead of "what?"

No doubt you realize that an oral board sees many, many applicants when a department is in a hiring phase. Most oral boards typically schedule five or six applicants in one day for interviews. Some departments schedule boards for one day during the week and some departments have oral boards set for every day of the week. You are talking to people who are more than likely quite tired of listening. That means the little things take on an extra importance.

Yes, It All Matters

What you have read so far may seem inconsequential. This is far from the truth. You walk a fine line when you appear before an oral board. They want you to appear self-confident and poised, but not cocky or arrogant. You are expected to be nervous, but not so nervous that you can't communicate beyond an occasional grunt or nod. You are expected to be polite, but you're not expected to fawn all over the board. Above all, you are expected to be yourself and not who you imagine the board might want. That brings up another point—what exactly is the board looking for in an applicant?

▶ What Is the Oral Board Looking For?

Today's departments expect officers to attend neighborhood meetings, get to know the people living and working in their patrol areas, and be accessible to the public. This concept is known as community policing. Community policing is being embraced by most medium to large police agencies and is designed to get the officers out of the squad car and back into the community. The days of riding around in a car waiting for the next call to come out are over for most officers.

Officers nationwide feel that community policing is simply a return to the basic idea behind policing—public service. Therefore, oral interview boards are faced with the formidable task of hiring men and women with the skills and talents equal to the demands of modern policing.

The men and women most highly sought after by police departments are those who can handle the demands placed on them by advanced technology and changes in policing concepts. Computers are here to stay—in the office and in the patrol car. If you haven't already, now's the time to brush up on your typing skills and sign up for a computer class.

Then there's the liability issue. Lawsuits and threats of lawsuits have law enforcement agencies scurrying to find applicants who have specific qualities and skills that will keep them out of the headlines and civil courtrooms.

Yes, law enforcement agencies want it all. There's always room for men and women who can leap tall buildings and do the speeding train thing, but even if your cape isn't red, you can still compete if you can convince the board you have the following qualities:

- maturity
- common sense
- good judgment
- compassion
- integrity
- honesty
- reliability
- the ability to work without constant supervision

These qualities aren't ranked in order of importance because it would be hard to say which should come first. They are all of importance in the eyes of the board, and your task in the oral interview is to convince them you possess these qualities. You will do your convincing through how and what you say when you respond to questions.

Youth and Inexperience—Plus or Minus?

The question here is, will an oral board think you have enough life experience for them to be willing to take a chance on hiring you? Law enforcement agencies have never been as liability conscious as they are today. Incidents like the Rodney King trial and the subsequent Los Angeles riots, as well as the controversial shooting of Amadou Diallo by four NYPD officers have heightened the awareness of city legal departments around the country.

This concern ripples straight through the department and eventually arrives to haunt recruiters, background investigators, oral boards, and everyone who has anything to do with deciding who gets a badge. The first question you hear when trouble hits a police department is, "How did that person get a job here anyway?" As a result, police departments are scrutinizing applicants more closely than ever before, and they are clearly leaning toward individuals who have proven track records in employment, schooling, volunteer work, and community involvement.

Youth and inexperience are not going to disqualify you from the process. You should be aware that if you are 21 years old and have never held a job, you will have a more difficult time getting hired on your first try at a larger police department than someone who is older, has job references to check, and is able to demonstrate a history of reliability, responsibility, and community involvement.

Maturity is a huge concern with police departments. They can no longer afford to hire men and women who are unable to take responsibility for their actions or the actions, in some cases, of those around them. Although maturity cannot be measured in the number of years an individual has been alive, departments will want to see as much proof as possible that you have enough maturity and potential to risk hiring you.

Get Out in the World

Make it as easy as possible for the oral board to see how well you handle responsibility. Sign up for volunteer work if you don't have any experience dealing with people. If you are still living at home with parents, be able to demonstrate the ways in which you are responsible around the home. If you are on your own, but living with roommates, talking to the board about this experience and how you handle conflicts arising from living with strangers or friends will help your case.

You may want to work extra hard on your communication skills before going to the board. The more articulate you are, the better you will be able to sell yourself.

Older and Wiser Can Pay Off

Being older certainly is not a hindrance in police work. Oral boards are receptive to men and women who have life experience that can be examined, picked apart, and verified. Maturity, as has been mentioned before, is not necessarily linked with how old you are. Older applicants can be either blessed or cursed by the trail they have left in life. Many applicants have gone down in flames because they were unable to explain incidents in their past and present that point to their immaturity and inability to handle responsibility.

Applicants of any age who have listed numerous jobs and have turned in personal history statements too thick to run through a stapling machine should be extra vigilant about doing homework before the oral board stage. If you fall into this category, you should carefully pore over the copy of the application your background investigator used to do your background check. Be fully aware of the problem areas and consider what you will most likely be asked to explain. And decide now what you are going to say. Prepare, prepare, prepare.

Don't Leave the Meter Running

The longer your history, the longer you can expect to sit before an oral board. If a board is not required to adhere strictly to time limits, you may be required to endure a longer session than other applicants simply because there's more material to cover. The more you know about yourself and the more open you are about your life, the more smoothly your interview will run. This advice holds true for all applicants.

▶ The Types of Questions You Will Be Asked

What kind of questions are they going to ask? Isn't that what everyone is really worried about when they are sitting in the chair outside of the interview room? You will hear all kinds of questions—personal questions about your family life, questions about your likes and dislikes, questions about your temperament, your friends, and even a few designed to make you laugh so you will get a little color back into your face. Don't look for many questions that can be answered with simply "yes" or "no," because you won't get that lucky. Let's look at the types of questions you are likely to be asked.

Open-Ended Questions

The open-ended question is the one you are most likely to hear. An example of an open-ended question is:

Board Member: "Mr. Jones, can you tell the board about your Friday night bowling league?"

Board members like these questions because it gives them an opportunity to see how articulate you can be, and it gives them a little insight into how you think. This is also a way for them to ease into more specific questions. For example:

Board Member: "Mr. Jones, can you tell the board about your Friday night bowling league?"

Jones: "Yes ma'am. I've been bowling in this league for about two years. We meet every Friday night around 6 P.M. and bowl until about 8:30 P.M. I like it because it gives me something to do with the friends that I might not get to see otherwise because everyone is so busy. This also gives me time to spend with my wife. We're in first place right now, and I like it that way."

Board Member: "Oh, congratulations. You must be a pretty competitive bowler."

Jones: "Yes ma'am, I am. I like to win and I take the game pretty seriously."

Board Member: "How do you react when your team loses, Mr. Jones?"

That one question generates enough information for the board to draw a lot of conclusions about Mr. Jones. They can see that he likes to interact with his friends, he thinks spending time with his wife is important, and that competition and winning are important to him. Mr. Jones's answer opens up an avenue for the board to explore how he reacts to disappointment, how he is able to articulate his feelings and reactions, and they'll probably get a good idea of his temperament.

Open-ended questions allow the board to fish around for information, but this is not a negative situation. You should seize these opportunities to open up to the board and give them an idea of who you are as a person.

Obvious Questions

This is the kind of question boards ask when everyone in the room already knows the answer. For example:

Board Member: "Ms. Rasheed, you were in the military for four years?"

Rasheed: "Yes sir, I was in the Marines from 1982 until 1986."

Board Member: "Why did you get out?"

The obvious question is used most often as a way to give the applicant a chance to warm up and to be aware of what area the board is about to explore. It's also a way for the board to check up on the information they've been provided. Board members and background investigators can misread or misunderstand information they receive. Understanding this, board members will usually be careful to confirm details with you during the interview.

Interview boards ask two other types of icebreaker questions for which you should be prepared. They may ask you something like, "What have you done to prepare yourself to become a police officer?" Or, you may be asked, "Why do you want to become a police officer?" These icebreakers are your opportunity to impress the board with your qualifications for the job, so be prepared to answer them.

Why do you want to become a police officer? You should be thinking about this question now. A good candidate will often answer that he or she likes working with and helping people and solving problems, and is attracted to the idea of facing different challenges on a daily basis. A good candidates may answer that he or she prepared for the oral and the job by interviewing other police officers, working as a volunteer, or reading books and websites on police work.

Fishing Expeditions

The fishing expedition is always a nerve-racking kind of question to answer. You aren't certain why they are asking or where the question came from and they aren't giving out clues. For example:

Board Member: "Mr. Yang, in your application, you stated that you've never been detained by police. You've *never* been detained?"

If your nerves aren't wracked by this kind of questioning, someone probably needs to check you for a pulse. In the example above, if the applicant has been detained by police and failed to list this on his application then he'll be wondering if the board knows this happened. The odds are high that the board does know the answer before asking the question. If the applicant has never been detained, then paranoia is certain to set in. Did someone on his list of references lie to the background investigator? Did someone on the board misread his application? These questions race through his mind as the board scrutinizes him.

Chances are, the board is simply fishing to see what he will say. In any event, don't let these questions cause you a dilemma because if you are honest there can be no dilemma. You simply must tell the truth at all times in an oral board. Your integrity is at stake, your reputation, and, not least of all, your chance to become a police officer is at stake. Don't try to guess at why the board is asking a question. Your job is to answer truthfully and openly.

Situational/Ethics Queries

Who doesn't dread these? You hear the words, "What would you do if . . ." and your heart pounds wildly. For example:

Board Member: "Ms. Nixey, assume you are a police officer and you are on your way to back up an officer who is on the scene of a burglary alarm at a clothing store. You walk in just in time to see him pick up a small bottle of men's cologne and put it into his pocket. What do you do?"

Some oral boards almost exclusively ask one situational question after another. Other departments may ask one, then spend the rest of the interview asking you about your past job history. Your best defense here is to decide ahead of time what your ethics are and go with how you honestly feel. The only possible right answer is your answer. If the board doesn't like what they hear, then you may be grilled intensely about your answer; however, you cannot assume that you've given the incorrect answer if the board does begin questioning you hard about your answers. Boards have more than one reason for challenging you, and it's never safe to assume why they are doing it.

Keep in mind, too, that it's not uncommon on police boards for one board member to be assigned the task of trying to get under an applicant's skin. The purpose is to see if the applicant rattles easily under pressure or loses his or her temper when baited. The person assigned this task is not hard to spot. He or she will be the one you thoroughly detest after you've had to answer such questions as, "Why in the world would we want to hire someone like you?"

Expect boards to jump on every discrepancy they hear and to pick apart some of your comments—all because they want to see how you handle pressure. Not all departments designate a person to perform this function, but someone is usually prepared to slip into this role at some point in the interview.

Role-Play Situations

Answering tough questions is stressful enough, but doing it under role-play conditions is even tougher. Many departments are using this technique more and more frequently in the oral board setting. A board member will instruct you to pretend you are a police officer and ask you to act out your verbal and/or physical responses. For example:

Board Member: "Mr. Patel, I want you to pretend that you are a police officer and you are chasing a fleeing suspect. The suspect is running from you now and I want you to stand up and instruct him to stop by yelling, "Freeze! Police!"

Board members may set up more elaborate role-playing scenes for you. Try to enter into these situations with a willingness to participate. Most people are aware that you are not a professional actor or actress, so they are not looking for Academy Award performances. Do the best you can. Role-playing is used heavily in almost all police academies and training situations today, so expect to do a lot of role-playing during your career as a law enforcement professional. Shy, reserved people may have difficulty working up enthusiasm for this kind of interaction. Practice how you'd handle this scene, and prepare yourself mentally as best you can.

Highly Personal Questions

The members of the oral board can indeed ask you just about any question that comes to mind. Applying for a job in public safety puts you in a different league than the civilian sector applicant. Yes, federal and state laws may prohibit civilian employers from seeking certain information about their applicants. But law enforcement agencies are allowed more freedom of movement within the laws for obvious reasons.

For example, you will rarely find a space for an applicant's birth date on an application for employment in private industry. This is the result of age discrimination litigation. Law enforcement agencies, as well as other agencies dealing with public safety, need such information to perform thorough background investigations and do not have many of the same restrictions. You will be expected to provide your date of birth and identify your race and your gender before you get very far in the application process for any police department. You are applying for a sensitive public safety job and must expect information you may consider highly personal to come to light.

In short, law enforcement agencies can ask you any question that may have a bearing on your mental stability, ability to do the physical tasks common to police work, integrity, honesty, character, and reputation in the community. There's not much left to the imagination after all of this is covered. If some of the questions are probing and perhaps even offensive, it is because you are being held to a higher standard by both the courts that allow these questions to be asked and the departments that want to hire you to protect life and property.

▶ Answers—How Many Are There?

While you are sitting in the interview hot seat, you may feel like only two kinds of answers exist—the one you wish you had given and the one you wish you could take back. Most law enforcement officers in uniform today have war stories about the one thing they wish they hadn't brought up in the oral interview board. And this is to be expected. Nerves and pressure often conspire at the most inappropriate times. To help you be on guard for these moments, let's look at the mysterious wrong and right answers.

The Wrong Answer

The wrong answer to any question is the answer you think you should say because that's what you've been told the board wants to hear. Do not take well-meant advice from friends or officers who haven't been before an oral board in the last five years. Boards will often overlook answers they don't like if they feel you have good reasons for what you say and if you are being honest with them.

If the board fails you, it will not be because you gave the wrong answer. It will be because you are not the kind of person they are looking for, or there are some things about your life or yourself you need to work on. The board just feels you need some time to work on these matters before they consider you for a job in law enforcement.

The Right Answer

The answers the board wants to hear are the ones only you can give. They want your opinion, your reasons, your personal experiences, and they want to know what you would do under certain circumstances. No one else matters but you and how you present yourself in the oral interview. If you try to say what you think the board wants to hear, you will almost certainly give them a shallow, unsatisfying response to their question.

What Do I Say?

It's not so much what you say as how you say it. The best way to answer any question is with directness, honesty, and brevity. Keep your answers short, but give enough information to fully answer the question. The board won't be handing out prizes for conserving words, but they also don't want to have to pull answers out of you just so that they can get enough information.

Avoid skirting the issue when answering questions. For example:

Board Member: "Ms. Abdul, I see you've been arrested once for public intoxication while you were in college? Is that true?

Abdul: "No, sir."

Board Member: "Really? That's odd. It says here on page seven that you were arrested and spent the night in the city jail."

Abdul: "Yes, well, I wasn't exactly *arrested* because the officer didn't put handcuffs on me."

Don't play word games with the board. You won't win. In this case, the applicant clearly knows that the board is aware of her arrest record, but she's trying to downplay the incident by ducking the question.

You should also elaborate as much as as possible when answering questions so you don't come across as difficult. For example:

Board Member: "Mr. O'Malley, tell the board why you left the job you held at Tread Lightly Tire Shop."

O'Malley: "I was fired."

Board Member: "Why were you fired?"

O'Malley: "Because the boss told me not to come back."

Board Member: "Why did the boss tell you not to come back?"

O'Malley: "Because I was fired."

Board Member: "What happened to cause you to be fired?"

O'Malley: "I was rude."

Board Member: "Rude to whom and under what circumstances?"

You get the picture. This question could have been answered fully when the board member asked O'Malley why he left the tire shop job. The board would prefer that you not rattle on and on when you answer questions, but they would also appreciate a complete answer. An oral board's patience is usually thin with an applicant who uses this answering technique.

Make sure you are answering the question the board is asking you. Try to avoid straying from the topic at hand. For example:

Board Member: "Well, Ms. Goldstein, we know about some of the things you are good at, now tell us something about yourself that you'd like to improve."

Goldstein: "I'm really good with people. People like me and find it easy to talk to me for some reason. I guess it's because I'm such a good listener."

If she is a good listener, Ms. Goldstein didn't demonstrate this quality with that answer. It's important to listen to the question and answer directly. If you duck the question then the board will assume you have something to hide or you are not being honest. If you don't understand how to answer the question, tell the person who asked it what you don't understand. They will be happy to rephrase the question or explain what they want. Be specific and above all, answer the question you are asked, not the one you wish they had asked instead.

Sample Interview Scenarios

By now, you should have a reasonable idea of what an oral board is looking for and how best to not only survive the experience, but come out ahead on your first oral interview. You've had a lot of material to absorb in this chapter. Read the following scenarios illustrating the wrong way and the right way to tackle an oral interview. As you read, try to put yourself in the shoes of the oral board member who is asking the questions.

Scenario #1

Marie Garcia is sitting before the Friendly Police Department oral interview board. She is wearing a pair of black jeans, loafers without socks, and a short-sleeved cotton blouse. As the questions are being asked, she is tapping her foot against the table and staring at her hands.

Board Member: "Ms. Garcia, can you give the board an example of how you've handled a disagreement with a coworker in the past?"

Garcia: "Nope. I get along with everybody. Everyone likes me."

Board Member: "I see. So, you've never had a disagreement or difference of opinion with anyone you've ever worked with."

Garcia: "That's right."

Board Member: "Well, I see by your application that you were once written up by a supervisor for yelling at a fellow employee. Can you tell us about that situation?"

Garcia: "That's different. It was his fault! He started talking to a customer I was supposed to wait on so I told him off."

Now read the second situation.

Scenario #2

Marie Garcia is sitting before the Friendly Police Department oral interview board dressed in a gray business suit. She is sitting still with her hands folded in her lap and is looking directly at the person asking her a question.

Board Member: "Ms. Garcia, can you give the board an example of how you've handled a disagreement with a coworker in the past?"

Garcia: "Yes sir. I can think of an example. When I was working at Pools by Polly I had an argument with a coworker over which one of us was supposed to wait on a customer. I lost my cool and yelled at him. My boss wrote me up because of how I handled the situation."

Board Member: "I see. How do you think you should have handled the situation?"

Garcia: "If I had it to do over again, I'd take James, my coworker, aside and talk to him about it in private. If I couldn't work something out with him, I would ask my supervisor to help out."

Board Member: "What have you done to keep this sort of thing from happening again?"

Garcia: "I've learned to stop and think before I speak and I've learned that there is a time and place to work out differences when they come up. I haven't had a problem since that incident."

So, which scenario makes the better impression? In scenario #1, the applicant is obviously unwilling to accept responsibility for her actions, she isn't showing any evidence that she is mature, and she isn't honest with herself or the board members when she says everyone likes her and she's never had disagreements with coworkers.

On the other hand, in scenario #2, the applicant is able to admit her mistakes and take responsibility for her part in the incident. Although she may have wished she could present herself in a better light, she did illustrate maturity by being honest, open, and straightforward in talking about the disagreement. In scenario #2, the applicant may have had to endure a long, hard interview in order to sell herself, but she was able to articulate what she did to correct a fault.

On the other hand, you can bet she had a very short interview and a "We're not interested, but thanks" from the board in scenario #1. Differences in the applicant's appearances and mannerisms would also affect the board's perception of their levels of professionalism.

These two situations may seem exaggerated, but applicants all over the country are making these same mistakes.

► Your Chance to Practice

Now that you are all warmed up, read the following situation. Decide which response you think is most appropriate for each question.

Alfred Watanabe's oral interview board is today at 9 A.M. at the police academy. He's sitting in a chair outside of the board room by 8:40 A.M. waiting to be called.

When it is time, Alfred is ushered into the room and introduced to all of the board members. He sits where he's told and waits. It begins.

Board Member: "Mr. Watanabe, what would you like for us to call you this morning?"

Watanabe:
(A) "I don't know. It doesn't matter. Alfred is okay, I guess."
(B) "Alfred is fine, sir."
(C) "I go by Al."

Board Member: "Why do you want to be a police officer?"

Watanabe:
(A) "I don't know. I guess because it's fun and you get to help people. I want to be there when somebody needs something."
(B) "I'd like to be a police officer because I'm very interested in the work. I love to be around people. I like the variety of duties. And I like the challenge of trying to figure out

what's really going on in a given situation."

(C) "Police work is what I've always wanted to do."

Board Member: "I see. Well, we have a few questions for you and I know a few others will crop up as we go along. First, can you tell us about your personality. What are you like to be around on a social basis?"

Watanabe: (A) "Oh, I don't know. I'm okay, I guess. My friends like me."

(B) "My friends tell me I'm usually fun to be around. I'm not particularly shy. I'd say I'm outgoing. I like meeting new people, talking, and I can be a pretty good listener, too. I am even-tempered. I get mad sometimes, but if I do I get over it quickly. I have a good sense of humor and don't mind being teased as long as I get to tease back."

(C) "I'm easy to talk to, friendly, very social—I like being around lots of people—and I'm laid-back."

Board Member: "I see here that your background investigator found that you once got thrown out of a friend's house during a party because you were picking fights with the other guests. Tell us about this experience."

Watanabe: (A) "Well . . . that was just that once. I had a little too much to drink I guess. I walked home from there."

(B) "That happened about five years ago in my very early college days. I had just discovered beer and I don't think I handled myself well at all in those days. At that party, I kept trying to get everyone to agree to switch the stereo to another station and was quite a jerk about it. My friend asked me to leave so I walked home. I was a jerk again the very next weekend and had to be asked to leave again. That wised me up. I realized I didn't need to be drinking like that so I did something about it."

(C) "Yes, that did happen. I got into an argument with friends over what music we'd listen to. I had been drinking. My host asked me to leave. I did."

Board Member: "What steps have you taken to make sure this type of situation doesn't happen again?

Watanabe: (A) "I guess I just watch how much I drink. I don't go to that guy's house anymore, either."

(B) "I learned to eat before I went to parties where there was alcohol being served and then carried around the same drink for a while. I limited myself to two beers during an evening. I went home happy that way and so did all my friends. I still follow the same rules for myself today."

(C) "I limit myself to two beers at a party and I don't drink much any other time. I'm responsible about the way I drink now."

All of the choices you read are responses that candidates have made in oral board situations—not verbatim, but awfully close to it. If you chose option (A) for all your responses, you will be guaranteed to grate on the last nerve of every board member. It's not hard to see why. Phrases like *I don't know* and *I guess so* and *I think so* tell the listener that the speaker isn't sure of himself. It says the speaker probably has never thought about what you asked and is giving the answer without bothering to think about it now.

The choice (A) answers do not give the board much to go on. The answers don't offer explanations, although the open-ended question gives the applicant all the necessary room to do so. The board would be left with a wishy-washy impression of this candidate at best.

If you liked choice (B) for each of the questions, you've kept yourself awake for most of this chapter. Choice (B) shows the applicant has manners, but he doesn't go overboard. He is direct, but not so direct that he comes across as blunt. He has either thought about the kinds of questions that will surface in the interview, or he thinks about what he wants to say before he speaks.

He comes across as confident, willing to discuss his past life, and not ashamed to admit mistakes. He also has a detailed explanation for how he's handled the drinking situation and the potential for future problems. It's at this point that the applicant needs to be the most vocal. Board members are especially interested in how you handle your life in the present and what you will most likely do in the future.

If choice (C) is what you chose for most of the questions, you probably won't blow the interview but you may want to reassess how you come across to others. The candidate is not rude, but he walks a thin line. When answering the second question, he should elaborate more on how he feels about police work because this is one of his opportunities to show the board how well he can express himself. People have different reasons for wanting to go into police work. Some are good and some are marginal, but for the most part this question is designed to warm you up and let the board warm up, too.

It'd be hard to come up with a truly wrong answer for this question, although people have managed to do so. ("I love to shoot guns" would not win extra points here.) The board gets a feel for how you are going to be as an interviewee with this standard question. You don't have to deliver the Gettysburg Address, but give them something to go on.

Choice (C) is the type of response quiet, self-assured people often tend to give. They don't use a lot of words and usually answer questions with directness. The danger here is that this applicant may not say enough to convince the board that he will deal well with the public and with other officers and supervisors.

These kinds of answers will most often force the board to switch to different kinds of questions that will force the applicant into lengthier responses. Don't make them work too hard getting the answers, though, unless you want a really short interview.

▶ Pulling It All Together

Don't let all of this information become overwhelming. Make yourself step back and look at the big picture. You know what kind of overall impression you are most likely to make. If you don't, you should. And cut yourself a little slack: The people who interview you aren't perfect and have no real desire to hire someone who is, considering they may have to work with you someday.

Keep your sense of humor intact while you're going through this process. Don't go into the board cracking jokes, but if you can keep your sense of humor close at hand, you might actually be able to come out of interview shock long enough to react if the board jokes with you about something. It wouldn't be unusual for this to happen. Most law enforcement personnel like to tease or joke around to relieve stress. Let the board lead the way in this area, though.

Self-confidence is key. Relax, believe in yourself, and act naturally. If you feel like you are blowing it during the interview, show the board your self-confidence by stopping yourself. Take a deep breath and tell them that's not exactly what you'd like to say, then tell them what you'd like to say. Now that's self-confidence. Be firm if a board member tries to rattle your cage. Firm doesn't mean inflexible—change your mind if you need to, but just don't do it every other sentence. You don't want to appear indecisive.

You are as ready as you will ever be if you follow these suggestions. There are no secrets to give away when it comes to oral interview boards. You can't change your past, your job history, or your educational status at this point in the process, nor can you change your personality or go back and do a more thorough job on your personal history statement. And you can't fake maturity if you are not a mature individual. But you can put your best foot forward and be as well-prepared as possible.

Many police officers you see on the street today failed on their first attempts to be hired by their department's oral board and then passed the board after working on shortcomings and correcting problems. Your goal, of course, is to make it through the process on the first try. If that doesn't happen and you decide to try again, you owe it to yourself to come fully prepared the next time around.

If you follow the tips you've read so far, you should not make the kinds of mistakes that tend to eliminate otherwise well-qualified candidates. You will certainly be ahead of the applicant who has the same qualifications you have, but who hasn't prepared for an oral interview board.

Some Final Words of Advice

Dr. Rick Bradstreet is a 20-year veteran psychologist for the Austin Police Department in Austin, Texas. He holds a law degree from Stanford University and a PhD in counseling psychology from the University of Texas at Austin. His specialty is communication skills and conflict resolution. Throughout his career with APD, Dr. Bradstreet estimates that he's sat on about 250 to 300 oral interview boards and has had plenty of opportunity to observe applicants in oral interviews. He offers the following advice to those who see an oral board in their future.

- Make eye contact. Applicants who fail to make eye contact with interviewers can expect a negative reaction from the board. Making eye contact makes the speaker feel like what he or she is saying is being heard and is being taken seriously.
- Sit erect in your chair, but not too stiff. You should not have the same posture that you would have if you were sitting at home in your living room, yet you want to appear somewhat relaxed and alert.
- Keep your hands in your lap if you have a tendency to wring your hands together when agitated. Wringing hands are generally perceived as signs of nervousness.
- Try not to drum your fingers on the table. Although this behavior is most often interpreted more as a sign of someone who has excess energy and is not necessarily seen as nervous behavior, it can be distracting to those around you.
- Feel free to shift positions periodically. It's perfectly natural to move around as you speak and is expected during normal conversation. An oral board is not meant to be an interrogation, so you are not expected to sit frozen in place for the duration.
- Speak up. If a board member lets you know you are mumbling, then project your voice. Speaking in a voice so soft that no one can hear you does nothing to enhance the image you want to project—that of a self-confident, take-charge person who knows what you want.
- Focus on explaining how you are as a person; do not respond to questions defensively. Once again, this is not an interrogation. Try to have a normal, respectful conversation with the board members and your body language will take on a more natural, confident look.
- Get out of the self-conscious mode. Your goal is to let the board see you and your experiences as unique. Do not try to mold your experiences and answers to questions according to what you think the board may want.

► Additional Resources

Websites

- Five Tactics for Taking Civil Service Exams
  www.hitechcj.com/id139.html
- Police Chat, Forum, and Information
  www.policeone.com
- Police & Law Enforcement Chat Boards
  www.policeworld.net
- Criminal Justice Forum Moderated by Professionals and Subject Matter Experts
  www.criminaljustice-online.com
- Wealth of Information, Discussion Boards, Chat Rooms, and Links
  www.copseek.com
- General Interview Tips and Strategies
  www.myfuture.com/toolbox/aceinterview_all.html
- Tips for Successful Interviews
  www.alljobsuk.com/ivtips.shtml
- How to Prepare for Interviewing
  www.uky.edu/CareerCenter/interviewhowto.html
- Public Speaking Tips
  www.uncommon-knowledge.co.uk/public_speaking/tips.html

Books

- *Best Answers to the 201 Most Frequently Asked Interview Questions* by Matthew J. Deluca (McGraw-Hill Trade).
- *101 Great Answers to the Toughest Interview Questions* by Ronald W. Fry (Career Press).
- *Sell Yourself! Master the Job Interview Process* by Jane Williams (Principle Publications).
- *Last Minute Interview Tips* by Brandon Toropov (Career Press).
- *101 Ways to Improve Your Communication Skills Instantly* by Jo Condrill (Goalminds).

CHAPTER

22 Additional Law Enforcement Opportunities

CHAPTER SUMMARY

There are many areas of law enforcement to consider as career options in addition to being a city police officer. You may be interested in becoming a state trooper or a deputy sheriff or in working for the federal government. This chapter gives a brief overview of these law enforcement areas along with additional resources where you can find more information about these options.

▶ County Police

Most counties in each state have an elected official who serves as that county's sheriff. Depending on the size of the county, the sheriff may have only a few or as many as several hundred deputy sheriffs. Since the size of each county varies, the entry requirements and specific duties for deputy sheriffs vary significantly from place to place. The range of duties for deputy sheriffs is broad. They may patrol particular regions, enforce traffic laws, enforce laws in county parks, transport suspects throughout the county, participate in criminal investigations, and serve subpoenas and garnishments for the county courts.

Some sheriff's departments have a wide range of areas of specialization in which a deputy sheriff can work, such as

- crime lab
- detectives
- jail

- K-9s
- narcotics patrol
- water patrol
- radio

A deputy sheriff must meet minimum qualifications. Applicants must be between the ages of 19 and 29, and they must have

- U. S. citizenship
- high school diploma or GED
- written, physical, or oral exams
- medical and psychological exams

For more information on becoming a deputy sheriff, visit the National Sheriffs' Association website at www.sheriffs.org, or go to the Police Employment website for deputy sheriffs and see if the sheriff's office you are interested in applying to has a link, www.policeemployment.com/sheriff. You can also check your telephone book to get the contact information for the sheriff's office near you.

▶ State Police

Working as a state police officer is much like working for the city except that your job encompasses a much broader geographical scope. You would be responsible for statewide law enforcement of criminal activity and traffic violations as well as citizen protection.

Your job as a state police officer would include

- providing emergency assistance
- conducting investigations
- writing reports
- presenting testimony in a court of law
- enforcing traffic laws

State police officer applicants must be at least 21 years of age (a few states will accept officers who are 19 or 20). In addition, a state police officer must have

- good vision and hearing
- drug free status (at least one year, usually)
- good physical health
- a high school diploma or GED
- residency in the United States
- a valid driver's license
- passed any qualifying exams and a background investigation

Testing

Testing for state police work is very similar to testing for city police work. Multiple-choice tests that cover basic writing, reading, observation, and memory are usually included. Abilities that are examined include human interaction, handling authority, situational judgment, social maturity and ethics, unbiased law enforcement, and reactions under pressure. There is also a physical ability test, an oral interview, a background investigation, a polygraph test, and medical and psychological evaluations.

For more information about state police jobs in your area, contact your local state agency or visit www.statetroopersdirectory.com for a listing of websites across the country.

▶ Federal Law Enforcement Careers

There are numerous departments and agencies that employ federal law enforcement officers or agents. In this section, you will find brief descriptions of some of these agencies as well as basic requirements and contact information for the most popular federal law enforcement jobs.

The Federal Bureau of Investigation (FBI)

The Federal Bureau of Investigation deals with violations of federal law in all areas except for those covered by other federal departments. Bank robberies, civil rights violations, blackmail, kidnapping, treason, and federal employee murders or assaults are all things that would be investigated by the FBI.

Working for the FBI is an interesting job and those who are a part of this organization may find themselves doing a wide variety of different tasks.

An applicant for special agent for the FBI must be no younger than 23 and no older than 37. The minimum qualifications for being a special agent for the FBI include

- U.S. citizenship or citizenship in the Northern Mariana Islands
- a valid driver's license
- a polygraph test, a drug test, and a color vision test
- a four-year college degree

The background investigation for FBI applicants includes contacting current and former employers, checking out references, talking to neighbors and other social acquaintances, reviewing your credit history, checking for any criminal activity or arrest records, looking into your educational background, and checking your military and medical records.

If you want to be a special agent for the FBI, there is an online application you can fill out in the employment section of their website. If you do not have Internet access, you can get an application by contacting the Applicant Coordinator or Special Agent Recruiter at the FBI field office nearest you. (Check your local telephone book.)

For more information, visit the FBI website at www.fbi.gov.

The Federal Drug Enforcement Administration (DEA)

The DEA enforces laws related to the illegal use, distribution, and sale of narcotics such as cocaine, opium, heroin, marijuana, hallucinogens, and synthetic narcotics such as methamphetamines or barbiturates. The DEA works to limit and halt incoming narcotics from other countries as well as their use within U.S. borders. They work to infiltrate drug trafficking organizations, arrest violators who are dangerous criminals, confiscate illegal drugs, collect and prepare evidence, and often testify in criminal court cases.

Working for the DEA is both exciting and dangerous at times, and much of the work is done undercover. There may also be long hours spent doing surveillance as well. Every aspect of the job is important and those who wish to apply to the DEA should know that they will be expected to perform well on both physical and written exams.

Applicants for DEA must be between 21 and 36 years of age. They also must have

- U.S. citizenship
- a valid driver's license
- the ability to obtain a top secret security clearance
- excellent physical condition, good vision, and good hearing ability
- a college degree with an overall GPA of 2.5 or better

Diversion Investigators for the DEA

Investigators in this agency work to uncover illegal activities within the manufacturing and distribution of pharmaceuticals and related chemicals. They collect and analyze information and work closely with DEA special agents to apprehend criminals in the drug/chemical market.

The minimum qualifications for being a DEA diversion investigator include

- U.S. citizenship
- a valid driver's license
- the ability to distinguish shades of color
- the ability to hear a conversational voice from a distance of 20 feet with both ears
- a bachelor's degree (any major)

DEA diversion investigators must be willing to accept assignments anywhere in the United States, depending on the needs of the agency.

For more information on either of these positions, contact a recruiter at the DEA field office nearest you or a special agent recruiter at DEA headquarters.

Special Agent Recruitment
Drug Enforcement Administration
2401 Jefferson Davis Highway
Alexandria, VA 22301
Telephone: 800-882-9539

The U.S. Marshals Service

The U.S. Marshals Service is in charge of the much publicized Witness Security Program. They also transport federal prisoners to court proceedings and inmates from one prison or facility to another. Additionally, they supervise federal court proceedings by maintaining security and order, guarding prisoners, and serving orders of the courts.

U.S. marshals also pursue federal fugitives, manage assets seized from criminal enterprises, and work to protect those who live within the witness protection program system. This job can also be dangerous at times, like most law enforcement positions. U.S. marshals are paid well and there is ample opportunity for career advancement.

U.S. marshals applicants must be U.S. citizens between the ages of 21 and 36. In addition, they must have

- U.S. citizenship
- excellent physical condition
- a bachelor's degree or three years of qualifying experience
- a valid driver's license with a good driving record

For more information about how to enter this law enforcement career field, contact

U.S. Marshals Service
Human Resources Division
Law Enforcement Recruiting
Washington, D.C. 20530-1000
202-307-9400

For more information, log onto www.usmarshals.gov.

The Federal Bureau of Prisons

Corrections officers within the Federal Bureau of Prisons work to enforce the rules and maintain order in prisons where inmates have been sentenced by the federal court. There is opportunity to transfer to most any area of the country. This job provides a stable work environment and ample opportunity for advancement. This agency of the federal government is one of the fastest growing, especially because of the many opportunities for career advancement.

Federal corrections officer applicants must not be older than 37. Other minimum qualifications include

- U.S. citizenship
- a high school diploma or GED
- at least two years of work experience
- no felony convictions
- good physical fitness, eyesight, and hearing

For more information, you can call the Federal Bureau of Prisons at 202-307-3198 or visit their website at www.bop.gov.

Bureau of Alcohol, Tobacco, Firearms, and Explosives (ATF)

ATF agents investigate violations and enforce laws relating to firearms, explosives, alcohol, and tobacco. Much of the work may be done undercover, as agents infiltrate groups who are suspected of smuggling arms or explosives into the country.

ATF agent applicants must be between 21 and 37 years old. In addition, the minimum qualifications for being an ATF agent include

- U.S. citizenship
- a valid driver's license
- good physical condition, with good hearing and vision
- a bachelor's degree or three years of qualifying experience

For more information, you can contact:

Bureau of Alcohol, Tobacco, Firearms, and Explosives
Human Resources Division
Room 4100
650 Massachusetts Avenue, NW
Washington, D.C. 20226
202-927-8610
www.atf.treas.gov

Department of Homeland Security (DHS)

After the terrorist attacks of September 11, 2001, it was clear that no one federal agency had the sole responsibility for providing homeland security. Indeed, responsibility for protecting the country was dispersed among over 100 different federal agencies. The Homeland Security Act of 2002 merged many different federal agencies into the newly created Department of Homeland Security (DHS). If you are considering a job with Customs, the Border Patrol, the Secret Service, or the Air Marshals, you are actually looking at working in the DHS.

U.S. Immigration and Customs Enforcement (ICE)

When the DHS was created, the Customs Service and Border Patrol were merged into U.S. Immigration and Customs Enforcement (ICE). As the largest investigative arm of the Department of Homeland Security, ICE is primarily a law enforcement agency. Its mission is to protect America and uphold public safety by targeting the people, money, and materials that support terrorist and criminal activities. ICE enforces the nation's customs and immigration laws and provides security for federal buildings.

There are a large variety of law enforcement and law enforcement-related jobs at ICE. For instance, the Customs and Border Protection branches of ICE have both investigators and a uniformed presence at border crossings and points of U.S. entry. While certain ICE jobs require a college degree, the minimum qualifications for all ICE jobs are

- U.S. citizenship
- at least 21 years of age and younger than 37 at time of appointment
- excellent health and physical condition
- complete background investigation including in-depth interviews, drug screening, medical examination, and polygraph examination

For more information about ICE, visit its website at www.ice.gov. However, job descriptions and job applications are available only at USA Jobs, the official employment website of the U.S. government, at www.usajobs.opm.gov.

Transportation Security Administration (TSA)

The Federal Air Marshal Service (FAMS) is a department under the Transportation Security Administration (TSA), which helps secure the nation's civil aviation system through the effective deployment of federal air marshals to detect, deter, and defeat hostile acts targeting U.S. air carriers, airports, passengers, and crews. Federal air marshals work to enforce federal laws, make arrests without warrants for any offense against the United States with probable cause, and identify and interview witnesses and suspects. Federal air marshals also participate in multiagency task forces and surveillance, and carry out undercover and covert work assignments.

While certain FAMS jobs require a college degree, the minimum qualifications for all FAMS jobs are

- U.S. citizenship
- at least 21 years of age and younger than 37 at time of appointment
- excellent health and physical condition
- complete background investigation including in-depth interviews, drug screening, medical examination, and polygraph examination

For more information about FAMS, visit its website at www.tsa.gov. However, job descriptions and job applications are available only through USA Jobs, the official employment website of the U.S. government, at www.usajobs.opm.gov.

The U.S. Secret Service

The U.S. Secret Service is also part of the DHS. The Secret Service carries out two significant missions: protection and criminal investigations. The Secret Service protects the president and vice president, their families, heads of state, and other designated individuals; investigates threats against these protectees; protects the White House and other buildings within Washington, D.C.; and plans and implements security for national special security events. The Secret Service also investigates violations of laws relating to counterfeiting, financial institution fraud, identity theft, computer fraud, and computer-based attacks on our nation's financial, banking, and telecommunications infrastructure.

The minimum qualifications to become a member of the Secret Service include

- U.S. citizenship
- at least 21 years of age and younger than 37 at time of appointment
- (1) bachelor's degree from an accredited college or university; or (2) three years of work experience in the criminal investigative or law enforcement fields that require knowledge and application of laws relating to criminal violations; or (3) an equivalent combination of education and related experience
- excellent health and physical condition
- complete background investigation to include in-depth interviews, drug screening, medical examination, and polygraph examination

For more information about the Secret Service, visit its website at www.secretservice.gov. However, job descriptions and job applications are available only through USA Jobs, the official employment website of the U.S. government, at www.usajobs.opm.gov.

Special Agents for the Fish and Wildlife Service

Special agents of this agency enforce federal wildlife laws throughout the United States. They investigate matters such as the illegal capturing, killing, or selling of protected species, and illegal exporting and importing of such species. This is a job that includes frequent travel and agents are often away from home for extended periods of time.

Applicants for Special Agent for the Fish and Wildlife Service must be between 21 and 37 years of age. Other minimum qualifications include

- U.S. citizenship
- a willingness to relocate if necessary
- excellent physical condition

A four-year degree in wildlife management, criminal justice, or a related field is preferred. Agents spend 18 weeks of training in Georgia, after which they are assigned to an area in the United States.

▶ Additional Resources

Websites

- Federal, State, and Local Law Enforcement Jobs
  www.copcareer.com
- Law Enforcement Employment and Hiring Information
  www.policeone.com/careers
- Information on Local, State, and Federal Law Enforcement Jobs
  www.policeemployment.com

Books

- *Law Enforcement Career Starter,* 2nd Edition (LearningExpress).
- *Guide to Careers in Federal Law Enforcement* by Thomas H. Ackerman (Sage Creek Press).
- *Federal Careers in Law Enforcement* by Russ Smith (Impact Publications).
- *Treasury Enforcement Agent Exam*, 2nd Edition (LearningExpress).
- *FBI Careers: The Ultimate Guide to Landing a Job as One of America's Finest* by Thomas H. Ackerman (Jist Works).
- *Guide to Careers in the FBI* by John Douglas (Kaplan).

Special FREE Offer from LearningExpress!

LearningExpress will help you be better prepared for, and get higher scores on, the police officer exam

Go to the LearningExpress Practice Center at www.LearningExpressFreeOffer.com, an interactive online resource exclusively for LearningExpress customers.

Now that you've purchased LearningExpress's *Police Officer Exam, 3rd Edition*, you have **FREE** access to:

- **A full-length law enforcement practice test** based on the official police officer exams
- **Questions that cover** judgment and problem solving, memorization and visualization, reading comprehension, verbal skills, **and much more!**
- Immediate scoring and **detailed answer explanations**
- Benchmark your skills and focus your study with our **customized diagnostic report**

Follow the simple instructions on the scratch card in your copy of *Police Officer Exam, 3rd Edition*. Use your individualized access code found on the scratch card and go to www.LearningExpressFreeOffer.com to sign in. Start practicing online for the police officer exam right away!

Once you've logged on, use the spaces below to write in your access code and newly created password for easy reference:

Access Code: ________________ Password: ____________________